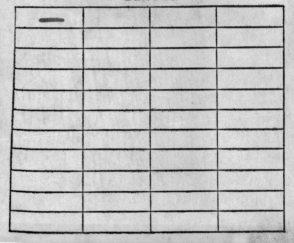

"What Is the Good of History?"

SELECTED LETTERS OF
CARL L. BECKER,
1900–1945

Carl L. Becker, early 1930's. (Department of Manuscripts and University Archives, Cornell.)

"What Is the Good of History?"

SELECTED LETTERS OF
CARL L. BECKER, 1873 – 1945.
1900–1945

Edited, with an Introduction, by
MICHAEL KAMMEN

Cornell University Press | ITHACA AND LONDON

First published 1973 by Cornell University Press.
Published in the United Kingdom by Cornell University Press Ltd., 214 Brook Street, London W1Y 1AA.

International Standard Book Number 0–8014–0778–8
Library of Congress Catalog Card Number 73–2849

Printed in the United States of America by Kingsport Press, Inc.

Librarians: Library of Congress cataloging information appears on the last page of the book.

This book is for
Sandra and Walter LaFeber

Contents

Preface   ix

Editor's Note   xiii

Abbreviations   xiv

Introduction: The Inner World of Carl Becker   xv

Chronology   xxxi

Recipients of Becker Letters   xxxiii

The Letters

  1. Apprentice and Journeyman Historian, 1900–1916   3

  2. Cornell, War, and the Productive Professor, 1916–1919   39

  3. Disillusionment and Thoughts on Politics, 1920–1924   66

  4. Quiet Years as Teacher and Friend, 1924–1930   101

  5. Everyman, the Heavenly City, and the Hospital, 1931–1933   144

  6. In Sickness, in Health, and in California, 1933–1935   189

  7. "A Well Known Communistic Writer," 1935–1939   228

  8. War, Retirement, and Renewed Vigor, 1939–1943   270

  9. Retrospection and Reflection on a Better World, 1943–1945   304

Appendix: Eight Letters to and about Carl L. Becker   348

Bibliography   359

Index   365

Illustrations

Carl L. Becker, early 1930's   *Frontispiece*

                                                        Following page 152
  I. Leonard Sarvay, Carl L. Becker, and Randolph Wright, early
       1890's
 II. Carl L. Becker, 1916
III. The Arts Quad at Cornell, 1917
 IV. The Cornell History Club, 1921
  V. The Cornell History Club, 1922
 VI. Carl Becker's home in Ithaca, New York
VII. History graduate students before Becker's retirement dinner, June
       10, 1941
VIII. Carl L. Becker and his grandson, Carl Jadwin Becker, summer
       1941

Preface

The year 1973 marks the one-hundredth anniversary of the birth of Carl Lotus Becker, one of the most philosophical and literate of American historians. Common sense meant more to Becker than sentimentalism; but common sense, as well as sentiment, suggests that the centennial is an appropriate occasion for the appearance of his letters. Only a handful have been published before; and this is surprising, because they are very interesting letters indeed. They deal extensively with historical writing and the historical profession, universities and higher education in America, war and peace, domestic politics, family and friendships.

Several of my colleagues at Cornell, familiar with Becker's intellectual acuity and literary grace, have asked from time to time, "Will the letters disappoint me?" I have been sanguine in assuring them that Becker's letters, unlike those of many academics, are not disappointing. Both in substance and style, they are vintage Becker, and therefore richly rewarding.

When I embarked upon this project several years ago, I found that a number of difficult editorial decisions would have to be made: how many of Becker's letters to publish; whether to include letters to, as well as from, him; how to organize the volume. My decisions were to publish 317 of Becker's letters—more than half of those collected; to include only eight letters to him, in an appendix; and to organize the volume chronologically rather than topically. Each decision was shaped by a singular rationale: that this book should present a self-portrait, or "autobiography," of the man and his mind. Becker's most enduring interests concerned "the growth and decline of opinion" and "finding out so far as possible what men are like & how they think."[1] Consequently, I

1. To Wallace Notestein, [1911?], and to Thomas Reed Powell, Dec. 3, 1944, below.

have tried to select and present the letters to reveal best what Becker was like and how he thought, as well as to show the growth and decline of certain segments of opinion concerning liberalism, historical relativism, and related matters during the first half of the twentieth century.

This rationale has had practical editorial consequences: most perfunctory notes and bland, routine correspondence have been omitted; some good letters that resemble or repeat included letters have been omitted; almost all letters here are presented in their entirety, but from a very few brief excisions have been made in order to protect the privacy of persons still alive or simply to eliminate trivia. All excisions are indicated by ellipses.

Whether to include letters to Becker, and, if so, whether to intersperse them among his own, presented a serious problem. Ultimately, I decided to include only a few, and to put them at the end. If this collection is to serve as a self-portrait—showing the development of a mind, a personality, and a style—the reader should be distracted by other minds and styles as little as possible. Whenever the purpose or substance of a letter from Becker requires contextual clarification, however, I have provided it in editorial notes; and where necessary I have paraphrased or quoted in the notes from letters to Becker. Therefore, those letters to Becker included in the Appendix are not necessarily the most interesting ones written to him, nor were they from the most important of his correspondents. I selected them because of what they reveal about Becker rather than about the writer: the impact of his personality and publications, and the way he was regarded by those he influenced.

This volume, then, contains more than a representative sampling of Becker's letters. I would call it comprehensive without being complete. Becker's former students and colleagues, as well as scholars interested in the "climate of opinion"—to use one of his favorite phrases—should find it adequate. Future biographers, however, as well as students specializing in historical thought in America, will want to consult the larger corpus of Becker's papers. To facilitate their work, I have deposited in the Olin Library, Cornell University, copies of all the Becker letters I have gathered from private individuals, public repositories, and various collections.

Numerous individuals have contributed generously of their time and energies to the completion of this project. I want to thank the many colleagues, friends, and former students of Carl Becker for their cooperation. This book would not have been possible without their help. I am indebted to Frederick DeWitt Becker, who granted permission to publish his father's letters; to Giles F. Shepherd, Jr., and Phil L. Snyder, who gathered a large collection of correspondence from and about Becker during the 1950's. C. Herbert Finch, the Cornell University Libraries' Assistant Director for Special Collections, and Nancy Dean, Kathleen Jacklin, and Barbara Shepherd, staff members in Cornell's Department of Manuscripts and University Archives, have all been cheerfully cooperative.

I am also grateful to the many institutions and individuals who have granted permission to publish letters: Miriam Beard Vagts and William Beard, Morris Bishop, Gussie E. Gaskill, Leo and Ida Gershoy, Louis Gottschalk, Carl G. Gustavson, Oron J. Hale, W. Stull Holt, Alfred M. Kazin, Alfred A. Knopf, Richard M. Leighton, Anita M. Lerner, May Elish Markewich, Mary Nevins, Robert R. Palmer, Wilma J. Pugh, Arthur Schlesinger, Jr., Gayle S. Smith, Florence and Morton Yohalem; the Columbia University Library, the Cornell University Libraries, the Harvard College Library, the Henry E. Huntington Library and Art Gallery, The Johns Hopkins University Library, the New York Public Library, the North Carolina State University Archives, the Pennsylvania State University Library, the State Historical Society of Wisconsin, the University of Kansas Library, the University of Minnesota Library, the University of Wyoming Library, the Yale University Library; and the editors of the *Cornell Alumni News* and *Cornell Daily Sun.*

I would especially like to thank Terry L. Dash and Mary H. Mall for their careful work in preparing a thorough checklist, and for transforming Becker's difficult handwriting into a workable typescript; Carol Kammen, Mary Jo McNamara, and James Hijiya for endless proofreading; the staff of Cornell University Press for meticulous copy-editing; reference librarians at Cornell for helping to solve many perplexing little problems; Leo and Ida Gershoy, Louis Gottschalk, Anita M. Lerner, Richard Polenberg, Paul W. Gates, Morris Bishop, Harlan Banks, and Winthrop Wetherbee for patiently responding to obscure questions; Angela Morse for expeditious typing; the Cornell University Research Grants Committee for generous financial support that made possible the collecting, transcribing, and editing of these letters.

My greatest obligations are to my colleagues Cushing Strout and Frederick G. Marcham, who carefully read the entire manuscript; to Gussie Gaskill, who did so twice and who has with infinite kindness answered literally hundreds of questions about Becker and his students; and most of all to my friend Walter LaFeber, who first suggested this project some years ago, who undertook a special diplomatic mission on my behalf, who helpfully read the manuscript, and who has been a sustaining source of advice and encouragement throughout, in this as in many other matters.

M. K.

Ithaca, New York

Editor's Note

The Carl L. Becker Papers in Cornell University's Olin Library (Department of Manuscripts and University Archives) include the manuscripts and typescripts for many of his publications, lecture and research notes, various personal documents, letters to him, and letters from him in three forms: drafts and carbon copies, originals that have been given to Cornell, and photocopies of originals in other repositories and collections. A number of Becker's letters may be found in several locations: e.g., originals of his letters to William E. Dodd and Felix Frankfurter are in the Library of Congress, and photostats of them are at Cornell. Wherever this duplication occurs, I have given the Carl L. Becker Papers at Cornell as the location (other locations are listed under "Manuscript Collections" in the Bibliography). The Becker Papers are so neatly organized in chronological order that it will be easier, in most cases, for researchers to find these letters at Cornell than in their original archives.

A fairly large number of Becker's letters are undated. In many cases I have been able to date them, at least as to month and year, from internal evidence. In other instances they have been dated by recipients. In a few cases it is simply impossible to attribute a proximate date with any degree of assurance. Whenever a date has been ascribed, it appears in square brackets.

Becker's orthography was often rather whimsical, and he also made inadvertent or trivial mistakes in composition. Therefore, I have silently corrected obvious typographical errors and inconsequential slips of the pen but have left his idiosyncratic spelling.

The first time a person is mentioned in the letters I have identified him or her in a brief biographical footnote. Readers wishing to reread that note upon encountering the person's name subsequently should refer to the first entry under that name in the index.

Abbreviations

AAK   Alfred A. Knopf Papers, Purchase, N.Y.
AHR   *American Historical Review.*
AML   Anita Marburg Lerner Papers, Columbia, Md.
CBCU Carl L. Becker Papers, Olin Library, Cornell University, Ithaca, N.Y.
CLB   Carl L. Becker.
COL   Columbia University Library, New York, N.Y.
CU   Cornell University, Ithaca, N.Y.
DAB   *Dictionary of American Biography* (New York, 1927–1958).
DWH   *Detachment and the Writing of History: Essays and Letters of Carl L. Becker,* ed. Phil L. Snyder (Ithaca, 1958).
ESS   *Encyclopaedia of the Social Sciences* (New York, 1930–1935).
FMY   Florence and Morton Yohalem Papers, Washington, D.C.
GEG   Gussie Esther Gaskill Papers, Ithaca, N.Y.
HEH   Henry E. Huntington Library and Art Gallery, San Marino, Calif.
HU   Harvard University, Cambridge, Mass.
LC   Library of Congress, Washington, D.C.
LIG   Leo and Ida Gershoy Papers, New York, N.Y.
SHSW State Historical Society of Wisconsin, Madison.
UM   University of Minnesota, Minneapolis.
YU   Yale University, New Haven, Conn.

Introduction:
The Inner World of Carl Becker

Becker would not have approved of a self-portrait for purposes of glorification. But he would, I think, have approved of autobiography for purposes of exemplification. Certainly he so used elements of his own life story on at least three occasions: once to illustrate the process of "Americanization" in the nineteenth century; once to demonstrate Frederick Jackson Turner's dramatic impact as a teacher; and once to indicate the tradition of freedom and responsibility at Cornell.[1] Since the first of those three "reminiscences" may introduce the reader to Becker's family background and early boyhood, it is worthwhile to incorporate some of it here.[2]

> My own parents were descended on the one side from Dutch and German ancestors who came to New York probably in the eighteenth century, and on the other side from English and Irish ancestors who came there—I have no idea when. My paternal great-grandfather could not speak anything but German; my father could not speak anything but English, nor could any one have guessed, either from his appearance or from any tone or quality in his speech, that he was of other than English descent. In 1867, having served three years in the Civil War, he decided, like thousands of others, to abandon the state of his birth in order to acquire much better land at a much lower price in the new West. He accordingly went, first to Illinois, and afterward to Iowa, where he bought eighty acres of as good farm land as there is anywhere to be found, for which he paid, I think, about eight

---

1. CLB, *The United States: An Experiment in Democracy*, 239–242; *Everyman His Own Historian: Essays on History and Politics*, 192–212; *Cornell University: Founders and the Founding*, 197–199. For bibliographical information about CLB's works, see the Bibliography.
2. *The United States: An Experiment in Democracy*, 239–242; copyright, 1920, by Harper & Brothers.

dollars an acre, and to this he afterward added two other "eighties." It was on this Iowa farm that I was born.

One of my earliest recollections was the appearance in our neighborhood, it must have been about 1878, of a strange family that came to live in the house across the road. To me, a "typical" American boy, they seemed outlandish folk whom one would naturally avoid as suspicious and yet wish to see from some safe point of vantage as a curiosity. The reason for this primitive attitude of mind toward the new-comers was that they were Germans who could barely speak a word or two of English; and a "typical" little American boy, who was himself descended from English, Irish, Dutch, and German ancestors, and whose great-grandfather could not speak English, had never in his life seen nor heard of a German, and now learned for the first time this marvelous thing—namely, that there were people in the world who could not talk as he did, but spoke a kind of gibberish which it was alleged they understood, although no one else did. The typical little American boy doubted, like Doctor Johnson, whether they could really understand themselves; and he wondered why they had not been taught to speak like other people.

Naturally enough, the little American boy had no desire to learn this strange gibberish, nor would he ever make the slightest effort to learn it. Afterward, when he became the daily companion of the children of this German family, and sometimes found himself inveigled by them into their house in order to get something to eat "between meals," the grown-up Kate, of whom he was much afraid, would perhaps make it a condition of his getting anything that he should say, "*Bitte, ein stück Brot.*" But the little American boy would never even try to make these strange sounds; not even the great desire for bread and molasses (which he always got, anyway, in the end) would bring him to it. Never, on any occasion, would he say even a single word, such as *Brot,* or *Messer,* or *Tish;* for the truth is that the little American boy could see no sense in these words, or any good reason for learning to pronounce them.

And indeed, in his own way, the little American boy was quite right. He never needed to speak German; and no one in that Iowa farming community ever needed to speak Ger-man. To speak nothing but German was as great a handicap as any one could well have; and the German family knew this better than anybody. They had to learn English, and all of them did, except the mother. The father soon learned to say all that he needed to say, in a strange, throaty fashion that never lost its interest for the little American boy, and the children learned more easily still to speak English as well as German, and no doubt much better in the course of time. They went with the little American boys and girls to the "district school," where they studied the same books and played the same games and acquired the same manners as other boys and girls. Between this German family and other families there was no difference, except the difference in origin. The man paid for his farm, just as my father paid for his. He ultimately "retired"—that is, he rented his farm and went to live in town on the rental of his farm—just as my father did. His children married, either the children of other German-Americans or else native Americans (one of them married my cousin), and they now have children of their own who go to the schools, join the Methodist or the Baptist or the Congregational Church, will become Democrats or Republicans, as the case may be, and probably cannot in any case speak any language but English. Such was the process of Americanization throughout the farming communities of the great Middle West.

Becker added subtle strokes to his self-portrait, on occasion, by noting in others those qualities that were precisely the obverse of his own. In 1930, after some years of intermittent depression, he remarked almost enviously that Benjamin Franklin "took life as it came, with the full-blooded heartiness of a man unacquainted with inhibitions and repressions and spiritual *malaise*." And in 1943, writing of Jacob Gould Schurman, Cornell's third president, Becker observed that "life was to him essentially neither a comic nor a tragic enigma, but a challenge to serious endeavor. Never greatly troubled by doubt, he enjoyed in a high degree the will to believe."[3] Having been suffocated by Methodism during his midwestern youth, the mature Becker lacked the will to believe and had always the inclination to doubt.

We are fortunate that Becker did, on occasion, plumb his memory for historical purposes, because his letters do not tell us very much about his origins or formative experiences. There are, in fact, a number of important things about the man and his make-up that we do not learn from these letters; and since the aim of this introductory essay is to discuss Becker and the nature of his inner world, it would be wise to indicate at the very outset what still re-

3. *Benjamin Franklin*, 32; *Cornell Alumni News*, XLVI (July 15, 1943), 27.

mains uncertain. Readers of this volume should not hope to understand fully why Becker was so shy and indifferent to most people; or why he acquired and retained an antipathy to organized religion and religious belief; or why he became quite so uninterested in conventional historical research among primary sources; or why he was as money-conscious (though hardly materialistic) as his letters seem to suggest.

Readers will derive a sense of what Becker owed to Frederick Jackson Turner, his mentor; but the nature of that crucial relationship remains obscured by Becker's romantic idealization of his great teacher. The influence upon Becker of his earliest colleagues cannot be adequately determined, although it surely must have been considerable. Historians have commonly remarked upon the oddity of Becker's writing mainly about American history while teaching almost entirely in the field of modern European history. In part this professional cleavage resulted from his having been trained by Charles Homer Haskins and James Harvey Robinson, two Europeanists, as well as by Turner and Herbert Levi Osgood; and also in part from the accidents of early job opportunities at Pennsylvania State College, Dartmouth College, and the University of Kansas. But the bifurcation—if that is the proper word—must have owed something, too, to the stimulation of such colleagues as Wilbur Cortez Abbott, with whom Becker taught at Dartmouth and Kansas. Like Becker, Abbott was interested in both European and early American history, and particularly like Becker, Abbott worked extensively on the history of colonial New York while holding major professorships in early modern European history.[4]

We do not learn from these letters as much as we would like about Becker's reading and its impact upon his thinking. We know that he absorbed and admired the work of such literary figures as Henry James, William Dean Howells, and Hamlin Garland; that he was influenced by such philosophers as Benedetto Croce, William James, John Dewey, and Alfred North Whitehead; and that in 1938 he included books by William Graham Sumner, Sigmund Freud,

4. See Wilbur Cortez Abbott's *Colonel John Scott of Long Island, 1634–1696* (New Haven, 1918); *New York in the American Revolution* (New York, 1929); and *Adventures in Reputation* (Cambridge, Mass., 1935), 149–208.

and Bertrand Russell among those "which have impressed me or influenced my thinking."[5] But the explicit nature and relative importance of their impact remain vague.

Different people will glean different things from these letters, to be sure, depending upon what they are looking for or what they are predisposed to "learn." Students of historiography and the philosophy of history, devotees of American thought and culture, former students and friends will derive varied impressions. But all, I think, will come away with a very real sense of the "climate of opinion" peculiar to Becker's professional and inner worlds. For his letters are revealing in many obvious ways. They were not written for posterity—indeed many are almost illegible—yet what they lack in formality they compensate for in candor, wit, compassion, and insight about people, situations, and the human condition.

I indicated at the outset that the publication of Becker's "autobiography" would be justified for purposes of exemplification. What then, does his intellectual odyssey illustrate? Many moods and trends, certainly, but above all the contrapuntal tendencies of historical thought in the English colonies and the subsequent United States. American scholars have vacillated between moods of ebullient optimism and profound pessimism. If Thomas Jefferson, George Bancroft, and Daniel Boorstin have celebrated the rising glory of America, Cotton Mather, Henry Adams, and Perry Miller have lamented the tragedy of America's unfulfilled promise. Within Becker's own development we find cycles of both confidence and cynicism. Between 1900 and 1920 his writings were girded by faith in the democratic system and the good will of its participants. During the next two decades, however, his outlook shifted to disillusionment bordering at times upon despair. Between 1940 and 1945 his doubts gave way to cautious but hopeful reaffirmation. These cycles of psychic emphasis, then, even more than his fabled

5. See CLB to the editor of the *New Republic*, autumn 1938; Wilkins, *Carl Becker*, 57–58; Strout, *The Pragmatic Revolt in American History*, 14, 26–27, 39. Unless otherwise indicated, letters referred to are in this collection. For bibliographical information about books on CLB and his contemporaries, see the Bibliography.

detachment, make him a sensitive measure of the historical mind responding to the meaning of America.

Long before Becker became known as a writer, he was a teacher; he "professed" history at Penn State, Dartmouth, Kansas, Minnesota, and Cornell from 1899 until 1941. It is clear from his letters that he enjoyed teaching the very brightest students, graduate and undergraduate, but that the general routine of lectures and run-of-the-mill students bored him (incidentally, his lectures bored many such students). "Everything as dull here as usual," he wrote in 1929. "Handing out the same old stuff in M[odern] Hist. and mystifying ten seminarians with the old jokes and paradoxes."[6] Some of his better students continued to look to him for guidance and support long after they had left Cornell; and Becker usually responded with a delicate mixture of deft criticism and warm encouragement. "I have read your paper," he wrote to Leo Gershoy in 1934. "It is of course so cut up, and some of it so difficult to make out, that it should not be judged on the basis of its present form. However, I got the main drift of the current, even if there was a good deal of broken floating ice and debris to obscure it. I feel sure that when you work this over until it unfolds naturally in terms of your chief ideas it will be a very fine piece of work."[7]

Despite the growing number of students who came to his classes, and his very poor health throughout the 1930's, Becker was conscientious about his teaching obligations. "I am in the midst of reading papers for H. 44," he wrote to a friend, "interspersed by students who come in wanting to know what they can do about 'that final grade'—which turns out to have been 45 or something like that. It is hard to answer these people convincingly, because obviously nothing is easier than to cross out the number 45 and write 85. I always want to do it, because it's easy to do, and would make them happy. But some vestige of a conscience prevents."[8] Understandably, then, Becker was vexed but also amused when *Time* reported that he opposed "such academic restrictions on liberty as roll calls, examinations, required papers," and that he

6. CLB to Leo Gershoy, Feb. 28, 1929, LIG.
7. CLB to Leo Gershoy, Jan. 4, 1934, LIG.
8. CLB to Val R. Lorwin, [Jan. 1934?], CBCU.

"requires no work at all in his seminars, but gets it nonetheless."
Becker's sardonic response to the editors of *Time* is printed in this
volume.[9]

However many students Becker taught in the classroom or
"seminary," his broadest impact as a teacher occurred through
his writings. He frequently received letters from high school teachers and students who were appreciative of his *Modern History*
(1931). But even as early as 1910, with the publication of his
doctoral dissertation, *The History of Political Parties in the
Province of New York, 1760–1776,* and his essay "Kansas," people
began writing congratulatory letters to and about him.[10]

Becker's work on prerevolutionary New York stressed the importance of social classes and economic interests in politics, an
emphasis that has caused historians to lump him casually with
Charles Beard and others of the "Progressive generation." Actually,
Becker had a subtler and deeper sense of human motives and behavior than did Beard; and he was less an economic determinist.
"One thing I think we have to avoid," he wrote in 1918, "which I
have always felt that Beard & people of his way of thinking do not
altogether do: and that is the assumption that the men who had
property & sought to protect it were somehow conscious hypocrites.
This comes from an inadequate psychology. . . . We all have a
wonderful talent for identifying our interests with the cosmic purpose, but we do it honestly enough for the most part.—& the men
who profess principles designed to enable them to keep their
property are not any the less, on that account, good patriots, than
those who profess principles designed to get it away from them."[11]

Most of Becker's scholarly writing concerned the eighteenth
century in general and the Enlightenment in particular. His own
qualities of mind—skeptical and rational, with a love of cerebral
exploration—suited him perfectly for immersion in the Age of
Reason. Like the philosophes, he respected the past but distrusted
tradition and cliché. He appreciated intellectual innovation and
was fascinated by "states of mind." Equally important, in Becker's
view, was the character of eighteenth-century prose. "The kind of

9. Sept. 17, 1934.
10. See Jacobs, ed., *The Historical World of Frederick Jackson Turner,* 208–209.
11. CLB to Arthur M. Schlesinger, [late 1918?].

felicity most admired and cultivated in the Age of Enlightenment,"
he wrote, "had the common sense, that is to say the obvious, if
fundamental, virtues of all good writing—simplicity, clarity,
logical order."[12]

From the letters we learn that Becker agonized over his writing—not merely to achieve simplicity, clarity, and logical order,
but also to avoid glibness and superficiality. "I wish to write
well," he remarked in 1914, "but I have a horror of being thought
rhetorical."[13] From time to time the letters discuss his own painful
process of writing, the need to fashion a literary style to suit the
individual personality, and the difficult art of book reviewing.
Ultimately, he concluded, "no one can teach anyone else anything
about how to learn to write."[14]

If Becker was self-conscious about being a literary craftsman, he
was equally aware that his distinctive style depended on a pervasive tone of irony, cynicism, and detachment. Those qualities were
certainly not the product of a pose or contrived posture; yet Becker
realized that they were central in his literary personality and
perspective, that they were attributed to him and, in a sense, expected of him.[15] Certainly his well-known tendency toward skepticism in matters of faith was simply part of a larger inclination to
be skeptical about all claims to absolute certainty, whether by
theologians, philosophers, or historians.

Becker's skepticism as a historian and his search for meaning in
history together provide the single most pervasive theme in these
letters. After presenting his famous presidential address before
the American Historical Association in 1931, "Everyman His Own

12. CLB, *The Declaration of Independence*, xiii. See also Becker's
comment on Franklin: "He was a literary artist of rare merit, the
master of a style which for clarity, precision, and pliable adhesion to
the form and pressure of the idea to be conveyed has rarely been
equaled" (*Benjamin Franklin*, 35).

13. CLB to Wallace Notestein, Nov. 1, 1914.

14. CLB to Anita M. Lerner, April 25, 1937. See also CLB's remarks in
his essay "Labelling the Historians": "Any style worth attention cannot be separated from the matter of which it is, in the measure of its
excellence, merely the most appropriate form" (*Everyman His Own
Historian*, 137).

15. See CLB to William E. Dodd, June 17, 1920; to Felix Frankfurter,
[May 1927]; and to Livingston Farrand, Jan. 25, 1929.

Historian," Becker was troubled by the extent to which he had been misunderstood, especially by his contemporaries and senior colleagues. "I was led to this address," he told William E. Dodd, "by the necessity, from long back, of finding some answer to the frequent question: 'What is the good of history?' The answer was not always easy, all the more so since it must be obvious that much of what is called historical research is a dreary waste of meticulous determination of facts the importance of which is difficult to see."[16]

Despite Becker's enduring commitment to historical study, he remained wary of the inflated claims made by some on behalf of history as a discipline. "About all I can see in history," he wrote in 1922, "is change from one situation to another situation, better or worse, as the case may be. . . . The object of historical study, as I see it, is to represent this change in such a way that it can be understood in terms of human purposes, motives and actions. . . . The chief value of history is that it is an extension of the personal memory, and an extension which masses of people can share, so that it becomes, or would ideally become, the memory of a nation, or of humanity."[17]

Becker wisely did not claim any particular predictive powers for history or the historian—wisely, because he was not himself, for all his understanding of history, a very good prophet. In October 1920 he was sure that the Treaty of Versailles and the League of Nations would soon be approved by the Senate. In January 1933 he saw evidence "of the new era of prosperity which I am sure is just around the corner." In October 1939 he felt confident that the European Allies "will defeat Germany if the war goes on, more easily than the last time, because Germany is in no condition to stand a long war." And in May 1942 he predicted that "this summer will show that Germany has found her peak & is bound to be defeated in 1943."[18]

Perhaps, irony of ironies, it was precisely Becker's early and excessive optimism about the possibilities of a democratic system,

16. Jan. 27, 1932.
17. To Henry Johnson, [Dec. 1922].
18. See CLB to William E. Dodd, Oct. 25, 1920; to Mr. Norton, Jan. 8, 1933, COL; to May Elish Markewich, Oct. 17, 1939; to Max Lerner, May 2, 1942, Max Lerner Papers, YU; to Mary Elizabeth Bohannon, Dec. 16, 1942, CBCU.

the justness of World War I, and the new era of prosperity dawning in 1933 that caused his bitter disillusionment with Woodrow Wilson and his periodic disenchantment with democracy and capitalism.[19] By 1944, certainly, there was at least a kernel of truth in one critic's caustic observation that "Mr. Becker is an old-fashioned liberal with a kind of abstract political realism but no very immediate sense of what is going on in the world in our time."[20]

In Becker's make-up, then, there was an interesting blend, perhaps especially midwestern, of sound common sense and naïve innocence. He partook of the practical idealism that he attributed to Kansas and Kansans: "an idealism that is immensely concrete and practical, requiring always some definite object upon which to expend itself."[21] And he also was affected by the very same collective individualism that he associated with frontier life in nineteenth-century America. "Of course the frontier promoted initiative and self-reliance," he wrote to Charles A. Beard. "You had to have guts to survive. But conformity was essential too. Individual liberty could be exercised only within a narrow framework of conduct and thought. And cooperation in the community was absolutely essential too. . . . I think this is the explanation of the fact that in the west, which produces individuals with plenty of initiative and independence, eccentricities which go beyond the narrow limits of the common mores are likely to be more frowned on than elsewhere."[22]

Becker's belief in collective individualism is less clearly visible than his practical idealism; but it shaped his temperament to a very great degree. A reserved and quiet man, sedate and considerate, he had grown up first on a working farm and then in Waterloo, Iowa, the heart, as he later put it, of "the Methodist menace."[23] He lived the most conventional and uneventful of academic lives, unmarked by scandal or by vices more serious than

19. See CLB to William E. Dodd, [late spring 1920]; June 17, 1920; and Oct. 25, 1920.
20. Edmund Wilson, "World Federation and the Four Fidgets," *The New Yorker*, XX (April 15, 1944), 68.
21. *Everyman His Own Historian*, 17, 19.
22. [Feb. 1939]. See also *Everyman His Own Historian*, 6, 9.
23. To E. R. B. Willis, June 13, 1928.

billiard-playing, fast driving, and excessive smoking of Camel cigarettes. He believed strongly in the need for collectivism in political society. Yet he had, from his college days at least, a "countervailing" attitude, a tendency to "think otherwise," and a penchant for friendships with radicals and what he liked to call "wild ones." Teaching at Stanford in the summer of 1928, he remarked that the students were too earnest. "They laugh, but only at the proper things. I long to meet a crazy person, like Morton Yohalem or Helen Sullivan"—two of his liveliest undergraduates at Cornell.[24] Among former students and younger associates of whom he was proud, Becker displayed special warmth for the unpredictable "live wires," such as Leo and Ida Gershoy, Max and Anita Lerner, Morton and Florence Yohalem, and Gussie Gaskill. One can almost measure the degree of Becker's affection and admiration by the severity of his needling. He only teased the ones he loved.

His favorites, in turn, were devoted to him, sending him scarves and ties, cigarette cases and books, and praising his writings effusively. Becker was in many respects a modest man and unpretentious; but he enjoyed praise and even fame as much as anyone. Although he often insisted that he was indifferent to reviews and reviewers, he followed the response to each of his books with intense interest and occasional complaint.[25] He enjoyed being mentioned in the press or receiving special citations; and he was candid about his ambitions and attendant sense of urgency: "I haven't many years left," he wrote in 1933, "and I should like to do something more than the little I have done, and something really good." By 1941, aged sixty-eight and about to retire from teaching, he conceded that "an old man lives on praise, having nothing else much to support his ego."[26]

Outside the inner circle of his affectionate former students, Becker cared for a small cluster of colleagues, most of them as-

24. To E. R. B. Willis, [summer 1928]. See also CLB to Guy Stanton Ford, Jan. 13, 1934; to Anita M. Lerner, May 24, 1934, AML; and to Ida Gershoy, June 10, 1941.
25. See CLB to Leo Gershoy, Jan. 13, 1933, LIG; to William E. Dodd, Nov. 13, 1915; to Claude Halstead Van Tyne, July 12, 1919; and to Dodd, Oct. 25, 1920.
26. CLB to Leo Gershoy, April 1933, April 1941, LIG.

sociated either with his luncheon group at Cornell[27] or with a little club called The Circle which met once a month to listen to a learned paper and drink beer. E. R. B. Willis the librarian, Henry W. Edgerton the lawyer and judge, Herbert J. Davenport the economist, Walter F. Willcox the statistician, Loren Petry the botanist, Othon Guerlac the professor of Romance literature, George Sabine the philosopher, and Eugene Bradford the university registrar—these were his close friends, and he was quite devoted to them.[28]

What Becker most enjoyed he revealed in writing about his relationship with George G. Andrews, a former graduate student: "a free-ranging discussion of things in general—academic gossip, the state of the nation, the nature of the universe, the devious behavior of the human mind."[29] He loved professional baseball, detective stories, movies and theatre, Shakespeare, Tolstoy, and especially *Anna Karenina*. He actively disliked few things, preferring to say that he was "indifferent." Bad writing irritated him, and the use of clichés most of all. He could not bring himself to send a letter of condolence to Turner's widow in 1932, because he "found it extremely difficult to say anything except the conventional things one does say."[30] When he resorted to clichés, he did so with a vengeance and made sure that his correspondent knew that he knew that the words were threadbare: "Excuse these novel & original phrases, I can't keep inventing them."[31]

Four figures from the American past commanded Becker's special respect: Benjamin Franklin, Thomas Jefferson, Abraham Lincoln, and Henry Adams. With one of them, in particular,

27. Founded by Walter F. Willcox in the later 1920's and presently known as the "Willcox group." Willcox always wished it to be called the "Becker group."
28. See CLB to Leo Gershoy, Jan. 17, 1933, LIG; to Robert Morris Ogden, Oct. 15, 1938; to Walter Francis Wilcox, [May] 1943; to Louis Gottschalk, Feb. 23, 1944.
29. Introduction to *Napoleon in Review*, by George G. Andrews (New York, 1939), vi.
30. CLB to William E. Dodd, Oct. 25, 1920; to Max Farrand, May 16, 1932.
31. See CLB to Florence Yohalem, [fall 1933], FMY; and to Ida Gershoy, May 5, 1939, LIG.

Becker shared qualities of mind and character to such a marked degree that the connection is worthy of notice. Becker was a Jeffersonian. His particular interest in the sage of Monticello was manifest in many of his writings, but especially in three: *The Declaration of Independence* (1922); "Thomas Jefferson," written for the *Encyclopaedia of the Social Sciences* (1932); and "What Is Still Living in the Political Philosophy of Thomas Jefferson?" an address given before the American Philosophical Society in 1943.[32]

Both men had roots in the soil and retained an abiding affection for agrarian things.[33] Both were reserved men of detached temperament, religious skepticism, high idealism, and an Enlightenment faith in the power of ideas. Both were notable for their wide-ranging interests, subtlety of mind, and felicitous prose style. What Henry Adams once wrote of Jefferson—"His instincts led him to widen rather than narrow the bounds of every intellectual exercize" —was equally true of Becker, as was Albert Jay Nock's view of Jefferson: "He was a man disillusioned about politics. He knew the real business of life was neither the governing of men nor the piling up of treasure, but the discipline of self and the study of man."[34]

Like Jefferson, Becker was a bookish Francophile. Both men, however, discovered in Paris how very American they were; and for both men, trips to Europe merely strengthened their personal sense of American nationality.[35] Both Becker and Jefferson had a rational rather than an emotional apprehension of experience; and neither man was socially at ease with most women.[36] Both were

32. In *DWH*, 214–240.
33. See CLB to Reuben Gold Thwaites, April 25, 1909.
34. Quoted in Merrill D. Peterson, *The Jefferson Image in the American Mind* (New York, 1960), 286, 413–414.
35. See CLB to Frederick D. Becker, Aug. 28, 1924; and Peterson, *Jefferson Image*, 415.
36. CLB to Louis Gottschalk, Feb. 23, 1944; Winthrop D. Jordan, *White over Black: American Attitudes toward the Negro, 1550–1812* (Chapel Hill, N.C., 1968), 461–469. Cf. Fawn M. Brodie, "Jefferson Biographers and the Psychology of Canonization," *Journal of Interdisciplinary History*, II (1971), 162–167.

democrats by instinct but elitists by inclination.[37] Both were deeply committed to the humanistic importance of higher education. And finally, both were profoundly aware of what Becker called "the uses of posterity."[38]

What use will posterity make of Carl Becker? Only time will tell; but it is certain that he haunts American historiography as no other historian can. There was some justice in Edmund Wilson's critique, which Becker called a "lulu," in 1944: "Mr. Becker makes some observations that are good enough common sense, but he also unloads upon us a great many very familiar platitudes; and the only real distinction of the book lies in the fact that contemporary platitudes have been endowed by Mr. Becker with a patina that gives them the dignity of museum pieces."[39] But ultimately Wilson missed a glimpse of the inner world of Carl Becker, and thereby the reasons why Becker will endure. In 1898, as a graduate student at Columbia, Becker wrote a paper for James Harvey Robinson on the physiocrats, and in so doing he "acquired an abiding interest in why people think as they do."[40] For the rest of Becker's life, his greatest fascination was the phenomenon of "intelligence at work"; or, as he put it in 1934, "the way in which minds seem to work."[41] Only a noble spirit would address itself persistently for half a century to this difficult calling.

Becker endures, then, because more than any American historian he persistently confronted questions of transcendent importance—sometimes with hope and sometimes with despair, but always eloquently and humanely, fearlessly and honestly. He sought historical perspective on eternal verities and contemporary

37. See CLB to William E. Dodd, May 22, 1917, CBCU; CLB, "Liberalism—A Way Station," in *Everyman His Own Historian*, 98; and Peterson, *Jefferson Image*, 308.

38. See CLB, *The Heavenly City of the Eighteenth-Century Philosophers*, ch. iv; and "The Earth Belongs in Usufruct to the Living," in Julian P. Boyd, ed., *The Papers of Thomas Jefferson*, XV (Princeton, 1958), 384–398.

39. *The New Yorker*, XX (April 15, 1944), 68, reviewing CLB's *How New Will the Better World Be?* (1944).

40. CLB's review of Robinson's *The Human Comedy*, in *The Nation*, CXLIV (Jan. 9, 1937), 48–50.

41. *Everyman His Own Historian*, 199; CLB to Leo Gershoy, [Jan. 1934].

realities: the meaning of progress and power, the future of democracy, the nature of historical knowledge, the relationship between freedom and responsibility. He attempted to understand the mind and destiny of man, and he was determined to present his ideas in a form that Everyman could read and contemplate. What more can we ask of any man?

Carl Lotus Becker: Chronology

1873   Born (September 7) to Charles and Almeda Becker, on a farm in Blackhawk County, Iowa, the second of four children.

1884   The Becker family moves to Waterloo, Iowa.

1892   Graduates from high school; enrolls at Cornell College, Mt. Vernon, Iowa.

1893   Enrolls as a freshman at the University of Wisconsin.

1894   Enrolls in his first history course, under Frederick Jackson Turner.

1896   Receives a B.Litt., with honors in history; begins graduate study at Wisconsin.

1897   Teaches a freshman history course at Wisconsin.

1898   Becomes a graduate fellow in history and constitutional law at Columbia University.

1899   Becomes an instructor in history at Pennsylvania State College.

1901   Marries Maude Hepworth Ranney of New York City; becomes an instructor at Dartmouth College.

1902   Becomes assistant professor of European history at the University of Kansas.

1907   Receives a Ph.D. from Wisconsin; is promoted to associate professor at Kansas.

1908   Is promoted to professor.

1909   Publishes his dissertation, *The History of Political Parties in the Province of New York, 1760–1776.*

1910   Publishes "Kansas" and "Detachment and the Writing of History." A son, Frederick DeWitt Becker, is born.

1914   Joins the editorial board of the *American Historical Review,* serving until 1922.

1915   Publishes *The Beginnings of the American People.*

1916   Becomes professor of European history at the University of Minnesota.

1917   Becomes professor of European history at Cornell University.

1918   Publishes *The Eve of the Revolution;* advises the Committee on Public Information in Washington, D.C.

1920 Publishes *The United States: An Experiment in Democracy.*
1921 Is elected a fellow of the Royal Historical Society.
1922 Publishes *The Declaration of Independence: A Study in the History of Political Ideas.*
1923 Is elected to the American Academy of Arts and Sciences.
1924 Undergoes stomach surgery; spends the summer in Europe with Charles Hull, Wallace Notestein, and others.
1927 Publishes "The Spirit of '76."
1931 Publishes *Modern History: The Rise of a Democratic, Scientific, and Industrial Civilization;* gives his presidential address, "Everyman His Own Historian," to the American Historical Association.
1932 Publishes *The Heavenly City of the Eighteenth-Century Philosophers;* receives a D.Litt. from Yale; becomes a member of the American Antiquarian Society.
1933 Is elected to the National Institute of Arts and Letters.
1935 Publishes *Everyman His Own Historian: Essays on History and Politics;* is offered but declines the Harmsworth Professorship at Oxford. The Committee of the Federation of Citizens' Associations petitions the Board of Education of Washington, D.C., to ban his allegedly communistic *Modern History* from the schools.
1936 Publishes *Progress and Power;* is elected to the American Philosophical Society.
1937 Joins the editorial board of the *Yale Review.*
1938 Receives a D.Litt. from the University of Rochester.
1939 Receives a D.Litt. from Columbia University.
1940 Undergoes major intestinal surgery.
1941 Publishes *Modern Democracy* and *New Liberties for Old;* retires from teaching at Cornell; is appointed university historian.
1942 Spends the spring term at Smith College as Neilson Research Professor.
1943 Delivers the Messenger Lectures at Cornell, published as *Cornell University: Founders and the Founding;* goes to Washington as a consultant on American bombing and German morale.
1944 Publishes *How New Will the Better World Be?;* delivers the Cook Lectures at Michigan, published posthumously, in 1945, as *Freedom and Responsibility in the American Way of Life.*
1945 Dies of uremic poisoning (April 10).

Recipients of Becker Letters

	1900	
October 15	Gaëtan Combes de Lestrade	3
	1902	
June 23	Frederick Jackson Turner	4
	1904	
January 6	Frederick Jackson Turner	6
February 22	Frederick Jackson Turner	7
	1906	
July 1	Wendell Phillips Garrison	8
	1908	
September 27	Wallace Notestein	9
	1909	
March 19	Frederick Jackson Turner	11
April 25	Reuben Gold Thwaites	11
November 21	Frederick Jackson Turner	12
December 14	Frederick Jackson Turner	13
	1910	
May 16	Frederick Jackson Turner	15
November 23	The editor of The Dial	17
	1911	
February 1	Frederick Jackson Turner	20
[1911?]	Wallace Notestein	21
	1912	
January 1	Claude Halstead Van Tyne	22
April 23	Frederick Jackson Turner	24

November 10	Frederick Jackson Turner	26
	1913	
March 3	William E. Dodd	27
[Late 1913]	William E. Dodd	28
	1914	
[March]	William E. Dodd	28
November 1	Wallace Notestein	29
[1914 or 1915]	Frederick Jackson Turner	30
	1915	
[Early summer]	William E. Dodd	31
July 23	William B. Munro	33
[October]	William E. Dodd	36
November 13	William E. Dodd	37
	1916	
[Early 1916]	Wallace Notestein	38
November 20	James W. Gleed	39
	1917	
January 4	George Lincoln Burr	46
January 8	Charles Hull	48
January 18	George Lincoln Burr	49
January 18	Charles Hull	51
January 24	George Lincoln Burr	52
February 25	George Lincoln Burr	53
March 23	Charles H. Blood	54
[June]	Frederick Jackson Turner	56
[Summer]	Clarence C. Crawford	56
	1918	
August 31	George Lincoln Burr	58
[Late 1918?]	Arthur M. Schlesinger	59
	1919	
[Early 1919]	William E. Dodd	60
February 15	William E. Dodd	61
March 8	William E. Dodd	62
April 14	Richard Ager Newhall	63
July 12	Claude Halstead Van Tyne	63
December 2	William E. Dodd	64

1920

March 24	Richard Ager Newhall	66
June 5	Alexander Meiklejohn	66
June 6	Alexander Meiklejohn	68
June 8	J. Franklin Jameson	68
[Late spring]	William E. Dodd	69
June 17	William E. Dodd	71
[Summer]	William E. Dodd	74
July 23	Jared Treman Newman	75
October 24	Frederick Jackson Turner	75
October 25	William E. Dodd	77

1921

June 7	J. Franklin Jameson	78
[Summer]	Arthur M. Schlesinger	78
[Autumn]	William E. Dodd	79
[Autumn?]	William E. Dodd	81
December 24	Carl Van Doren	82

1922

[1922?]	William E. Dodd	82
October 24	Henry Johnson	84
[December]	Henry Johnson	85

1923

| [February 26] | William E. Dodd | 86 |
| [1923] | Henry Holt | 88 |

1924

May 10	Everett E. Edwards	88
June 15	Frederick D. Becker	89
July 4	Maude Ranney Becker	90
July 16	Maude Ranney Becker	91
July 27	Maude Ranney Becker	92
August 5	Maude Ranney Becker	93
August 24	Maude Ranney Becker	94
August 25	Maude Ranney Becker	95
August 28	Frederick D. Becker	96
September 6	Frederick D. Becker	97
September 8	Frederick D. Becker	99
October 22	Leo Gershoy	101

1925

January 24	Leo Gershoy	102
February 4	Leo Gershoy	103
April 10	Alfred A. Knopf	104
September 20	Frederick Jackson Turner	105

1926

February 26	Harry Elmer Barnes	105
April 28	George Lincoln Burr	107
[1926?]	Harry Elmer Barnes	107
December 9	Gussie E. Gaskill	108
December 10	The editor of the *Cornell Daily Sun*	109
December 15	The editor of the *Cornell Daily Sun*	112

1927

January 11	Harry Elmer Barnes	114
February 13	Leo Gershoy	114
April 2	Leo Gershoy	115
May 10	J. Franklin Jameson	116
May 18	Frederick Jackson Turner	117
[May]	Felix Frankfurter	118
June 2	Felix Frankfurter	118
[Late summer?]	Merle Curti	119
September 27	Leo Gershoy	120

1928

[Winter?]	Leo Gershoy	122
March 27	Richard Ager Newhall	124
June 13	Elias R. B. Willis	124
July 20	Mabel Perry	125
[July]	Leo Gershoy	126
July 30	Gussie E. Gaskill	128
[Summer]	Elias R. B. Willis	128
October 14	Frederick Jackson Turner	129
[November]	Frederick Jackson Turner	131
[November]	August C. Krey	131

1929

January 25	Livingston Farrand	132
[June?]	Charles Hull	133
[Summer]	Leo Gershoy	133

1930

[1930?]	Anita M. Lerner	135
April 18	Anita M., Max, and Constance Lerner	136
July 5	Constance Lerner	138
[1930?]	Constance Lerner	138
[1930?]	Anita M. Lerner	139
[Summer]	Constance and Anita M. Lerner	140
[September?]	Leo Gershoy	141
September 20	H. L. Mencken	141
October 12	Arthur M. Schlesinger	142
[December?]	Anita M. Lerner	143

1931

January 29	William E. Dodd	144
[Summer]	Leo Gershoy	145
October 6	Leo Gershoy	146
October 9	Constance Lerner	147
October 16	Leo Gershoy	148
October 20	Frederick Jackson Turner	148
November 13	Constance Lerner	150
December 6	Geoffrey Bruun	150
December 25	Anita M., Max, and Constance Lerner	151
1931	Ida and Leo Gershoy	152

1932

[Early 1932]	Leo Gershoy	153
January 15	Norman V. Donaldson	154
January 19	Frederick Jackson Turner	154
[January]	W. Stull Holt	155
January 27	William E. Dodd	156
[February]	William E. Dodd	157
[February 12]	Anita M. Lerner	158
May 16	Max Farrand	159
[Spring?]	Leo Gershoy	161
[Summer]	Oron J. Hale	163
[Summer?]	Constance Lerner	164
August 6	Fruma Kasdan Gottschalk	164
[August]	Leo Gershoy	165
[Autumn]	Leo Gershoy	166
October 27	Leo Gershoy	167
November 1	James Truslow Adams	168
November 10	Louis Gottschalk	169

November 21 James Truslow Adams 169
November 29 William E. Dodd 170
[December] Leo Gershoy 171

1933
January 22 Mary Elizabeth Bohannon 172
February 8 Mary Elizabeth Bohannon 173
February 14 Arthur M. Schlesinger 174
February 23 Ida Gershoy 176
March 1 Leo Gershoy 177
March 9 Livingston Farrand 178
March 19 Frederick Lewis Allen 179
May 3 Guy Stanton Ford 180
May 10 Norman Spitzer 181
[May 10] Conyers Read 182
May 15 Leo Gershoy 184
June 11 William E. Dodd 185
[Summer] Florence Mishnun Yohalem 186
July 15 Livingston Farrand 186
July 25 Mary Elizabeth Bohannon 187
September 12 George Lincoln Burr 189
[September] Val R. Lorwin 190
October 4 Leo Gershoy 191
October 16 The editors of *The Nation* 192
October 30 Leo Gershoy 194
[November] F. S. Rodkey 194
December 9 Ida and Leo Gershoy 196
December 20 Leo Gershoy 197

1934
January 13 Guy Stanton Ford 198
[January] Leo Gershoy 199
[Winter?] Val R. Lorwin 200
March 9 Carl Van Doren 201
March 15 Mary Elizabeth Bohannon 202
June 2 Leo Gershoy 202
[Summer] Louis Gottschalk 203
July 15 Ida Gershoy 204
[September 5] Ida Gershoy 205
September 17 The editors of *Time* 206
November 7 Florence Mishnun Yohalem 208
[Fall or winter] Morton Yohalem 209
December 14 Leo Gershoy 209

1935

January 5	Merle Curti	210
January 6	Leo Gershoy	211
January 10	Felix Frankfurter	212
January 15	Leo Gershoy	213
[January]	Val R. Lorwin	214
January 30	Ida Gershoy	215
[February]	Ida Gershoy	216
March 4	Leo and Ida Gershoy	217
March 16	Leo Gershoy	217
April 13	Gussie E. Gaskill	218
April 13	Anita M. Lerner	220
May 3	Elias R. B. Willis	221
May 5	Ida Gershoy	222
[July 26]	Anita M. Lerner	223
August 24	Leo and Ida Gershoy	224
October 5	Max Lerner	225
October 12	Merle Curti	226
November 8	Isaiah Bowman	228
November 11	W. Stull Holt	228
November 18	Leo Gershoy	229
November 26	W. Stull Holt	231
November 26	The editor of the *Washington Herald*	232
November 26	Wilma Pugh	236
December 26	Leo and Ida Gershoy	237

1936

January 8	The editor of the *New Republic*	239
February 6	Leo and Ida Gershoy	240
February 12	Florence Mishnun Yohalem	240
February 13	Leo Gershoy	241
February 29	Harry Elmer Barnes	242
April 10	Guy Stanton Ford	243
September 30	The editor of the *New Republic*	244
November 8	Florence Mishnun Yohalem	245
November 22	Morris Bishop	246
November 29	Leo and Ida Gershoy	248
December 25	Leo and Ida Gershoy	249

1937

January 3	Felix Frankfurter	249
[February]	Val R. Lorwin	251

February 7   Leo and Ida Gershoy   252
[Late February]   Val R. Lorwin   254
March 30   Florence Mishnun Yohalem   255
April 11   Max Lerner   256
[April]   Max Lerner   257
April 25   Anita M. Lerner   258
August 20   Leo and Ida Gershoy   259

1938
March 25   Max Lerner   260
[September]   Charles A. Beard   261
September 29   Guy Stanton Ford   261
October 15   Robert Morris Ogden   262
October 22   Harry Elmer Barnes   263
[Autumn]   The editor of the *New Republic*   263
December 26   Louis Gottschalk   264
December 27   Charles A. Beard   265
December 29   Henry W. Edgerton   266

1939
[February]   Charles A. Beard   267
June 9   Alfred A. Knopf   269
October 17   May Elish Markewich   270

1940
April 29   Carl Horwich   270
May 3   Louis Gottschalk   271
[June 11]   Carl Horwich   272
August 28   Louis Gottschalk   273
August 30   Leo and Ida Gershoy   274
September 28   Ida Gershoy   274
October 16   Leo Gershoy   275

1941
April 23   Alfred A. Knopf   276
May 1   Leo Gershoy   277
May 9   Max Lerner   278
June 10   Ida Gershoy   278
July 18   Louis Gottschalk   279
August 7   Alfred A. Knopf   280
September 24   Leo Gershoy   281
[Late December]   Henry W. Edgerton   281
[December]   Leo and Ida Gershoy   282

1942

February 12	Anita M. Lerner	283
March 4	Mary Elizabeth Bohannon	284
March 11	Max Lerner	285
March 13	Alice Durand Edgerton	286
[March]	Alice Durand Edgerton	287
March 30	Ida Gershoy	288
[April]	Ida Gershoy	288
June 5	Richard M. Leighton	289
June 26	Jessie Becker	290
July 10	Thomas Reed Powell	291
August 5	Leo Gershoy	292
[September]	Louis Gottschalk	293
October 7	Leo Gershoy	294
December 25	Leo and Ida Gershoy	295
December 27	Florence and Morton Yohalem	295

1943

March 19	Florence and Morton Yohalem	296
March 26	Alfred A. Knopf	298
April 13	Alfred A. Knopf	299
May 4	Alfred Kazin	300
May 10	Charles A. Beard	301
[May]	Walter Francis Willcox	304
July 10	Leo Gershoy	306
September 4	Leo Gershoy	307
October 18	Alfred A. Knopf	308
October 24	Leo and Ida Gershoy	308
October 25	Merle Curti	309
November 1	Edmund Ezra Day	310
November 4	Alfred A. Knopf	311
November 6	Richard M. Leighton	311

1944

January 15	Leo Gershoy	312
February 23	Louis Gottschalk	313
March 20	Leo and Ida Gershoy	314
May 26	The editor of the *Cornell Bulletin*	315
June	The editor of *Common Sense*	316
June 12	Leo Gershoy	317
July 13	Alfred A. Knopf	319
September 3	Louis Gottschalk	320

October 1	Robert N. Campbell	322
October 7	Louis Gottschalk	323
October	The editor of the *American Magazine*	324
October 20	Alfred A. Knopf	325
November 20	Leo and Ida Gershoy	325
November 29	Thomas Reed Powell	326
December 3	Thomas Reed Powell	327
December 14	Mildred J. Headings	327
December 20	Alfred A. Knopf	329
December 22	James Duane Squires	331
December 22	Leo and Ida Gershoy	332
December 30	Anita M. Lerner	332

1945

January 12	Rudolph E. Freund	333
January 15	Carl G. Gustavson	334
January 26	Mrs. Max M. Kesterson	335
January 29	Leo Gershoy	337
January 31	The editor of the *American Historical Review*	338
February 14	Carl Jadwin Becker	339
February 16	Mrs. Max M. Kesterson	340
March	The editor of the *Cornell Alumni News*	343
March 14	H. L. Mencken	344
March 14	Leo Gershoy	345
March 21	Jessie Becker	346

THE LETTERS

1. Apprentice and Journeyman Historian, 1900–1916

To Gaëtan Combes de Lestrade

State College, Pennsylvania, October 15, 1900[1]

Dear Sir,[2]

You will allow me to thank you for the communication which you have done me the honor of writing me with reference to my review of the Droit Politique Contemporain.[3]

I take pleasure in acknowledging the misapprehension I was under as to your use of the phrase *"Ce que nous appelons."* I well understand that the parliamentary regime on the continent is far from being the parl. regime in England. Neither have I the least ambition to determine which is the "genuine" one.

Referring to your work again I find the expression "Angleterre n'a pas de constitution politique." But I do not find that any distinction is there made between a formal constitution and any other. Since earlier in the work you had defined pol. constitution to mean the whole political organization of a people, I could not, and you will pardon me if I cannot now, perceive the significance of the latter statement.

Finally I am as far as possible from desiring any one to have a thesis to prove, or to present their conclusions in advance.[4] My main criterion was that the fairly well established terminology of constitutional Law had been more or less ignored without sufficient grounds, and that for the old terminology no well defined or consistent terms had been substituted. It seemed to me for instance that "constitution" & "govt" were used interchangeably; that "sovereignty" was defined not from a legal point of view at all, but in a purely sociological sense; and that "state," if it is to be a legal conception should be made objective.—I say it seemed so to me; it

may be that here also I was under a misapprehension. If I am in error I shall be most happy to be the recipient of further correction.
     I have the honor of assuring you of my most
                                    Distinguished consideration,
                                    Carl Becker

     1. CBCU, draft.
     2. Vicomte Combes de Lestrade (1859–1918), political scientist and sociologist, was the author of *Droit Politique Contemporain* (Paris, 1900).
     3. *Annals of the American Academy of Political and Social Science,* XVI (Sept. 1900), 127–129. CLB's review began: "A striking feature of this work is the confusion of thought which pervades it."
     4. CLB had written: "The want of some central, governing principle is most pronounced. The results of this defect are almost disastrous, for law can be profitably studied only in connection with some fundamental conceptions, round which the great multitude of facts can be more or less arranged."

To Frederick Jackson Turner

New York, New York, June 23, 1902[1]
My Dear Professor Turner[2]
     I do not know whether you have learned in any way that I am going to Kansas with Abbott next year.[3] Through Abbott's influence I had the refusal of a position there until about the last of May, and as the Mo. place was not settled then and there was little chance for me there I concluded that I could not take the chance though it was a much better place in some ways than the one at Kansas. At Mo. they decided to make the position a Professorship and relieve Loeb of History work entirely.[4] The last I heard it was offered to Dow of Michigan.[5] I do not know whether he accepted or not. The president assured me that after Dow I stood high in a list of younger men whom they were considering. The Kansas place is an assist Prof. with a salary of only $800 the first year; it is however permanent with a very good chance of a raise in salary up to $1200. I inquired whether the place was an Assist Professorship in every thing but salary or an instructorship in every thing but name, and was assured that it was the former in name and salary. The arrangement is that Abbott and I divide the European

History between us. I have Greek & Roman, Mediaeval, Renaissance & Reformation, & English, and Abbott takes the Modern period. On the whole it is not a bad position; I am told that $800 is as good in Kansas as 1000 or 1200 in Hanover. I can well believe it—it costs as much to live in Hanover as it does in New York City.

I shall be here for two or three weeks working in the libraries. Through Osgoods influence[6] I have secured access to the DeWitt Clinton MS letters, which the Columbia library recently purchased from Dodd Mead & Co for $2500, although they have not yet been bound or indexed. I do not find as much in them as I expected to. They seem valuable mostly for the matter of the Erie Canal, etc. They contain some letters on the La. purchase, but only a few, and as to their value I cannot say. Osgood has also secured me access to the John Lamb Papers in the Hist. Society library—a very great privilege as any one will agree who has ever worked in that library. These I know are very valuable for my purpose. There is also MS material in the Lenox [New York Public Library] which I shall examine, and if I have time I shall go to Albany for some odds & ends. I expect to finish up getting my material while here, for I cannot say when I may come east again.

This summer I shall be in Waterloo [Iowa] until about the first of September when I have to be at Lawrence.

The positions at Dartmouth have not been filled, & will not be, so the President said, until the close of the summer. They have adopted the group system there & made history elective. I do not think I stood any chance there; why, I cannot say, as Abbott was very well pleased with my work. Everything is however in the hands of the President and I fancy he requires other qualifications than those I possess.

By the way has your [?] address before the historical association on the Diplomatic Antecedents of the La. Purchase been published?[7] I suppose it will come out next year in the publications. As you are interested in that subject perhaps you might like copies of the letters in the Clinton papers bearing on it. I cannot vouch for their value, but I have kept exact references to them all and can give you the references if you would care to have them. You could have them copied through the libraries I think if worth while.

The weather is delightful here and we are enjoying our stay greatly.

With best wishes for Mrs Turner & yourself

Very Sincerely,

Carl Becker

1. CBCU.

2. Turner (1861–1932) taught history at the University of Wisconsin (1889–1910), where he was Becker's principal mentor, and at Harvard (1910–1924). One of Becker's most charming essays, "Frederick Jackson Turner," appeared in 1927 and was reprinted in his *Everyman His Own Historian: Essays on History and Politics.*

3. Wilbur Cortez Abbott (1869–1947) taught history at the University of Michigan (1897–1899), Dartmouth (1899–1902), the University of Kansas (1902–1908), Yale (1908–1920), and Harvard (1920–1937). His special interests were early modern England and colonial New York.

4. Isidor Loeb (1868–1954) taught history and political science at the University of Missouri (1892–1925), political science and constitutional law at Washington University, St. Louis (1925–1940).

5. Earle W. Dow (1868–1946) taught European history at Michigan (1892–1938).

6. Herbert Levi Osgood (1855–1918) taught history at Columbia (1890–1918). His special interest was early American history, particularly colonial New York. Becker studied with Osgood from 1898 to 1899.

7. Presented in Washington on December 28, 1901; published as "The Diplomatic Contest for the Mississippi Valley," *Atlantic Monthly,* XCIII (1904), 676–691, 807–817.

To Frederick Jackson Turner

Lawrence, Kansas, January 6, 1904[1]

Dear Professor Turner,

I wanted to talk with you about the requirements at Wisconsin for the Ph.D., but forgot it whenever I had an opportunity.[2] Could I elect to be examined wholly in history, and if so could I elect the periods, or would it be necessary to take examination in the whole field of history and in Economics as a minor. In a word just what would be the nature of the examination. And do you require publication of thesis. I could be ready with a thesis very soon but should not want to publish it I think just yet. Finally is there any examination in languages, and am I in any case eligible for the doctoral examinations? Doubtless you can send me a pamphlet that will satisfactorily answer all these questions.

Yours Cordially
Carl Becker

1. CBCU.
2. On July 3, 1896, Turner wrote to CLB about graduate study in general and the choice of minors in particular. Turner replied to this inquiry on January 9, 1904, and again on February 24, 1908. All three letters are in Jacobs, ed., *The Historical World of Frederick Jackson Turner*, 88–90, 200–201.

To Frederick Jackson Turner

Lawrence, February 22, 1904[1]

Dear Professor Turner,

I have been unduly long in answering your very kind letter. I think it doubtful whether I shall be able to get up to Madison for examinations this spring though I should like much to be present at the celebration you are planning there for June. We are beginning a course in Mediaeval History this term in which I have 130 students and that bids fair to keep me busy, with my other classes. I am getting my thesis in shape as fast as I find time but hardly think it will be ready by June. I am hardly prepared to take an examination in German and shall meantime be doing some thing with that. Another year at latest I hope to come up. I suppose if I should be ready this June, it would be possible to make the application later in the year perhaps? I have had quite sufficient economics for one minor, and as I understand you the other two— first minor & major—may be chosen in History. Probably my major would be in the same field as my thesis, and the first minor in some field of European history—say Mediaeval history or the Reformation Period, or, if you think best even a narrower field, like the 13 century.[2]

Mr. Crawford is applying for a fellowship at Wisconsin.[3] I know him formally and he seems an attractive man, a man of energy, and what they call a good "mixer" here. I do not mean that he has all the instincts of the politician by any means, but that he is the kind of a man who will come to the front as fast as his abilities justify. As to his ability I know very little. I have read a small part of his thesis & it seems a good piece of work—excellent in fact, under the circumstances. He is taking a course with me in "methods," this term and I have been favorably impressed with his ability. Finally I know he wishes to take the advanced degree either at Wisconsin or in the East, and expects to prepare for College work. I think he is a man who will *grow,* and I am sure he will do faithful work.

Yours truly,
Carl Becker

1. CBCU.

2. Becker's special interest in the thirteenth century would come to fruition twenty-eight years later in his most famous book, *The Heavenly City of the Eighteenth-Century Philosophers,* in which he stressed similarities in the medieval and Enlightenment "climates of opinion."

3. Clarence C. Crawford (1879–1962) received his B.A. and M.A. from Kansas (1903, 1904), and his doctorate from Wisconsin (1906). He taught history at Kansas (1907–1950). His specialty was English institutional history.

To Wendell Phillips Garrison

Lawrence, July 1, 1906[1]

My Dear Mr. Garrison,[2]

The announcement of your retirement from the editorial control of The Nation comes with the shock almost of a personal bereavement. No one, I am sure, has ever more fairly than yourself won relief from the strain of the world's work; but in my own case at least you have so constantly repaid a slight official service[3] with genuine personal kindliness that I cannot readily separate the one from the other. Accept my congratulations on having fought, for so many years, and no less uncompromisingly than your illustrious father,[4] the enemies of the Republic—with what results, who shall say? May your remaining years be many in the land, bringing you the rewards which distinguished services always merit. I shall always cherish the memory of your friendship in the past, as I shall in the future always strive to measure up to the high privileges which it confers.

Most cordially yours,
Carl Becker

1. Wendell P. Garrison Papers, Houghton Library, HU; by permission of the Harvard College Library.
2. Garrison (1840–1907) was literary editor of *The Nation* and author of occasional books for home and family.
3. Between 1903 and this date, Becker published thirty-five reviews in *The Nation*.
4. William Lloyd Garrison (1805–1879), antislavery reformer.

To Wallace Notestein

Lawrence, September 27, 1908[1]

My Dear Notestein,[2]

You will doubtless be glad to hear that there were eight bridesmaids and a maid of honor, a flower girl and a best man, and that the bride looked lovely and the groom manly. It may also be of moment that the bridesmaids dresses were of yellow satin,—to match the groom's hair I have no doubt—, with trimmings and everything necessary. Strangely enough there was a reception afterwards, and cream and cake, and punch on the front porch, and when they went away rice was thrown. It was, in short, everything a wedding should be; and I may add that the punch was *not* like the punch served at the Chancellor's receptions; the difference may have been due to some German custom or other. The groom played his part well, with jaw set, and a look of grim determination, as who should say, "The President expects every man to do his duty." For all that, I think it was not at all a matter of duty with him; I think he was very hard hit. Many people have said "If Moore is half as nice as Miss Wilhelmi, it will be all right." I don't profess to know Miss Wilhelmi very well, but I know Moore, and if I had any reservations to make as to the success of the event, I think I should put it the other way.[3]

Moore's place here is taken by a certain Mr. Humble, of Cornell and Cincinnati and Chicago.[4] I gather that he is a Political Science man who took this job because it was open rather than for any inclination to teach law. I have not met him yet, but Uncle Jimmy[5] says he shows no inclination to reform the Law School the first year at any rate. He is doubtless wise in going slow, but if he has no desire to reform the Law School the second year, or the third, there must be something the matter with him. The Law School is as much in need of reform as ever, but who is to do it is the question.

The University has a registration of 2200, about 400 more than last year at this time; and the department of history has its share. In all courses there are about 700 registrations. You can imagine this pleases Hodder[6] very much, for his deep fear was that students would drop off and it would be ascribed to Abbott's leaving. You doubtless know that Patterson of Wisconsin is here as an Associate-Professor.[7] He is altogether of the right sort, personally and as a teacher. He has not done much research yet, and how much he will do I can't say. If he has any weak side it will be that, but I have every reason to think that he will do very good work if he does any.

Bates is doing excellent work.[8] Everyone likes him. He is an excellent teacher, and gets into the "life of the University" in a way that ought to satisfy the Chancellor.[9] In connection with Bates there is a little joke on the Chancellor that I must tell you. When Abbott went away there was some question as to retaining Crawford for your place, and the Chancellor would not consent to a permanent appointment. As a compensation for the one year's appointment, the Chancellor was induced to make his salary 1200. After this was settled both Hodder and myself observed to the Chancellor that Bates was getting only $1000; but, that as his was

[*The last page is missing.*]

1. Wallace Notestein Papers, Yale University Library.

2. Notestein (1878–1969), taught history at Kansas (1905–1908), Minnesota (1908–1920), Cornell (1920–1928), and Yale (1928–1947). His specialty was seventeenth-century England.

3. William U. Moore (1879–1949) taught law at Kansas (1906–1908); he married Henelia Wilhelmi, who had received her B.A. from Kansas (1904).

4. Henry W. Humble taught law at Kansas (1908–1921).

5. James W. Green (1842–1919) was dean of the law school at Kansas (1891–1919).

6. Frank H. Hodder (1860–1935) taught history and economics at Cornell (1885–1890, 1928–1929), American history at Kansas (1891–1933).

7. David L. Patterson (1884–1963) taught European history at Kansas (1908–1947).

8. Frank G. Bates taught American history and political science at Kansas (1907–1911).

9. Frank A. Strong (1859–1934), chancellor of the University of Kansas (1902–1920), a lawyer and constitutional historian.

To Frederick Jackson Turner

Lawrence, March 19, 1909[1]

My dear Professor Turner,

I never quite understood until last night, when I read your paper on the Old West,[2] why there was no marked conflict in New York, as in other colonies, between the interior & the coast. It seems that New York was all coast, and the struggle was one of classes only, rather than of classes & regions combined. I am immensely confirmed in my idea that the Revolution was only incidentally a matter of home rule, and primarily a matter of democratization of politics & society.[3] The history of revolutionary parties must be rewritten on that line, I think, and your paper points the way unmistakably for that as well as for other ventures.

We are much pleased with Patterson. I think he hasn't yet mastered the "Kansas Language," which develops steadily at the expense of the English.

With best wishes,
Carl Becker

1. Frederick Jackson Turner Papers, HEH; by permission of The Huntington Library, San Marino, California.
2. "The Old West," *Proceedings of the State Historical Society of Wisconsin . . . 1908* (Madison, 1909), 184–233.
3. See Becker's influential dissertation, *The History of Political Parties in the Province of New York, 1760–1776*, esp. p. 22.

To Reuben Gold Thwaites

Lawrence, April 25, 1909[1]

My Dear Dr. Thwaites, [2]

I have read with much interest the little pamphlet on the "Reaper" which you have sent me.[3] During the summers of 1888–91, I enjoyed the great pleasure of following a McCormic selfbinder about a forty acre oat field for ten hours a day, in the humble capacity of a "shucker." And I can remember when my father cut his wheat with the old fashioned 'reaper' which [raked] the single unbound 'bundle' on to the ground. I recall, too, when this was replaced by the 'platform' reaper, which carried two men who bound the 'bundles' before they were thrown to the ground. Finally came the 'self binder.' The "bundle carrier" is at least twenty years old, for I remember it very well in the 80's. Do not the stationary guards, which you mention at page 241, project forward *under* the knife, or 'sickle' as we used to call it, being bent backwards over it? At least, these are the kind I am familiar with.

Excuse the zeal of a one time practical farmer in these small matters.

Yours very truly,
Carl Becker

1. CBCU.

2. Thwaites (1853–1913), historian and editor, directed the State Historical Society of Wisconsin. His specialty was early American history, especially the exploration and development of the Old Northwest.

3. Thwaites, "Cyrus Hall McCormick and the Reaper," *Proceedings of the State Historical Society of Wisconsin . . . 1908* (Madison, 1909), 234–259.

To Frederick Jackson Turner

Lawrence, November 21, 1909[1]

My dear Professor Turner,

I have just received a marked copy of the Harvard Bulletin which says that the Fellows, whoever they may be, have appointed Professor Turner to be professor of history in Harvard University. It does not say that Professor Turner has accepted. I suppose at Harvard they think that when the Fellows appoint a man the incident is closed: the acceptance is a matter of course. I wish some one would surprise those Fellows once by refusing; perhaps the Bulletin might then take trouble, the next time an offer had been accepted, to remark casually that it had in fact been accepted.

Well, I congratulate Harvard sincerely; and I congratulate you too, though I don't know why, except that since you have accepted, as I must suppose you have, your new position must have some advantage over your old one. I had got in the habit of thinking that Wisconsin was a fixture with you, probably because of the notion that it was as good a university as any in the country, if not better than any, and your position in it all that could be desired, or at least all that could be anywhere attained. You will see by all this that I am jealous for the west, and proud for Wisconsin, and very provincial into the bargain. However, I wish for you everything that you deserve, and that is everything good.

Everything is going on here as usual, and the history department seems to be flourishing. I shall be in New York Christmas, together with three other members of the department, and hope to see you then. My thesis has brought me a number of letters, some of which say the conventional thing, and some a little more than that. I am now doing a little critical stunt on Walpole's *Memoirs of George III,* which I shall try on the Review although the Review probably has better stuff and will not care for it.[2] I have also produced a kind of fulmination which the editors of the Atlantic Monthly say they are disposed to print if it can be reduced to ten pages, ten pages being the limit—for articles of a 'literary or scholarly nature.' You see they are not just sure whether it is literary or scholarly. I suspect it is neither, and you will think so too I dare say—if you ever see it, which isn't certain.[3]

With kindest regards to all of you,

Most sincerely,
Carl Becker

1. Turner Papers, HEH.

2. "Horace Walpole's Memoirs of the Reign of George III," *AHR*, XVI (1911), 255–272, 496–507.

3. "Detachment and the Writing of History," *Atlantic Monthly*, CVI (1910), 524–536.

To Frederick Jackson Turner

Lawrence, December 14, 1909[1]

My dear Professor Turner,

You may be sure that I highly appreciate your letter of confidence. My only fear is that there was something in my letter that seemed to call in question your action in leaving Wisconsin, or that seemed to assume on my part a right to any explanation of your motives. I assumed, as I always do, that you had very good reasons for your action, and I meant only to express my regret that there could be, in the case of Wisconsin, good reasons for your leaving. As soon as I heard of your resignation, I said to myself— *Politics!* Your letter has justified my judgment, and I need not say that, in my opinion, it has entirely justified your action; and though I did not need that justification, and hope my letter did not seem to demand it, I am glad indeed to have it. I have long realized that that terrible *average man*—good creature—was bound, sooner or later, to thrust his sharp nose into our universities; but I confess I did not realize how rapidly it would come.[2] We have often been assured, especially in Kansas, that the state Universities are to "standardize high education," because they alone are thoroughly in touch with democratic ideals, and because they have one great advantage over endowed institutions—they have the wealth of the state back of them. It is fine to have the people under for support, but when they get out on top and begin to bear down—well, that is another matter. We have a "fine board of regents"—they do everything the Chancellor wants.[3] What the Chancellor wants, is to be a "power in the State." Rightly so, of course. But as rapidly as we become a "power in the State," our regents will be less docile, and we shall have the same difficulties you have.[4]

There are some things in your letter that I can't agree to. It is not you who have had a *share* in building up the Department of history at Wisconsin; it is the other people who have had the *share*, and a small share, too, in most cases. Wisconsin's position in the study & teaching of history will, of course, not be lost by 'one man's going or coming'; but your going will weaken it for some time; no question of that. If, however, it teaches the Regents something, as I have no doubt it will, perhaps, as you say, you are, in the long run, doing Wisconsin a service. Service or not, you are right in wanting to "do your work"—and may your years be many in which to do it—and in going where you can do it to best advantage. Of course a man never thinks he *has done* his work, and from that point of view, you are again quite right; but I must say that if you should do no more work, it would still be supposed by most of us that your work had been done, and very well done.

I have just sent off, by request, a short sketch of your work for the *Wisconsin Alumni Magazine,* inadequate enough, but I hope

I have caught the point of view in respect to your study of the "West."[5]

Cordially yours,
Carl Becker

1. Turner Papers, HEH.
2. Similar problems would subsequently cause Becker to leave Kansas in 1916. See his letter to James W. Gleed, Nov. 20, 1916.
3. The chancellor at this time was Frank Strong.
4. See CLB, "The Value of the University to the State," *University Press Bulletin* (Lawrence, Kan.), Dec. 3, 1910.
5. "Frederick Jackson Turner," *Wisconsin Alumni Magazine,* XI (1910), 143–144.

To Frederick Jackson Turner

Lawrence, May 16, 1910[1]

My dear Professor Turner,

It was in 1894 that I took my first course with you—that general course based upon the Epoch Series. Until then, I had never been interested in history; since then, I have never ceased to be so. For this effect, I hold you entirely responsible; the things that impressed me, that remained with me permanently, were incidental to the course, but inseparable from the teacher. I learned but few facts. So far as I recall, I answered correctly only one question during the year. The answer was 1811; the question I have forgotten. I think you gave us to understand that no one, not even Mr. Thwaites, knew "exactly what happened," that you did not yourself know; but to me at least you seemed mightily interested in selecting, from the infinite number of things that were said to have happened, things that had meaning and significance. Some of the things you said, often enough but casual remarks, my mind has held fast, and they have since become keys to open many locked doors. I do not remember whether South Carolina nullified the Laws of the United States; but I learned that minorities are everywhere likely to be nullifiers; and the latter point opened up so much the larger field of speculation than the former, that I have never ceased considering it. It seems that minorities can at best have only right on their side, whereas majorities have generally fact on theirs, and in the end therefore invariably prevail; which has puzzled me much, so that I have sometimes asked whether there is any difference between fact and right. I do not remember whether sovereignty resided with the States or with the nation in 1789; but I remember you drew a diagram on the board to illustrate the problem (which I had never seen anyone do except for geometry), and that you said you hadn't a logical mind, which one ought to have if one wanted to be positive about such a question. That remark I have often recalled, and have pondered, in a desultory way, the difference between the logical and the historical mind; and have come to the conclusion that logic and history are two distinct ways (and perhaps the only ways) of apprehending 'reality'; history being, however, the more comprehensive, since there is no logic of history but [there] is a very interesting history of logic. Then I remember you said once that it was all very well to poke fun at the Philosophy of history, but that after all it was impossible not to have some kind of a Philosophy of history, the vital point being only whether one's Philosophy amounted to anything. And more than once I have heard you say: "History is the selfconsciousness of humanity." That, at the time, meant absolutely nothing to me, but the phrase must have been working in the "fringe" of *my* consciousness all these years, for I have recently hazarded in print the thesis that "we must have a past that is the product of all the present." That, I take it, is the same as saying that history is the selfconsciousness of humanity. Thus you see you are responsible even for what I publish, although, as they say in the prefaces, while quite agreeing to give you the credit for the little good there may be in it, I hold you in no way liable for the much that is bad. I remember that you tried to interest us in the Blue Ridge, and the Cumberland Gap, and the Old Cumberland Road, (or some such road.) What it was you said, I have forgotten; but I remember precisely the manner in which you said it. It was a manner that carried conviction—the manner of one who utters moral truths; and somehow it has ever since stuck in my mind that the Blue Ridge, and the Cumberland Gap, and the Old Cumberland Road, (or whatever road it was) are threads that will unravel the whole tangled skein of American history.

To me, nothing can be duller than historical facts; nothing more interesting than the service they can be made to render in the effort to solve the everlasting riddle of human existence. It is from you, my dear Professor Turner, more than from anyone else, that I have learned to distinguish historical facts from their uses.[2]

With best wishes and most cordially,

Carl Becker

1. Turner Papers, HEH.

2. On the occasion of Becker's retirement in 1941, he received a similar letter from Louis Gottschalk, one of his earliest doctoral students at Cornell. See CLB to Gottschalk, July 18, 1941; and Gottschalk to CLB, July 15, 1941, Appendix.

To the editor of *The Dial*

Lawrence, November 23, 1910[1]

(To the Editor of THE DIAL.)

I have been interested in the letter of Mr. Hutson on "The Writing of History," and in the replies called out by it.[2] Mr. Hutson tells us that history never has been a science, and that it is in a fair way of ceasing to be literature, and he advises us to get back to the spirit and methods of Macaulay as soon as we conveniently can.[3] Those who reply to Mr. Hutson say that while history may not be a science, it is scientific in its methods. They deny that any historian tries to write badly, and they contend that many historians since Macaulay's time, such as Renan and Luchaire,[4] have written well, and that if we do not all write like Macaulay it is not because we do not wish to do so. They maintain that Macaulay was a genius, that England has produced but one Macaulay, and that it is too much to expect us so-called historians to be geniuses like Macaulay, and to have a style like his; they think that, even if we attempted to imitate him, our books, doctor's theses and the like, would probably not displace the latest novel on the young ladies' dressing-tables.

Probably they would not. But what interested me most was that your correspondents, differing at so many points, were quite agreed that there never was a style like Macaulay's. I have been waiting to hear someone say that he could not endure Macaulay's style. I remember well the first time I read of Macaulay's History having been found, by the young ladies, when it first came out, more interesting than the latest novel. I was in college then, and I ran to the library to get Macaulay's History, hoping against hope that no one had drawn it out before me. No one had. I was elated at the thought that the history of England might be taken on so easily, and with the same pleasure I had experienced in learning about Athos and Porthos. I went home prepared to make the acquaintance of an English Dumas.[5] Well, I was disappointed. I did not keep the book on my dressing-table, but returned it to the library. Since then, I have tried again and again to read Macaulay's History; and, by dint of much perseverance, I have succeeded in reading most of it. Imagine the whole history of England written by Macaulay! I cannot imagine it; but I have often tried to imagine what the Pilgrim's Chorus, adapted to fife and drum, would be like.

One of your correspondents, "J. W. T.," in his reply to Mr. Hutson, brought forward Renan, and set him up, with some timidity, I thought, by the side of Macaulay, to show that there had been some good writing since Macaulay's time. He seems to say that Renan writes very well indeed, and cites one passage which even Macaulay might have envied; and he mentions others, such as Lavisse[6] and Luchair, who write well, though of course not as well as Macaulay. England, as he says, has produced but one Macaulay. Well, I should think that one was enough. Of course it would be a distinct loss not to have had one Macaulay,—to observe the average middle-class Englishman raised to the nth power is certainly worth while; but one such will do very well. Now, if it comes to style, or to matter either, or to manner, or to philosophy, I much prefer Renan. It is true that he has not the wealth of allusion to all the literatures of the world that Macaulay has. But I think I must care less for literary allusions and quotations than some readers. I despise a Greek quotation because I cannot read it, and I am suspicious of a Latin quotation because I cannot always read it easily. *O tempore! O mores!*—if this is apropos here.

Mr. Hutson complains that the new school turned its back on Macaulay. "They drowned their thought with an endless tangle of modifications," as he so aptly says. "Those who still stood by rhetoric looked on Macaulay's style as crude and sometimes as cacophonous, and aimed at effects which we call, after the French, 'precious.' Of these were Walter Pater and Robert Louis Stevenson.[7]

Well, what of the result? Perhaps we have greater exactness as to facts, in many cases new points of view, a more cautious summing up of the evidence; but nowhere is the clear and flowing current of narrative, the allurement of style, the wonderful touch of art in the presentation of truth."

Incidentally, I am not convinced that Robert Louis Stevenson is "precious," at least not in the sense Mr. Hutson means. I do not wish to enlarge on that; but since Mr. Hutson has mentioned Walter Pater, I would like to quote, apropos of "allurement of style, the wonderful touch of art in the presentation of truth," the following passage from that writer. It is taken from the essay on Leonardo da Vinci, and is an interpretation of the famous picture "La Gioconda": [8]

"The presence that thus rose so strangely beside the waters, is expressive of what in the ways of a thousand years men had come to desire. Hers is the head upon which all "the ends of the world are come," and the eyelids are a little weary. It is a beauty wrought out from within upon the flesh, the deposit, little cell by cell, of strange thoughts and fantastic reveries and exquisite passions. Set it for a moment beside one of those white Greek goddesses or beautiful women of antiquity, and how would they be troubled by this beauty, into which the soul with all its maladies has passed! All the thoughts and experience of the world have etched and moulded there, in that which they have of power to refine and make expressive the outward form, the animalism of Greece, the lust of Rome, the revery of the middle age with its spiritual ambition and imaginative loves, the return of the Pagan world, the sins of the Borgias. She is older than the rocks among which she sits; like the vampire, she has been dead many times, and learned the secrets of the grave; and has been a diver in deep seas, and keeps their fallen day about her; and trafficked for strange webs with Eastern merchants: and, as Leda, was the mother of Helen of Troy, and, as Saint Anne, the mother of Mary; and all this has been to her but as the sound of lyres and flutes, and lives only in the delicacy with which it has moulded the changing lineaments, and tinged the eyelids and the hands. The fancy of a perpetual life, sweeping together ten thousand experiences, is an old one; and modern thought has conceived the idea of humanity as wrought upon by, and summing up in itself, all modes of thought and life. Certainly Lady Lisa might stand as the embodiment of the old fancy, the symbol of the modern idea."

Meanwhile, I sympathize with Mr. Hutson in the matter of doctor's theses. I have written one and read several. Professor Sioussat,[9] in his defence of doctor's theses, gives good reasons for their existence, some of which are, at the same time, the best reasons in the world for not printing them.

Carl Becker

1. *The Dial*, XLIX (Dec. 1, 1910), 454.

2. Charles W. Hutson, "The Writing of History," *ibid.* (Oct. 1, 1910), 225.

3. Thomas Babington Macaulay (1800–1859), English historian, Liberal M.P., Whig partisan.

4. Ernest Renan (1823–1892), French historian and philosopher; Achille Luchaire (1846–1908), French medievalist.

5. Alexandre Dumas (1802–1870), author of *The Three Musketeers* (1844), concerning the adventures of D'Artagnan, Athos, Porthos, and Aramis.

6. Ernest Lavisse (1842–1922), French historian.

7. Pater (1839–1894) was a British historian, literary critic, and humanist; Stevenson (1850–1894), a British author and traveler.

8. Leonardo (1452–1519), a Florentine artist and scientist, painted "La Gioconda" ("Mona Lisa") in 1504.

9. St. George L. Sioussat (1878–1960) taught history at Smith (1899–1904), University of the South, Sewanee, Tennessee (1904–1911), Vanderbilt (1911–1917), Brown (1917–1920), and the University of Pennsylvania (1920–1938), and was Chief of the Manuscripts Division of the LC (1938–1948).

To Frederick Jackson Turner

Lawrence, February 1, [1911?][1]

My dear Professor Turner,

It is now 1st February, a beautiful bright morning with the thermometer at 60°. I have just turned off the furnace, and opened the windows. That is Kansas. Meanwhile, you are in Cambridge [Mass.] with fur cap and umbrella. But that does not prevent you from harboring kind thoughts of us, and sending us what we would most wish to have—a likeness of yourself, which came yesterday; which we have long desired to possess, never expecting, however.

to possess one so excellent. It looks down on me from over my books, and you will see it there when next you visit us, which will be soon I hope, and every time you visit us, which I wish might be often.

That you and those dear to you may live long and enjoy every good thing, is the wish of all who live in this home.

Most sincerely,
Carl Becker

1. Turner Papers, HEH.

To Wallace Notestein

Lawrence, [1911?][1]

My dear Notestein,

I have just been looking through, and reading carefully some chapters, of your witchcraft.[2] It is little to say that it is the best prize essay which the association has published. It is an excellent argument in favor of not requiring doctor's theses to be published until they are put in proper shape. I believe that two thirds of the theses published in this country are not worth publishing, and in many cases the prime reason is that they are rushed into print before the author has mastered his subject or attained maturity enough to see it in any sort of perspective. The thing I like about your work is a certain maturity, a kind of poise and restraint, which leaves the impression that you have not exhausted either your mind or your notebook in order to make four hundred pages of copy. The literary form is excellent—something more than clear and direct English: there is a certain individuality about the manner of expression, and the choice of words, an apt turn of the phrase every now and again, that puts it out of the class of 'conventional' writing. The minute accuracy of detail, the thorough knowledge of the sources examined as well as of the existence of sources left unexamined, the careful moderation in drawing conclusions—all this is apparent to every reader, and I have no doubt will prove a reality to those who are competent to judge. Doubtless you have been wise to be chary of theorizing, but personally I am not averse to theorizing, and would have been pleased if you had given us a little more of it. I believe your explanation of the influences that weakened the belief is sound. It seems to have been in much the same way that the new 'philosophical' ideas spread in France in the 18 century: it became the fashion among the smart set in Paris & other cities to be thought 'advanced,' and to be 'advanced' meant to be emancipated from the conventional religious beliefs. From the court set, the new ideas permeated the middle class; only, the middle class bourgeois was essentially moral and sentimental, and here, about the third quarter of the century, the new ideas began to take on an emotional and sentimental cast which reaches its culmination in Rousseau.[3] Few things are more interesting (perhaps I should say, to me) than the growth and decline of opinion, and few things more difficult to get at or explain. I believe that this is one of the fields which will be cultivated more and more; and one which will bring much grain to the historian's mill. I hope you have not given up the intention which you express of treating separately the aspects of witchcraft which you mention in your preface, particularly the part played by the physicians, & the use of torture, & the general causes of the decline of the belief. These subjects appeal to me much more than the committee of Both Kingdoms, which I have not yet read, though I have no doubt that is well done and important too.

With all our best wishes,

Sincerely yours,
Carl Becker

1. Notestein Papers, YU.
2. *A History of Witchcraft in England from 1558 to 1718* (Washington, D.C., 1911), awarded the American Historical Association's Adams Prize for 1909.
3. Jean Jacques Rousseau (1712–1778), French social philosopher and writer.

To Claude Halstead Van Tyne

Lawrence, January 1, 1912[1]

My dear Van Tyne,[2]

The readiness with which you have accommodated your plans to my preferences is very agreeable to me, you may be sure; and the two courses you mention—the French Revolution and the Methods—are those I would most prefer to give. I give you a free hand in announcing them as you think best. The Revolution I have hastily sketched an outline for, which I send you. The Methods will be adapted to whatever class of students elect it, but naturally would go best with a moderately small class and with students who have had some modern history. As I said, I think, in my previous letter, it will consist of a sketch of the development of the study of history since the Renaissance, together with some practical exercises in critical problems, and, if desirable, with studies of particular historians as illustrating the methods and purposes of historical study prevailing in different periods. The lectures on the general development of historical study will not be in any sense learned or technical, but will merely endeavor to show how the study of history has responded to the changing influences that have successively shaped European thought and history. This part will close with a survey of conditions of historical research & study in the principal European countries today. The practical problems, especially the study of representative historians, might, if desirable, be occupied mainly with the 18 century; and so the relation of the interest in history and the method of writing it in that century to the Revolution itself could be brought out. I make these suggestions to show that the course is susceptible of considerable adaptation to the interests of whatever class of students may take it. If for instance those who took it should also elect the Revolution, the two could be made to work together very well.

You ask me to state frankly what I can afford to pay for a house. I take you at your word, and I say, my dear sir, that I am of that numerical majority of the Eminent tribe of teachers which cannot *afford* to pay anything. Seriously, we had heard that people who went away for the summer were frequently glad to get someone in their houses for a nominal rent,—$20 was mentioned to us by someone who had been there. We had thought, if so low a price was to be secured for a small house, we would take our meals out if there is any good place, in which case the house would not need to be so well equipped as would be desirable if we did our own housekeeping. However, our information is probably incorrect, and in that case we shall have to pay more than we expected. This is no new experience with us in our summer arrangements, and I dare say other people have found the thing true also. It is very kind of you to take any trouble in the matter, and I hope you will not go out of your way in the business. I may say there are three of us, and a two year old besides,—and my daughter says the only really necessary thing is a sleeping porch,—if you who have not the advantage of living in the "progressive" state of Kansas, know perchance what that is. The gist of all this is that we should like a house large enough for three people and a baby, are not at all particular about its being a fine house, care relatively little about location, would like a sleeping porch if it comes without too much sacrifice of other things, and wish to pay as little as possible above $20.00. This is what we desire, but please remember that we do not hold you responsible in the slightest degree for getting it, and shall be greatly obliged to you if you will only gather in what information comes your way and send it to us.

You do not say when your Summer session begins. And if you could give any approximate estimate of the probable size of classes I should like to have it.

Cordially yours,
Carl Becker

1. CBCU; misdated 1911.
2. Van Tyne (1869–1930) taught history at Michigan from 1903 until his death. His specialty was the period of the American Revolution.

To Frederick Jackson Turner

Lawrence, April 23, 1912[1]

My dear Professor Turner,

Professor Dodd, of Chicago,[2] has just written requesting me to contribute the first volume of a series of four volumes to be published by Houghton as a College text on American history. The period to be covered is from the beginning to 1783,—a volume of 60000 words.[3] Probably he has already consulted you about it, and you may have mentioned me to him as a contributor. I should like your opinion as to whether I ought to try the thing. My own idea is that it is absurd. I have never known enough about the period to write any kind of a book on it. It is rather remote from my interests, and would require an immense amount of work. Probably in the end it would be a mediocre book; it is bound to be, for a summary like that simply can't be well done except by one who has studied the subject long, and thought about it for years. If the plan is to skimp the first part and give the main part of the volume to the Revolution, there would be more reason for trying it. Besides, what is the demand for such a series? Your book is coming out soon —last Fall the publishers said 'immediately'—and I understand there is a two volume history in preparation, of which the last is by Fish, and is nearly completed.[4] What is your idea of all this? Professor Dodd did not give me many details of the scheme, but I will probably stop off in Chicago in June on my way to Ann Arbor and talk it over with him.—

A certain Col. Roosevelt has been in Kansas the last few days, I don't know what for, since he is not "making any campaign." There are thousands of people out here who are turning away from the Col.—men who formerly voted for him. It looks like a democratic year and I should not be surprised to see our friend from Nebraska elected after all.[5] He has been the man of the hour so long, that his hour ought to strike. I mean it seems only poetic justice. I'm agin him. I hope for a chance to vote for Wilson. I suppose you are perfectly hide bound now, a mere "easterner," stand patter, friend of Col. Harvey, and [protege?] of the "Interests."[6] You see I have the Kansas point of view.[7]

With best wishes,
Sincerely,
Carl Becker

1. Turner Papers, HEH.

2. William E. Dodd (1869–1940), American historian and later a diplomat, one of Becker's closest professional friends during the next quarter-century. See Robert Dallek, *Democrat and Diplomat: The Life of William E. Dodd* (New York, 1968).

3. CLB, *The Beginnings of the American People.*

4. See Evarts B. Greene, *The Foundations of American Nationality* (New York, 1922), and Carl R. Fish, *The Development of American Nationality* (New York, 1913).

5. Theodore Roosevelt (1858–1919), author, historian, and politician; William Jennings Bryan (1860–1925), politician and lecturer.

6. Woodrow Wilson; George Harvey, editor of the conservative *Harper's Weekly.*

7. One of Becker's most charming essays, "Kansas," first appeared in
1910. It was reprinted in *Everyman His Own Historian*, 1–28.

To Frederick Jackson Turner

Lawrence, November 10, 1912[1]

My dear Professor Turner,

I am much obliged to you for the copy of the new guide.[2] A
hasty glance has enabled me to understand that it is much better
than the old one, particulary for the later period where I see
more attention has been given to social & industrial matters. I
suppose this is an evidence of the "Influence of the social concept
on history" about which Professor Small[3] wishes me to speak at the
Sociological Association meeting. I have been writing on this, and
I find, what I should have known from the first, that I am altogether incompetent to do it as it should be done. One difficulty is
than I am not quite certain just what it is that they expect me to do;
and as I understand you were largely responsible for procuring me
this honor, that is to say for getting me into this box, I am going
to ask you what you understood from Small to be the purpose of
the paper. I have in mind to discuss the conditions of European
politics, industrial & social development, & intellectual changes
about 1850–75 which contributed to turn the attention of historians to more exact methods, to enlarge their ideas of the subject matter of history, & to establish the present ideal of continuity
& development etc. Then I expect to illustrate, in the work since
1875, the increasing emphasis on economic & social conditions,
and to close perhaps with some remarks on the difficulties from
the point of synthesis, and the recent tendencies towards a different method of interpretation etc. Do you think this will at all
fill the bill? I would be much obliged if you would write me your
notion of what is desired. I fear it will be wonderfully thin—my
knowledge of historical literature is so strikingly inadequate to
the task.[4]

I am looking forward with great pleasure to seeing you at
Cambridge in December.

With best wishes,
Carl Becker

1. Turner Papers, HEH.

2. Turner collaborated with Albert Bushnell Hart and Edward Channing in compiling a revised *Guide to the Study and Reading of American History* (Boston, 1912).

3. Albion W. Small (1854–1926), sociologist, taught at Chicago from 1892. He was editor of the *American Journal of Sociology* after 1895.

4. CLB, "Some Aspects of the Influence of Social Problems and Ideas upon the Study and Writing of History," *American Journal of Sociology*, XVIII (1913), 641–675.

To William E. Dodd

Lawrence, March 3, 1913[1]

My dear Dodd,

I am sending you, by separate cover, the first chapter of the first volume[2] of the series which, as you well know, is to set the world aflame. I don't like it very well, but on the whole it is about the best I can do. I send it to you as a sample, and I send it to you to criticise,—subject matter, arrangement, details, style, everything. Do not be sparing: I am not so pleased with my work as to be upset by adverse remarks, or so thin skinned as to be offended by frankness. I expect to make corrections & changes of detail, and will be obliged for any suggestions of that sort; but what I want to know particularly is whether the conception and general style of the chapter is at all the kind of thing you want. If it is I will go on grinding out the rest of the book along similar lines.

Very Sincerely,
Carl Becker

1. CBCU.

2. CLB, *The Beginnings of the American People*.

To William E. Dodd

Lawrence, [late 1913][1]

My dear Dodd,

I shall be ready by April 1915, if all goes well, and probably before. It would of course be better to publish all at once. If my book were not the first one it would not matter so much. But to write an editor's introduction a year after most of the series is out would be a little odd. However, I do not wish to hold anyone back: and if it is merely to do me a service, by no means would I have you delay.

What do you think of printing the bibliographies at the end of the book instead of at the close of each chapter? I would like it better, & it would improve the looks.

I think you mentioned some books on the religious influence & spirit of the back country in the 18 century. I am about ready to tackle my chapter on the Colonies in the period of about 1760.[2] & I want especially to get hold of anything that will throw light on the intellectual & religious & political point of view of the *frontier* as distinguished from the tidewater. I hope this will be the best chapter in the book. If you can suggest anything I shall be glad.

Very truly
Carl Becker

1. CBCU.
2. Entitled "The American People in the Eighteenth Century."

To William E. Dodd

Lawrence, [March 1914][1]

My dear Dodd,

I am returning the two books you sent me. I have found them extremely useful, and am much obliged for your trouble. I have been a good deal interested in the "Great Awakening" and its results. Not enough attention has been given to the religious aspects of the 18 century. In America, as in France, the old religious conceptions were in a sense being transformed into a kind of civil religion, and in this change is to be found much that helps explain the revolution—so I think at present.

Very Sincerely,
Carl Becker

P.S. Have just been requested to write three chapters to the supplementary volumes to the Cambridge History of Eng. Lit. which are to deal with American Literature—it was cut out that I should do the historians & memoir writers.[2] But I had to give it up—so you see I have something credited against your series: however, I should hardly have wished to do it anyway.

C. B.

1. William E. Dodd Papers, LC.
2. See John Erskine to CLB, March 14, 1914, CBCU.

To Wallace Notestein

Lawrence, November 1, 1914[1]

My dear Notestein,

The ms. came all intact; with the letter. I need not say that I am greatly obliged to you for taking the trouble to read it.[2] Your few— all too few—cautions pencilled in the margin, I shall turn to good account. Your general criticism, as well as that of Ford,[3] and I take it that you agree fundamentally, is entirely just: the book should be more purely an interpretation, or more purely a narrative of fact. And yet my experience has been that without a good deal of fact, your "interpretations" are likely to be very disappointing except in the hands of a genius; and I think perhaps my difficulty has been rather in lack of skill in fusing fact with interpretation. In respect to the chapter on Puritanism, some of the notions are undoubtedly over subtle; particularly that short section on the origin of the Puritan state of mind. I have often thought it would be well to cut that out entirely: and if you think it is too far fetched, don't hesitate to say so. Of course I know the book has some merits; but I am fearful that it is fundamentally superficial, and that in places it verges closely on fine writing. I wish to write well; but I have a horror of being thought rhetorical. I hope you & Ford will be frank to say so, if you thought so. I don't want you to think I have read in the sources more widely than I have. It is true that I have read a good many things, at one time and another, and most of my quotations are, as it were, my own. But sometimes, I have taken quotations from secondary writers, always verifying them when possible. The quotation from Raleigh—"I shall yet live to see it an English nation,"—is a case in point; I notice that you ask about it in the margin of the ms. It was quoted by Tyler, in his volume of the American Nation series.[4] He says it was written in 1603 just before his imprisonment. This is one of the things I have not been able to verify. The publishers do not wish footnotes, or I should give the source of my quotations in order not to leave the impression that I have an intimate acquaintaince with the sources, which is far from true.

We are all glad to know where Lord Jim[5] came from. There was no card, and I overlooked the fact that it was addressed to my wife, or I might have surmised that you sent it. I supposed that it came from the publishers. None of us has read it yet: but I hope to get to it soon. Mrs. Becker sends thanks for the book, and we all send best wishes. Frederick informed me the other day that "God didn't think it necessary to make giants any more." I wish I had his means of communication.

Cordially,

Carl Becker

1. Notestein Papers, YU.
2. CLB, *The Beginnings of the American People.*
3. Guy Stanton Ford (1873–1962), historian, taught at Yale (1901–1906), Illinois (1906–1913), and Minnesota (1913–1938); he served as executive secretary of the American Historical Association (1941–1953).
4. Lyon G. Tyler, *England in America, 1580–1652* (New York, 1904), 33.
5. Joseph Conrad, *Lord Jim: A Tale* (London, 1900).

To Frederick Jackson Turner

Lawrence, [1914 or 1915][1]

My dear Professor Turner,

I was very glad to get your paper on the "Massachusetts Frontier,"[2] for I am just finishing up the next to the last chapter of my sketch of colonial history. I have made great use of your "Old West,"[3] as you will see,—and I intend to read the present paper at once to see if I can't borrow something from that. Maybe it is plagiarism to borrow so freely; but knowing so little about the subject you must understand that I have to construct my work out of other men's books. Writing a book is a terrible job, and if I finish this one I am at present resolved never to attempt another. In fact, I don't think I have written a book, but only a series of more or less connected essays. Whatever it is, it is absolutely *not* a textbook; and yet I believe that is what the publishers are expecting.

I shall be teaching in the Minnesota summer session, June 15–July 24.

With best wishes,
Carl Becker

1. Turner Papers, HEH.
2. "The First Official Frontier of the Massachusetts Bay," *Publications of the Colonial Society of Massachusetts,* XVII (Boston, 1915), 250–271. The paper was presented on April 23, 1914.
3. "The Old West," *Proceedings of the State Historical Society of Wisconsin . . . 1908* (Madison, 1909), 184–233.

To William E. Dodd

Lawrence, [early summer 1915][1]
My dear Dodd,

I have taken time between the regular & the summer session to read your book with some care, and also rather more hastily, Paxons [sic]. Of Johnson's I have read only some chapters.[2] Everything considered, your book is in my opinion the best of the series. My own style probably has more movement, but I feel that it is less natural than yours; it is perhaps more brilliant, but it doesn't reflect the complex reality so well. One of the things that struck me more & more as I read was that what we call, for lack of a better term, the spirit or atmosphere of the period, that peculiar union of strength & futility, of efficiency & vulgarity, of idealism and fustian demogogery, which is so characteristic of the 30's & 40's, you manage to reflect far better than any other writer I know of. That is partly a matter of style, and that is where your style is far more successful than a superficial reading might lead one to infer. But it is a result not so much of literary ability as it is of your minute & sympathetic knowledge of the subject. And this is the respect in which your book is without any qualification better than mine, or Paxons, & better I suspect than Johnsons, although I have not read much of Johnsons yet. The most excellent point of the book I should say is the way in which you develop the politics of the period out of the conflicting economic interests of the three sections.

The Letters

It is the most intelligible & convincing interpretation of the period
that I have ever read. Your intimate knowledge of the south is the
only thing that would lead me to suppose you a southerner; but if
I were a prejudiced southerner I might suppose you were born in
the North, except for the fact that you do not play up the abolitionists. From the point of view of the civil war conflict I think it
is as fair as a book can be. For this reason there are many readers
who will not be pleased with it, but they are not the judicious. I
like your Jackson, and your Calhoun especially. Jackson, a man
without a policy who succeeded instinctively, Calhoun, a man who
failed in spite of, or perhaps because of, his very definite policies.
That is a fine phrase about Calhoun being a "combination of up-
country ideals and low country purposes." Generally, your leading
men are well portrayed.—Webster comes off perhaps less well than
others. I think your book, like mine, assumes on the part of the
reader a familiarity with a great deal that most readers will not
possess. The continuity, from the chronological point of view, of
the chief external political events, is not very clear. I suspect your
powers of analysis, description, and exposition, are much greater
than your power of narrative. But then, my dear sir, you can't expect to possess every excellence in the catalogue of virtues.

You may be interested to learn that Bancroft[3] & his friends—
notably Latané[4]—have given you up. Latané wrote to Hodder that
you had become a backslider. Their explanation of your article is
amusing: you were naturally pieved because Bancroft blocked your
nomination to the Board of Editors; and besides that, your position,
with McLaughlin[5] as head of your department, is a delicate one.
How they square this estimate of your mental & moral make up
with Bancroft's former statement to Hodder that you were one of
the most conscientious & independent men in the Association, I
can't conceive. I have just received a card from Jameson[6] saying
that B's letter is not to appear for some weeks.[7]

With sincere congratulations on your book, & best wishes for
you all,

Very cordially
Carl Becker

1. CBCU.
2. Dodd, *Expansion and Conflict* (Boston, 1915), concerning the
period 1828–1865; Frederic L. Paxson, *The New Nation* (Boston, 1915),

concerning the period 1865–1914; Allen Johnson, *Union and Democracy* (Boston, 1915), concerning the period 1783–1828. These are volumes in "The Riverside History of the United States."

3. Frederic Bancroft (1860–1945), historian and lecturer, was especially interested in American political history during the nineteenth century. He served on the literary staff of *The Nation*.

4. John H. Latané (1869–1932) taught history at Randolph-Macon (1898–1902), Washington and Lee (1902–1913), and Johns Hopkins (1913–1930). His specialty was the history of American foreign relations.

5. Andrew C. McLaughlin (1861–1947) taught history at Michigan (1887–1906) and Chicago (1906–1929), directed the Bureau of Historical Research at the Carnegie Institution of Washington (1903–1905). His specialty was American constitutional history.

6. J. Franklin Jameson (1859–1937) taught history at Johns Hopkins (1882–1888), Brown (1888–1901), and Chicago (1901–1905), directed the department of historical research at the Carnegie Institution (1905–1928), and was chief of the Manuscript Division at LC (1928–1937). His specialty was early American history.

7. For tensions within the American Historical Association in 1915, see Ray Allen Billington, "Tempest in Clio's Teapot: The American Historical Association Rebellion of 1915," *AHR*, LXXVIII (1973), 348–369.

To William B. Munro

Lawrence, July 23, 1915[1]

My dear Mr. Munro,[2]

Your proposed history might be practicable if you don't imply too much by "literature." It would be possible to get perhaps 20 men who could write good history in a straightforward and readable manner; but if they should be expected to raise their work to the level of real literature—to the level of Green or Parkman, for example,—I fear it can't be done.[3] Men of high literary talent unfortunately do not go in for the serious study of history very often; and the study of history, as conducted in our universities, is unfortunately not designed to develope such talent as exists. Besides, history is I should say one of the most difficult subjects in the world to make literature out of; I mean history in the general sense, as distinct from biography or the narrative of some particular episode. Yet it is possible, and in my opinion highly desirable to come as near doing just that thing as possible. With all our busy activity history has less influence on the thought of our time than it had in the second quarter of the nineteenth century, and one principal reason is that it isn't read. Every one benefits from science even without knowing anything about it; but people don't benefit from historical research except in so far as they read history, and they wont read it unless it is readable.

I can off hand think of the following men who are good historians, and who are accounted good writers, that is for historians. You may judge whether they could produce "literature" such as your friend would think necessary. Colby, Thayer, Roosevelt, Gamaliel Bradford, Rhodes, Cheyney, W. L. Grant, Van Tyne, Dunning, C. M. Andrews, W. E. Dodd, Carl Fish, Paxon.[4] No doubt there are others less well known, I know a few such, who could do as well or better. Yet few of these have produced anything that would be called literature in the strict sense. If such work as these men could do would be satisfactory, I should think the thing might be practicable.

It would, however, even on this basis, be worth doing I should think only on condition: (1) that the right editor could be found; (2) that a good deal of time were allowed in order to get the right men and to allow them time to do their very best; (3) that every man, particularly the editor, should clearly understand that literary excellence, beyond that ordinarily expected in cooperative histories, is a primary consideration. Otherwise, the result would be another American Nation, and we do not need another American Nation, excellent as that is in its way.[5]

As to the editor, I haven't much of an idea. He should be a man with a good grasp of American history as a whole, a man of literary ability, able to select the right man to do the right task, a man who could direct and criticise and shape their work rather rigorously yet without offense, and a man who could direct and who believes strongly in the value of such a work as you suggest. In fact, he should be a man with all the virtues. For that reason perhaps two or three editors, with one directing, would not be a bad thing. Men in the "profession" who occur to me as possessed of certain desirable qualities do not possess the others, or would not be sufficiently interested to take it up. I have a feeling that some one outside the profession, so to say, with less specialized interests, and more literary talent, would be the right man if one could be found who appreciates sound scolarship and is sufficiently in touch with students and writers of American history. Such a man as Bradford, whom I know only by his works, occurs to me, but he may be wholly unfitted for such a task, for all I know. Dunning, Turner, Van Tyne come to mind only to be dismissed for one reason or another.

As to the division into volumes, that is a matter of great importance, and would depend much upon the ideas of the editor. My own opinion is that 20 volumes would be better than 40, volumes of about 75,000 words. (1) It would be easier to get the men to write them. (2) I rather think the subject would divide better, or at least equally well. (3) The volumes would present a better appearance I should think. I don't particularly like the idea of particular volumes for particular subjects, such as Literature, American Industry, The Navy in the Revolution, etc. The historical importance of American Literature, for example, or railroad building, can be best shown by introducing them in their actual historical setting. Besides, would it not be rather difficult to make literature out of the Panama Canal? It could be done.

The main question, as I see it, is this: Would it be worth while to get out a fairly elaborate history of the United States which would be literature in a higher sense than the American Nation, yet something less so than, say, Green's English People? I think that much at least could be done. The second question is whether the editor is procurable. In respect to the last point, I have a feeling that the right man exists somewhere, but my acquaintance is too limited to enable me to say where he is to be found.

I am sure this advise is worth much less than ten dollars; I hope I need not say that I should have been glad to give it for nothing. If anything more pertinent occurs to me I will let you know.

Cordially,
Carl Becker

1. CBCU.

2. Munro (1875–1957), a political scientist, taught at Harvard (1904–1929) and at the California Institute of Technology (1930–1945), and was Schiff lecturer at Cornell in 1926.

3. John Richard Green (1837–1883), popular historian of England; Francis Parkman (1823–1893), popular historian of North America.

4. Frank Moore Colby (1865–1925), historian and editor; William Roscoe Thayer (1859–1923), author, historian, and editor; Theodore

Roosevelt (1858–1919); Gamaliel Bradford (1863–1932), author and
biographer; James Ford Rhodes (1848–1927), historian; Edward Potts
Cheyney (1861–1947), historian; William Lawson Grant (1872–1935),
Canadian historian; Claude H. Van Tyne (1869–1930), historian;
William A. Dunning (1857–1922), political scientist and historian;
Charles M. Andrews (1863–1943), historian; William E. Dodd (1869–
1940), historian and diplomat; Carl Fish (1876–1932), historian; and
Frederic L. Paxson (1877–1948), historian.
    5. Albert B. Hart, ed., *The American Nation: A History* (27 vols.;
New York, 1904–1908).

To William E. Dodd

Lawrence, [October 1915][1]

My dear Dodd,

Congratulations on the fine letter in the Nation,[2] which I have
just read! By bringing your historical knowledge to bear on the subject, you have managed to say something extremely relevant. Yet I
think somewhat the same danger threatens if the Universities are
controlled by the "People," excellent folk, as from the "Interests."
Perhaps we feel that danger here a little more than you do at Chicago: the danger that Universities may be turned over to the ped-
dlers of quack nostrums, pedagogical ineptitudes, and the like. No
doubt young men should be trained to social service rather than to
self realization, but the danger is that if "Herr Owner" gets control
he will think that the YWCA secretary, the organizer of play-
grounds, and the leader of "Gospel Teams" represent the sort of
man who performs the most effective social service. He will be
likely to think your learned historian a parasite on the body politic,
whereas your Special Interest man will think the radical economist
a dangerous disease germ—that is about the difference.

    There is a story hereabouts that the Trustees will not fill Hen-
dersons place at Chicago because he was too radical.[3] Is there anything in it.

    With kind regard to Mrs Dodd

Cordially
Carl Becker

    1. CBCU.
    2. "Democracy and the University," *The Nation,* CI (Oct. 14, 1915),
463–465.

3. Charles R. Henderson (1848–1915), a sociologist and Baptist minister, was university chaplain and professor of sociology, University of Chicago (1892–1915).

To William E. Dodd

Lawrence, November 13, 1915[1]

My dear Dodd,

I hope you are right about the people having regard for learning, and I rather think you are. They need desperately to have right minded leaders, however, and in any case I was only pointing out that our danger was different from yours. It goes without saying that universities should be concerned, however indirectly, with the vital problems of society. Where they come under the influence of the popular demagog the great danger is that they will be concerned with the second best sort of solution, the cheap and popular panacea, etc. I have lately been scribbling some light and desultory remarks for a paper which I may entitle "On Being a Professor: Some Remarks on Education by one Whose Early Training was not of the Best."[2] My aim is to poke a little gentle fun at the people who conceive of education as a matter of method and machinery. If I can hit on the right tone, I may try to get it printed.

I am far from regreting that you induced me to write a book[3] in your series. On the contrary! About the only way I contrive to get anything done is to bind myself down to it. I know the limitations of my book, but I should never have done anything half so good if you hadn't got me where I had to do something. I am really much obliged to you therefore. Why should I care what the reviewers say when I have, carefully preserved, such letters as you have written me about it, and similar letters from Van Tyne, Haskins,[4] Burr,[5] and others? The only review which I have seen lately is a long four page notice in the Dial by Pooley,[6] who says nothing at all in the most uninteresting manner possible. If I can find it I will send it to you. Van Tyne was given the series for the Historical Review, but his health compelled him to refuse it and I don't know who has it. Van Tyne would have given us a fine send off.

I shall be in Washington Christmass so far as I know now.

Cordially,
Carl Becker

1. CBCU.
2. "On Being a Professor," *Unpopular Review,* VII (1917), 342–361.
3. *The Beginnings of the American People.*
4. Charles Homer Haskins (1870–1937) taught history at Wisconsin (1890–1902) and Harvard (1902–1931). His special interest was European medieval history. He was second only to Turner as an influence upon Becker's development as a historian.
5. George Lincoln Burr (1857–1938), librarian and historian, taught at Cornell (1888–1922). His special interest was in medieval and early modern European history.
6. William V. Pooley, "The Making of America," *The Dial,* LIX (Oct. 28, 1915), 367–371.

To Wallace Notestein

Lawrence, [early 1916][1]

My dear Notestein,

Many thanks for your cordial note. Of course I should have appreciated a little better offer: but my visit at Minneapolis convinced me that they are doing the best they can under the circumstances. I should not feel comfortable getting more than White[2] does, and I was told that he gets only 3000. I was much surprised at that. I have put the question of salary aside, and am considering the matter on other grounds. I have heard nothing from Cornell, & do not expect to. Besides Cornell does not look so attractive to me as it did. I have a characteristic incident to tell you about Burr when we meet. I am considering your offer very seriously, and I may say favorably—

Cordially,
Carl Becker

1. Notestein Papers, YU.
2. Albert B. White (1871–1952) taught English constitutional history at Minnesota (1899–1940).

2. Cornell, War, and the Productive Professor, 1916-1919

To James W. Gleed

Minneapolis, Minnesota, November 20, 1916[1]

Dear Mr. Gleed,[2]

In reply to your letter of inquiry, I wish to say first of all that personally I have no grievance of any kind against the university or any one connected with it. I came to the university fourteen years ago, as Assistant Professor, at a salary of $800. During those years, the recognition I received, in the way of promotion and raise of salary, and in every way, was all that I could hope for and more than I could reasonably expect. My relations with the students, the faculty, and the university administrative officers, have been of the most friendly and cordial character. I liked the people of Kansas, and have many good friends in the state, and particularly in Lawrence where I had come to feel, as you can well imagine, very much at home. Under the circumstances, therefore, it is hardly necessary to say that I left the university with great regret, after mature deliberation, and on account of conditions which seemed to me most deplorable and not likely to be corrected in the near future.

I take it that a good university is primarily a question of getting first rate scholars and teachers for its faculty. Of course you have to have buildings and equipment, but you may have the finest material plant and still have a very poor university; whereas, if you have a faculty of able scholars and teachers you will have a good university even with very inferior buildings and equipment. When I came to Kansas there were then, or had recently been, connected with the university a number of men who gave distinction to the institution. I recall Chancellor Snow, Professors Williston, Franklin, Kellogg, McClung, Caruth [sic], Marvin, Barber, Hodder,

Templin, and A. T. Walker;[3] there may have been others whom I do not now think of. Hodder, Templin, and Walker are still there. The others are no longer there, and it is not too much to say that they have not been replaced by men of equal, or nearly equal distinction. There are many good men on the faculty, it is true, but it would be impossible now to duplicate the above list, whereas, since the faculty is so much larger now than it was then, it should be possible to double it. For fourteen years there has been much talk of the marvellous growth of the university, meaning always growth in numbers, forgetting that quality is the essential thing. Taking the institution as a whole, considering it from the point of view of the quality of its faculty, and this means the quality of the work done, both in teaching and in productive scholarship, the university is not, in my opinion, as good an institution as it was fourteen years ago.

What is the cause of this deterioration? Some would say lack of money. I do not think so. No university has all the money it needs, and Kansas has been no exception to this rule. But during fourteen years the appropriations have steadily increased; and it is a well known fact that for many years Chancellor Strong[4] got precisely what he asked for, which was what he regarded as essential. With these funds in hand, it was possible to do one of two things; either to apply them to maintaining and strengthening the departments already established, or to apply them, or a considerable part of them, to establishing new departments. The latter policy is the one that has been more or less consistently followed. Now, inasmuch as the number of students has increased as steadily as the appropriations, new departments could not be taken on without neglecting the legitimate needs of those already existing. It seems to me obvious, therefore, that the Medical School, the Extension Department, the Department of Journalism, and the School of Education were established at the expence of the legitimate needs of the College, the Graduate School, the Law School, and the School of Engineering.

It would have been bad policy, under the circumstances, to undertake this expansion even if there had been some real need for it. I cannot think there was any real need for it. A good medical school is a good thing; but a poor one is worse than none. A medical school is immensely expensive; no other sort of education is anything like as expensive; and yet there never was, and never was much prospect of there being, a tithe of the money necessary for a good four year medical course at Kansas. Even now it is a fair question whether it would not be wise policy to abandon the most expensive part of the school, the last two years, and concentrate upon the first two years. There was, in my opinion, even less need of an extension department. Evidently the legislature thinks so too; for, so I was credibly informed, it has refused, during the last two bienniums, to pass the special appropriation asked for this department. For certain kinds of extension work, there is a real demand; but this work was done, and still is done I am told, by the particular departments concerned. It would seem, therefore, that the only reason for organizing a special department of extension was to push out upon the state a kind of activities for which there was no real demand, scarcely any demand at all except a fictitious demand manufactured largely at the university. What is the need of a special department of journalism? Young men are there taught, for the most part, precisely what they would have to learn, and would easily learn, in a newspaper office—the mechanics of printing, the knack of getting news, and of warping facts to make a good story. They ought to get in the university the things they can't get in a newspaper office, the things they never will get adequately if they do not get them in a university. What they need, if they wish to be anything more than smart reporters, is a fundamental grounding in history, economics, English literature, politics and law. A very good course for prospective journalists could be made on the basis of these subjects; but a department of journalism, by stressing the superficial things, makes it less possible for the student to get as much of these subjects as he should. What does the School of Education do that was not done by the Department of Education which we formerly had? Formerly one professor and perhaps two assistants offered the courses necessary to enable prospective teachers to get the 12 hours of education required for the teacher's diploma. Now four professors and three assistants offer the courses enabling prospective teachers to get the 15 hours of required education. As far as I can see, the chief result of establishing a school of education was to make seven men grow where only three grew before. Last spring I sat on a committee of which the chairman was the Dean of the School of education; and he made a strong plea for lowering the requirments for the degree in Education on the ground that otherwise the professors could not get students enough to keep them busy. He did not put it in those words, but that is what his proposal came to.

What pressure Chancellor Strong was under, from the alumni, the regents, or the legislature, to adopt a policy of expansion, I do not know; but it seems to me that it would have been much wiser to have devoted the resources of the university to the departments already existing, and to two things particularly, to procuring the very ablest scholars to be had, and to building up a library adequate to their needs. A first rate mathematician, Professor Young, came to Kansas for a year; he went to Dartmouth with little if any increase in salary.[5] One of the ablest men Kansas ever had was M. A. Barber, a man whose scientific work is better known in Germany than it is in Kansas. I knew him well, and I think he would have remained if there had been any proper attitude towards scientific research. A few years ago Dick Scammon[6] was at Kansas; they let him go for a triffling salary, and he is now full Professor here in Minnesota, and is regarded as one of the ablest men in the university. They tried to get rid of W. U. Moore; he now draws a salary of 6000 in the Columbia Law School. Professor Kay,[7] a man of force, and highly regarded by geologists throughout the country, was allowed to go to Iowa. These men should have been kept; they would have been of more value to Kansas than a wilderness of extension departments and schools of education. And most of them could have been kept had there been a proper attitude towards productive scholarship and a proper effort to encourage it.

But if you wish to get good men and to encourage scholarship and research, the library is of primary importance. A good library, and plenty of money for books, are as attractive as high salary to the genuine scholar. What is the situation of Kansas in respect to the library? There is scarcely a weaker spot in the university. Amherst College, with a student body of about 500, has a better library than Kansas. For fourteen years it has been impossible to get anything done about it, that is to say, about the very thing that can not be neglected without serious prejudice to any university. Money for books is a crying need at Kansas, and second to that a competent librarian. Last year the budget carried $3,000 which we were told could be used for a librarian. A first rate man could almost certainly have been had, Mr. Koch, formerly of Michigan.[8] Millis and Hodder and some others did their level best to have him offered the position. But nothing was done. At least $50,000 a year for books would not be too much, it would not be enough, but it would do much to remedy a situation that is the dispair of every scholar on the faculty. If this seems a big sum, it must be remembered that all new state universities are at a tremendous disadvantage compared with such schools as Harvard and Yale. Those institutions got the great sets and collections long ago when they were much easier to be had than now, and they profit constantly by munificent private donations. If Kansas would concentrate on men, books, and scientific equipment, she would soon gather there, to reinforce the real scholars which she now has, a group of men who would initiate the activities and create the atmosphere that go to make a real university.

What chance is there of this being done under the present management? None whatever. On the contrary, the present management has accentuated, and will continue to accentuate, the very evils which I have mentioned. A paid board, I say a *paid* board and not a single board, is a great mistake. The reason is simple. First, you cannot get the ablest men in Kansas to abandon their professions to give all their time to this business. Second, those who do take the positions, giving all their time and receiving a high salary, are almost bound to feel that it is necessary to justify their highly paid position. They feel that they must earn their salaries. And they know no other way to do it except by taking an active and responsible part in the management of the university, in directing its policy, in employing its faculty, in applying its funds.

Now, these men, in spite of the best intentions which are admitted, are not competent to take the initiative. I don't suppose Mr. Hackney would think himself competent to take over the management of a highly specialized, and intricate business industry, of which he had only such a general knowledge as any good lawyer might be supposed to have.[9] But a university is a far more difficult, as well as a far more important matter than, let us say, a meat packing industry. Men who have all their lives been intimately associated with universities, who have given all their intelligence and energy to the problem of education, find that problem an extremely complex and difficult one. How is it possible that Mr.

Hackney (and this is nothing to the disparagement of Mr. Hackney), how is it possible that Mr. Hackney, who wouldn't think himself competent to run a meat packing industry, should be thought competent to run a university? A board of Regents such as we formerly had, under no obligation to justify their job, under no obligation to any body, composed of men to whom the state was rather under obligation for giving their time for nothing, such men, working in harmony with the Chancellor and the faculty, leaving them the initiative but giving them the benefit, and the very great benefit, of the practical layman's point of view, were of the highest assistance. But a paid board, setting the Chancellor aside, leaving him without power and without responsibility, is bound to do things on its own hook, and so far as it does is bound to make a mess of it.

The present board deserves credit for what it has not done. It has not done many things on its own hook. But it has virtually set the Chancellor aside, with this result: in so far as the Board doesn't take a hand the university simply drifts; in so far as it does take a hand the result is deplorable for the most part. The Board has made a number of high appointments in the university contrary to the Chancellor's advice; these appointments have been, to put it mildly, very unfortunate, with one possible exception. I never saw any evidence that the Board ever took any intelligent interest in, or was really aware of the existence of, the genuinely valuable work done at the university; but they have almost invariably exhibited, in their enthusiasms and in their official decisions, a marked partiality for the superficial aspects of educational activities. I was told that an official report of the Board, published last fall, found its way into the faculty club at the University of Chicago, and was read there to his colleagues by one of the members, to an accompaniment of derisive laughter. I can well believe the story. There is not a line in the report which indicates that the author had the faintest conception of what a university should be, or that he had any knowledge of the real scholarly work that is being done in the University of Kansas. It was apparently designed to show that everything was now quite as it should be, and that this happy result was due largely to the changes effected by the Board of Administration.[10]

This is the way the situation looks to me; and so far as I can judge it is much the way it looks to the good men on the faculty. I am forty three years old. The next ten or fifteen years are important ones for me. Why should I, having a fair opportunity to go elsewhere, have remained in an institution so largely at the mercy of the incompetent, an institution without wise and farsighted leadership, an institution where the genuine is so largely ignored while the sham and the shoddy are exhalted. The University of Minnesota is by no means one of the best universities in the country. In many ways it suffers from the same weaknesses as Kansas. But it is largely directed by the President and the Faculty. In the last six years it has been going forward instead of backward; and the prospects here for the next ten years are, so far as one can judge, very good. I have many good friends throughout the country, east and west, whose advice I asked; every one of them, without hesitation, gave it as his opinion that it would be wise for me to make the change.

It may be that I have misjudged the situation. It may be that Kansas will get rid of her paid board, and that during the next ten years she will forge ahead and attain the position among the universities of the country which the intelligence of the people of Kansas and the traditions they have inherited lead one to think she ought to occupy. If this should come about, no one would be more pleased than I would be.

Very sincerely,
Carl Becker

1. James W. Gleed Papers, University of Kansas. The letter has been published, without annotation, in *DWH*, 145–154.

2. Gleed (1859–1926), a lawyer, taught Latin and Greek (1879–1883) and law (1884–1903) at Kansas. He practiced law from 1884 until his death, and served as a regent of the University of Kansas. In October 1916, the Visiting Committee of the Alumni Association of the University of Kansas invited Becker and several other former Kansas professors to comment on conditions within the university. In a covering note, Becker wrote: "I have spoken freely, and I need not say that when I am outside of Kansas I do not give expression to these views, but make out the best case I can for the state and the university for which I have a real regard."

3. Francis H. Snow (1840–1908), professor of mathematics, natural science and natural history at Kansas (1866–1889), president and chancellor (1890–1901), professor of organic evolution (1901–1908);

Samuel W. Williston (1852–1918), professor of geology and anatomy, dean of the medical school (1890–1902); Edward C. Franklin (1862–1937), professor of chemistry (1888–1903); Vernon L. Kellogg (1867–1937), professor of entomology (1890–1894); Clarence E. McClung (1870–1946), professor of zoology (1897–1912); William H. Carruth, professor of Germanic languages and literature (1902–1913); Frank O. Marvin (1852–1915), professor of engineering (1878–1913); Marshall A. Barber, professor of botany and bacteriology (1894–1913); Olin Templin (1861–1943), professor of mathematics and philosophy (1884–1921); Arthur T. Walker (1867–1948), professor of Latin (1897–1942).

4. Frank Strong (1859–1934), president of the University of Oregon (1899–1902), chancellor at Kansas (1902–1920), professor of constitutional Law at Kansas (1920–1934).

5. John Wesley Young (1879–1932) was professor and head of the department of mathematics (1910–1911), then went to Dartmouth (1911–1932).

6. Richard E. Scammon taught zoology and anatomy at Kansas (1906–1911).

7. George F. Kay (1873–1943), professor of Geology and mineralogy (1904–1907); professor of geology at the University of Iowa (1907–1943).

8. Theodore W. Koch (1871–1941) prepared the annotated catalogue of the Dante Collection at Cornell (1895–1900); he was a librarian at the LC (1902–1904) and at Michigan (1904–1916).

9. Edward T. Hackney (1870–1953), A.B., Kansas, 1895. He practiced law in Wellington, Kansas (1897–1953); was in the Kansas House of Representatives (1897–1899); in the Kansas Senate (1930–1936); president of the State Board of Administration of Educational Institutions (1913–1917).

10. See CLB to Frederick Jackson Turner, Dec. 14, 1909, for a similar conflict at Wisconsin.

To George Lincoln Burr

Minneapolis, January 4, 1917[1]

Dear Mr. Burr,

In thinking over your offer, the thing that comes most often to mind is the fear that you may have over rated my attainments and abilities. The worst thing that could happen would be to accept your offer and then have it turn out that I was not after all precisely the man you supposed me to be. Mr Sill[2] said, after you left I think, that you found in me a rare combination of intellectual power, imagination, and teaching ability. I would not like to claim all this, but assuming that I possess these qualities in some degree I think it right to say explicitly, although doubtless you know it already, that I am not a learned scholar like yourself, nor have I that thorough grounding in the ancient languages and in the technique of paleography and diplomatic which you have, and which, in some lesser degree at least, a professor of European history probably should have. While I have read rather widely in general European history, my special researches, and my knowledge of the sources, are therefore mainly confined to the 18 century and the Revolution, including the American Revolution, and to the historiography of the 18 and 19 centuries. In these fields I think I may claim an adequate knowledge perhaps, although my forte, if I have any, is in having thought a good deal about the meaning of history rather than in having achieved erudition in it; and in these fields I hope and expect to do, and believe I am capable of doing, some work which you will not think badly of.

This is my confession, which I hope will be good for the soul if for nothing else. If this confession does not shake your faith in me, and you are still disposed to let your offer stand, may I ask a few questions?[3]

I have heard it said that for lack of funds, or for some other reason, the Cornell faculty is not as strong as it used to be, especially in the humanities, and that in fact the humanities are somewhat sacrificed in favor of the sciences. I have hardly thought this true, but would like to know whether there is any ground for the statement.

In case I came to Cornell, would the following schedule, or something near it, meet your expectations?

1. Modern History, 3 hours, through the year, covering the period from about 1648 to the present, with the major emphasis on the 19 century, and particularly the period since 1870. If this class ran about 75 or 100 I should prefer to lecture once a week, dividing the class into two sections twice a week for discussion. This would then make five hours class work.

2. The Revolution and Napoleon, 2 hours through the year, perhaps alternating with other courses in different years, perhaps running 3 hours if that seemed best for any reason.

3. Seminary[4] in the 18 century intellectual movement, or in the Revolution.

Would there be any objection to placing my classes in the first hours in the afternoon? I am accustomed to that arrangement, and like it because it gives me undisturbed mornings for study and writing. If I come to Cornell I feel that I must do something really good to justify myself and you.

Is the climate of Ithaca regarded as normally healthfull, particularly for people with nervous temperaments? I have heard that on account of dampness it is very cold in winter and very hot in summer.

Mr. Ford has asked me particularly not to make a hasty decision, and you will understand that if I take a little time before deciding the matter the delay does not arise from any lack of appreciation of the fine opportunity you have offered me.

Very cordially,

Carl Becker

1. George Lincoln Burr Papers, CU.
2. Henry A. Sill (?–1917), professor of ancient history at Cornell (1902–1917).
3. Becker's account of his "first contact with the Cornell tradition," at the American Historical Association convention in Cincinnati (Dec. 1916), is charmingly related in CLB, "The Cornell Tradition: Freedom and Responsibility," in *Cornell University: Founders and the Founding,* 197–199.
4. I.e., seminar.

To Charles Hull

Minneapolis, January 8, 1917[1]

Dear Mr. Hull,[2]

Your letter came this morning. I have already written to Mr. Burr a letter which you will already have seen. For my part, if Mr. Burr is not disturbed by what I have said in my letter to him, I may assure you that the offer of $4,000 only confirms me in the feeling, which has been gaining strength since I came home, that I ought to accept your offer. If I hesitate to do so at once, that is largely because Mr. Ford has asked me particularly to wait until Dean Johnston returns, which will be today or tomorrow. Besides, this is

a very important decision for me, and I am tempermentally inclined to be slow in the decision of important matters. I am anx-
ious, however, to get the matter settled definitely as soon as
possible, for my own peace of mind and in the interest of everybody concerned. I think, therefore, you may expect to have a definite decision, which at present I think will be favorable, in no
great time.

> Very cordially,
> Carl Becker

1. Charles Hull Papers, CU.
2. Hull (1864–1936) was a librarian at Cornell (1886–1890), taught
political science and political economy (1892–1901), and was professor of American History (1901–1931). In 1909, CLB had sent Hull a
copy of his published dissertation, *The History of Political Parties in
the Province of New York, 1760–1776,* as well as several articles. See
Hull to CLB, July 29, 1909, Hull Papers.

To George Lincoln Burr

Minneapolis, January 18, 1917[1]

Dear Mr. Burr,

I shall be entirely willing to begin the Modern History at 1600
or any date that best fits in with your work. If I began with 1648 I
should naturally have to say something about the Thirty Years
War, Richelieu, and Henry IV in the way of review at least. As
most courses are in the forenoon, I should think, as I found in fact
at Lawrence, that there were as few conflicts in the afternoon
hours as in the morning. Scheduling my courses at 2, or 3, oclock,
whichever seems to you best, would suit me very well. The entire
freedom which seems to obtain at Cornell I like immensely; but I
need not assure you that I shall always be willing to cooperate
cordially in whatever arrangements seem best adapted to attain
the ends we all desire. I am therefore quite ready to assist in the
two courses you mentioned. I don't count myself much pumpkins
as a popular lecturer, but will do the best I can. From what you
say, and from everything I can learn from the Treasurer's and

Librarian's reports, it seems to me that the humanities are very well taken care of, and very effectively guaranteed for the future; on which points I never had any serious doubts.

Your presidential address I have read with the pleasure I anticipated.[2] From talk I had about it with men at Cincinnati, I daresay many will misconceive your position in two respects: they will not quite understand what the distinction is which you draw between the freedom of history and the freedom of historians; and they will suppose that you wish to maintain that men are not influenced by economic or material conditions. I can't see that there is any great difficulty in either respect, although perhaps a little more in the first than in the second. If a man goes to church, you can say that the explanation is to be found in a certain series of sensory impressions which result in certain mechanically conditioned muscular reactions, the effect of which is that he puts on a coat, walks down the street, and comes finally to sit in a pew for an hour; or you can say the explanation is to be found in a sense of duty or the desire to be popular in the community and so in the end to sell more shoes. Both explanations are valid, and both are useful in their different ways. But the point is they are different ways, neither of which has anything to do with the other. As I understand you, history has to do with the latter order of interpretation of man's conduct. The historian tries to explain man's conduct and thinking by entering into a sympathetic understanding of the individual or group as a particular individual or group, living in a particular place and under particular conditions, and actuated by more or less conscious human purposes and desires. So you say, using commonly understood terms, and confining yourself to motives which men everywhere act upon and understand, that Mr. A. goes to church from a sense of duty. Let the psychologist explain how the sense of duty, abstractly considered, is a product of psychic responses to external stimuli. That is his business, and a good business it is, but it is not the historian's business. I have found this difference very happily put, as it seems to me, in Plato's *Phaedo,* in the paragraph, a little beyond the middle of the dialogue, beginning, "What hopes I had formed, and how greviously was I disappointed!" (Jowet's translation) I have tried to express this difference in a review of a worthless little book by Mr. Jane which appeared last year, which I send you under separate cover, on the chance that it might interest you.[3]

Cordially,
Carl Becker

1. Burr Papers, CU.
2. "The Freedom of History," *AHR*, XXII (1917), 253–271.
3. L. Cecil Jane, *The Interpretation of History;* reviewed by CLB in *The Dial*, LIX (1915), 146–148.

To Charles Hull

Minneapolis, January 18, 1917[1]

Dear Mr. Hull,

As I have already indicated in a letter to Mr. Burr, I have decided to accept your offer. You may therefore take this as an expression of my determination to accept the professorship of Modern European History at Cornell, in case the Regents are disposed to offer me that position at the salary mentioned in your letter of January 3. I have never had any doubt that I should like Cornell as an institution, or Ithaca as a place to live; and certainly if I had ever felt in the slightest degree that I should not find congenial colleagues there, which in fact I have never felt, I could not fail to be reassured by the many cordial letters received during the last two weeks. My family is very enthusiastic over the prospect of coming to Ithaca to live, particularly so since looking at the picture book which you sent. Professor Ogden[2] has kindly consented to keep his eye open for a house. I might say that our lease is up here May 1. I can probably get an extension for a few months. I don't know whether houses are more likely to be available at Ithaca early or late in the summer. But if a house can be obtained, we should like to break up here in June; and if we could get a house in Ithaca about the first of July that would suit us best. Any information you can give me in this matter, without putting yourself to too much trouble, will of course be greatly appreciated.

Very sincerely,
Carl Becker

1. Hull Papers, CU.
2. Robert M. Ogden (1877–1959) taught psychology at Tennessee (1905–1914), Kansas (1914–1916), and Cornell (1916–1945), where he was also dean of the College of Arts and Sciences (1923–1945).

To George Lincoln Burr

Minneapolis, January 24, 1917[1]

Dear Mr. Burr,

Your letter makes certain, what I had little doubt of, that I had understood your position rightly. My remarks were not in the nature of a rejoinder to anything in your address, but were rather addressed to an imaginary objector, or perhaps to some men whom I talked with at Cincinnati. One man said he wasn't sure he would agree that history dealt only "with the concrete." And after some talk I gathered that he feared if he admitted that history had to do with the concrete, he would not be allowed, on your theory, to make general statements; would not be permitted, for example, to say that the failure of the wheat crops in Kansas in the early nineties tended to make men populists. This seemed to me so absurd that I did not try to enlighten him further than to say that I was sure you had something entirely different in mind. In talking to historians about such matters as you discussed in your address I have commonly found three difficulties. First, most historians assume at once that I am advocating something that deserves the name of "Philosophy of History," which of course they have long ago dismissed as moonshine. Second, if we nevertheless go on discussing the matter, they think, never in fact having thought much about the matter, that in saying that history does not use the method of abstraction I mean that the historian should not generalize, and to them this means that I am advocating a purely narrative treatment, mainly the story of kings or other important representative individuals. Third, if I try to distinguish between history and the exact sciences, they think I am trying to rob history of a scientific character, the result of which is that I must be maintaining that it is a "branch of literature." And so, through the discussion, I realize that my opponent is not really answering any position I have taken, but is always really combatting certain dreadful bogies in his own mind, such as "Philosophy of History" or "Branch of Literaure," which he was taught as a graduate student to beware of. It is all rather amusing, but sometimes rather irritating too.

Cordially,
Carl Becker

1. Burr Papers, CU.

To George Lincoln Burr

Minneapolis, February 25, 1917[1]

Dear Mr. Burr,

Whatever announcements you may have made with respect to my courses I am sure will be satisfactory; and before April I will send you announcements for the College catalogue. About the Assistant, I don't at present know of any one here, and as for that I don't remember very well what the Assistant is expected to do or what the compensation is, although Hull doubtless did explain those points. For the Fellowship there is a Mr. Hedger here who hopes to go east and study in modern European history, but particularly I think in very recent English and European history.[2] He is a good, mature man and student. I haven't talked with him yet about his plans, but shall do so soon, and may advise him to apply for the position. Stephenson, I confess not to remember well enough to express any judgment about. I should like to say that in general I am quite ready to waive my "equities" in the matter of Fellowships; for my idea is that Fellowships should always go to the best candidates, whatever fields they may be working in. If you care to have me do so, I shall be glad to look over the papers of applicants; but I shall be perfectly content to leave the whole matter of appointments to you who are on the ground.

Of course I could have no objection to van Loon's coming back for some lectures;[3] on the contrary, I should be glad of it for every reason, and particularly if his lectures might be worked into the general course on the History of Civilization in such a way as happily to relieve me of my share. Isn't this a bare-faced proposal! But you know the first year in a new place is bound to be a difficult one; or rather, you don't know it, I suppose, since you have never had these adjustments to make.

The "sketch" didn't bother me at all. You are quite right about the name. It was originally "Lotus Carl." The Lotus was given me for my uncle. An odd, unusual name, connoting somnolence too appropriately by far! Besides, the men in college couldn't remember it, and so I left it off, an act which my mother deprecated with as little mildness as she was capable of.

Cordially,
Carl Becker

1. Burr Papers, CU.
2. George Andrews Hedger (1877–1955) was an instructor in history at Minnesota (1915–1917), took his doctorate at Cornell in 1919, taught at Miami of Ohio (1919–1921) and at the University of Cincinnati (1921–1947). His specialty was modern European history.
3. Hendrik Willem Van Loon (1882–1944), lecturer, author, and journalist, received his A.B. at Cornell in 1905, and was lecturer in modern European history there, 1915–1916.

To Charles H. Blood

Minneapolis, March 23, 1917[1]

Dear Mr. Blood,[2]

I have just received your two letters, of the 21 and 22, together with the plans. I am much pleased with everything about the house so far as the plans show what it will be like, except the study, which is too small. It has occurred to me that by extending the part of the house in which the study is so that it would come sheer with the outside wall of the living room, and then throwing about two or three feet of the living room into the study, the latter would be a very respectable room. As I do a good share of my work at home, the study is important. This change would of course cut out the end window in the living room, but it would also enlarge the up stairs sewing room, and although I know little about building I should think the change would not add a great deal to the cost. In any case, as it would make two fairly good sized rooms out of two pretty small ones, I should feel that the additional expense would probably be worth while. I suppose the finishing down stairs will be hard wood, as also at least the floors up stairs. I am somewhat interested to know what heating you plan, whether hot air or steam or hot water. Your winters are not so severe as our winters are, but of course hot air, although cheapest to install, is the most expensive to operate and the least satisfactory. I think I should like to buy the place if it proves as satisfactory as I should imagine from all I know, but you can understand that a person does not like to agree to buy a place he has never seen in a town he knows nothing of personally. If we could arrange to rent it for a year, I could then have, if everything goes well, the two thousand dollars to pay down, and probably should like to pay rather more than the amount you mention per month. I understand, though you do not say so, that whatever is paid on the principal in any year is subtracted from the principal at the end of the year, and the interest for the next year is reckoned on the diminished principal. The basement is I assume under the whole house, cemented, and provided with the ordinary rooms of a modern basement. If you gave me the privilege of renting, and I should not wish to buy, I should expect to keep it until you could sell, or at least to give you a reasonable number of years to sell; but if the change I suggest can be made without great additional expense and the house is what I suppose it to be, I should think a better opportunity to buy would not be likely to present itself. If I should rent, and find that it is the place I wish to buy, I should probably be ready to make the arrangements for buying before the end of the year. If you can answer the points suggested in this letter, and let me know the lowest terms you could manage to rent for the year, I can then give you a definite answer, so that in case we come to an arrangement no time need be lost in beginning.

Sincerely,
Carl Becker

P.S. My wife would like to know whether it would be practicable from the architectural and the builder's point of view to make a sleeping porch over the kitchen porch, and if so, what would be the estimated additional expense?

1. CBCU.
2. Blood (1866–1938) was a lawyer, district attorney, and judge in Tompkins County, New York; a bank official and director of local cor-

porations in Ithaca (which is in Tompkins County); a trustee of Cornell University; a landowner and developer of Cornell Heights and Cayuga Heights, suburbs of Ithaca.

To Frederick Jackson Turner

Ithaca, New York, [June 1917][1]

Dear Professor Turner,

Before I knew that you had been ill I learned that you had successfully undergone an operation and were coming on famously. I sincerely hope there will be no relapses and that you will soon be better than ever.

Do you know that you are a great man? It is so. The Editor of the Dial is about to run a series of special articles on famous American historians, of whom you are one, and he has asked me to do you. I shall shortly be interviewing you therefore, desiring to know the full list of your publications, the date & place of birth, how you made your first dollar, and all other necessary information to enable me to make you attractive to the general reader.

As you will see, I am already here at Ithaca, and my family will be here today. It is a beautiful spot certainly, and I think we shall like it. Mr. Burr spends himself unreservedly in my behalf, calls me "Boy", and will make us feel at home if any one can. Delightful man!

Cordially,
Carl Becker

1. Turner Papers, HEH.

To Clarence C. Crawford

Ithaca, [summer 1917][1]

Dear Crawford,

I was glad to get your long letter of some weeks ago, and intended answering it, although I don't recall there was anything in it especially calling for answer, before now. We are located at the above place [a cottage on Cayuga Lake] for the summer while a house is being built for us on the heights north of the campus. From the point of view of scenery, and general attractiveness as a place to live, this is certainly a most splendacious spot. I think we shall like it immensely. They have lost about 2000 students, and are much exercised over the prospect for next year. The loss in tuition will be considerable, but I do not see any ground for thinking the falling off will be anything like 2000. Due to the uncertainty, however, they are economizing in every way possible; and for that reason have not attempted to fill Lunt's place permanently, but have given his work to a young chap by the name of Sweet—a year's appointment only.[2] —Cornell has a good endowment, with an income of over 3 millions annually,—but it has not increased much for twenty years whereas the enrollment has gone up rapidly so that it is becoming relatively poor.

I hear that Davis has deserted his wife for glory or the grave, and that W S Johnson is about to take on one—from other motives than to escape the draft I hope.[3]

I am sending you a short squib on Being a Professor, which may not be good for much but which at least helped to move me from Minneapolis to Ithaca—a fairly expensive business.

Cordially
Carl Becker

[*Written in the margin*]

I suppose you know your old friend Vic Coffin[4] has resigned his job at Wisconsin to go into business.

1. CBCU.
2. William E. Lunt (1882–1956) taught English history at Cornell (1912–1917), and Haverford (1917–1952); Alfred H. Sweet (1890–1950) received his Ph.D. at Cornell (1917), taught English history there (1917–1920), and later at Washington and Jefferson College (1925–1950).
3. William W. Davis (1884–1960), professor of history at Kansas (1910–1954); William S. Johnson (1877–1942), professor of English literature at Kansas (1908–1942).
4. Victor Coffin (1864–1942) studied at Cornell (1887–1893); while at Wisconsin (1893–1917), he taught Becker European history; he was on "leave" 1907–1917.

To George Lincoln Burr

Washington, D.C., August 31, 1918[1]

Dear Mr. Burr,

I certainly expected to be home long before this when I came down here; but I find that it is easier to come than to get away. When the revision of the Cyclopedia was finished, Ford asked me to stay on and write a pamphlet on German deviltries in Belgium,[2] and now that that is done a new job is looming on the horizon. How long it will keep me I can't say, but I hope to get away towards the middle of September. If that should come to pass I shall probably stop off at Branford,[3] where Jameson tells me the Board of Editors is to have a meeting, for a few days on my way home. Information which we get here seems to indicate that the new draft law will make a considerable readjustment of college work necessary. The draftees are to come to college at Government expense and to be held to a course largely under the control of the military authorities. It also seems that the men will be called away at intervals of three months so that courses in history will need to be arranged on a three month's basis, as will also the War Aims Course which all will be required to take, including the boys from Grammar school who will be present. I wonder if the simplest way all round wouldn't be to put the university on a three or four term basis and organize all courses accordingly? Doubtless you have all considered the situation much more carefully than I have, and certainly with more knowledge of the local situation.

Sincerely,
Carl Becker

1. Burr Papers, CU.
2. CLB, "German Attempts to Divide Belgium," *World Peace Foundation*, I (Aug. 1918), 307–340; subsequently issued as a separate pamphlet.
3. Connecticut, near New Haven.

To Arthur M. Schlesinger

My dear Schlesinger,[2]

I have, by dipping into your book at intervals, managed to find time to read the greater part of it, and some parts, notably that on the Non-Importation Experiment of 1768–70, and the adoption of the Association, rather carefully.[3] It seems to me an unusually thorough and careful work, intelligently put together, and clearly presented. It should be of great value to any one who wishes to understand the character of colonial society & politics or the origins of the Revolution. Someday some one will show the connection between this conservative influence in the Revolutionary period & the Federalist party, & for that task your study will also be highly valuable. I notice that you suggest the connection at the close of your work and refer to Beard.[4] One thing I think we have to avoid, which I have always felt that Beard & people of his way of thinking do not altogether do: and that is the assumption that the men who had property & sought to protect it were somehow conscious hypocrites. This comes from an inadequate psychology. Every class acts in general, taking men by & large, along the line of its economic interests; & yet the great majority are honest & sincere enough in their profession of "principles." We all have a wonderful talent for identifying our interests with the cosmic purpose, but we do it honestly enough for the most part.—& the men who profess principles designed to enable them to keep their property are not any the less, on that account, good patriots, than those who profess principles designed to get it away from them. But I don't know any reason for impressing this on you, as I have not seen any evidence of animus against the merchants in your excellent book.

Sincerely,
Carl Becker

1. Arthur M. Schlesinger Papers, HU.
2. Schlesinger (1888–1965) taught at Ohio State (1912–1919), the University of Iowa (1919–1924), and Harvard (1924–1954). His specialty was American social history.

3. *The Colonial Merchants and the American Revolution* (New York, 1918).
4. See Charles Beard, *An Economic Interpretation of the Constitution* (1913); *Economic Origins of Jeffersonian Democracy* (1915).

To William E. Dodd

Ithaca, [early 1919][1]

My dear Dodd,

I have read your letter with much satisfaction, as you can imagine, the more so as you could not have felt called upon to say anything about it on account of having received a copy "with the author's compliments."[2] The reason you have not received such a copy is that I have only one copy as yet, and that of the Abraham Lincoln edition, which is so far above the resources of professors that I must content myself, for presentation copies, with the simpler edition which is to appear sometime—I don't know when. Perhaps it has appeared—if so I have not been notified. The book is not so fine as you say, but it may pass.—and anyway, as W. J. Bryan once said on being introduced to an audience, "You don't have to believe everything you hear in order to enjoy it."

I have been reading recently with great pleasure and some exasperation the "Education of Henry Adams," which Jameson gave me last summer for review: and I have just finished a rather longish review which will probably appear in the April number.[3] —If Jameson is satisfied with it and doesn't think it too long. The book suggests so many things that an article would hardly do justice to it, and I have found it harder than common to know what to omit.

I ran off to Washington this fall from October to January at the call of the Committee on Public Information, and so escaped the S.A.T.C. mess.—I judge it was much of a mess everywhere, and as I expected it would be, I was glad to go. We are through with it here, and are once more back to normal condition.[4]

Have you read Veblen's new book on the Higher Learning? It is much more to the point than mine. Beard recently reviewed it in New Republic under the caption "The Hire Learning"—It is understood that Veblen got much of his thunder from Chicago. But if

Chicago gives him so much thunder, I wonder what some other institutions would do.—[5]

Cordially,

Carl Becker

P.S. If it takes you the better part of a half hour to make out this letter—and if you then fail in parts—I shant regret it!!! I understand your wife copies some of your things on the typewriter. Why not your letters!

1. CBCU.
2. CLB, *The Eve of the Revolution.*
3. *AHR,* XXIV (1919), 422–434.
4. For the Students' Army Training Corps at Cornell, see Morris Bishop, *A History of Cornell* (Ithaca, 1962), 430–431.
5. Thorstein Veblen, *The Higher Learning in America* (New York, 1918). Veblen (1857–1929), economist and social theorist, taught at the University of Chicago from 1892 until 1905, when he had to leave because of extramarital affairs.

To William E. Dodd

Ithaca, February 15, 1919[1]

Dear Dodd,

Greene[2] has written me that he is going to resign as Secretary of the Council; that the Council agreed to suggest to the committee on Policy (of which you and Munro and Ford[3] are members with Haskins as chairman and myself as fifth member) that it might be willing to take up in a preliminary way the discussion of policy before Haskins returned; and he turns over to us, as something that we might like to consider in connection with our main question, the advisability of uniting the two secretaryships—of Council and Association.

I think it would be a great gain to have the work of the two secretaryships center in one office, and to have that office next to the editor of the Review. Whether Leland[4] would think his work in the Carnegie Institution would permit taking on the additional job, I of course don't know.

If you have any ideas on the question of general Association

The Letters

policy, and the question of secretary, you might send them in duplicate to the other members of the committee in this country, and we could at least be thinking the matter over, although it will I imagine be difficult to do much without getting together. I am writing the substance of this request to Ford and Munro.

Cordially,
Carl Becker

1. CBCU.
2. Evarts B. Greene (1870–1947) taught history at Illinois (1894–1923) and Columbia (1923–1939). His specialty was American colonial history.
3. Guy Stanton Ford.
4. Waldo G. Leland (1879–1966), American historian, was with the department of historical research of the Carnegie Institution (1903–1927), and secretary and director of the American Council of Learned Societies (1927–1946).

To William E. Dodd

Ithaca, March 8, 1919[1]

Dear Dodd,

Sorry you did not go up to Princeton. I assumed that you were going whether I did or not, and so in my letter to Munro I mentioned that you were of the opinion that a good deal of dissatisfaction still existed in the association, and that you were yourself not altogether content with the outcome. I asked him to keep it in confidence. He writes me that he was not aware of any dissatisfaction; but he suggests that it would be well to send out a statement or questionaire to 75 or 100 men in the Association. He adds: "Why not let Dodd draft it, and suggest as long a list as he thinks desirable of the dissatisfied, and, in addition, put on a list of representative men from all over the country?" Such a statement or questionaire ought to touch upon the matter of how the Association is run, that is to say upon all the points in which you think there is dissatisfaction, and also upon the question of general policy of the Association in respect to its activities. I wish you would prepare such a statement or questionaire, at least on those points which interest you, and also suggest a list of men to whom it should be sent. If you will do this, I will send it on to the other members of the committee for their suggestions and additions, so that the thing can be got started as soon as possible.

Sincerely,
Carl Becker

1. CBCU.

To Richard Ager Newhall

Ithaca, April 14, 1919[1]

My dear Newhall,[2]

The Reprints haven't arrived yet; but when they do I shall be glad to send you one.[3] The last part of the book bored me a good deal, but the other parts I found particularly fascinating. The philosophy is discouraging—hopeless, in fact, if you take it seriously. For my part, I have been fed up on so many philosophies that none of them makes any great impression. I study what interests me and don't inquire too curiously whether it is worth doing. I believe it is as well worth doing at least as some other things—such as making War and Peace.

I am glad to have your address; and if you are looking for a job next year I should like to know it.

Cordially,
Carl Becker

1. CBCU.
2. Newhall (1888——) taught European history at Harvard (1912–1919), Yale (1919–1924), and Williams (1924–1956).
3. "The Education of Henry Adams," *AHR,* XXIV (1919), 422–434.

To Claude Halstead Van Tyne

Ithaca, July 12 [1919][1]

Dear Van Tyne,

I am glad that you liked my book.[2] At least your review of it seemed to indicate that you liked it, although I suppose one member of the Board, reviewing another member, *must,* in the interest of solidarity, puff him up. You ought, in any case, to have pointed out some defects which are obvious enough. Our beloved ex-president, Mr. Thayer,[3] said that the book left the impression of "smartness." I think it may do that in some places. Now that the war is over, I hope you will stop propaganding and get out your own book.

Sincerely,

Carl Becker

1. CBCU.
2. *The Eve of the Revolution.*
3. William Roscoe Thayer was president of the American Historical Association in 1918.

To William E. Dodd

Ithaca, December 2, 1919[1]

Dear Dodd,

I was much surprised and much flattered that you should wish to have me at Chicago; but, while I am not quite ready to say at present that I would not accept an offer from there, I must confess that I do not feel disposed to leave Cornell. In most respects I think Chicago is a better institution than Cornell; its students, so far as I can judge, are a more serious class of people; and accordingly a more serious spirit prevails there. I also have a great many friends there, and have no doubt of the agreeable character of a position there in that respect. The work which you outline is attractive. So you see I do not underestimate the attractiveness of the proposal you wish to make me, and I am quite aware that you are doing me a quite exceptional honor in making it. On the other hand, there is the library here, which in my field is the best in the country; there is the location, which is very convenient; and there is the place, which we are all very much in love with, while we would be, I am quite sure, not very happy in a place like Chicago. My work here is very agreeable, five hours and a seminary; aside from which there is a tradition of liberty for the individual professor which leaves little to be desired. Altogether, we are very well content, and the prospect of pulling up again and again getting adjusted to a new place makes us all very solemn. As to salary, they raised me here last June to $4500, without my asking or expecting it, and for no reason that I can see except the realization that salaries must be raised. They are now raising $5,000,000 for increase of salaries alone; and I think my prospects of going to $5,000 in the near future are good. Amherst offered me $5500 last July. Of course Amherst is not Chicago; but it is a very good college, and you can judge that Cornell is attractive from the fact that I was willing, or able in these days, to sacrifice a $1000 to remain here.

If you take this as ending the matter, I shall not blame you; but if you do not, I shall be glad to talk it over with you more fully at Cleveland. But in all honesty I ought to say that I would find it very difficult to make up my mind to leave Cornell.

As to the Spanish-American place, I do not know of any men. Burr said there was a good man at Texas; and doubtless, as you have come from there, you will have learned all the possibilities from Barker.

The trip to Waterloo was very sudden. Millis[2] did not know I was in Chicago till afterwards. I stopped at your house but no one was at home, and I saw Mrs. Millis but for a few moments on my way through. My father's death was quite sudden, and without pain. He was an old man, who had lived a good life, had got much what he wanted out of life by dint of hard labor, was much respected and much mourned, and left his affairs just as he would have done if he could have forseen his death. On the whole, therefore, it was a good end, and there is nothing to regret.

I shall hope to see you at Cleveland.

With regards to your family,

Sincerely,
Carl Becker

1. CBCU.
2. Harry A. Millis (1873–1948), professor of economics at Kansas (1912–1916) and Chicago (1916–1938).

3. Disillusionment and Thoughts on Politics, 1920–1924

To Richard Ager Newhall

Ithaca, March 24, 1920[1]

My dear Newhall,

You may indeed give your brothers letter to me. I shall be very glad to see him. It is true that American politics is at a pretty low stage. It isn't what it used to be in the good old days—and it never was! But then, what politics is better? Gt Britain? France? Italy? The world is in that state of confusion, irritation, and disillusionment which always follows great revolutions or great wars. We are confronting problems of peace with a war psychology. Maybe we shall elect Hoover. I don't know what his political philosophy is; but he is an honest man and an able one, and I am ready to gamble on him.

I am more than delighted to get Notestein down here,—he is a very good man and a particular friend of mine. We feel that we have made a good haul for one year.

I had heard of your marriage; but haven't heard how that arm is doing. Sincerely hope you have the use of it.

Cordially,
Carl Becker

1. CBCU.

To Alexander Meiklejohn

Ithaca, June 5 [1920][1]

Dear Mr. Meiklejohn,[2]

Your letter of June 1 has just come. The delay I do not understand, although we live out here in Cayuga Heights Village with only one rural mail delivery each day. Your telegram speaks of the situation having changed in respect to the offer. I am wondering whether this means that you withdraw the offer, or whether you are only pressing for an immediate decision. The second paragraph of your letter might imply the latter, but the concluding paragraph leaves me with the impression that you wish to convey the former. I should be sorry if you think that I did not serious[ly] consider coming to Amherst. I endeavored to make it clear to you, as I did to the people here, that my attachment for Cornell was such that a pretty high differential in favor of Amherst would be necessary to induce me to leave here; but I felt that if they could not come within reasonable approach to your offer I could not afford to decline so advantageous an offer. I realize that there has been considerable delay here in dealing with the matter, but that has been due to the circumstance that President Schurman[3] was away and acting Pres. Smith[4] naturally did not wish to assume any responsibility until the Trustees met. I therefore said to you that I would probably not be able to make a decision until about the 1 June when Pres Schurman was expected home, & which could be the approximate date of the meeting of the Ad. Com. of the Trustees. Your second letter led me to suppose that an earlier decision was not indispensable. The Trustees meet this morning and Pres. Schurman will arrive at noon. Your letter leaves me in the anomalous situation of not knowing whether I still have an offer at Amherst at the moment when the Trustees are acting upon the assumption that I have.

Sincerely,
Carl Becker

1. CBCU, draft.
2. Meiklejohn (1872–1964), philosopher and educator, received his Ph.D. at Cornell in 1897, taught philosophy at Brown (1897–1912), at Amherst (1912–1924), and at Wisconsin (1926–1938). He served as president of Amherst (1912–1924).
3. Jacob Gould Schurman (1854–1942), scholar, teacher, educational administrator, and diplomat, taught philosophy at Cornell (1886–1892) and served as its third president (1892–1920). He had diplomatic service in Greece, Montenegro, China, and Germany.
4. Albert W. Smith (1856–1942), professor of mechanical engineering at Cornell (1887–1891, 1904–1921), and acting president (1920–1921).

To Alexander Meiklejohn

Ithaca, June 6, 1920[1]

Dear Mr. Meiklejohn,

Late yesterday Acting President Smith informed me that the Administrative Committee had recommended a certain increase in my salary, and asked me to state on behalf of the committee whether I would remain on those terms. In view of the changed situation consequent upon the inferences I drew from your letter, there was nothing for me to say except that I would. I cannot say whether the result would have been different apart from that letter. Probably not in the end. I am sorry to have caused you trouble and inconvenience, perhaps I should say annoyance, which have led to nothing; but I still doubt, as I did last year, whether I should have been as helpful for your purposes as you were inclined to think I would. Theoretically I think your scheme an excellent one; but I am temperamentally inclined to be too much aware of practical difficulties to be a good reformer. As an observer of courageous experimenters, my interest in your projects is as great as it ever was; and I sincerely hope and believe that you will find someone more helpful in putting them over than I should have been.

Very sincerely,
Carl Becker

1. CBCU.

To J. Franklin Jameson

Ithaca, June 8, 1920[1]

Dear Jameson,

I am sorry to say that I do not expect I shall be able to come to Branford—unless the Committee on Policy should meet there, which is not likely. This reminds me that there would be some advantages in being at Amherst, which is so much nearer Branford. Mr. Meiklejohn has been trying to tempt me away from Cornell, and to that end held up before me a lot of glittering lucre which was hard to resist in these days of H. C. L. However, I am not going. Every one is most kind in desiring me to remain here, and they have done what they could in the way of salary; all of which is due in no small part to letters written to the President on my be-half by some good friends, of whom I am told you are one. I mean I was told you wrote a letter; I did not need to be told you were a good friend, of which you have given too many evidences for me ever to be unaware of it. I am surely much obliged. Everything is most agreeable here at Cornell. I have a very good lot of graduate students, who seem to be under the illusion that I do a good deal to help them on their way. There is the library which is a joy for-ever, as well as a thing of beauty. Above all, there are such men as Burr and Hull, who are the finest of the wheat. I cannot see any reason at all for going to Amherst, except the money; and although I give up a good deal of that to remain here, I feel very comfortable about it.

Cordially,
Carl Becker

1. CBCU.

To William E. Dodd

Ithaca, [late spring 1920][1]

Dear Dodd,

It was very good of you to send me a copy of your book on Wood-row.[2] I have read it with great interest, but not always with agree-ment. It shows your usual grasp of American history, & your usual infernal insight into the mole-like interests that burrow underneath the resounding platitudes of politics. But your Woodrow somehow escapes this penetration which you bestow on others. He has been a powerful force unquestionably; but the inconsistencies, egoism, & other weaknesses are too much concealed. Because Lincoln was damned and misunderstood is no ground for saying that Woodrow will some day be exalted as Lincoln is.[3] Lincoln had humility, and humor, and a warm and generous love of men. Woodrow has none of these. Compared with Lincoln, his speeches & addresses sound something hollow & rhetorical. That he got something at Paris I

will admit. The peace is less bad than it would have been without him. But to say that the Peace conforms with the 14 points is either the result of dishonesty or an egoism that enables him to see black as white. In 1918 he saw that the kind of new international order he dreamed of required a peace without victory. It was the truest thing he ever said. But later he said that since the Germans would have it, we would give them force without limit; and the war ended in victory. Still he goes on calmly assuming that the new international order can be attained by precisely the kind of peace which he formerly said would make it impossible. I don't say he could have done differently,—but I say if he was right in 1918 he is wrong in 1920. The man has no humor, no objectivity, no abiding sense of or contact with reality. If he would talk reasonably about the treaty & the League [of Nations]; if he would say that it was not all that we had hoped, but that it was after all the best that could be got, if he should argue that the best hope of the League becoming something & the best hope of improving the treaty, lay in the adherence of the U.S.—such talk a man might not agree with but he could understand. But to go on talking about the Peace of Versailles as embodying the principles which he proclaimed while fighting the war—this is to be ridiculous to the point of sublimity.—I can understand being for the treaty or against it,—but I can't understand being for it to the point of refusing to accept any reservations whatever, or of being against it only if these reservations are not made. The thing will be neither worse nor better by a few reservations. What does it matter anyway. It won't last; it is not being observed, and the people who made it never expected it would be. If anything ever comes of the League, Woodrow will have the credit of having launched the experiment and that will have been much; but future generations will never exalt him for having handicapped the new experiment with such a millstone as the Peace of Versailles.

Are you correct about McKinley's not having gone on the stump in the 1896 campaign? I distinctly recall that the only time I ever saw the man was at the Wisconsin Gym, making a speech towards the close of that campaign.

Cordially,
Carl Becker

1. CBCU.
2. *Woodrow Wilson and His Work* (New York, 1920).
3. Note that Becker, like Lincoln, was from the Middle West, while Dodd, like Wilson, was a southerner.

To William E. Dodd

Ithaca, June 17, 1920[1]

Dear Dodd,

If I could always count on getting a good long letter by writing a short carping one, I would keep on writing that kind. My dear man, you take me too seriously. I am not worth it. But I do not think your book a bad one; quite on the contrary. I do not accuse you of partisanship. You are one of the two or three most honest and straight thinking men I know. You do not offend me by anything you say about Lincoln, or about anything else. I cannot, at least I hope I cannot, be offended by any one so fine and genuine and generous as you. You say there must be "something more subtle operating in you or in me." There is. There was something more subtle operating with me at Cleveland; very subtle, but yet very simple, which was that it was nine o'clock in the morning, and I had not yet had my coffee, and was accordingly, as my wife would abundantly assure you, very cross grained.

But perhaps that was not all. The war and what has come out of it has carried me very rapidly along certain lines of thought which have always been more congenial to my temperament than to yours. I have always been susceptible to the impression of the futility of life, and always easily persuaded to regard history as no more than the meaningless resolution of blind forces which struggling men— good men and bad—do not understand and cannot control, although they amuse themselves with the pleasing allusion that they do. The war and the peace (God save the mark!) have only immensely deepened this pessimism.

It is of course easy to explain the war in terms of the sequence of events, or the conflict of interests, or the excited state of the public mind, etc. But in itself the war is inexplicable on any ground of reason, or common sense, or decent aspiration, or even of intelligent self interest; on the contrary it was as a whole the most futile and aimless, the most desolating and repulsive exhibition of human power and cruelty without compensating advantage that has ever been on earth. This is the result of some thousands of years of what men like to speak of as "political, economic, intellectual, and moral Progress." If this is progress, what in Heaven's name would retardation be! The conclusion I draw is not that the world is divided into good men and bad, intelligent and ignorant, and that all will be well when the bad men are circumvented and the ignorant are enlightened. This old eighteenth century view is too naive and simple. Neither good men nor bad wanted *this* war (although some men may have wanted *a* war); yet neither good men nor bad were able to prevent it; nor are they now apparently able to profit by their experience to the extent of taking the most obvious precautions against a repetition of it. The conclusion I draw is that for good men and bad, ignorant and enlightened (even as enlightened as Mr. Wilson), reason and aspiration and emotion —what we call principles, faith, ideals—are without their knowing it at the service of complex and subtle instinctive reactions and impulses. This is the meaning, if it has any, of my book on the Eve of the Revolution, and particularly of the chapter on Adams and Hutchinson.[2] You may see something of the same philosophy in the New Europe for May 13;[3] and I hope before I die to write a story of the French Revolution which will convey, to those who can read between the lines, the same idea on a larger scale.[4]

The men recently convened in your city of Chicago were mostly good and honest men enough.[5] Senator Harding is a good and honest man enough—born on a farm, member of the Baptist Church, (against which no one can say a word, you least of all,) upright citizen, never said or did anything ignoble.[6] They are all honorable men, with clear consciences, loving their country and their fellow men, and firm in the belief that they are working for the welfare of all, including themselves. Yet the whole business there strikes me, in view of the state of the world at large and of America in particular, as so unreal, so false, as so all compact of bunk and fustian and petty intrigue that one can only turn away in disgust or cynicism. And in a less degree I feel the same about politics and government in general. Politics predisposes the men who engage in it to self deception, it immerses them in such a dense and unrelieved atmosphere of obfuscation that they become dishonest in effect while remaining somehow for the most part honest in intention. I do not doubt that Lodge[7] is as honest in his own mind and conscience as Wilson is. Both convince themselves that they are working disinterestedly for the welfare of their country and the good of humanity; yet neither one will, or apparently can, discuss the treaty or the league or European or American politics directly, disinterestedly, or intelligently. Their talk about these things is unreal talk. It is puerile talk. In a word, it is bunk.

And this is why I cannot get up any enthusiasm for or against the treaty or the league, for or against Wilson. The whole business is so saturated with self deception and nonsense, that it is only sickening when it is not merely diverting. The other night I attended a concert by your Chicago orchestra: and as I listened to these men what came over me with overwhelming force was the honesty and genuineness of what they were doing. The same is true of all genuine art, scholarship, craftsmanship, and of all human activity which has for its primary object the creation of something beautiful or useful, or the discovery of some truth, or the doing of something helpful to others. But the most of politics, and much of business, has none of these for their primary object; their primary object is the gaining of some advantage over others; and hence there is a subtle taint of unreality and accordingly of dishonesty about these enterprises that warps and falsifies the minds of their followers. And so in my present temper politics strikes me as serving chiefly to illustrate and confirm the ancient saying: "The human heart is deceitful above all things, and desperately wicked." Don't suppose because I can't be enthusiastic about Wilson that I have any sympathy with the Senators who oppose him. I read your article in the N. R. [*New Republic*] with interest and found it well argued; my only comment would be that it is useless to defend Tweedle Dum against Tweedle Dee. A plague on both your houses!

What really irritates me, I will confess to you, is that I could have been naive enough to suppose, during the war, that Wilson could ever accomplish those ideal objects which are so well formulated in his state papers. A man of any intelligence, who has been studying history for 25 years, and to some purpose if I am to believe your high opinion of him, should have known that in this war, as in all wars, men would profess to be fighting for justice and liberty, but in the end would demand the spoils of victory if they won. It was futile from the beginning to suppose that a new international order could be founded on the old national order.

Cordially,
Carl Becker

My present intention is to vote, if I vote at all, for Debs.[8]

1. CBCU.
2. *The Eve of the Revolution.*
3. CLB, "Europe through the Eyes of the Middle West," *New Europe,* XV (May 13, 1920), 98–104.
4. See Becker's unpublished allegory, "The King of the Beasts" [1920], CBCU; and cf. Wilkins, *Carl Becker,* 143–144.
5. The nominating convention of the Republican Party.
6. Warren G. Harding (1865–1923), Ohio senator (1915–1920), President (1921–1923).
7. Henry Cabot Lodge (1850–1924), Massachusetts senator (1893–1924).
8. Eugene V. Debs (1855–1926), Socialist Party candidate for President.

To William E. Dodd

Ithaca, [summer 1920][1]

Dear Dodd,

Many thanks for your long letter. It amounts to saying, what you said before, that Wilson did the best he could. I admit it. Nevertheless, he largely failed. I am willing to give him credit for doing the best he could, but am not willing to say he succeeded where he obviously didn't. My chief quarrel with him is that he is perfectly blind to the failure.

But come up to Branford in September. I will give you hours and hours in which to defend him, while I throw in a cynical remark now and then. The committee on policy(?) is to meet at Branford: I know you don't care for that. No more do I. But I expect to be there for three or four days, and it would be awfully jolly to have you there for a long uninterrupted chewing the rag. Do come up. We don't get together very often, and life is short, and this is a fine chance. Besides, it's your duty to come on the chance of making me see reason. If you shirk your duty your conscience (Baptist [?]) will come down on you something bad.

> Very sincerely,
> Carl Becker

1. CBCU.

To Jared Treman Newman

Ithaca, July 23, 1920[1]

Dear Mr. Newman,[2]

This spring, through Mr. Curtis, I got a small cedar tree from your woods on the west side of Cayuga Heights Road. Mr. Curtis assured me that he had your permission on condition of paying you the price (of $1.00) which you had stipulated. I am enclosing the dollar, and am much obliged for the permission.

> Sincerely yours,
> Carl Becker

1. Jared T. Newman Papers, CU.
2. Newman (1855–1937) was an Ithaca attorney, bank official, Cornell trustee (1895–1903, 1907–1933), and developer of Cayuga Heights.

To Frederick Jackson Turner

Ithaca, October 24, 1920[1]

Dear Professor Turner,

Your book came yesterday, and although the Nation had already sent me a copy, I was glad indeed to have your autographed copy, with its generous expressions of regard.[2] Your 'share' in my stock, whatever the stock may be worth, is no small one, as I have often assured you. Whatever I have written in American history shows the influence of ideas which are expressed in these essays and addresses; and in my last book,[3] as you will see if you look at it, I have appropriated your interpretations without scruple, without fear also, without reproach I hope, and certainly without research.

This share in my stock is I fear not very profitable to you, since I have thus embezzled it. But you have other shares, less palpably docketed, but not I hope less worth while. It was you more than any one, you and Haskins, who shunted me into the scholar's life. I always wanted to write. From the age of twelve I had the writer's itch, the models which then fascinated me being the wonderful fictive adventures appearing in the Saturday Night and the New York Family Story Paper, and such journals of established reputation; admirable stories no doubt in their kind, but perhaps not after all representing the 'best that had been thought and said in the world.' Later I became interested in the realistic novel, the sort that, without chapter headings, were intended to illustrate the 'art for art's sake' theory of life and letters. In fact I had in me the making of a scrubby journalist and third rate literary fellow. The literary fellow I have still with me; but I try to keep him in his place, and I hope I succeed passably. If I do it is because I got at an early age a kind of grip on the idea of scholarship. The holy fear of the dishonest and the second best, of words without sense, of easy generalizations unballasted with knowledge—this was what I desperately needed, and this was what I got from you and Haskins, and from the study of history as you taught me to study it. You may be surprised to learn that to this day, whenever I write anything, sooner or later, before I let it go, I read it over, with you and Haskins and certain others at my elbow listening; and it often happens that one or other of you, or all of you together, send me to the library for further researches, or wisely suggest that this sentence be cut out, or that paragraph be recast, in order that the thing may not be too brash or superficial or otherwise unworthy of my good masters.[4] You may say you would never have suspected it. Fact nevertheless; and if I have not profited more by the procedure, the fault is wholly mine. Thus your share in my stock is large and steadily increasing; and I live in hope that the stock may some day go to par, or perhaps above. All things are possible, and this may come to pass when we eventuate from our present involvements and retropedate back to normalcy.

I hope you may find it convenient to come on to Washington in December.

With best wishes,
Carl Becker

1. Turner Papers, HEH.
2. *The Frontier in American History* (New York, 1920). Becker's review appeared in *The Nation,* CXI (Nov. 10, 1920), 536.
3. *The United States: An Experiment in Democracy.*
4. *The Heavenly City of the Eighteenth-Century Philosophers* is dedicated to Haskins and Turner.

To William E. Dodd

Ithaca, October 25, 1920[1]

Dear Dodd,

It was very good of you to take the trouble to write about my book,—and charitable to find nothing but good to say about it.[2] I have had a number of appreciative letters, & the reviews have not been unfavorable so far as I have seen them. I could write a critique of it that would leave some holes. It is not a scholarly book like yours; but I suppose popularization of an elementary sort is worthwhile sometimes. I realize the importance of the reactions you speak of, but as this was not a narrative history I couldn't very well find a place for them.

I wish you could have got up to Branford, but I can understand the difficulty. I am dreadfully afraid you will not be coming to Washington for the Christmas meeting. Do come if you can: there is no one I wish to see more, and I know many people in the same boat.

You will of course vote for Cox:[3] and I confess my sympathies, when I read the newspapers, are instinctively with him. I shall be glad if he wins, although my intelligence tells me it is a case of Tweedle and Dum. Whichever party wins we will have the treaty & the League, with some reservations, very shortly. That is my guess at least. And in any case I don't see that the world will be helped out of its "involvements," or will get back to "Normalcy" any sooner, from the election of one party rather than the other. I am becoming extremely unpolitical; so much so that it is a matter of complete indifference to me whether I vote or not. I know you will think my case is one that calls for prayers; but I tell you frankly I am "standing out," for the Devil is hardening my heart. Poor lost soul!

Sincerely yours,
Carl Becker

1. CBCU.
2. *The United States: An Experiment in Democracy.*
3. James M. Cox (1870–1957), congressman (1909–1913), governor of Ohio (1913–1915, 1917–1921), Democratic nominee for President in 1920.

To J. Franklin Jameson

Ithaca, June 7, 1921[1]

(Confidential)

Dear Jameson,

I am writing to ask what information you may have relative to the qualities of Preserved Smith as a teacher.[2] We have him in mind as a possible man for Burr's place, and while we are disposed to think that in respect to scholarship he is the best man available for the particular field, we should like somewhat more definite information about him as a teacher, both of undergraduates and of graduates. From your knowledge of Amherst men, and things, it occurred to us that you might help us in this matter. I realize that you are on the eve of going abroad; and if it suits your convenience better, there is no reason why you should answer until you are safely stowed on the boat.

Sincerely yours,
Carl Becker

1. CBCU.
2. Smith (1880–1941), the tenth member of his family to bear the name Preserved, taught history at Amherst and Harvard before coming to Cornell in 1922 as a lecturer; he was later professor of history. His specialties were the history of the Reformation and early modern cultural history.

To Arthur M. Schlesinger

Ithaca, [summer 1921][1]

My dear Schlesinger,

Much obliged for the reprint of your interesting article on Immigration.[2] I go along with everything I think, except perhaps your "unwavering toleration of all creeds and opinions"—I have a notion that Americans for the most part are extremely tolerant—that is, indifferent to—of all opinions within certain boundaries; but that outside these boundaries there is a different story to tell. After all, the numbers of people who are tolerant on principle is extremely small: most people are intolerant of the things they dislike if they thoroughly dislike them, & especially so if they the [sic] matter in question is thought to be important.

I suppose you are duly irritated at the delay in getting out the July Am H. R. [*American Historical Review*]. Printers strike is the reason, as I don't doubt you know. Just got a note from Leland, who says the Printers say it will be out in a few days. Hope to have the October number out by the middle of October.

Shall hope to see you at St. Louis.

With best regards,
Carl Becker

1. Schlesinger Papers, HU.
2. "The Significance of Immigration in American History," *American Journal of Sociology*, XXVII (1921), 71–85.

To William E. Dodd

Ithaca, [autumn 1921][1]

Dear Dodd,

Our library has at last got a set of the Chronicles, and I have been reading your volume.[2] It is really a masterly little sketch of a big subject, and gives evidence at every page of having been written by one who knows his subject down to the ground—something my books never show, whatever other merits they may have. The chapter on the Philosophy of the Old South interested me especially. Of course I had read your article on the same subject; but I am interested just now because I am writing a book on the Declaration of Independence in which my chief task is to show where the Natural Rights philosophy came from and where it went to and why. This last takes me into the slavery controversy. By the way, did you know that we have a splendid collection of anti-slavery literature?[3] And plenty of your pro-slavery stuff too—Harper, and Dew and Simms and Hammond and Sawyer and Bledsoe and Seabury and W. A. Smith and dozens of others of whom I never heard. I have been going through all this literature with a good deal of interest. I wondered why you did not mention Calhoun?[4] It seems to me that he was the Moses that led them out of the Natural Rights wilderness. His definition of Nature in the Disquisition did the business. He says to find what is natural to man you have to find what it is that he tends to become; he tends to become civilized and to establish government and complex legal relationships, etc; and hence the natural state of man is the actual political state of history. This was to identify the natural with the historical and the prescriptive, and the natural rights of the slave were thus the same as his legal rights, which weren't many. What interests me especially is this: Calhoun's conception of Nature is precisely the same as that of Bonald and most of the continental critics of Rousseau and the 18 century Natural Rights philosophy. In general it is marvellous how similar the whole pro-slavery philosophy is to that of the historic-rights school on the continent. You mention Dew's having studied on the continent; but do you know of any other direct influence of European thought on southern leaders? Especially Calhoun. Did Calhoun read French or German political speculation? His Concurrent majority theory is also similar in some respects to the philosophy on which the Tories opposed the Reform Bill.

I hope to see you at St. Louis.

Sincerely,
Carl Becker

P.S. Intended to send you an offprint of my *Wells;* but they were all gone before I knew it.[5]

1. CBCU.

2. *The Cotton Kingdom: A Chronicle of the Old South,* Chronicles of America Series, XXVII (New Haven, 1919).

3. Based upon the bequest of Samuel J. May in 1870. See Crawford B. Lindsay, "The Cornell University Special Collection on Slavery: American Publications through 1840" (Ph.D. dissertation, Cornell, 1949).

4. John C. Calhoun (1782–1850), politician and philosopher from South Carolina, author of a *Disquisition on Government* (published after his death).

5. "Mr. Wells and the New History," *AHR,* XXVI (1921), 641–656.

To William E. Dodd

Ithaca, [autumn 1921?]]¹

Dear Dodd,

The book of Prince which you wish to see we have not in the library. We have a sermon of Dr. Thomas Prince² on the taking of Louisburg—*Extraordinary Events the Doings of God, etc.* 1745. But I suppose that doesn't interest you. I quite agree with you about the importance of the preachers and the Revolution, but I think it was a different sort of preachers than Samuel Davies³ who contributed to popularize the doctrine of natural rights. I also think the religious revulsion from the Revolution in the early nineteenth century helped to discredit the Declaration and Jefferson. Southern writers make a good deal of Jefferson having got his ideas from the "atheistical French school." Of course I don't think he did. My whole contention is that the Revolution, both in theory and practice drew its inspiration from the parliamentary struggles of the 17 century. Natural rights was essentially an English doctrine. In the nineteenth century, when the French Revolution and the doctrines on which it was based were in disgrace in England the myth grew up that the natural rights doctrine, being particularly vicious must be peculiarly French, and that the Americans must have taken it from France. In fact Jefferson copied Locke⁴ and Locke quoted Hooker.⁵ You are quite right about Calhoun. I looked into his Disquisition the day after I wrote you for the first time since I was a student in Turner's classes. Somehow it got fixed in my mind that it was written about the time of the nullification controversy. The same ideas about the Declaration are in the speech on the Oregon Bill 1848, but as yet I have not located them in any speech of 1833. If you can put me on the track of that speech I should be obliged—not that I want you to go to any special trouble.

Sincerely yours,
Carl Becker

1. Dodd Papers, LC.
2. Prince (1687–1758) was a New England theologian and bibliophile.
3. Davies (1723–1761), a Presbyterian clergyman in Virginia, became fourth President of Princeton.

4. John Locke (1632–1704), English philosopher.
5. Richard Hooker (1554?–1600), English theologian.

To Carl Van Doren

Ithaca, December 24, 1921[1]

My dear Van Doren,[2]

I am sending by American Express the ms. of the Dec. of Ind.[3] I welcome your criticism and suggestions; and I believe I am right in thinking that I am not sensitive in such matters. The last chapter is what has given me most trouble, and I don't like it much yet, although I have rewritten it two or three times. If you can tell me what is the trouble with it, I will gladly try once more to make it right. And the same applies to any other parts of the ms.

In printing chapter four, particular pains will have to be taken with the printers to be sure that the various texts of the Declaration are printed exactly as given, with all erasures, interlineations, spelling, capitalizations, etc. For this purpose I have pasted instructions to them at the important points.

This is a sad Christmas present I send; but so God made the world.

Faithfully yours,
Carl Becker

1. CBCU.
2. Van Doren (1885–1950), an editor and author, taught (1911–1930) at Columbia and The Brearley School; was an editor of *The Nation* (1919–1922), *Century Magazine* (1922–1925), and the Literary Guild, a book club (1926–1934). He first suggested to Becker that he write a book about the Declaration (Jan. 8, 1920).
3. *The Declaration of Independence: A Study in the History of Political Ideas.*

To William E. Dodd

Ithaca, [1922?][1]

My dear Dodd,

Your letter interested me much, and the inclosed separate, which I think I have already read, I read again with great pleasure, and with agreement. I saw Andrews[2] last summer, and he raised the question of my statements in the "Eve of the Revolution," [and] "Dem. an Experiment."[3] We discussed the matter for some time, and I did not see that we differed much except that he thought I had used the term democracy without considering whether that was the precise term that they would have used, or rather whether they would have meant by government by the people just what we mean by the word democracy. He did say that he thought the Revolution had been entirely misconceived, and was writing, or preparing to write, a book which would give a different view.[4] I really don't think he has anything new. Of course there were plenty of people who supported the Revolution and used the conventional ideology while it was going on, who did not relish government by the people much, just as there were plenty of people who thrilled with pride and emotion when President Wilson's fine words were quoted in 1917–18, and quite sincerely, who nevertheless were ready to think in 1920 that it was all idealistic and 'visionary'. In both states of mind they were quite sincere—I am speaking now of thousands of the plain people who don't think very much or consistently about these things. The truth is few people care much for equality unless they are trying to climb up to the other fellow's level. Andrews' discussion of whether people in 1776 really wanted democracy or not struck me as largely futile, because it missed the point that democracy or aristocracy are, like war, not objects in themselves which people want or don't want; people want or don't want a great variety of things, against which or for which they struggle, and war, democracy, etc., are instruments, sometimes no more than words, which they lay hold upon as a means of obtaining what they want or safeguarding them against what they don't want. Thousands of people now lay hold of the word democracy as a safeguard against Bolshevism, democracy being of course the word which describes the government we have and which they are satisfied with. If the danger of Bolshevism disappeared and they suddenly found themselves pinched by the Beef Trust, they would easily turn round and demand a democratic government in place of government by the interests. Very few people think with their minds. That is an unusual accomplishment, like objectivity, or always telling the exact truth, or reading a foreign language. People commonly think with their emotions; and these periods of ebb and

flow which you point out in our history are, I think, less the results
of a more or less effective struggle of the people consciously aiming
at democracy than they are the result of shifting emotional reactions of the same people, or the same kind of people. I don't see
history quite as much in terms of a conscious class struggle of conflicting economic interests, as you seem to do. People's minds are
far too muddled to carry on any such struggle for more than a short
time. Besides the overwhelming majority of people give on an
average only an infinitessimal part of their time to social or political aims or thought. You can take any average man and find that
on one side of his mind, if you introduce the subject in the right
way, he is a democrat, but introduce the subject in another way
and you will find another side of his mind which is pure aristocrat.
But he is not conscious of any inconsistency. What historical research needs is a more subtle psychology.

With apologies,
Carl Becker

1. Dodd Papers, LC.

2. Charles M. Andrews (1863–1943) taught history at Bryn Mawr
(1889–1907), Johns Hopkins (1907–1910), and Yale (1910–1933),
specializing in early American history.

3. *The Eve of the Revolution* and *The United States: An Experiment
in Democracy.*

4. *The Colonial Background of the American Revolution* (New Haven,
1924).

To Henry Johnson

Ithaca, October 24, 1922[1]

My dear Johnson,[2]

I have very little belief in the value of teaching history in schools
as now taught, in so very many cases, by immature young women
without experience, who do not know the subject and have never
reflected to much purpose on any subject. If taught by competent
teachers I think it could serve in the main to teach us "how we do
live together"; if it taught how we ought to live, etc., that would be
something the teacher would put into it—not that I object to his
doing so. Certainly history should give the idea of continuity—I
suppose that is the essential meaning of the term; and I believe

that it is highly desirable for all of us to be aware of the fact that all of our most valuable social possessions are rooted in the past, and that however much society may need reforming you cannot tear it up by the roots without loosing more than you gain. On the other hand history equally teaches that this is a changing world, and that it is useless to try to keep what is good in any society by keeping everything just as it was "when I was a boy." Considering how little students actually get out of the study of history in schools, I sometimes wonder if it wouldn't be better to throw all of the high school instruction in history, economics government, etc., into one three year course consisting of (1) one year devoted to the history of Europe and America during the period since about 1776; (2) two years devoted to a careful descriptive study of the geography, governments, party politics, economic resources, industries, international trade, 'backward country' exploitation, international conflicts and alliances, etc. Such a course carefully organized and well given would give students a good deal of precise and concrete knowledge of the world in which they live. Of course it all comes back to the question of competent teachers. If you could get competent teachers, my inclination would be to stop telling them what to teach and how to teach it, and let them go ahead and teach what they could do best. But this is a counsel of perfection, and I realize that this brief screed won't help you any.

> Yours pessimistically,
> Carl Becker

1. CBCU.
2. Henry Johnson (1867–1953) was professor of history at Columbia Teachers' College (1906–1936); a member of the committee on history in the high schools, New York State Board of Regents; chairman of the editorial committee of the *History Teachers Magazine;* and author of *Teaching of History in Elementary and Secondary Schools* (New York, 1915) and *An Introduction to the History of the Social Sciences in Schools* (New York, 1932).

To Henry Johnson

Ithaca [December, 1922][1]

My dear Johnson,
    The statement you sent around relative to the unique contribution of history seems to me to be about as good as it could be within

the space. The term progress I don't like, because it implies change toward something better; and so far as scientific history is concerned this is begging the question. Development is not so bad, but even that word has taken on, without any warrant that I know of, a connotation of upwardness that is misleading. Perhaps the same criticism may be made of 'becoming.' About all I can see in history is change from one situation to another situation, better or worse, as the case may be; or better for some people and for some purposes, or otherwise. The object of historical study, as I see it, is to represent this change in such a way that it can be understood in terms of human purposes, motives and actions. When you attempt to explain it by the method of scientific 'law,' you are running into Sociology or something else. The chief value of history is that it is an extension of the personal memory, and an extension which masses of people can share, so that it becomes, or would ideally become, the memory of a nation, or of humanity. In so far as it does or can do this it should serve to steady the activities and fortify and fructify the purposes of mankind. This of course is a wild ideal. What actually happens is that the mass of a nation cares nothing for history until they have a particular purpose to carry through which can be justified by reference to the past, to their traditions, (American 'principles,' etc) and then they proceed to make these traditions, this past, to suit their purpose. In other words the "history" that actually has an effect on the course of events is almost always an idealized history. The idealization of classical republicanism & of stoic & Roman Virtue in the latter 18 century is a good example.

Sincerely yours,
Carl Becker

1. CBCU.

To William E. Dodd

Ithaca, [February 26, 1923][1]

My dear Dodd,

The Nation sent me your letter to them apropos of the Baker article.[2] I am glad you liked the article, especially since you know as much about Wilson and what he did as most people, more than

Villard ever can know on account of his ingrained and quite violent prejudice against him.[3] From something he said to me once, I suspect that there is a purely personal reason for his animosity, although of course he does not know it and would stoutly deny it. He thinks Baker is prejudiced in favor of Wilson, and cannot see that he is himself even more prejudiced against him. I, naturally, like every one else, think I am prejudiced neither for nor against. When Wilson came back I had a grudge against him which lasted for some time. I was indignant at something I supposed he had done or left undone. But one day I said to myself: Why are you angry with Wilson? What has he done to you? Are you then a party man, with a cause to serve? Perhaps you ought to be out putting up the barricades, or get yourself a stilleto so that you can stab the enemy in the back? But if you are a historian, endeavoring to understand this damnable world, what have you to do with anger? You will never understand Wilson by getting angry with him. Then I realized that what I was angry with was myself; I was angry to think that having studied history for twenty five years I was still so stupid as not to have foreseen that after such a war the peace of Versailles was precisely what one might have expected. I had had a moment of optimism, had experienced a faint hope that Wilson might do what he wished to do. When he failed, I was angry because I had failed to see that he must fail; and took it out on Wilson. But that is all over. I told Villard that I did not wish to be severe on Wilson, even if there were a justification for being, because even if he was wrong-headed, he was wrong-headed in the right direction—and I added, "as Emerson said of some of your ancestors." How he liked that I don't know. His editorial only amuses me.

Sincerely yours,
Carl Becker

P.S. Your estimate of me as a historian is calculated to increase my conceit beyond its present limits: it will do for a private letter, but if you will put it in print it would damage your reputation for sanity.

1. CBCU.
2. CLB, review of Ray Stannard Baker, *Woodrow Wilson and World Settlement,* in *The Nation,* CXVI (Feb. 14, 1923), 186–188.

3. Oswald Garrison Villard (1872–1949), journalist with the *New York Evening Post* (1897–1918); editor and owner of *The Nation* (1918–1932).

To Henry Holt

Ithaca, [1923][1]

My dear Holt,[2]

I am glad you liked my review of Baker. My little satire, read to the Philosophical club, or whatever it was called, was intended to draw the distinction which most of us, "The man of the people everywhere," including politicians, are not aware of—viz: the distinction between our fine educational ideals and our very prosaic actions. The satire was a little too hard on Wilson, and I confess I was a little sore at him then; but I have since realized that what I was really sore at was myself for having had a moment of optimism, for having had a faint belief that he might do what he thought he could. An old student of history should have known that the Peace, after such a war, could not be the expression of brotherly love.

The review evidently pleased a good many people, judging from letters I have received about it.

Sincerely yours,
Carl Becker

1. CBCU.
2. Henry Holt (1840–1926) was employed by G. P. Putnam (1863–1873), president of Henry Holt & Co., publishers (1873–1926), editor of the *Unpopular Review* (1914–1921).

To Everett E. Edwards

Ithaca, May 10, 1924[1]

Dear Mr. Edwards,[2]

I am sorry that I cannot be present at the banquet you have arranged in honor of Professor Turner. It is now more than thirty years ago that I first spoke to him, in his class room in University

Hall at Wisconsin, one day in 1893, when I had occasion (or did I only make it?) to ask him some question or other. What the question was, I know not, or what the answer; but I well remember the peculiar lifted flash of the eyes that seemed to look me through, the engaging quality of the voice that replied. From that moment I was Professor Turner's man—a confessed and devoted disciple. Such I have remained ever since: and if I have studied much and with any discrimination, if I have taught others not wholly in vain, if I have written anything not badly, these things I have done in no small degree because Professor Frederick Jackson Turner, throughout life my teacher and friend, has had for me both this stimulus and the restraint of a noble example. May the latter years of his life be many, and filled with honor and satisfactions!

> Very sincerely yours,
> Carl Becker

1. Turner Papers, HEH.
2. Edwards (1900–1952) studied with Turner at Harvard, taught at Northwestern (1923–1925), and became agricultural historian with the U.S. Department of Agriculture (1927–1952). A founder of the Agricultural History Society, he edited its journal.

To Frederick D. Becker

> T.S.S. "Columbia," June 15, 1924[1]

Dear Frederick,[2]

I am going to keep a kind of record of my trip in the form of a daily journal & I want to keep it on these little cards so that I can file it away in cases when I get home. So instead of describing things in my letters I will send you these little cards from time to time,—but I wish you would be careful to keep them in good shape, so that I can use them later.

> Your loving daddy.

1. CBCU.
2. Frederick DeWitt Becker (1910——), CLB's son, received his B.A. and M.A. at Cornell (1933, 1934), and has been with the Silver Burdett publishing company since 1935.

To Maude Ranney Becker

York, England, July 4, 1924[1]

Dear Maude,[2]

I got your letter forwarded to me at Durham, together with the doctor's letter about Edith.[3] Monday we leave here for London, and I hope to find more mail waiting me there.[4] My first address is 17 Brunswick Square, W.C.—but send your letters to Brown Shipley Co., & they will forward them. Besides, I don't know how long we shall stop there. We had difficulty in getting any place at all, as London is crowded on account of the Imperial Exhibition going on there at Wembly. Our plan is vague yet, but at present the idea is to stop in London a week or two, & then move to some more quiet place in the country. At least Prescott & Notestein do not want to remain long in London. I may have enough of it in two weeks. There is some talk of a walking trip, but that is still all uncertain. I think they will both, later in the season, go to France with me. We are talking of going through Holland & Belgium & then to Paris. But all is uncertain. Notestein has several different plans every day. Both York & Durham are very interesting, as I have explained in my notes to Frederick.

I hope you will make some satisfactory arrangements for the summer which will give you a rest. I suppose you will try taking Edith with you,—but I don't think it will work very long.—you need a change and rest more than Edith does.

English cooking is nothing to brag of,—but I find the cool moist climate gives me a fine appetite, and I am I think much better than when I left. I sleep nearly every afternoon, and generally pretty well at night.

With much love,
your husband

1. CBCU.
2. In 1901, Becker married a young widow, Maude Hepworth Ranney, the daughter of a New York physician. She was several years older than CLB, with a seven-year-old daughter. He had met Mrs. Becker during his year at Columbia in 1898–1899. She died on June 2, 1957.
3. Edith, Mrs. Becker's daughter by a previous marriage, suffered

from mental incapacity resulting from serious illness and improper medication during late adolescence.

4. Becker made his only trip to Europe during the summer of 1924. He traveled with his colleagues Wallace Notestein and Charles Hull, Hull's sister Mary, and Frederick C. Prescott (1871–1957), professor of English at Cornell. Becker's main purpose in going was to recover from mental depression and nervousness. He had recently undergone surgery.

To Maude Ranney Becker

Oxford, England, July 16, 1924[1]

My dear wife,

I have had no letter from you since you left Boston. But I suppose you were busy getting settled. We came to Oxford today after a ten day stop in London. It was hot there, and I shall be glad to get to the country & rest,—but for all that I had a good time in London, and feel now that it is something more than a name to me. Oxford is not so beautiful a place as I expected. In fact, aside from the University there is little in it that would be worth coming to see. I have not seen much of the University yet. As it is divided into colleges, & each college is walled in, it is impossible to see the University as a whole. You can only go into the separate colleges. Some of these have very beautiful "quads"—that is grass & trees— or campuses.

We are staying at the quaintest old Inn you ever saw,—an old old building, containing the room in which Cranmer & Ridley slept before they were burned for heresy in the 16 century.[2]—The rooms are very clean & quiet however, & it is a good place to stop. I like English hotels. They are quiet, clean, & cheap. One great difference over here is that everyone you have to do with is polite & accommodating & good natured. Even in London the Bus men & policemen & car conductors are all extremely obliging. I don't think I saw or heard anything that showed irritation or ill temper. It is the climate.

> With much love
> your husband

1. CBCU.

2. Thomas Cranmer (1489–1556), Archbishop of Canterbury, and Nicholas Ridley (1500?–1555), Bishop of London, leaders of the Prot-

estant Reformation in England, were both burned at the stake, Ridley with a bag of gunpowder tied to his neck.

To Maude Ranney Becker

Winchcombe, Gloucestershire, England, July 27, 1924[1]

Dear Maude,

I have been here a week now, and plan to stop on for another week certainly, and probably two or three. Travelling about is tiring, and I find this quiet place very restful. A walk of three or four miles, a sleep in the afternoon, and a good rest at night, with really good food, is probably doing me good. It seems to me that I have been away for months, and sometimes I am ready to come home at any time. I am enjoying it, and expect to do so; but even now, although I feel well enough physically, I can't stand much, and I have little zest of life. I think my mind is slower in recovering from the effects of the operation than my body. I am more & more convinced that the dope they gave me had not worn off. I am apathetic, I dislike the idea of working, or reading anything serious, even the talk of people wearies me, and I am easily bored with everything. So sometimes, I feel that it is useless being here, but I know that I should be even more apathetic and bored at home. Prescott said that after his operation he felt the same way, half dead mentally, for about a year, & then the effect began to wear off. Notestein's enthusiasm for everything English is sometimes refreshing and sometimes childish & tiresome. All in all, I think the best thing for me is to stay here for some time, where I can rest all day if I feel like it, or stay in my room, or go off by myself as I like. Later I shall doubtless go over to France, although it is pretty clear now that neither Notestein nor Prescott will go with me. The truth is I don't care much whether I go or not. I oughtn't to feel that way, & since I am in Europe it would be foolish not to go to Paris at least. But I know a week or ten days in Paris would be all I could stand, and I dread the exertion. The difficulty of making any effort is appalling; but still I don't regret coming, and I am having as good a time as I could have under the circumstances. I wish you and Frederick were here with me, or in my place, because you would enjoy everything so much more than I do.

This is rather a depressing letter; but I want you to know just how I feel. Don't think I am not as well as I was, for that is not true. I am better than when I left Ithaca. I sleep well, and have a very good appetite. The main trouble is depression, & a lack of interest in anything.

I am glad you are having a rest and a good time, & I hope Edith continues to be so easy to manage. I sent her a card yesterday.

With much love,
your husband

1. CBCU.

To Maude Ranney Becker

Winchcombe, August 5, 1924[1]

Dearest Maude,

Your letter of July 23 has just come, in which you say that Edith is so docile that you have sent the nurse away, and speak of going to Ithaca in August. I don't see why you do not remain where you are. It can't be much more expensive to live at Ocean City than at Ithaca: but I suppose this letter will not reach you before you make your change. It may be that Edith is, according to the course of D. Praecox[2] as we were told, becoming quiet & apathetic. Or, it may simply be the welcome change, which would wear off, especially if you returned to Ithaca. If she is going to settle down and be perfectly immobile and tractable, she could live at home; but I greatly fear that once in the old environment the old trouble would recur. However, you must do what you think best.

Am sorry about Frederick's knee. Of course he couldn't go into salt water with it until it is pretty well healed.

Am having a fine time here, and the rest and quiet are doing me a world of good. I feel more like myself than at any time since my operation. Yesterday I walked 12 miles, without any ill effects; but today I am lying all day about [in] the sun. The idea of leaving here does not appeal to me much, but I suppose I must go to Paris for at least a week or so.

With much love,
your husband

1. CBCU.
2. Dementia praecox, schizophrenia.

To Maude Ranney Becker

Paris, France, August 24, 1924[1]

Dearest Maude,

Just got your letter addressed from the cottage on the Lake, but not dated. Am glad to learn that Frederick's knees are all right once more. I was a little worried; and am delighted that you are having a not too hard time there. I hardly supposed Mrs. Gottschalk[2] would be so keen about that kind of life.

There is any amount of interesting things to see here, and I am putting in my time seeing them; but I am not overdoing it. The most I hope to do, or expect to do, is to get a kind of familiarity with the place as a whole, so that I can carry away a mental picture of its streets & buildings, etc. It will at least be something more to me than a name on the map: —But two weeks will be quite enough: it is rather tiresome being here all alone. Miss Dielmann[3] I see a good deal of, and she is very helpful, but not a particularly interesting person. I shall be quite ready to come home when the time comes, and should be glad if the two weeks were up now. My foreign travel has come too late to be of any great benefit. I should have come to France at the age of 25; then it would have been an experience of incalculable benefit. Well, it is too late for regrets now, and I shall get something out of it at least.

I got a letter from Edith in which she says she has become thin again on account of being constantly on the go. She has stopped each of her two paragraphs in the middle of a sentence, & has left the letter unsigned. It seemed to indicate that she was falling back again into an earlier condition. But of course the main thing is whether she runs away.

I will send Frederick some more notes of my wanderings tomorrow.

> With much love to all,
> your husband

1. CBCU.
2. Laura Reichenthal Gottschalk Riding Jackson (1901——), Amer-

ican-born poet and humanist, went to England in 1926, where she collaborated in writing and publishing with Robert Graves and others.

3. Rita H. Dielmann (1892——) a student of Becker's, received her Ph.D. at Cornell in 1924, and taught at Wilson College in Chambersburg, Pennsylvania.

To Maude Ranney Becker

Paris, August 25, 1924[1]

Dearest Maude,

This is my fourth day in Paris, and I am getting adapted to the place and the strangeness of it. For beautiful streets and architecture & gardens there is nothing like it. One thing you would enjoy is the lively and festive character of the streets & especially the avenues & boulevards. What contributes to this gaiety is chiefly the restaurants. There are restaurants everywhere, and all of them nearly, even the cheapest and tiniest, are almost sure to have tables outside on the sidewalk with tubs of plants round partially screening them off from the street,—& over these tables will be awnings, usually of yellow or orange stripes which makes a pleasing effect against the gray buildings. The food is invariably good. Today I was wandering round the other side of the River near the Pallais Royal, when a shower came on, & as it was about 1 oclock, I slipped into a dingy looking restaurant, which was nevertheless packed with people. There they offered a table d'hote, which gave me first a sardine, then a choice of roast beef (Ros. Bif.) or veal with french fried potatoes, next a dessert of fruit or pastry. With this went a basket of bread, from which I freely helped myself, and the inevitable half bottle of white wine. Although the place was a little dingy & noisy, the food was good,—and it all cost, including wine, 3½ francs. The franc is worth about 6 cents, which made my lunch 21 cents. A tip of one franc, which was really too large, since the custom prescribes 10% only, brought the total up to the tremendous sum of 27 cents. In ordinary restaurants it is difficult to spend a dollar for a dinner. After dinner the thing to do is to stroll along the avenue & stop at one of the innumerable places where little round tables & chairs are out on the sidewalk and order a coffee or a chocolate or a syrup & sit & sip & watch the people etc.

I do sometimes get depressed, but it is usually at night,—& in any case I am enjoying my stay here and shall find plenty to do that will be worth while.—

I don't object to anything you have decided about Edith,—and I am certainly glad you went to the sea shore & had a rest. You will have to do what seems best for the time being, & if it doesn't work out then something else will have to be done. If she keeps quiet and doesn't run away or break things, most of the difficulty is avoided. Of course she may fall back into her old ways.

You had better not send any letters or mail later than Sept 3, unless you want to send a last letter about Sept 4 addressed to me at Steamer Assyria, Anchor Line, Glasgow, Scotland.

With much love,
Carl

1. CBCU.

To Frederick D. Becker

Paris, August 28, 1924[1]

Dear Boy,

It rains every day here in Paris,—but never very long or exceptionally hard. It does not interfere seriously with what I want to do, except that I have to carry my rain coat about wherever I go. Today I visited the Bibliotheque Nationale, the great library of France, & one of the three or four most famous in the world. Not much of it was open to the public, but I got at least an idea of what it was like. Afterwards I visited one of the less notable museums,—the Carnavalet,—which interested me however because it contains two or three rooms devoted to things relating to the French Revolution. They had there a model of the old Bastille, the prison which was destroyed in the Revolution, and some of the clothes, dishes, rasors, etc used by Louis XVI and Marie Antoinette when they were in prison previous to their execution. Many old guns, pikes, etc. were there, and some of the red caps worn by the Jacobins or *sans culottes*. "Sans culottes" means without britches. The old nobility wore knee britches, but the common workers wore blouses & pants,

—and as the revolution was made by the common people against the nobles, they took pride in calling themselves "sans culottes." Knee britches, lace sleeves, and powdered wigs, went out of style at the time of the Revolution because those things were the distinctive dress of the nobles. The Revolution thus brought in a democratic dress, which is pants, as well as a democratic form of government and society. Or at least it aimed to do so; but in fact neither the new government nor the new clothes were altogether democratic.

I have a hard time getting any good cigarettes here. The kind they have displayed in the window are mostly English and American, but on account of the tax they are very expensive—about ¢50 for a packet of Camels, which cost ¢15 in the U.S. The French cigarettes I don't know the name of, and I have only French enough to ask for something I know the name of. One or two kinds I know; but neither is very good. I shall be glad to get back to the U.S. where the best cigarettes are made, and the cheapest. If food was only as cheap & as good there as here, we could live like princes. A franc is worth about 6 cents in our money, but it is divided, like our dollar into 100 centimes; & they have as small as 5 centime pieces, and are as careful of them as we are of pennies, or nickels.—

I am having a good time, but shall be glad to get back to a country where the people speak English. There are hundreds of Americans here of course, & some in this hotel,—& it really sounds pretty good to hear the voices & the accents.

Lovingly,
Daddy

1. CBCU.

To Frederick D. Becker

Antwerp, Belgium, September 6, 1924[1]

Dear Frederick,

Well, here I am in Anvers (Antwerp), after a six hour ride from Paris. The train was crowded, and the country not very interesting.

Through northern France, where the Germans invaded the country, many houses and villages were destroyed, and new brick houses have now been built, so that it looks more like Indiana than France. After we passed Brussells, the country becomes flat, because you know this is near the sea, and it is in the region of the Dykes. Holland is the great country of dykes & canals, but northern Belgium is much like Holland, & was once part of the same Netherlands, or Low Countries (Pays bas). As Belgium lies between France and Holland, the people are partly like the French & partly like the Dutch. The Walloons of the south speak French, but the Flemish of the North & east speak Flemish which is much like Dutch. But in towns like Antwerp, where so many English & American tourists come, I find that a great many people, in hotels & shops, speak English. In this hotel all the waiters & clerks & even the bell boys speak English, or at least enough to be understood. Even my cab man spoke it. Here all public notices are posted in two languages—French & Flemish. In one shop I saw three signs—"Hoedenmakery—Chapellerie—Hatter." The first word you see is practically the English Hoodmaker. The second is French & much like our cap.—

I had dinner on the train, and I must tell you what they gave me. Their dinners here on trains are table d'hote.—First there was on the table the course called Hors d'oeuvre (side dishes) of potato salad, fish, a slice of bologna sausage, & a slice of musk melon. A waiter came around with a big cloth apron bag affair & handed out bread. Then came a kind of oyster pattie or something of the sort. Then roast beef & potatoes, with a second helping if you wanted it. Then a little slab of ice cream. Then choice of three kinds of cheese. Then a bunch of grapes, & then coffee. This was all 12 fr. for the dinner, & 2 fr. for the "cover" (all restaurants in France charge for the "cover" i.e. bread, napkins, plate, etc.). I ordered a pint of wine which was 1 fr (6 cents) extra. The whole thus came to 15 fr. which with a tip of 1 fr. 50 c. came to 16 fr. 50 centimes= $1.00. What would such a dinner cost on an American diner?

With love,
Your Daddy

1. CBCU.

To Frederick D. Becker

Antwerp, September 8, 1924[1]

Dear Frederick,

Antwerp is a most interesting city, and I have had a pretty good sight of it now. Today, among other things, I visited the old castle, built about 500 years ago to defend the city against the Spaniards during the Revolt of the Netherlands against Philip II. It is built on the River Scheldt, which is the great harbor of Antwerp in from the North Sea. Now the Castle is a museum. It was also used by the Spaniards as a prison and court of Inquisition for Protestant heretics; and they have still the bed in which condemned heretics slept, the chapel where they worshiped, and some of the instruments of torture that were used. One room, which would have interested you, was filled with models of ships of the 16 and 17 century. There must have been twenty or thirty models, some nearly five feet long, and four or five feet to the top of the sails, all fully rigged, & of all different sorts.

Another thing which would amuse you are the carts pulled along the streets by dogs. There are a great many small delivery carts on two wheels pushed along by handles, some small, & some pretty large. They put the dogs in harness under the cart, under the axle if it is high enough, and fasten the traces to a whiffle[tree?] that is fastened to the standard running down from the handle bars. Thus the man, or more often a woman pushes & the dogs under the cart pull. They pull quite heavy loads & sometimes at good speed, so that the man or woman has to run to keep up.—

Yesterday I got in touch with the Hulls who are stopping with a relative, Mr. Mitchell, who is manager here of the Red Star Line. In the afternoon he took us all in his high power car over into Holland, on to one of the Islands of Zeeland, to a town called Goes, about 30 miles from Antwerp. I got a fine view of the flat Dutch country with its Dykes & canals. This was close to the sea, which runs far into the country in great inlets, as you will see if you look on a large map,—& so there were Dykes running in every direction. One place we ran along a road on top of a dyke where the sea comes in at high tide. It was low tide at the time, and as far as you could see there was nothing but a flat stretch of mud.— When they need more land they run a dyke across a patch of this low tide country, & there is a fine stretch of very fertile land won from the sea. They build their railroads & wagon roads on the dykes sometimes, & line the road with trees. After we had gone on some distance into Holland, we suddenly came upon people wearing the old fashioned Dutch peasant costumes of the 17 century. All the women coming home from church wore long black skirts, with colored waists, and on their heads those white caps with great stiff white wings sticking out on both sides, something like the head gear of sisters of charity & in front on either side of the forehead, a kind of gilt spangle sticking out, like the blinders on horses. The men, many of them wore black courduroy suits with the little low crowned hats with brims turned up all around, something like a clowns cap, only without the pointed top,— exactly like the garb worn by the players of Dutch parts in Weber & Fields Vaudeville years ago.—There is nothing of this in Belgium, and only in some parts of Holland.

Tomorrow I am thinking of taking a train to Rotterdam & Delft, & possibly to the Hague. Distances are not far in this country. Tomorrow night I sail for Harwich & London.

Daddy

1. CBCU.

4. Quiet Years as Teacher and Friend, 1924–1930

To Leo Gershoy

Ithaca, October 22, 1924[1]

Dear Gershoy,[2]

I think it is too late to get on the programme this year.[3] It is nearly time to print the first edition. Next year it could be managed perhaps. If you will remind me about June or July, I will write to the chairman of the programme committee.

Don't worry about your teaching. It comes hard at first, but easier at last. For years I had to keep my nose to the grindstone, working up every lecture or class room exercise beforehand, thinking out carefully what I was going to say. A terrible grind, and the thing rarely done with any satisfaction. The first years in Cornell I was a rank failure half the time, and felt as if I were on the edge of a collapse. The difficulty was that I was over impressed with Cornell and felt that I had to do twice as well as anywhere I had been before or lose my job. But I haven't lost it yet, and so I have gained confidence, and it goes easier. This will come to you too. After the first year you will begin to feel Rochester under your feet instead of on your back, and then you will have time for something else. Let your other work go, give your time to your courses, but do it leisurely. Don't cram, but take time to reflect. Confidence, then, and above all de l'audace, toujours de l'audace!

Awfully sorry about Hatch.[4] The ingenious cruelties and refined tortures called life have given him a full dose for his age. I hope there are better times coming.

Hope to see you soon,
Sincerely yours,
Carl Becker

1. LIG.
2. Gershoy (1897———) received his A.B. (1919) and Ph.D. (1925) at Cornell under Becker's guidance. He taught European history at the University of Rochester (1924–1926), City College of New York (1928–1929), Long Island University (1929–1938), Sarah Lawrence (1938–1946), and New York University (1946–1969), and held various fellowships.
3. Of the American Historical Association, in late December.
4. Lloyd Hatch, a graduate student in English history at Cornell.

To Leo Gershoy

Ithaca, January 24, 1925[1]

Dear Gershoy,

I heard of Packards[2] going to Amherst from Miss Young,[3] who knows everything. It surprised me a bit. As to your thesis,[4] I read it, as well as I could, soon after you were here, and wrote some pages of useless comment; & then laid it aside on the chance that you might come down. I don't know that it is worth your while to come down for that alone. I will send the thesis and comment to you. You can take the exams if you wish, and leave the thesis till later; or leave the exams till you have the thesis. If you wish to take the exams I suppose you should notify the Dean's Office to that effect.

Why don't they take you on in Modern European history? Or, if they want someone with more experience and a degree (Oh, invaluable degree!) there is Gottschalk.[5] They might do a lot worse. I know this slants at Zionist propaganda, to mention two members of the chosen people for one university.

Sincerely yours
Carl Becker

1. LIG.
2. Laurence B. Packard (1887–1955) taught at the University of Rochester (1913–1925) and at Amherst College (1925–1955), specializing in early modern European history.
3. Catharine E. Young (later Mrs. Masters), a graduate student in modern European history, who took her Ph.D. at Cornell in 1927.
4. "Barère, the Mediator of the Revolution," Ph.D. dissertation, Cornell, 1925.
5. Louis Gottschalk (1899———) received his A.B. (1919) and Ph.D. (1921) at Cornell under Becker's guidance. He taught modern European

history at the University of Louisville (1923–1927) and the University of Chicago (1927–1966). Both Gershoy and Gottschalk were of Jewish parentage.

To Leo Gershoy

Ithaca, February 4, 1925[1]

Dear Gershoy,

I didn't really *read* much of your thesis—I couldn't. I merely tried to get an idea of how you had blocked out the material. I didn't intend, by my comments, to suggest any radical changes in order, except possibly at the beginning. As for the main body of the thing, I merely suggested that by keeping the main thesis in mind the problem of selection and emphasis would perhaps simplify itself.

The reason you find it difficult to do the thing is precisely because you have a fine feeling for what is really excellent. An ordinary dumbell would already have put it together in a rough, wooden way, with footnotes properly allocated and disposed, and it would have passed as a thesis. But your feeling for literary form, and real constructive, organic thinking, is such that you can't be satisfied with the third rate, or even the second rate. If I had your knowledge of Barère, and had done all the preliminary work which you have done, it would take me eighteen months, or two years, of steady, laborious grinding to put it in form—that is, in a form that would satisfy me. If I can average a page a day of completed ms, working three or four hours in the morning, with nothing to distract me, I do well. I usually write and throw away ten pages to get one that will pass. And I am fifty one years old and have been practicing the damnable art for thirty years. At your age I couldn't write anything that would bear the light of day.

Now the point of all this. You are one of the very few students, almost the only one, I have ever had who has a fine and subtle feeling for what is really good in form and substance. So for God's sake don't think it is lack of ability that makes it difficult for you to get things done quickly. . . . You are going to do something that is really fine in the way of writing before you are through.

So keep pegging away, and be discouraged as much as you like, but remember this—you are going to write something better than the others.

Incidentally, Notestein came back from Richmond saying that Packard was extraordinarily well pleased with you. Well, I knew he would be.

Sincerely yours,
Carl Becker

1. CBCU.

To Alfred A. Knopf

Ithaca, April 10, 1925[1]

Dear Mr. Knopf,[2]

It is very good of you and Van Doren to think of me in connection with a book on Disraeli. The subject is attractive—extremely so; and in fact there is nothing so ill done as biography. Besides, to do the life of some one interests me. For all these reasons I ought perhaps to accept your offer; but there are two particular reasons against it. The first, and insuperable one, is that I am working on a book now which will take me two years at least to finish. The second is that 19 century English history is too far out of my field. I should have to work up English politics & society from the ground before I could begin. Some 18 century worthy, such as T. Jefferson, would be more in my line.

But I must say that Disraeli is an intriguing subject.

Isn't Prof. Bell,[3] of Bowdoin doing a life of Disraeli? Or is it Palmerston?

Sincerely yours,
Carl Becker

1. AAK.
2. Knopf (1892——) founded his distinguished publishing house in 1915.
3. Herbert C. F. Bell (1881–1966), professor of history at Bowdoin College (1912–1926), and then at Wesleyan, wrote *Lord Palmerston* (2 vols.; London, 1936).

To Frederick Jackson Turner

Ithaca, September 20, 1925[1]

Dear Turner,

There is, as perhaps you know, a project afoot for a book intended to be "an approach to the Social Sciences." Sounds like a stalking party; and in a way it is, for the approach is to take the form of hunting down the leading "masters" in the social sciences and putting them for exhibition in this book, each one in a chapter by himself. You are one of the "masters"; and I have been asked to exhibit you in a chapter of 8–10,000 words.[2] Do you object to being thus exhibited; and, if not, do you object to me as your particular barker? Whatever I write I should wish to submit to you for your comments, suggestions, etc. If you have no objections to my going ahead, would you mind sending me any late things you have done, if you have reprints of them—I mean anything you have not sent me. (I am leaving here on the 28 Sept. and perhaps you might send in care of Jameson, 1144 Woodward Bld. Washington). I ought to say the chapter is supposed to include something of personality, something of teaching methods, and something of productive work.

If you do not already know of this nefarious plot, perhaps you are not expected to, in which case please be a deep well from which nothing escapes.

Sincerely yours,
Carl Becker

1. Turner Papers, HEH.
2. "Frederick Jackson Turner," in Howard W. Odum, ed., *American Masters of Social Science* (New York, 1927).

To Harry Elmer Barnes

Ithaca, February 26, 1926[1]

Dear Barnes,[2]

I have read your chapter with interest,—and have raised a query about the relative expences of France & Gt. B. for armies. After returning home from your talk at the University Club here,

I received a request from the Editor of the Christian Century to write a series of articles in reply to yours. I wired that I could not reply to you because I was in *essential* agreement. I am, so far as the brute facts are concerned, and that means that it is no longer possible to lay upon Germany the responsibility for the war. Where I differ from you is in this: you are inclined to believe that some special persons are criminally responsible in some what the same sense that a man is criminally responsible when he commits a murder for personal advantage: and you are inclined, I take it, to think that by exposing the criminals the world can be enlightened & induced to take a radically different attitude towards war: I on the other hand can't see either of these things. It's a matter probably of temperament—some lack of vitality or glandular secretions on my part. You said yourself here that Poincare et alii no doubt were, or thought of themselves as being, honest highminded gentlemen who were doing their duty to their countries and therefore to the H. Race—and that if *we were* in their positions with their training and traditions we would doubtless have done as they did. That is exactly what I think: —"But for the Grace of God, there go I." etc. Well, if that is the case, I don't quite see how they can be held responsible in the sense in which you hold them so. Another point is that "we the people" are perhaps quite as responsible. A people in peace is one thing; a people in war, or under conditions in which war is imminent, is quite another set of animals.

Well, this is why I couldn't write in the vigorous, superlative, sledgehammer way you do; but that doesn't mean that I protest, or that I don't enjoy what you write. I do. It can't I think do any harm. On the contrary it is probably the only way to jar people loose & make them think a little. You have done more probably to keep this question alive and make the people, or some of them realize that there are two sides to the question than anyone else. Fay's kind of writing is probably more judicious & water tight than yours; but Fay might write to the end of time and no one the wiser except a few university professors.[3]

So I say, more power to your arm—and perhaps it would have more power if it were a bit more supple, & not quite so heavy.

Sincerely yours,
Carl Becker

1. CBCU.
2. Barnes (1889–1968) taught sociology and history at the University of Syracuse (1913–1915), Columbia (1917–1918), Clark (1918–1923), the New School for Social Research (1919–1920, 1922–1926), and Smith (1923–1930), and was a lecturer, journalist, and author (1930–1968).
3. Sidney B. Fay (1876–1967) taught European history at Dartmouth (1902–1914), Smith (1914–1929), and Harvard (1929–1946). In 1928 he published *The Origins of the World War*, 2 vols.

To George Lincoln Burr

Ithaca, April 28, 1926[1]

Dear Mr. Burr,

I enclose check for $500.00 in payment of the loan you so kindly made me two years ago. I have been a long time about it; and it is only right that I should pay you interest. If you only say the word I will be glad to. It has been a great convenience to me, and I do appreciate your kindness.

Very sincerely yours,
Carl Becker

1. Burr Papers, CU.

To Harry Elmer Barnes

Ithaca, [1926?][1]

Dear Barnes,

I have just finished your *Genesis of the World War*.[2] It is, I think, the best thing you have done—a marvellously straight, swift, cogent presentation of facts and conclusions, with less unnecessary baggage of adjectives than your writing often carries. It is I think the most *effective* statement of the position than anything I have seen, although I haven't read a great many books. It is perhaps an oversimplification of the psychology of individuals like Poincaré, Ed. Grey,[3] etc.:[4] but substantially the fundamentals are right, and this simplification will do no harm since without it you could not get the attention of many readers. No one can seriously study the beginnings of the war without taking account of your book. I congratulate you.

Sincerely yours,
Carl Becker

1. CBCU.

2. *The Genesis of the World War: An Introduction to the Problem of War Guilt* (New York, 1926).

3. Edward Grey (1862–1933) was British foreign secretary (1905–1916), and chancellor of Oxford University (1928–1933).

4. See CLB to the editors of *The Nation*, Oct. 16, 1933.

To Gussie E. Gaskill

Ithaca, December 9, 1926[1]

Dear Gussie,[2]

We were glad to hear from you, & especially to know that you were getting on well and enjoying the experience. Paris is really a wonderful place, which I enjoyed and would like to see again. But after all I got homesick & was glad to come away after four weeks. I am too old for a first venture abroad. The glamor & romance of it is not there. But you are young enough to get what one should get—viz. the pot of gold at the foot of the rainbow.

We have had a horrible fall & winter. Since the first week in August, it has been cloudy and raining without cessation; & now we have a foot of snow come down on us the 6 of Dec. with a coat of ice on top of that. The Ford I have put away for the winter. It is more bother than it is worth this kind of weather.

The Gershoys have been here this fall. He is trying to write his book for Knopf,—not getting on with it very fast I think. He is still looking for a job.

Catherine [sic] Young took her final exam on the thesis[3] and is now a full fledged PhD. She had a letter from Robert Graves,[4] who writes to her for Laura (formerly Gottschalk). He said that he and Laura were in Vienna, leaving Martha (that's his wife) in England. The reason for going to Vienna was so that Martha could have quiet for her drawing, in which she is much interested. He closed by saying that he & Laura liked Vienna, but after all they "did miss the children." You had better take note of this *menage* if you want to be up to date. Gottschalk visited them last summer, & now he is about to marry again—a girl he met in Minneapolis last summer school, I understand: a girl with the bluest of eyes & the goldenest of hair.

I am grubbing away on my text book;[5]—have meantime written out a lecture delivered by request at the Brookings School in celebration of the anniversary of 1776. The subject they asked me to talk about was "the Spirit of '76."—fancy! Well, I wrote a little story, purely fictitious, relating, through the pen of a friend, the activities & opinions of Mr. Jeremiah Wynkoop of New York. It will be printed they tell me.[6]

We all send love, & would like to see you.

Sincerely yours,
Carl Becker

1. GEG.
2. Gaskill (1898———) took her B.A. (1918) and M.A. (1919) at Kansas; she came to Cornell as Becker's assistant and graduate student (1919–1923), and became curator of the President White Historical Library and also of the Wason Collection on China and the Chinese (1924–1963).
3. Catharine E. Young, "A Comparison of the Letters and the Memoirs of Madame Roland: An Introductory Study for a Biography," Ph.D. dissertation, Cornell, 1927.
4. Robert R. Graves (1895———), poet, novelist, and essayist. Graves' first wife was Nancy Nicholson, his second Beryl Pritchard.
5. *Modern History: The Rise of a Democratic, Scientific, and Industrial Civilization.*
6. "The Spirit of '76," published in *"The Spirit of '76" and Other Essays* (Washington, D.C., 1927).

To the editor of the *Cornell Daily Sun*

Ithaca, December 10, 1926[1]

To the editor of the *Cornell Daily Sun:*

I was interested in the letter of Five Bewildered Freshmen and in the discussion it gave rise to.[2] The freshmen say they have been engaged in the intellectual life for more than two months and don't know what it's all about. This is bad, but who is to blame? Some say the students are to blame, and some say the professors.

What is to be done about it? You suggest . . . an orientation course such as is given in other universities.

For my part, I don't blame anyone—not the freshmen, certainly. It's not especially the student's fault if he doesn't know what it's all about. If he did, he wouldn't need to come to college. That's why, I have always supposed, young people come to college—to get some notion, even if only a glimmering, of what it's about. They come to get "oriented." But why expect to be oriented in two months, or a year? The whole four years' college course is a course in orientation. It isn't a very satisfactory one, indeed. Four years isn't enough. Life itself is scarcely long enough to enable one to find out what it's all about.

Neither do I blame the professors—not particularly. Many people appear to think that professors possess some secret of knowledge and wisdom which would set the students right as to the meaning of things if they would only impart it. This, I do assure you, is an illusion. I could write you a letter on behalf of Five Bewildered Professors which would make the five bewildered freshmen appear cocksure by comparison. The professors are in the same boat. They don't know either what it's all about. They tried to find out when in college, and they have been trying ever since. Most of them, if they are wise, don't expect ever to find out, not really. But still they will, if they are wise, keep on trying. That is, indeed, just what the intellectual life is—a continuous adventure of the mind in which something is being discovered possessing whatever meaning the adventurer can find in it.

This effort to find out what it's all about is, in our time, more difficult than ever before. The reason is that the old foundations of assured faith and familiar custom are crumbling under our feet. For four hundred years the world of education and knowledge rested securely on two fundamentals which were rarely questioned. These were *Christian philosophy* and *Classical learning*. For the better part of a century Christian faith has been going by the board, the Classical learning into the discard. To replace these we have as yet no foundations, no certainties. We live in a world of incredibly rapid change, a world of naturalistic science and of physico-chemico-libido psychology. There are no longer any certainties either in life or in thought. Everywhere confusion. Everywhere questions. Where are we? Where did we come from? Where do we go from here? What is it all about? The freshmen are asking, and they may well ask. Everyone is asking. No one knows; and those who profess with most confidence to know are most likely to be mistaken. Professors could reorganize the College of Arts if they knew what a College of Arts should be. They could give students a "general education" if they knew what a general education was, or would be good for if one had it. Professors are not especially to blame because the world has lost all certainty about these things.

One of the sure signs that the intellectual world is bewildering is that everywhere, in colleges and out, people are asking for "Orientation" courses which will tell the freshmen straight off what it is all about. If we were oriented we shouldn't need such courses. This does not mean that I am opposed to an orientation course for freshmen. I would like an orientation course for freshmen. I would like one for seniors. I would like one for professors and trustees. I would like one for President Farrand[3] and President Butler.[4] Only, who is to give it? And what is it to consist of? I asked Professor Hayes. "What about your orientation course at Columbia?"[5] He said, "It's a good thing for the instructors who give it." I asked a man whose son had taken the course, "What did he get out of it?" The reply was, "He read three books in three unrelated fields of knowledge and got a kick out of one of them." Who knows the "background" or the "general field of knowledge?" If the course is given by many professors the student will be taking several courses as one course insead of several courses as separate courses. If one man gives it what will it be? It will be as good as the man is. If we could get a really top-notch man to give a course, no matter what, and call it an orientation course, I should welcome it. H. G. Wells might give such a course, and it would be a good course.[6] I doubt if it would orient anyone or settle anything, but it would stir the students up and make them think. That would be its great merit. That is the chief merit of any course—that it unsettles students, makes them ask questions.

The Five Bewildered Freshmen have got more out of their course than they know. It has made them ask a question—What is it all about? That is a pertinent question. I have been asking it for thirty-five years, and I am still as bewildered as they are.

Carl Becker

1. *Cornell Daily Sun,* Dec. 10, 1926; in *DWH,* 155–158.
2. In the *Cornell Daily Sun,* Dec. 6, 1926, "Five Unhappy and Bewildered Freshmen" observed that their first term was concluding without their understanding the purpose of a college education any better than they had in September. The editors of the *Sun* then offered two editorials advocating an orientation course. CLB's letter responds to both the bewildered freshmen and the editors' proposal.
3. Livingston Farrand (1867–1939) taught psychology and anthropology at Columbia (1893–1914); was president of the University of Colorado (1914–1919), chairman of the Central Committee of the American Red Cross (1919–1921), and president of Cornell (1921–1937).
4. Nicholas Murray Butler (1862–1947), president of Columbia University (1901–1945).
5. Carlton J. H. Hayes (1882–1964) taught modern European history at Columbia (1907–1950) and was U.S. ambassador to Spain (1942–1945).
6. Herbert George Wells (1866–1946), English author of many works of fiction, history, and social commentary.

To the editor of the *Cornell Daily Sun*

Ithaca, December 15, 1926[1]

To the editor of the *Cornell Daily Sun:*

May I take a little space to say that Mr. Knappen has apparently misunderstood me in two important respects.[2] First, as to "certainties in life and thought," and Christian philosophy "going by the board." Of course there are certainties in life and thought for the individual. I have many of my own, although Mr. Knappen appears to think not. Of course there are many people who have an assured Christian faith and an assured Christian philosophy. But which of these so many and conflicting certainties in life and thought, which of these so many and diverse versions of Christian faith shall the college teach? Formerly the educated and learned world was fairly well agreed as to what a college should teach in order to give the student a "general education." It should teach Latin, Greek, Mathematics, and the Evidences of Christianity. Is it not evident that there is no longer any agreement, either in college or outside of it, that these are the essentials of a college course? My point is only that Christian philosophy and Classical learning are "going by the board" as the commonly accepted foundations of a "general education." This seems to me merely the statement of obvious fact. Personally, I am strong for the teaching of Latin and Greek, and mathematics; and I think that a philosophy of life, whether Christian or other, is what a student should mainly seek in his college course.

The second point. Mr. Knappen appears to think that I wish students to accept my "findings"—my ideas, my point of view, my philosophy of life. Heaven forbid! The main point of my letter was that college offers the student an opportunity (not so good an opportunity as we all wish) to enlarge his experience, extend his knowledge, to be initiated into many points of view, many philosophies of life. I would not have the student tamely accept any professor's "findings." He cannot accept all that are offered since there are so many and conflicting ones offered. The student must, with whatever aid he can get from professors, work out his own philosophy. The college does not offer all these various and conflicting points of view in order to confuse the student. It offers them because they exist in modern thought, and the college necessarily reflects the conditions of modern thought. In any case, a philosophy which the student accepts on authority, whether the authority of a professor or of a faculty, is not in my opinion worth much. The student who manages to work out any sort of philosophy of life during his four years has got the most a modern college can give him. Mr. Knappen has obviously done just that. It is what I wish every student to do.

Carl Becker

1. *Cornell Daily Sun*, Dec. 15, 1926; in *DWH*, 158–160.

2. In the *Sun* of December 13, 1926, Marshall M. Knappen, a graduate student in history and later (1928–1929) a Congregational minister, took exception to CLB's view that Christian faith no longer provided modern life with certainty, and that skepticism was inevitable in contemporary culture and education. Knappen (1901–1966) received his Ph.D. at Cornell in 1927, taught history at Chicago (1927–1939) and Michigan State (1939–1948), political science at the University of Michigan (1948–1957) and the University of Delaware (1958–1966). His special interests were English history and American foreign policy.

To Harry Elmer Barnes

Ithaca, January 11, 1927[1]

My dear Barnes,

I have not seen the review of Fabre-Luce[2] which you refer to. But if I protested to the editors about every stupid review, my hands would be fuller than they are of work to be done, and I find them overflowing as it is. Besides, while I hope an "honest" student of War guilt, I am not really a very "well-informed" one. And again besides, as you know, I have much less faith in the possibility of setting the world right than you have.

Sincerely yours,
Carl Becker

1. Harry Elmer Barnes Papers, University of Wyoming Library.
2. Alfred Fabre-Luce (1899———), French journalist, historian, and novelist.

To Leo Gershoy

Ithaca, February 13, 1927[1]

Dear Gershoy,

We learned of your appointment[2] from Schlesinger, who is a member of the board. Glad I was able to help, but I didn't say anything that wasn't true. I hope you can keep the place for a second year if you want it. What will be the fate of the text book? You can't very well write that and research at the same time?

So Ida[3] was tardy? Well, its doubtless due to the lax discipline at Cornell. Still I'm glad at least that she wasn't discharged: no one can say she lost her job because she was a "bad girl"—if you know what I mean.

We all rejoice with you, and everyone does here. I hope it will be the beginning of the end of all your worries—worries, I mean, on account of not having something to do. Worries you will have, no doubt, not being people with thick skins.

Knappen has been questioned by some Mission Board for not believing in the "literal Inspiration" of the Scriptures. So he is looking for a job. That is what comes from "bowing[?] out of existence something that is dearer than life"—to the Mission

Board. Still, this is only a Board which doubtless has no soul, so I don't blame him much.

I should have syndicated my letter to the Sun.[4] It has been copied in Syracuse, in New York, and now H. E. Barnes has quoted it in full in an article in the Smith College Monthly, in which he refers to me as "next to J. H. Robinson,[5] the most thoughtful of American historians." I tell you I'm becoming famous. How is it that you never realized that? Do look me up. You will see that I am somebody.

Ever faithfully yours,
Carl Becker

1. LIG.
2. A fellowship from the Social Science Research Council.
3. Ida Prigohzy Gershoy (1905——) received her B.A. from Cornell in 1927.
   CLB to the editor of the *Cornell Daily Sun,* Dec. 15, 1926.
4. James Harvey Robinson (1863–1936) taught European history at Columbia (1892–1919) and wrote extensively on historical thought and historiography. Becker studied with Robinson in 1898–1899, and was first exposed to European intellectual history by him.

To Leo Gershoy

Ithaca, April 2, 1927[1]

Dear Gershoy,

I haven't read Guedalla's latest. I read his Second Empire, & thought it clever, but perhaps too clever—too much dragged in in order to top it off with an epigram. Perhaps his Palmerston is better—I dare say it is.[2] An admirable subject.

About me there is nothing, except that I drone along in the same old way. Have done my textbook up to 1825—but shall have to break off for a month or so to do a 5000 article on Sam Adams for the new Ency. of Am. Biography.[3]

We had a sudden heavy wet snow of about 4 inches for April fool.

The Ford is out again sputtering along. Hope no one takes me for Henry & drives me over the bank.

Gottschalk has accepted a position at Chicago for a year at $4000. I think it will be permanent. He was to have resigned from Louisville in time; but in support of a collegue he kicked up a row and resigned *instanter*, or was dismissed, I can't make out which. The local papers seem to be on his side.

Well, I wish you joy of your trip, & would like to see you before you go. May do so, if, as is possible, I come down to N.Y. this Spring on some committee business. But that isn't certain. Have you read "The Sun also Rises"?[4] It would give you some points on how to be an American in Paris.

Sincerely yours,
Carl Becker

Mrs. Becker joins me in all good wishes.

1. LIG.
2. Philip Guedalla (1889–1944), author of *Independence Day: A Sketchbook* (New York and London, 1926); *The Second Empire: Bonapartism, the Prince, the President, the Emperor* (London, 1922); *Palmerston, 1784–1865* (New York, 1927).
3. "Samuel Adams," *DAB* (1928).
4. Ernest Hemingway (1898–1961), *The Sun Also Rises* (New York, 1926).

To J. Franklin Jameson

Ithaca, May 10, 1927[1]

Dear Jameson,

I never thanked you for sending me the Amherst Quarterly with your talk on history in it. If you did send it, as I suppose. If not, I thank you for writing the paper. I liked it much—hits the nail on the head without glancing off and hitting the thumb. I have a good deal of sympathy with Barnes and Robinson and their School (I am supposed to be a "Newer Historian" you know. See Barnes, passim), but they, especially Barnes, hit my thumb a great part of the time.

The publishers of Odum's volume on Masters of Social Science were so stingy as not to give us any offprints of our articles—otherwise I should send you a copy of my thing on Turner. Hope I have been sane, and not too much carried away by my admiration for the man.

May very likely be sending you an article on Mme. Roland soon.[2] Written five years ago, and I don't much fancy it now. Perhaps you won't. No harm done if you don't.

We go to Cazenovia this week end, and I wish you were going with us.

Best regards to all of yours,
Carl Becker

1. CBCU.
2. "Memoirs and Letters of Madame Roland," *AHR*, XXXIII (1928), 784–803.

To Frederick Jackson Turner

Ithaca, May 18, 1927[1]

Dear Turner,

I suspected you must be away, and not long since Max Farrand[2] told me you were in California. I am glad you think the article exhibits well enough the character of your work. As to the idealization of your personal influence—well, no doubt: but that doesn't bother me. I haven't so many enthusiasms but that I can afford this one. Besides, isn't the idealization the reality so far as the students are concerned? Even if we saw you in some golden light, the fact that we all did see you thus must mean that there was something there calculated to enable us to see you thus magnified. At all events the many who have read or heard my portrayal are agreed that the Turner they knew is there recovered for them. But I know how it strikes you, because many of my students think I have done great things for them, whereas I (so it seems to me) have done nothing but sit around and look wise and tell them they have more capacity than they think—more sometimes than I think myself. Usually they manage somehow not to turn me down.

I hope, for your sake, you can winter in California. For my sake I should wish to have you nearer—but then our paths don't seem to cross anyway. I wish they did. Couldn't you be induced to come to Ithaca for a lecture? Or just for some week end conferences with graduate students. I could easily get your expenses & a little wad besides.

Cordially yours,
Carl Becker

1. Turner Papers, HEH.
2. Max Farrand (1869–1945) taught history at Wesleyan (Connecticut) (1896–1901), Stanford (1901–1908), Cornell (1905–1906), and Yale (1908–1925), and was director of the Henry E. Huntington Library, San Marino, California (1927–1941). His specialty was American constitutional history. He was the brother of Livingston Farrand of Cornell.

To Felix Frankfurter

Ithaca, [May 1927][1]

Dear Frankfurter,[2]

Thanks for your dispute with Wigmore.[3] I admire your valiant championship of the oppressed, your courageous defence of lost causes, & only wish I had the generous spirit & the intelligent optimism which inspires your action. You are one of those of whom Mr. Garrison used to say—"They deserve well of the Republic." Truly! There's not a trace of irony or cynicism in this. I am with sincere admiration, yours always,

Carl Becker

1. CBCU.
2. Frankfurter (1882–1965) was professor of law at Harvard (1914–1939) and associate justice of the U.S. Supreme Court (1939–1962).
3. The public dispute with Dean J. H. Wigmore of the Northwestern University Law School occurred over Frankfurter's charges in "The Case of Sacco and Vanzetti," *Atlantic Monthly*, CXXXIX (April 1927), 409–432. See Liva Baker, *Felix Frankfurter* (New York, 1969), 125–126.

To Felix Frankfurter

Ithaca, June 2, 1927[1]

Dear Frankfurter,

Thanks for your kind words about the Turner article. I had good fun writing it: and many friends and old students of Turner have assured me that it described the Turner they know. Besides, a long letter from Turner indicates that he was well satisfied with my analysis of his work; and pleased also with what I said of him personally as a teacher. Of course he thinks I have idealized him. Doubtless I have. We would none of us be much good as teachers if our students didn't idealize us a little. Even my students perceive some wonderful thing I have done for them; when as a matter of cold fact all I do is to sit about & look wise and tell them they can do more than they think they can—often more than I think they can myself. Then they have a habit of going ahead and doing it. Without our best illusions life would be a poor thing. Illusion is after all the best reality; & [truth?] only the most convenient form of error.

Sincerely yours,
Carl Becker

1. CBCU.

To Merle Curti

Ithaca, [late summer 1927?]¹

Dear Curti,²

I think the history of the peace movement is an excellent subject.³ It is almost if not quite untouched. I shouldn't look at it as a negative or a positive movement,—that is, as a movement that "contributed" something or nothing to something else. I should regard it as a concrete manifestation of the way in which the human mind works, & correlate it with the general intellectual history of the century. It is I think no accident that the last fifty years has been at once a period of ruthless business & international competition, of devotion to material welfare & philosophy of the survival of the fittest, and at the same time a period of immense activity in humanitarianism & pacifism. The latter is a compensation for the former. During the War all Europe devoted itself with great energy to killing as many people as possible by the most ruthless methods; lies & deception was the order of the day. Yet how everyone talked of brotherhood, & making the world safe for democracy, and all the rest of it. The more ruthless the world is the more it needs idealistic compensations. Even on the ground of "contributing" to the League of Nations & the sentiment in favor of it, I think the peace movement was of great importance. It was in this late period that the peace movement ceased to be primarily identified with religious leaders & churches. That was important because it then ceased to be regarded as a thing for women & Sunday School Superintendants. Business men & lawyers & legislators could without ridicule associate themselves with it. That is why it is now possible to be a supporter of the League without being dubbed a "visionary"—

By all means go ahead—if it interests you. That's the main thing. Everything is "negative" in the long run, if it comes to that.

Sincerely yours,
Carl Becker

1. Merle Curti Papers, SHSW.
2. Curti (1897——), taught American history at Smith College (1925–1937), Columbia Teachers' College (1937–1942), and Wisconsin (1942——). His specialty is American intellectual history.
3. See Curti, *The American Peace Crusade, 1815–1860* (Durham, N.C., 1929).

To Leo Gershoy

Ithaca, September 27, 1927[1]

Dear Gershoy,

Glad to get your long letter, but sorry to learn that your summer was not all you hoped. But isn't that usually the case? With a more settled way of life you will get on with your work, and things will seem more as they should. You are a good deal like me—too easily discouraged. I have learned that truth after long years, and so allow for it. You must learn to go on even though things cost more (I don't mean merely in a financial way!) than you expect: You must learn to take this attitude toward opportunities, toward life itself—"Well, it wasn't so good as I expected, or so cheap, but then I didn't expect it would be." I recall when I was 19 I went with my father and mother to the Columbian Exposition at Chicago. I was a country boy who had never been anywhere, never to a large city. It was, in anticipation, a great adventure, and I expected immense things of it. I wandered about, day after day, saw millions of things that didn't thrill me much, got frightfully tired, and was greatly disappointed because the great thing, exhileration, uplift, joy, or what have you, didn't come off. I expected much & got only a little. I expected less of my trip to Europe, and wasn't so much disappointed. Thirty years of experience between the first and the second adventure had taught me a sense of proportion, had taught me to expect less than I hoped for. But after all, as I look back on both experiences—the Chicago Fair and the European trip—I realize that I really got more out of both experiences than I was aware of at the time. Life will treat you in the same way. The Holy Grail isn't what you think it is; and you will be finding it all the time without knowing it. The meaning of life is that we are always seeking some great object, some supreme joy, or whatever, only to learn in the end that satisfaction resides in the search not in attainment.

I have done nothing this summer except teach summer courses, & lie in bed carefully nursing lumbago & other treasured ills, & drive about the country to pass the time. For the last month we have been down on Cape Cod, where we had a good time. Frederick went with us, but on account of his school opening so early I had to take him to N.Y. & send him home by train. We went to a ball game, which meant suffocating for an hour or two in the subway, and so I caught a cold and when I returned to the Cape was in bed for two days, and have now just about recovered, so that now I am nearly as strong as before I took my vacation.

The principal news is that Miss Marie Becker,[2] whom I think you must have known, has contracted a slight touch of T.B. & has had to give up her exams & her job & go off to a sanitarium at Saranac. She hasn't any money, but Hull and the Student Loan Fund will between them take care of that. Dr. Unger thinks that six months or a year of treatment will cure her. Bruun[3] has gone to N.Y.U.; and Ferguson[4] took his exams yesterday and departed for Europe. I hate to begin work again, but there is no way out, even though the very sight of students and express vans full of trunks depresses me. I hope to get on with my text book and by spring to have got pretty well toward the end. If it doesn't make me some money I shall be frightfully sad.

Perhaps you hadn't heard that Louis Fuertes[5] was killed this summer in an automobile accident—hit by a train. Titchener is also dead—of stroke.[6] So time passes, the world moves on, beards grow and are shaved and we call it another day.

Sincerely yours,
Carl Becker

Mrs. Becker joins me in best wishes to you and Ida.

1. LIG.
2. A graduate student in history at Cornell (1924–1927), working with Hull and Becker. She was not related to CLB.
3. Geoffrey Bruun (1898———), Cornell Ph.D. in 1927, taught history at New York University (1927–1941), Sarah Lawrence (1943–1945), and Columbia (1945–1949).
4. Wallace K. Ferguson (1902———), Cornell Ph.D. in 1927, taught history at New York University (1928–1956) and the University of Western Ontario (1956———).
5. Louis Agassiz Fuertes (1874–1927), naturalist and painter of birds, lecturer in ornithology at Cornell.
6. Edward B. Titchener (1867–1927), professor of psychology at Cornell (1892–1927).

To Leo Gershoy

Ithaca, [winter 1928?][1]

Dear Gershoy,

I should have written a long time since, but I lost your address, if I ever had it. I am immensely pleased that you are having the time of your life. But what I want especially to know is what you plan for next year? My hope is that they will renew the fellowship. What do you do about getting it renewed? And is there anything for me to do about it? When is it decided, etc. A cascade of questions, but if you are returning next year I want to be on the lookout for a job. Let me know as definitely as possible whether you think it likely you will remain a second year. Of course Ida, with all her following, will want to; and you too, in spite of jealousy of the most green.

There is little news here. A most mild winter. Many graduate students and some good ones. Helen Sullivan is one of them.[2] Davenport says she is a brilliant girl in his "Theory."[3]

I have a distinction conferred on me this month—an article accepted for the "Columns," a sure enough literary college paper. It is a letter dialogue entitled "Napoleon in Utopia"—a conversation between Voltaire and Napoleon, who enter Utopia from the Past by different opportunities, and H. G. Wells, who enters from the Future by every opportunity. The upshot of it is that Utopia is a bore, even H. G. W. is almost bored.

Nevins, the new man in American history, is much liked I think

& is doing well.[4] Notestein has accepted a place at Yale. For several weeks the business was a profound secret known to everyone.

Miss Gibbons[5] is here working for Burr. I mean employed by him to help out with the revision of A. D. White's book.[6] Of course they will never finish it.

Definitions

Meaning of Life = the meaning of Life is that we should be always seeking the meaning of Life without ever finding it.

Honor = (1) Personal integrity, a feeling of self respect (obs.)
    = (2) A kind of pedestal, which one can step on to or off of at will. Eg. "In examinations students are placed on their honor"

Sincerely yours,
Carl Becker

My love to Ida. Mrs. Becker joins me so that makes it all ok.

1. LIG.

2. Helen Sullivan, later Mrs. Mims (1906——) received her B.A. (1927) and M.A. (1928) in history at Cornell and later taught at the University of Chicago.

3. Herbert J. Davenport (1861–1931) taught political economy at Chicago (1902–1908) and Missouri (1908–1916), and economics at Cornell (1916–1929).

4. Allan Nevins (1890–1971), journalist and historian, taught American history at Cornell (1927–1928) and Columbia (1928–1958). He was senior research associate at the Huntington Library (1958–1971).

5. Lois Oliphant Gibbons (1887–1950), Burr's last graduate student, received her Ph.D. at Cornell in 1920. She taught history at Agnes Scott College (Decatur, Ga.), Sweet Briar College (Sweet Briar, Va.), Western College (Oxford, Ohio), the University of Wyoming and the University of Utah. She assisted Burr with research in Ithaca in 1927–1928.

6. Andrew Dickson White (1832–1918) was the first president of Cornell (1865–1885), historian, diplomat, and author of the *History of the Warfare of Science with Theology in Christendom* (2 vols.; New York, 1896).

To Richard Ager Newhall

Ithaca, March 27, 1928[1]

Dear Newhall,

Gershoy is not only the ablest man I have had as a graduate student—the ablest, I mean, in respect to subtlety of mind—but he is as fine a gentleman in the best sense of that word as I know. There are persons of course who can't abide a Jew at any price. But those who judge a Jew as they would anyone else—as good, bad, or indifferent—would find that Gershoy has none of those disagreeable qualities which they dislike in Jews as they dislike them in other people. The last thing Gershoy will do is to push in, to be aggressive, to blow his horn. On the contrary he is secretive to a fault, and often holds back for fear someone will be thinking—"that's the Jew of it." In any group of cultivated gentlemen Gershoy would be accepted as one. He is the real thing.

As a teacher I think he is best with advanced classes and small groups. With introductory classes, of say 100 or more, he would probably do less well. But the Rochester people never intimated that he was in any sense a failure as a teacher: they said he was not as successful as some others are. I think your students would like him, & I think he would do them good. I don't think he would be a "howling" success. His achievements would make no noise.

Sincerely yours,
Carl Becker

1. CBCU.

To Elias R. B. Willis

Waterloo, Iowa, June 13, 1928[1]

Dear Willis,[2]

This is the very heart of the Methodist menace, but you will be relieved to learn that it is apparently gasping for breath. Two (2) big churches each capable of seating 2500 people, and every Sunday about 2 people per pew. Churches paid for, but badly maintained because not enough people interested to keep them going. Most of my relatives (except those who are over 80), although all brought up in the faith, never enter the Church, except for weddings or funerals. Another generation and the thing will be virtually dead. The auto, the movie, and fundamentalism are destroying the menace. Rejoice and be exceeding glad! For if Methodism is slowly dying in Iowa there is hope for the world. It may yet continue to go to the Devil in peace.

I am off tonight for California. I have been here four days saturating myself in an atmosphere of the respectable and platitudinous. It nearly suffocates me, but it is good for the intellect. A good lady of 80 years told me today that she would rather bury her granddaughter than see her smoke a cigaret: & that if Al Smith were elected she wouldn't wish to live any longer.

Dodd of Chicago thinks Smith[3] has a fair chance.

Sincerely yours,
Carl Becker

1. CBCU.
2. Willis (1879–1959) received a B.A. at the University of Pennsylvania (1901) and an M.A. in classics at Cornell (1915). After teaching Greek at Cornell (1918–1921), he joined the library staff, serving as associate librarian at Cornell (1930–1947). He became one of Becker's closest friends.
3. Afred E. Smith (1873–1944), governor of New York (1919–1920, 1923–1928), Democratic candidate for president in 1928.

To Mabel Perry

Stanford, California, July 20, 1928[1]

Dear Miss Perry,[2]

It was very good of you to send me a copy of your thesis. It seems to me an excellent piece of work, both in respect to the research and in respect to the presentation. The Cornell library would have provided you with a lot of pamphlets & newspapers which you have not had; but apart from that I can't think of anything of special importance you have not used. Of course, for an exhaustive study of Marie Antoinette, & of the royalist activities, there must be I should suppose a great deal of valuable unpublished material in the Swedish archives, & perhaps in the Austrian also, although those have been more used. Jensen must have [referred?] more to the Swedish government than is to be found in his published work. However, that is neither here nor there. I do not often see as good a masters thesis as yours.

What pleased me especially, I need hardly say, was the inscription on the fly leaf. Teaching seems often an unsatisfactory & futile business, without results that can be measured or even pointed to: and if I retain any illusions at all as to the value of what I have done in twenty five years of effort, it is because my students, so many of them, persist even after years have passed in thinking that I did them some good—did something to them which has made a great difference. I find it hard to understand what it could be; but since it is so pleasant to believe them I take their word for it without too much question. This support to my own confidence (and to my vanity I dare say) keeps me young, and enables me to do the job of teaching better than I otherwise could; so that if I have been in any sense a successful teacher I owe it in great part to you & hundreds of other students who have had & still have the notion that you owe me something.

We may be stopping in Los Angeles a few days on our way back. If so I shall certainly manage to see you even if only for a short visit. I will let you know if it is possible.—I am sorry you could not have been here this summer: but probably the rest will do you more good.

Give my regards to your sister, and to your mother, whom I remember meeting on the occasion of your graduation at Lawrence.

Very sincerely yours,
Carl Becker

1. CBCU.
2. Perry (1889–1959) received her B.A. in history at Kansas (1916) and her M.A. at Stanford (1926).

To Leo Gershoy

Stanford, [July 1928][1]

Dear Gershoy,

Have been here nearly three weeks. It is very fine—the climate, I mean, and it sets me up, or something does. I haven't been so well in a long time. I have written away on my book, and expect to get two chapters done, which will bring me to the World War, and then two more, or possibly three, will see it done.[2] Haven't met any very interesting people here, except possibly Golder.[3] They're cut off from the world, a bit provincial, earnest, bright students, who have the air of wishing to acquire culture without forgetting the home town folks, or what the preacher said about high ideals. Sometimes I wish to yell obscenities in the midst of the well kept, beautiful quad. It wouldn't do any good. I suggested a topic on Montesquieu to one of my seminary students—viz. to find out what he meant by "nature" & natural law. Student, a bright, round-eyed, good boy, said he like [sic] to try it, but might misinterpret Montesquieu "—That would be serious, wouldn't it?" he said. I said no: all interpretations were wrong, that all thinking was a falsification for a good purpose. The class smiled faintly, as much as to say, you shouldn't joke in class. People laugh here a good deal, but always at the proper things.

Well, I mustn't malign them. They give me a lot of money for doing nothing—3 hours a week, & a seminary once. I almost forget to go to class. Sleep a lot, & eat a lot. This week my family will be here. They'll drag me about no doubt.

I think Catherine's book is better than it was, but she's solid as a wall, & hasn't too much resiliency.[4] The light that never was doesn't shine on her much. If she could only on occasion have hysterics, or do perfectly wild, crazy things! She's too normal, too sensible. A bit of insanity is what she needs. Well, they like it anyway, and it will be published, and then the critics can have their say. A French woman, Madeline Clemenceau-Jacquemaire, is engaged on a substantial life, I'm told.[5]

It beats the devil that you of all my "disciples" (Christ, what a word!) shouldn't be able to get a good job. Anyhow, here's still wishing & hoping.

Love to Ida.

> Sincerely yours,
> Carl Becker

1. LIG.

2. *Modern History: The Rise of a Democratic, Scientific, and Industrial Civilization.*

3. Frank A. Golder (1877–1929), professor of modern history at Stanford (1921–1929), director of the Hoover Library at Stanford (1924–1929), and a specialist on Russian sources of American history.

4. Catharine Young, *A Lady Who Loved Herself: The Life of Madame Roland* (New York, 1930).

5. *The Life of Madame Roland* (London, 1930).

To Gussie E. Gaskill

Stanford, July 30, 1928[1]

Dear Gussie,

No need to ask how you are; you are always in the best of form. I suppose you are running down to N.Y. frequently now, if that plan of yours has not been abandoned.

We are having a fine time. The climate here is simply ideal for summer. Sunshine every day, no wind at all, no rain, & cool fresh air. I feel much better than for some years, and have written 50 pages on my book—something I don't ordinarily do at all in the summer. But the teaching is very light—3 hours of lectures, & a seminary one day a week—so I ought to do something. We have hired an old Buick roadster for two weeks, and are taking all the interesting drives within the region. There are not so many, but the drive over the Mts. to the sea, & up to San Francisco, is certainly gorgeous. I think if I ever have enough money to live on without teaching I will retire, like all good Iowa farmers, & live in California.—But not in Los Angeles. But on second lights, I think three months at a time would do me. There is something too awfully complacent & proper, monastic & sheltered & cloistered, about the place here to suit me for long.

Sincerely yours,
Carl Becker

Maude & Frederick send their best wishes

1. GEG.

To Elias R. B. Willis

Stanford, [summer 1928][1]

Dear Willis,

Thanks for the letter and the clipping. The latter I had already heard of. Women are evidently disturbing to the poor fellow: and nothing strange about that; but I don't think their legs would be less glamorous & exciting if they were across the gorge. I suspect ways would be found by which the boys could cross the gorge from one side, & the girls from the other. Poor old Sex! How much it's responsible for. How we all wish sometimes that it wouldn't trouble us, and how depressed we become if, by some happy chance, it lets up for an hour or a day. If the problem of education were only as simple as the naive gentleman seems to think!

This is a lovely climate. Bright sunshine every day, and all day, with very few exceptions; and besides something cool & fresh in the air that peps you up wonderfully. I sleep all night, and then again in the afternoon. You see I haven't anything to do, really, and no one to bother me, since no one knows me. Only three lectures a week, & a seminary on Monday. I am feeling fine, and am doing some writing on the damnable text book. People here— students and others—all admirable, and all much alike. No great variety of type. Mostly earnest bright capable people. They laugh, but only at the proper things. I long to meet a crazy person, like Morton Yohalem[2] or Helen Sullivan.

> Sincerely,
> Becker

1. CBCU.
2. Morton E. Yohalem (1904———), received his B.A. from Cornell (1929), became an attorney, joined the legal staff of the Securities and Exchange Commission (becoming director of the Public Utilities Division), was special deputy to the administrator of the Reconstruction Finance Corporation, and, since 1954, has been in private practice.

To Frederick Jackson Turner

> Ithaca, October 14, 1928[1]

Dear Turner,

Thanks for your kind letter of appreciation. The Mme Roland was written six years ago when Burr retired. Notestein had a scheme for a volume of critical studies by the members of the history group to be published in honor of Burr. He said he had an article "practically" ready. The rest of us got busy & wrote ours.

Notestein's is still unfinished.[2] The others wearied of waiting and printed their articles. The Mme. Roland, I do think, is a contribution, in a modest way, to history—*via* psychology. Doubtless if I had ever mastered formal psychology, á la Barnes, I could have done much better. Very many old students of yours, for the most part the good ones, such as Curti and Robinson, have told me how extremely much they liked the "Turner Article." When I express the fear that perhaps my critical judgment was a little betrayed by my affection, they are entirely unconvinced: they say it portrays the Turner they know. The marvellous hold you have on hundreds of men, former students and others, is something very real and very fine. It ought to make you happy.

Did you know we were in Stanford this last summer quarter? It was a real vacation for all of us. They were extremely generous, giving me but three hours & a seminary. The wonderful climate, or the change, or both was good for all of us, mentally & physically. And then they were all so hospitable. We were in Los Angeles a week on the return, where I had hoped to see you, but was told that you were in Maine. I am extremely glad to know that California is good for you. They tell me, and so do you, that the book is going on. Well, give the "data" a rest, and write the book.

It is very lovely here now, with the hills covered with multicolored foliage. The Hodders are here for the year. You know he was an instructor here in the 90's; & here he met his wife—the "brilliant" Florence Moon whom the old timers still recall. They are having a fine time renewing old acquaintances, & identifying the old landmarks.

My wife is sold on California. She wants to retire & live there. I'm not so keen for that, but if you will only remain there some summer I might be there—in which case even the magnificent distances of the place won't keep me from seeing you.

Ever faithfully yours,
Carl Becker

1. Turner Papers, HEH.
2. *Persecution and Liberty: Essays in Honor of George Lincoln Burr* (New York, 1931) eventually appeared, but without essays by either Becker or Notestein.

To Frederick Jackson Turner

Ithaca, [November, 1928][1]

Dear Turner,

. . . . .

I almost wish I lived in California now—snow & ice, & chains on the car, and all the worst annoyances of the most alluring and exasperating of modern conveniences. Still it promises to melt away tomorrow; so I'm a bit reconciled to staying on. Have to anyway. Early in life I learned that if you don't like what you have you've but little chance to have what you like. Is that a part of the "slave morality?"

Sincerely yours,
Carl Becker

1. Turner Papers, HEH.

To August C. Krey

Ithaca, [November 1928][1]

Dear Krey,[2]

Thanks for your invitation to discuss the report which you have sent me: but I think I must decline, for two reasons, both good as it seems to me. One is that I hardly think I shall be at Indianapolis this Christmas. The other is that I have no ideas on the subject of history teaching in the schools, partly because I have no experience in such work, partly because I have never thought much about it. The problem of high school teaching is one so very different from University teaching that I do not feel I have any grounds for an opinion that would be of any value. If I have any opinion it is that high school students would perhaps be better served if they were taught something else than history—but even of this I do not feel confident.

Very sincerely yours,
Carl Becker

1. August C. Krey Papers, UM.
2. Krey (1887–1961) was professor of medieval history at Minnesota (1913–1955); chairman of the American Historical Association's Commission on Social Studies in the Schools (1929–1934).

To Livingston Farrand

Ithaca, January 25, 1929[1]

Dear Mr. Farrand,

I know Ogden[2] will have expressed to you the thanks of the committee for your willingness to discuss with us the questions raised last night. But as I was perhaps as much responsible as anyone for imposing this additional burden on you, I wish to add my very cordial appreciation of the frank and lucid exposition of the entire situation. It made clear to me what I had before only vaguely apprehended. On the whole the situation is better than I thought it might turn out to be. As you discussed the matter I was struck with the fact that the Trustees find themselves confronted with problems which present the same sort of difficulties as are presented by those which confront the faculty. The truth is that a university is such a complex and intricately woven skein of vested interests and sentiments, of tangible and intangible values, of firmly held but vaguely defined purposes, and is dependent on so many different individuals and groups, on so many cooperating and conflicting wills, that it does what it wants or must rather than what any of us or all of us might think best. Concrete contingencies are always lying across the straight road to the general object. I find that in our committee, or in the faculty, we can't discuss policy with a big P for more than twenty minutes without in spite of the best intentions being diverted to the discussion of policy with a small p.

I don't think I am an over optimistic person. My friends seem not to think so at all events. I think I can see well enough the defects of universities, Cornell included. In my view universities commit three deadly sins—expansion, mecanization, standardization. I think most faculty men and most presidents and deans (although we of the faculties love to pass the buck to presidents and deans) are aware of these deadly sins and wish not to commit them. But in spite of the best intentions we commit them more or less. Yet if that gloomy pessimism in which I am supposed to be enveloped ever lifts it does so when I compare Cornell with other institutions with which I am familiar. I think Cornell is far less guilty of the deadly sins than most universities. It is at all events so much the place where I prefer to be that I sometimes think fate or Mr. White must have created it for my special benefit. I propose to stay here until you or my colleagues give some sign that my services would be more valuable elsewhere. And I should like to add, if you will permit me, that your unfailing frankness and courtesy in all matters and to all persons, and your cordial support of the intangibles that make Cornell what it is, are not the least of those contributing factors that make for my great contentment.[3]

Very sincerely yours,
Carl Becker

1. Livingston Farrand Papers, CU.
2. Robert M. Ogden.
3. Between 1929 and 1931, CLB was considered for a position at Yale, largely because of Notestein's initiative and the enthusiasm of a group in the law school. See Ulrich B. Phillips to Wallace Notestein, Aug. 30, 1929, and Jan. 2, 1931, Phillips Papers, YU.

To Charles Hull

Chicago, [June 1929?][1]

Dear Hull,

.   .   .   .

Everything is well here; even the weather has been cool except for a few days. This is a serious place in the summer; all the students want their money's worth, and they want it in their notebooks. One middle aged lady graduate student asked me if I did not think God created the universe for some high purpose. I didn't know. What do you think? If you don't know, ask Mary:[2] she ought to know.

Sincerely yours,
Carl Becker

1. Hull Papers, CU.
2. Mary Hull, Charles's sister.

To Leo Gershoy

Chicago, [summer 1929][1]

Dear Leo,

This is not B.E.S.[2] writing. It's only me. But finding this frightfully nice paper lying around, I couldn't resist the temptation to use it: and since such awfully nice paper called for someone awfully nice to write to, why——!

I'm living a bachelor life in Bernadotte's apt. at the top of Boucher's[3] home—quite free and spacious, with three rooms and bath. (Only one of the roomers on the second floor uses my bath.) Separated from my family and free to do as I like, I've been waiting ever so patiently for some stirring adventure to come my way. Alas, none has come so far. It's a great mistake to suppose that well brought up middle class people are in danger of "going astray." It really isn't so easy. With the best will in the world I can't break away from the virtuous dull habits of a lifetime. The most I've been able to achieve is to to seek out, on hot nights, a gilded palace of sin where they sell ice cream sodas. Once I took two unattached ladies to dinner, and afterwards a stroll through the park; but they were both members of the intelligencia, teachers in colleges, and the adventure turned out just as you might expect. I wish you and Ida were here: you are both young and emancipated, and perhaps you could successfully lead me into temptation.

This university is really an interesting place. Out of the oily Baptist soil of John D.[4] has grown a marvellous collection of gothic ecclesiastical buildings. Among them five or six chapels which are apparently but little used: but they give a strong flavor of religiousity to the place which keeps me subdued. I hesitate to make a cynical joke on the campus. I feel somehow oppressed and inhibited. But perhaps that is a good thing after all: since the students here in the summer are dreadfully serious. They want their money's worth, and they want it in their notebooks. I think I've discouraged them a little: they don't take notes now all the time. One grey haired lady (who is taking the M.A. in order to prepare for Junior College teaching, and get a 1000 dollars added to her salary) is in my seminary, & has had some heart to heart talks with me. About the "meaning of life" and whether I do not really think that "God created the universe with a noble purpose." I didn't know. What do you think? If you don't know, ask Ida. She ought to have an opinion. It's a pressing matter and needs to be settled before Sept. 1.

I forget where you are this summer, and am sending this to Getz in the hope it will be forwarded.

I hope you are doing something thrilling and are as happy as kings—far happier indeed.

I hear that Gottschalk is not having a very good time in Paris. He's living with Wm. Dodd, son of Prof. Dodd, and they are both lonesome and homesick—all as per information received through Martha [Dodd].

I'm working on the revision of my text book, and hope to get it done this fall. Publishers wish to get it off the press by February. What a relief it will be to get the thing off my neck. I think I'll never write another book.

Give my love to Ida.

Sincerely yours,
Carl Becker

1. LIG.

2. Bernadotte E. Schmitt (1886–1969) was professor of history at Chicago (1925–1946), specializing in European diplomatic history. Becker wrote this letter on Schmitt's letterhead.

3. Chauncey S. Boucher (1886–1955), professor of American history at Chicago (1923–1935), later chancellor of the universities of West Virginia and Nebraska.

4. John D. Rockefeller (1839–1937), capitalist and philanthropist who endowed the University of Chicago.

To Anita M. Lerner

[New York, New York, 1930?]¹

Dear Anita,²

I can't tell you how much we have enjoyed being here with you and Max and Constance.³ It often amazes me the trouble young people like you will take to be nice to me, but I appreciate it. You have captivated Fred also. We think Max lovely too, but that isn't a thing you can say to a man unless you are a woman. As for Constance, well we have made advances, & have got so far as to sit by her on the sofa, & put our arms around her & kiss the top of her head: but like any flirt she's off and on, and we never quite know where we are. Still we have hopes.

Ever faithfully
Carl Becker

P.S. Sorry that you had to go off to Philadelphia; but of course it was necessary, what with your bad temper and all. Since you went away I've learned that you hiss in the theater. I'm sure you do it nicely, and I would like to hear you; but you mustn't be surprised if others look daggers. You see they don't know you, & they don't pay good money to hear you hiss. Sooner or later you'll be taken firmly by the ear and led out. In spite of everything I will be your friend, & there's bail to be had in Ithaca whenever you need it.

C. B.

P.S. 2. If you must hiss, please hiss like a serpent & [not] like a goose.

P.S. 3. After all we have decided that we do like the breakfast room.

1. AML.

2. Anita Marburg Lerner (1900——) received her B.A. at Vassar (1921), Ph.D. at the Brookings Graduate School (1928); she taught economics and literature at Sarah Lawrence (1928–1945), sociology and English at Vassar (1924–1925, 1952–1955). The Lerners met CLB in New York City in 1929.

3. Max Lerner (1902——) received his B.A. at Yale (1923) and Ph.D. at the Brookings Graduate School (1927). He was an editor with *The Encyclopaedia of the Social Sciences* (1927–1932); taught at Sarah Lawrence, Harvard, Williams, and Brandeis; authored many books and has written for various newspapers and journals. Constance Lerner (later Mrs. Russell), whom CLB called Kornstox, was born on September 20, 1929.

To Anita M., Max, and Constance Lerner

Ithaca, April 18, 1930[1]

To the Lerners.
Anita, Max, and Kornstox (s.p.)

Dear Max,

I address you first just to preserve a semblance of that primacy which husbands once enjoyed over wives. (Tell Anita there's nothing else in it, and yourself there's nothing in it at all). Seeing the dread word Encyclopedia on your envelope I had a great fright. I thought you would want a biography or something. You are certainly a loveable man to think of me in some capacity other than as a writer of biographies.

The book[2] has been delayed owing to the necessity, discovered late, but better late than never, of cutting the MS about 200 pages. This is now done, and the last chapter only to write. I may be down to Newark in early summer. If and when I come I shall certainly see you and Anita and the delectable Kornstox; but I can't make your place my headquarters, and,

Dear Anita,

The reason is that your place is too far and far too pleasant. I shouldn't get to my work until noon. And so, much as I should love to stop with you and Max and, as aforesaid, the delectable Kornstox, I really couldn't. I have to remember that life's real, life is earnest. Be up and doing. Wilful waste (of time) makes woeful want. And so on. (If you see what I mean). But I will come up some evening. I had such a good time the last time that I am not likely to forget it. So much good talk, sense and nonsense. Of course I like the nonsense best. Max always gets the talk on abstrucities—very stimulating, but my head is not used to it. But listen, you're his wife, and if you would only let him finish what he has to say you would find that his remarks are often quite sensible.

(Special and Confidential).

Dear Kornstox,

Nothing in the way of invidious discrimination was intended in placing your name last. The words sounded better in that order—in short more euphonious. Nothing else I do protest. You can never be last in my affection. I beg therefore that you will accept the assurance of my most distinguished consideration, and believe me, my dear Kornstox,

> Ever your most humble devout.
> Carl Becker.

1. AML.
2. *Modern History.*

To Constance Lerner

July 5, [1930?][1]

Dear Kornstox,

I wonder where the Bilboes[2] are?
They often wander very far.
They may be in the Honey Pot,
Or in the Cooky Jar.
But I do *hope* they've not
Fallen down a penny slot!

Ever faithfully,
C. B.

I wonder if the Bilboes went
A hunting Snark with wrong intent?
Once I'm told they even snook
Jam and treacle in Lent.
But I do *hope* they haven't took
Anita's Private Prayer Book!

Ever faithfully,
C.B.

1. AML.
2. Bilboes are long iron bars with sliding shackles to confine the ankles of prisoners, with a lock to fasten one end of the bar to the floor; also, a bilbo was historically the name for a sword known for the temper of its blade. Presumably, however, CLB's bilboes are simply imaginary creatures.

To Constance Lerner

[1930?][1]

The Argument.

A Bilboe and a Tiger Cat
Went stalking in a Stove Pipe Hat.

The cat, he said, "I think," said he,
That you are growing round and fat—
A most disgusting thing to be!"
The Bilboe said: "You're very free!"

The cat replied: "I may be free,
But any one can surely see
That I am thin as is a rake."
The Bilboe said: "I quite agree,
But I do wish, for mercy's sake,
You wouldn't eat up all the Cake!"

> Very Sincerely Yours
> Carl Becker

1. AML.

To Anita M. Lerner

[1930?][1]

Dear Anita,

Thanks for the picture of Kornstox. It's a very nice one. Don't believe what the nurse says. It's a very low view of life to suppose that every emotion is the result of aching teeth, or inhibitions, or lack of glandular secretions. I think that Kornstox cries because her soul is troubled. She is obviously mourning over the poor duck. Of course it may be an unsatisfied desire for Bilboes. Just on the chance I send her another instalment.

Lines to Constance
on
Frustration.

The rain it raineth every day
Upon the Bilboes and the clay:
So that their bulbous, tender feet
In muddy vesture of decay

Enclosed are. It makes them bleat
To find themselves not clean & neat!

C. B.

To Constance and Anita M. Lerner

[Summer 1930][1]

To Kornstox.

A Bilboe and a Big Black Ant
Went swimming down at Lynn-Nahant.
The Ant remarked: "I can't see why
The water's wet. I really can't.
Or why the sand's so very dry."
The Bilboe said: "No more can I!"

C. B.

Dear Anita,

   I'm sorry you have to come second. But of course you always will.
It can't be helped. The old generation gives way, necessarily, to the
young. But do you mean you have moved out into the country forever and ever? Or only for the summer? I can't tell when, if at all,
I shall be in New York. It depends on the will and pleasure of the
publishers. They said they expected to have a final conference on
the MS of the book after summer school (ends Aug 15). But
whether at once, or in September, or later, I don't know. If and
when I come to New York, I will do my possible to see you. A spare
room with clean sheets & towels, is just what I've always wanted
—always.

Give my love to Max.
Sincerely yours
Carl Becker

1. AML.

To Leo Gershoy

Ithaca, [September 1930?][1]

Dear Gershoy,

By all means send on your Ms.[2] I am not reading proofs yet, and in any case I can read your Ms. in some of my numerous leisure hours. I shall be very glad to do it.

I hope Ida's story proves a best seller and discovers in her a streak of very vile money-making talent which she can exploit to the advantage of everyone concerned. If it's a detective story proper I will gladly read it—I mean a story in which all the circumstances are common place (man found with a dagger in his heart and so on), & in which the interest rests on the cleverness of the deduction of conclusions from simple facts. But if it's a mystery story (in which "sinister" influences are diabolically at work, and skinny, claw-like talons materialize from behind closely drawn curtains, & strange atmosphers are created in order to raise the scalp etc.) I refuse to read it. Such stories don't raise my scalp; they only raise my gorge. However, I hope it sells whatever it may be.

I may be down to N.Y. sometime this fall on text book business, so keep me informed of your whereabouts.

Give my love to Ida, and all that.

Sincerely yours,
Carl Becker

1. LIG.
2. *The French Revolution, 1789–1799* (New York, 1932), a volume in Berkshire Studies in European History.

To H. L. Mencken

Cambridge, Massachusetts, September 20, 1930[1]

Dear Mr. Mencken,[2]

Several years ago I read at the meeting of the Historical Association at Rochester a 20 minute paper on Historical facts.[3] It has never been printed, and in fact is hardly worth printing—at least not in its present form. I merely pointed out the obvious truth that "historical facts," which we like to think of as "hard" and "cold" and something you "can't get around," are after all not substantial material objects like bricks or [gantlings?].⁴ Seemed hardly worth saying, but it was apparently thought by many people to be quite original.

Someday I may want to elaborate it a little, & take out the spoofing and have it printed. If and when, I will not forget the Mercury.

Very sincerely yours,
Carl Becker

1. H. L. Mencken Papers, Manuscript Division, The New York Public Library, Astor, Lenox and Tilden Foundations; by permission.

2. Henry L. Mencken (1880–1955) was a prominent journalist, author, editor, and social critic. At this time he edited the *American Mercury*.

3. Read in 1926, and posthumously published as "What Are Historical Facts?" *Western Political Quarterly*, VIII (1955), 327–340. See CLB to Harry Elmer Barnes, Feb. 29, 1936.

4. A gantline is a line rove through a block for hoisting rigging or hanging clothing.

To Arthur M. Schlesinger

Ithaca, October 12, 1930¹

Dear Schlesinger,

I am preparing the article on Hutchinson for the D. A. B.:² and am trying to recall what I know about his *History*.³ Am I right in supposing that its chief quality is that of a clear & precise & accurate antiquarian chronicle? There is in it very little of what we like to call "interpretation," is there? And am I right in supposing that it is still an original source in some measure, due to the loss of documents which he used, as well as to the fact that he used his personal knowledge of affairs in which he was concerned? I would like your comments on these points & on any other points that occur to you.—Just a brief statement, you understand, I don't want you to go to any special trouble.

Sincerely yours,
Carl Becker

I went through his papers at the State House[4] and it was well worth while.

1. Schlesinger Papers, HU.
2. "Thomas Hutchinson," *DAB* (1932).
3. *History of the Colony and Province of Massachusetts-Bay,* 3 vols.
4. In Boston.

To Anita M. Lerner

Ithaca, [December 1930?][1]

Dear Anita,

I am overwhelmed by the splendor of the ties and, especially, the neck scarf (it is a neck-scarf, isn't it?) you sent me; and flattered beyond anything by the implication in your note that I am fitted to wear "what the young men are wearing now." Fred is much pleased with the ties, chiefly because he says (sez you!) that I will not now need to steal his. As to the scarf, he has reminded me that it can be of no use to me, since I rarely wear a scarf. What he doesn't know is that the reason I rarely wear a scarf is that I have never before had a silk one, to say nothing of a perfectly gorgeous silk one. You shouldn't ought to have did it, but I am, nevertheless, very pleased that you did done it.

Every one is well, & everything here is like always.

We send all our loves,
Carl Becker

1. AML.

5. Everyman, the Heavenly City, and the Hospital, 1931-1933

To William E. Dodd

Ithaca, January 29, 1931[1]

Dear Dodd,

Thanks for your long letter, and the picture. You have certainly done much to the place since 1918 when I saw it. My health is very good really: in November I was laid up for a few weeks by some kind of intestinal disturbance (it's painful, but not serious: they don't seem to know what causes it). Aside from that I've felt better and more like work than for ten years past. My text book is going through the press, and with many maps and illustrations it's a big job. Besides, I'm writing four lectures to be given at the Yale Law School on the Storrs Foundation in April. I am trying to do something with the 18 century social & political philosophy: and will entitle the book (the lectures will I suppose be published) "The Heavenly City of the Philosophes." I am enjoying writing it more than I supposed, and I believe it won't be too bad.[2]

Adam's[3] death put me up a notch in the line of vice presidents, the result of which is that I have to write the address a year earlier than I had counted on. I'll have to do that this spring.

Gottschalk was here for a few days. We all like him, & we all liked his wife. She is quiet, but I think a very wise and nice person.[4] Stephenson told me he rather thought G— had one of the best papers at the meeting. He likes it there I think—I mean at Chicago: and so I believe does Knappen. Both are good men.

Well, I'll hope to see you at Minneapolis. Give my regards to Mrs. Dodd & Martha. They were very nice to me when I was in Chicago that summer.

Sincerely yours,
Carl Becker

1. CBCU.

2. The four lectures were given late in April 1931, and subsequently published as *The Heavenly City of the Eighteenth-Century Philosophers*.

3. Ephraim D. Adams (1865–1930) taught history at Kansas (1892–1902) and Stanford (1902–1930). His speciality was Anglo-American relations.

4. Fruma Kasdan Gottschalk was educated in Russia and Germany, was trained as a pianist, and taught Slavic languages at the University of Chicago.

To Leo Gershoy

Ithaca, [summer 1931][1]

Dear Gershoy,

A book between two letters! That's the pace to set. You're getting on: and I always said you would go far. You are one of the good Jews. Did you know there were some? No less an authority than Miss Professor Lucy Salman[2] of Vassar (formerly) once remarked: "After all there are some very good Jews"—and she supported the generalization by mentioning Lingelbach,[3] Schlesinger, Notestein, and Becker. She didn't know you—else there would have been five, and I think Ida ought to be in this too—that makes six: a very respectable number. I am glad you are both to have a vacation: but I hope you will be in New York in September. I have to go down there sometime in September to iron out a few sentences in the "Great Book" so that the Catholics on the board of approval in N.Y.C. will not object to putting it on the approved list. Williamson[4] first suggested Sept 4. Then said that perhaps he could not get a meeting of the proper persons until the 14th. I replied I could come at any time, but have not yet heard when it is to be. I will let you know as soon as it is settled.

Summer School is just closing. It hasn't been very hot, and the six weeks passed more rapidly than any summer session I remember. I haven't done a thing but talk two hours to classes in the A. M. Afternoons I have dozed away as any old man should. Now I will have to get to work again: two reviews, a life of Hutchinson for the D. A. B. and the completion of the blasted presidential address. I had it ⅔ finished in June, and there it stuck. I don't know how to end it. Maybe after all this rest I will have a brain storm & get an idea. Let me know when you and Ida will be back in N.Y. so that if I have any choice of dates for going down I can choose the right one. I want of course to see you.

Mrs. Becker sends her best wishes. And I am

Very Sincerely yours
Carl Becker

P.S. It's about time for you to give up the pernicious habit of addressing me as "professor."

P.S. If you are to be on a vacation maybe you will receive this when Ida is gallivanting somewhere else. You might send it on to her with my love.

C. B.

1. LIG.

2. Lucy M. Salmon (1853–1927), professor of history at Vassar (1887–1926), whose specialties were administrative history and the history of the newspaper.

3. William E. Lingelbach (1871–1962), professor of history at the University of Pennsylvania (1900–1946), librarian of the American Philosophical Society (1942–1958).

4. Robert D. Williamson (1876–1963) was editor-in-chief at the Silver Burdett Company (1918–1940).

To Leo Gershoy

Ithaca, October 6, 1931[1]

Dear Gershoy,

W. L. Langer[2] has been trying to get me to write the French Revolution for his series on Modern History. Convinced at last that I won't do it, he recently asked me to suggest a younger man who might do a good job: said that if I wouldn't write it he wanted one of my "students" (that speaks well for the chaps that were kind enough to come my way). To make an end of it, I told him that you were the nuts (theres all the difference in the world between "nut" and "nuts" in this connection). I said also that when you finished up your text you would be free I thought to take on something else. You had better think it over in case he approaches you which I expect he will. There's probably something in your contract with Crofts banning you from publishing any book that would duplicate the one you are writing:[3] but since this proposed volume isn't a text & doesn't cover Napoleon, I shouldn't suppose it would fall within the limitation. That you would have to settle with Crofts. Of course don't take on the book unless you want to.[4] You are a free man so far as I am concerned.

I'm writing my Pres. Address. The title is "Mr. Everyman his own historian," and it begins this way—"Once upon a time, long long ago——."[5]

I had a most nice time in New York, and seeing you and Ida was a large part of it. Rumor has it that there is to be a meeting of the A. H. A. Council in N.Y. in November which I am supposed to attend (I am *President*, don't ever forget that!). If so I will see you again. I wish you could come up to Ithaca sometime.

Maude and Frederick send their best regards to you and Ida. Fred, who takes to nice people, took a great shine to you all— naturally.

Sincerely yours,
Carl Becker

1. LIG.
2. William L. Langer (1896——) taught European history at Clark (1923–1927) and at Harvard (1927–1964), and was general editor of The Rise of Modern Europe series, 20 vols.
3. See Gershoy, *The French Revolution and Napoleon* (New York, 1933).
4. See Gershoy, *From Despotism to Revolution, 1763–1789* (New York, 1944).
5. "Everyman His Own Historian," *AHR*, XXXVII (1932), 221–236.

To Constance Lerner

Ithaca, October 9, 1931[1]

Dear Constance,

A Bilboe by the river's brim
A Bilboe is; and he is slim
Because he will not drink his milk.
How I do wish that you were him!

He'd drink it down as smooth as silk,
And never more have ache or ilke!

Uncle carl

1. AML.

To Leo Gershoy

Ithaca, October 16, 1931[1]

Dear Gershoy,

I am delighted that the volume Langer wants you to do is in the period which will fit in with your preferred study of classical influences. You can, I am sure, take your time. There is no great pressure to get the series out so far as I know; and I am sure Langer would prefer to wait any reasonable time in order to get a book of originality & distinction. That is the kind of book you can do if you have time enough. Ida will do her bit on it, and you will dedicate the book

> To my dear wife,
> without whose aid and
> encouragement, and
> tactful criticism, this
> book would never have
> seen the light of day.

Poor dear Ida!

Very Sincerely yours,
Carl Becker

1. LIG.

To Frederick Jackson Turner

Ithaca, October 20, 1931[1]

Dear Turner,

I sent you my book, not in the expectation that you would waste any time reading it (it's almost an impertinence to send a friend one's textbook), but merely for old times sake and as a friendly gesture. The indications are that it's being well received. I hope so, for if it doesn't sell I'm sold, since I've put so much time and effort on it.

I have just finished my Pres. Address—blast the thing! And now I'm preparing for the press four lectures delivered last April at the Yale School of Law. They deal, in a rather fantastic way I'm afraid, with the social and political ideas of the 18 century; and to match the substance I've invented an irritating title—"The Heavenly City of the Philosophes." I've dedicated the volume to you and Haskins —I hope you don't mind; I thought it only appropriate since both of you have been teaching me for thirty five years now.[2]

I saw Haskins for twenty minutes a year ago this summer when I was in Boston. I hadn't seen him since the St. Louis meeting, just before his illness. The contrast was a shock, although I was in a way prepared for it of course: but what marvelous courage, and how remarkable it is that he still retains the extraordinary memory & the swift incisive intellect unimpaired.

I hope your health is good, I hear that it is, and I take it that it must be so if you are working on your book. I think I didn't acknowledge a monograph I received some time since. I'm looking forward to your book, as many others are. Get it out, even if it isn't as good as you want it: it never will be as good as you want it, no good book ever is as good as the author wants it.

Hull retired last June, and we have Whittaker [sic][3] to replace him, although of course no one could ever quite replace Hull. Burr is working away on God only knows what. No one else ever will know, I fear, for it is extremely unlikely that he will ever publish the "great book" that many people have expected him to.

Very sincerely yours,
Carl Becker

1. Turner Papers, HEH.

2. The presentation copy which CLB gave to Haskins contained this inscription: "Dear Haskins, I hardly think this is history. Perhaps it's philosophy, but maybe it's only moonshine. . . . Carl Becker" (Cornelliana Collection, Uris Library, Cornell University).

3. Arthur P. Whitaker (1895——) taught at New York University (1922–1924), Western Reserve (1928–1930), Cornell (1930–1936), and the University of Pennsylvania (1936–1965). His specialty is Latin American history.

To Constance Lerner

Ithaca, November 13, 1931[1]
Dear Kornstox,

A Bilboe and a Bobolink
Stood sadly by the river's brink.
Bereft of anything to say,
The Bobolink could only blink.
The Bilboe said: "I think the day
Is quite serene, if somewhat grey."

The Bobolink remarked: "Let's play
That we are ancient Beasts of Prey.
You a Pleistocinean Mink
And I a Prehistoric Jay
Will be." The Bilboe said: "No Gink
Has ever thought so nice a Think."

Ever yours,
Carl Becker

1. AML.

To Geoffrey Bruun

Ithaca, December 6, 1931[1]

Dear Bruun,

I have read your St. Just[2] again, or more correctly those parts
that deal with his part in the Convention. It seems to me very good
—well put and solidly documented. I think you bring out pretty
well the fact that much of the factional fight was at basis a game
played to save their skins. Of course they rationalized it by appealing to liberty, Equality, the Sacred Revolution, Reign of Virtue,
etc. I think this later part of the Revolution 1792–94 needs to be
reexamined. The determining influence is an increasing emotional
strain arising from out of (1) the danger to the whole Revolutionary movement from foreign powers; and (2) the fear born of un-

certainty which each group and each individual experiences. Each group and each individual had to "do others before they do you." Someone with a flair for the unconscious influences that activate the human animal ought to trace the rise of this Revolutionary psychology. It goes back beyond 1792 of course. Unless this is made the basis, the whole story reads like an *opera bouffe*. Of course with men like St. Just and Robespierre, and many another, the fear was rationalized successfully. I don't doubt that they felt genuinely that they were standing for virtue and justice, for the Revolution and the welfare of humanity. Men like Barere and Billaud were less able to kid themselves, and hence they appear more clearly as opportunists working to save their skins in a difficult situation. I hope you will keep this in mind when you write your new book, and work it out. You have got hold of the thing in this book, but I think not yet sufficiently realized it—have not yet entirely and with complete sympathy put yourself in the place of the actors.

I have made a few comments on separate sheets.

I hope my comments will prove of some use. Before you are through you are going to do some first class work.

Sincerely yours,
Carl Becker

1. CBCU.
2. *Saint-Just, Apostle of the Terror* (Boston, 1932).

To Anita M., Max, and Constance Lerner

Ithaca, December 25, 1931[1]

Dear Anita,

Put into cold type it doesn't sound so good, but I have a new typewriter and I couldn't resist the temptation to use it. Maude left last night for Brattleboro, but she wished me to say for her, and I wish to say for myself, that your card was a thing of beauty and a joy forever—if you will permit me to coin a new phrase. Max is right, you ought to be devoting all your time to "ert." If I could only see you sticking out your tongue (you don't really do it; it interferes with talking) my Christmas joy would be complete. The

Dawgs are splendid. We haven't any doors to hold open, so we have
placed them on top of the clock that stands on the mantel over the
fire place. There they shall forever safeguard our home.

Dear Max,

I got five shirts and two handkerchiefs. Also seven neckties
which Fred had worn four times and were no longer good enough
for him. One advantage of having a son is that you don't have to
buy so many clothes: the old man gets the cast offs. I haven't anything to do now but write the 1000 word article on Jefferson for
your old omnibus.[2] What do you think I ought to write next—if
anything?

Dear Constance,

I am leaving for Minneapolis tomorrow. I hope to see some Bilboes, and if so I will let you know. Nite, nite!

Sincerely yours,
Carl Becker

1. AML.
2. "Thomas Jefferson," *ESS*, VIII (1932), 377–378.

To Ida and Leo Gershoy

Ithaca, 1931[1]

Ida   1931   Leo

> There was a chap who could not tell
> Why he loved not old Dr. Fell.
> It is not so at all with me.
> I love you both so very well
> Because, as I can plainly see,
> You're both as nice as nice can be!

C. B.

1. LIG.

I. Leonard Sarvay, Carl L. Becker, and Randolph Wright (top to bottom), in Waterloo, Iowa, early 1890's. (Department of Manuscripts and University Archives, Cornell.)

II. Carl L. Becker on the front lawn of his home on Mt. Oread, Lawrence, Kansas, spring 1916. (Department of Manuscripts and University Archives, Cornell.)

III. The Arts Quad at Cornell as it looked in 1917, when Carl Becker arrived. The figure in the foreground is Andrew Dickson White, Cornell's first president, who died in 1918 at the age of eighty-six. To the left is Goldwin Smith Hall, where Becker taught and had his office, 1917–1932. Boardman Hall, where Becker had his office from 1932 until 1941, is in the center. The University Library is at the right. (Department of Manuscripts and University Archives, Cornell.)

IV. The Cornell History Club, 1921. Seated, left to right: Julian P. Bretz, Nathaniel Schmidt, George Lincoln Burr, Charles Hull, Blanche E. Hazard, William L. Westermann, Carl L. Becker; standing: Ernest W. Nelson, George G. Andrews, Edgar H. Riley, William B. Graves, Wallace Notestein, Nellis M. Crouse, Gussie E. Gaskill, Louis R. Gottschalk, Harold Hulme. (Courtesy of Gussie E. Gaskill.)

V. The Cornell History Club, 1922. Seated, left to right: Preserved Smith, Julian P. Bretz, Charles Hull, George Lincoln Burr, Carl L. Becker, William L. Westermann, Nathaniel Schmidt; second row: David H. Willson, John H. Nelson, Amy A. Wilson, two unidentified women, Frances Relf, Catharine E. Young, John G. McGuire, Lloyd H. Hatch; third row: Thomas P. Harrison, Albert N. Thompson, Clifford Martin, Harold Hulme, unidentified man, Nellis M. Crouse, Leo Gershoy, unidentified man. (Courtesy of Gussie E. Gaskill.)

VI. Carl Becker's home (1917–1945) at 109 West Upland Road, Ithaca, New York. His study, where he wrote every morning until lunch time, was between the front door and the glassed-in porch. (Photographed in 1972.)

VII. History graduate students at Cornell before Becker's retirement dinner on June 10, 1941. Left to right: Seymour B. Dunn, David M. Ellis, Scott H. Lytle, Carl G. Gustavson, William H. McNeill, Walter Balderston, Virginia and James E. Seaver. (Courtesy of Gussie E. Gaskill.)

VIII. Carl L. Becker and his grandson, Carl Jadwin Becker, summer 1941. (Courtesy of Gussie E. Gaskill.)

To Leo Gershoy

Ithaca, [early 1932][1]

Dear Gershoy,

Thanks for your letter. I am especially glad to have your opinion (excuse me! I mean "reaction") of my address.[2] You are one of half a dozen men whose judgment in matters of form & substance I really value. If you think the thing really good I feel pretty confident it must be. Of course I discount the enthusiasm a little (the comparison to a symphony etc.) on account of friendship & old associations. I'm glad to see you didn't call my attention to the fact that $1017.31 (or whatever it was) was too much for 20 tons of coal. Many literal minded people have pointed this out to me. Perhaps you were bright enough to realize that this was an example of the "mythological adaptations" which we all indulge in—it represents the way our coal bill always looks when we get it. Many historians won't think much of the address. F. J. Turner was much pleased with it. C. A. Beard[3] and Jameson & Burr also.

Of course it isn't up to what I had in mind. But that's an old story.

I'm awfully glad you have a place of your own, but sorry that you haven't as entirely recovered as I hoped. For heaven's sake take care of yourself. You always look so blooming well that one can't really get the idea of your being ill. I think if you will just *do* what Ida tells you, you will be all right. I don't think many wives would measure up to this.

We all send love & best wishes.

Cordially yours,
Carl Becker

1. LIG.

2. "Everyman His Own Historian," Becker's presidential address to the American Historical Association, Minneapolis, December 29, 1931.

3. Charles A. Beard (1874–1948) taught political science at Columbia (1907–1917) and wrote many books concerning European and American history, American government, and contemporary affairs.

To Norman V. Donaldson

Ithaca, January 15, 1932[1]

Dear Mr. Donaldson,[2]

In your note of January 14 I am pleased to learn that the committee on publications has formally approved the publication of my lectures on "The Heavenly City of the Philosophes." But I am surprised to find that the committee feels that a different title would be desirable. The title seems to me a peculiarly happy one. It was suggested of course by the famous book of St. Augustine, "The City of God"; and the sum and substance of the lectures is to show that the Philosophes of the eighteenth century formulated a social and political philosophy which took over the cardinal preconceptions of the Christian philosophy as formulated in St. Augustine's work. The lectures are carefully built up around this idea, and many parts of the ms. would be ambiguous and irrelevant if a different title should be used. The title is moreover one that suggests in a striking way the central thesis of the lectures; and one that will be entirely intelligible to the readers of the book, who will be for the most part scholars who are quite familiar with [the] phrase Heavenly City which St. Augustine made famous. For my part I cannot think of any good reason for changing the title.

Very sincerely yours,
Carl Becker

1. CBCU; from CLB's draft.
2. Donaldson (1891–1964) was the director and chairman of the Yale University Press (1919–1964)

To Frederick Jackson Turner

Ithaca, January 19, 1932[1]

Dear Turner,

I need not say that your judgment on what I write has always been of the highest import to me: and it is a great comfort to know that you approve of my address. Like most efforts at writing, this one left me, when I was through, without any objective judgment of it.—I didn't know whether what seemed to me a sound idea at the beginning was good bad or eyewash. But it seemed to take very well at Minneapolis, and a number of good judges told me that it was good, so I think now that if not as good as it could be it is as good as I could make it.

There will be some offprints, & when they come (which they haven't as yet) I will send you one just in the way of friendship. Your note will serve as quite sufficient acknowledgement.

As always with great admiration and affection,

Very sincerely yours,
Carl Becker

1. Turner Papers, HEH.

To W. Stull Holt

Ithaca, [January 1932]¹

Dear Holt,²

Thanks very much for your appreciative note. I suspect there is some dynamite in the address, but I think also that there are a good many people in the association (younger people like yourself) whose ideas on this subject I did little more than formulate—perhaps more clearly than they could themselves have done. It is now pretty well admitted by all that interpretations change & that every age has to write its history anew: and yet the very people who admit this very often seem quite unaware of the implications— they appear to think that history must be rewritten because of the appearance of new "material" or a more expert technique, so that they can still believe that historiography presents a steady onward & upward march of progress in knowledge & "sound" interpretation. Of course the implications of my address are far more radical than that. There are a good many people outside the historical fraternity who will appreciate & understand the address better than some inside it. I'm told that Dodd of Chicago took it to be an argument for the futility of history couched in an ironical form. Misunderstanding could hardly go farther than that. I will send you a separate [i.e., offprint] when they come.

Cordially yours,
Carl Becker

1. CBCU.
2. Holt (1896———) taught history at George Washington University (1927–1930), Johns Hopkins (1930–1940), and the University of Washington (1940–1967), specializing in American diplomatic history and historiography.

To William E. Dodd

Ithaca, January 27, 1932[1]

Dear Dodd,

I am sending you a separate of my presidential address. I was told that you were inclined to regard it as advocating the futility of historical research under a thin guise of irony. But nothing could be farther from the truth. I was led to this address by the necessity, from long back, of finding some answer to the frequent question: "What is the good of history?" The answer was not always easy, all the more so since it must be obvious that much of what is called historical research is a dreary waste of meticulous determination of facts the importance of which is difficult to see. I could have much sympathy with the definition of research which I once heard: "If you take it out of one book, it's plagarism; if you take it out of many books, it's research." In seeking for an answer to the question, I was impressed by the fact that history as story is an old business. All children love stories. All primitive peoples cherish stories of their past, of their heros and great men. From earliest times all peoples have their histories, true or false. History as we practise it is an evolution of these early stories, a more expert and sophisticated treatment of the subject. On the other hand, sociology, economics, and the other so-called social sciences, are relatively late developments. I asked myself what is the reason for this? Why is history so old and so persistent an interest in the life of all peoples? It occurred to me that there must be some natural and instinctive basis for this universal and persistent preoccupation with history. It must, I thought, meet some well-grounded human need. What that universal need is I have tried to point out in all seriousness. It is simply the need of a conscious creature, who has memory and who can anticipate the future, to enlarge his present perceptions by remembering things that happened in the past. The individual does this constantly, primitive peoples do it more or less unconsciously, and without much attention to accuracy. Critical history is simply the instinctive and necessary exercise of memory, but of memory tested and fortified by reliable sources. The facts may be determined with accuracy; but the "interpretation" will always be shaped by the prejudices, biasses, needs, of the individual and these in turn will depend on the age in which he lives. Hence history has to be re-written by each generation. Even if the facts are the same, the slant on the facts will be different. You would certainly be the last to deny this I should think. At all events, my address was intended to find a natural and necessary basis in the nature of the human animal for the study and writing of history, to prove that history is a fundamental and most important branch of knowledge; to show that Mr. Everyman has and will have his history, true or false, and that one function of the historian is to keep Mr. Everyman's history, so far as possible, in reasonable harmony with what actually happened.[2]

Of course I don't object to any dissent which any one may feel to what I had to say, least of all do I object to any objections which you may have to make to it. But I don't want you to misunderstand what I was trying to do.

> Cordially yours,
> Carl Becker

1. CBCU.
2. For a thoughtful analysis of these same issues, see J. G. A. Pocock, *Politics, Language, and Time: Essays on Political Thought and History* (New York, 1971), especially chapter vii.

To William E. Dodd

Ithaca, December 25, 1931 [1]
Dear Dodd,

Thanks for your letter. The only circumstance which would make historical research & study futile would be the achievement of what is so commonly thought to be the aim of research—i.e. the attainment of final truth. If enough really "definitive" work could be written, then there would be nothing further to do in the way of research. Then historical research would indeed be futile. But my thesis—that nothing can ever be finally settled makes the effort to settle it ever necessary & useful.

I shall be glad to learn the result of your project to get the ideas discussed by Schevill[2] & students.

Of course I should like to have copies of your lectures.

My best regards to Mrs. Dodd and Martha.

Very Sincerely,
Carl Becker

1. CBCU.
2. Ferdinand Schevill (1868–1954) taught history at Chicago (1892–1937), specializing in modern Europe.

To Anita M. Lerner

Ithaca, [February 12, 1932][1]

Dear Anita,

We all send congratulations, if you want them, and in any case the very best of best wishes. For some reason, since you ask me, I wasn't troubled with nausea when Fred was coming, but I've had plenty of it since. The kind I had wasn't pleasant. I have always felt that a woman in that 'interesting condition' would want to punch her very dear husband's stomach exactly three times a day —or more if necessary. So far as I know women never do—they're so unoriginal.

I've thought of some names, if it's a boy.

Feodor Basarof
Nicolai Bodansky
Isvolsky Sazanof
Alexander Petrograd
Pierre Katuzoff.

Or how would you like Joseph Stalin Romanoff? The point is that when these foreigners[2] slip in and corrupt native American stock by marrying girls of old Philadelphia families, they ought to be open and aboveboard in naming their children.

Here's another, Iky Novogrudsky.

If it's a girl let her be Sonia Rostoff or Rachel Sapristi. Tell Max, the Philosopher, that there's nothing personal in these remarks.

Abstractly considered, he's a bad influence of course, but personally
I admire him greatly,

> Cordially,
> Carl Becker

1. AML.
2. Max Lerner was born in Russia.

To Max Farrand

Ithaca, May 16, 1932[1]

Dear Farrand,

I never saw very much of Turner after leaving Wisconsin, nor
did we keep up anything like a regular correspondence. Nevertheless, in the course of thirty five years I have accumulated a good
many letters from him. I have arranged them in chronological
order, and am sending them to you by way of American Express,
with heavy insurance. I may have destroyed some of his brief
notes, but I think I have kept practically all that Turner ever wrote
me. I haven't looked it through, but I feel sure that there is nothing
in it so personal that it might not be copied and kept in the Huntington Library. I am therefore leaving it entirely to you to make
copies of any or all of the letters, and make such use of them as
you think best. I should like the originals returned. You can well
understand that I prize them highly, and I often like to look at
them, if for nothing else than the sight of the characteristic handwriting. I have included the early letters as they show how much
pains Turner took for his students. The most valuable letters from
your point of view will probably be the long ones he wrote me when
I was writing the article for the volume on the Masters of the Social
Sciences. I told him about the article and asked him for any information about his early life, etc., that he cared to give. You will find
it interesting. Some of the letters, in which he acknowledges books
or articles of mine, while they must be taken as the cordial appreciation of a teacher for the work of his student, do I think show
something about Turner's idea of history and the writing of it. One
letter says something about his reasons for going to Harvard. I
had written rather regretting it; and there was something in the

public announcement of his acceptance (I've forgotten what) that aroused my ire (western) a little, for I thought it sounded as if [it] were taken for granted that an offer from Harvard would be accepted by any one. Turner explains that there was nothing in the situation to arouse any youthful sense of his having not been duly appreciated. I have also included two letters not from Turner, but about Turner. One from Phillips[2] and one from Allen [sic] Young.[3] I wrote to them at the time I was writing my article, desiring to have their impressions of Turner. These of course are private letters, and I suppose the writers have a certain right in them, so far as being made public is concerned. But I don't think there can be anything in them that either Phillips or Young, if he were alive, could object to having included in the Huntington ms. dealing with Turner. So I give you a free hand to do what you thing wise.

I needn't say that I was shocked to learn of Turner's death,[4] although I knew he was not in the best of health, and that he was getting old. But somehow it was always difficult to realize that Turner was ever old, or ever in bad health, so youthful and bouyant he always was. It's true I hadn't seen him for many years. I thought of writing to Mrs. Turner, but I scarcely knew her, and found it extremely difficult to say anything except the conventional things one does say. Anyhow I thought she would know, from my article, what I thought about Turner and what I must have felt when I learned of his death.

I wonder if his book was in a sufficiently advanced stage so that it can be published?[5] You know in 1925 he assured me (as you will see in one of his letters) that he was 'just finishing up a book' on the period 1830–1850—or was it 1840?

Very sincerely yours,
Carl Becker

1. Max Farrand Papers, HEH; by permission of The Huntington Library, San Marino, California.
2. Ulrich B. Phillips (1877–1934) taught history at Wisconsin (1902–1908),Tulane (1908–1911), the University of Michigan (1911–1929), and Yale (1929–1934), specializing in the American South.
3. Allyn A. Young (1876–1929) received his doctorate at Wisconsin in 1902, and taught economics at Stanford (1906–1911), the University of Washington ((1911–1913), Cornell (1913–1920), and Harvard (1920–1929).

4. January 26, 1932.
5. *The United States, 1830–1850: The Nation and Its Sections* (New York, 1935).

To Leo Gershoy

Ithaca, [spring 1932?][1]

Dear Gershoy,

It doesn't seem that my prophecy, some time since, that you were due for a good break, is coming true yet. I think you are right in not cutting loose at present from the Bronxville place.[2] Things may come out reasonably well at L.I. [Long Island University]. Still in replying to Anita Lerner, I left a kind of loophole by saying that you would be better able to take a definite line on the B— place at a later date, at the same time telling her that if they were in a hurry they had better not wait. I hope that was okay.

I've read your little *opus* on the F. R.[3] Its remarkably good as a generalized summary which takes account of everything, in a very excellent proportion, & with admirable subordination of minor things, etc. There's maturity in it, & a suggestion of having been thrown off easily by someone who has lived long with the subject & knows it comprehensively. It's certainly the best of the series so far as I know it. Of course if what they want is a brief factual manual, it isn't the thing; but if the reader is supposed to know something of the factual side, & wants the whole subject laid out for him to see as a whole & in its various relations, then this is the thing. The style is excellent—I mean suited to the purpose—it *moves* easily and rapidly along, there are no breaks, no changes in tempo. It's always clear & simple without being pedestrian or matter of fact.

There are as many facts in it as could be easily got into a running narrative which aims at making the facts fit into an intelligible whole. It's impersonal without being dead—without giving the impression of having been manufactured by a writing machine. There are admirable illuminating phrases in it, like "the sweating palm of the international Jew." This smacks of the man behind the book, and I think you might be well urged not to suppress things like this, as I fear you often do for fear you may appear *smart*.

Well, I don't want you to be smart, but there is a peculiar and fine, & fine edged, flavor that will someday be recognized as belonging to one person, and one only, viz: Leo Gershoy. Don't hide the flavor under a bushel (my images are getting mixed) too much. You will always avoid vulgarity & what you once spoke of as "another Jewish symphony in I"; but don't let your extreme dislike of exhibiting yourself keep you from putting your personality in your writing. It's there already, but very dim. A writer has to be something of an exhibitionist if he expects to develop a method of expression which people can recognize as definitely & individually his. Writers without taste or modesty can develop such an individual style by this or that kind of exaggeration, or by insolence, or what is called "frankness" etc. That grows wearisome very soon, but you are in no danger of that. Your danger is in not letting yourself go sufficiently. So I have no hesitation in advising you to be as individual and smart aleky as you can.

I am writing this in bed where I have been for three days with a double barrelled grip—head grip and intestinal grip, or whatever it is. Am expecting to be out again in a few days.

My assistant Val Lorwin,[4] has pulled down a $1400 travelling fellowship, and I hope he can see you either in New York or Ithaca before he goes to Paris. You could give him valuable tips. In any case you are sure to like him—he is a very fine gentleman and a man of subtle & humorous intelligence. His chief fault is a too great modesty & fear of putting himself forward—a fault of many Jews, I've noticed.

I've written a paper to be read at Columbia in its summer session public lectures. The title is "Liberalism; or Mr. Facing Both Ways."[5] It needs to be rewritten, and probably will be. I really haven't anything to do now and for a couple of months have had a regular debauch in old Shakespeare, and much fun reading the critics who disagree on everything. It's necessary, so I gather, to write monographs still to demonstrate that Hamlet was a thoughtful man not easily understood. You know after saturating yourself in that old guy for a month, you are aware as never before, when you try to write something that the pen is heavier than the sword. With what a spendthrift prodigality he scatters those unmatchable phrases about! "For look, the morn in russet mantle clad, walks o're the dew of yon high eastern hill." "We two alone will sing like birds in the cage: And when you ask me blessing, I'll kneel down and ask of you forgiveness." "The marigold that goes to bed with the sun, And with him rises weeping"—[6]

And so on without stint or limit.

I feel, that I never want to write again. However, this letter doesn't bear that out.

Sincerely,
Carl Becker

1. LIG.
2. Sarah Lawrence College
3. *The French Revolution, 1789–1799.*
4. Val R. Lorwin (1907——) received his B.A. (1927) and Ph.D. (1953) at Cornell, was an economist with the U.S. government (1935–1943, 1946–1949), taught at Chicago (1953–1957) and the University of Oregon (1957——). His specialty is comparative politics and social movements in modern Europe.
5. "Liberalism, a Way Station," *Saturday Review of Literature,* IX (Dec. 3, 1932), 281–282.
6. The quotations are from *Hamlet,* I, i, 166–167; *King Lear,* V, iii, 9–11; *The Winter's Tale,* IV, iv, 105–106. The first two are slightly misquoted.

To Oron J. Hale

New York, New York, [summer 1932][1]

Dear Mr. Hale,[2]

It was a great pleasure to get your very appreciative letter about my book.[3] I can say this, that I never took any piece of writing more seriously, or worked harder at it. It has been very well received by high school teachers, & those who have used it, so far as reports go, find that the pupils prefer it to other books. Considering the fact that it's a bad time to get any one to spend money that isn't absolutely necessary, the number of adoptions is very gratifying.

I haven't seen Andy[4] for a long time. He's a born crusader, and will always be happiest in the thick of the fight.

It's very nice to be able to go to Europe for a vacation—I wish I were going, but I never seem to have money enough to do anything except stay home, and hardly enough for that.

Very sincerely yours,
Carl Becker

1. Oron J. Hale Papers, Charlottesville, Va.
2. Hale (1902———), professor of European history at Virginia (1929–1972).
3. *Modern History.*
4. Andrew J. Biemiller (1906———), A.B., Cornell (1926), member of the 79th and 81st U.S. congresses, AFL-CIO official.

To Constance Lerner

New York, New York, [summer 1932?][1]

Dear Constance,

Be Nonchalant.

The Bilboes often run a lot.
They don't care if they do or not.
It doesn't weary them a bit,
Or bother them, or make them hot:
But when they've had enough of it
They simply spread their wings and flit!

Ever faithfully yours
Carl Becker

1. AML.

To Fruma Kasdan Gottschalk

New York, New York, August 6, 1932[1]

Dear Fruma,[2]

We are delighted to have the snaps of little Alexandre. He looks up and coming—with his dark hair, close cropped, growing low on the forehead, & his round alpine head, he looks intelligent and aggressive, and something of a tough guy. I'm afraid there's a strain of ruthless Tartar blood in him. A Bolshevik, another Lenin, probably—that's what he'll be. No professor, I'm sure of that. It's no good you're trying to make a gentleman of him. But how will you be able to leave him all the time you're abroad? The most intractable, rascally sons are the ones mothers are fondest of. Well, maybe you will stop off in Ithaca so that we can see you and the wonderful Alexandre,—and Louis of course, although now he is only of minor importance. I expect he's learned that by now.

We are living in Prof. Byrne's[3] house on 75 St., in quite grand style, which we are able to do only because he let us have it for paying the wages of the cook and the maid. They run the house and take most solicitous care of us. We feel like kings, and the world is filled with a number of things. We go to shows, and ride on busses, or drive up and down in the car. Fred has been at Plattsburg at a military camp, but is here now. Yesterday he went up into Connecticut to see one of his numerous girls, & he proposes to drag her down here tomorrow for a taste of New York life. He didn't like military camp much, but it did him good physically, and gave him a hunch that the military life was not for him.

Did you know Yale conferred a D. Litt. on me this June? I mention it so that you can prepare to treat me with the proper degree of respect in future. Maude has said half a dozen times that she is going to send that Alexandre—"something." So if she doesn't it isn't because she hasn't thought of it and doesn't want to. We will be here until Sept 1, I expect. I wish you & Louis were passing through now so that we could "entertain" you in right royal style.

Ever Sincerely Yours,
Carl Becker

P.S. I've asked Maude if she wishes to add anything, and she says only to say that she sends her love and very best wishes to you all.

1. CBCU.
2. Mrs. Louis Gottschalk.
3. Eugene H. Byrne (1882–1952), professor of history at Barnard, specializing in medieval economic history.

To Leo Gershoy

New York, New York, [August 1932][1]

Dear Leo,

I am glad you & Ida are to have the privilege of a rest on M.V.,[2] which I have never seen, but have been told is a splendid place to relax and rest. I am afraid we shan't be able to see you there. You will have received my letter saying that we are returning to Ithaca Sept. 3. Very, very sorry not to see you again.

Your suggestions for a title for the great book are good.[3] Nothing has been settled as yet. I am rather partial to the title *"Everyman His Own Historian, & Other Essays"*, or *Kansas & Other Essays*. I know these are both very conventional, but I dislike any title that seems to strain for originality: and it's very difficult to get a title that is descriptive of so varied a content. However,——

Tomorrow winds up the Summer Session. I haven't had your advantage of swanky clothes; but at any rate they have asked me to come again next summer.

Well, good luck & best wishes. I hope Ida will do something unseemly on M.V.

Carl Becker

1. LIG.

2. Martha's Vineyard, an island off the Massachusetts coast.

3. In the Preface to *Everyman His Own Historian: Essays on History and Politics,* CLB expressed his appreciation to "those former pupils who are so largely responsible for the appearance of the present volume."

To Leo Gershoy

Ithaca, [autumn 1932][1]

Dear Gershoy,

I am enclosing a letter to Gottschalk. I wish you would put in his street address, which I seem to have lost, and mail it. Will you also, the next time you write, send me his address. One of my letters failed to reach him last Spring, and others may have done so.

Nevins was here last week end, the same Nevins as ever—infinitely intelligent and everlastingly sane: the same as ever, only more so. He had a great time in the Far East I fancy. He said he had seen you and that you were getting on to the end of your text book. I know how easily people get that idea—that a book you happen to mention as "getting on" with is all but finished. So I suspect you are not yet sending off the Ms. What I fear is that when you do get to the end you will, being always too much enamored of perfection, after all conclude that the thing is absolutely too poor to think of printing without a thoroughgoing revision. The poverty of every book I ever wrote was most glaringly apparent to me at the moment of finishing it.

Mrs. Becker joins me in sending regards to you and Ida.

Very Sincerely yours,
Carl Becker

1. LIG.

To Leo Gershoy

Ithaca, October 27, [1932][1]

Dear Leo,

Of course I shall be delighted to have you dedicate your book to me,[2] although I am quite sure that you do not owe as much to me as you think. I realize that the book, written under unfortunate & moving circumstances, is not as good as you can do—but its a very good book of its kind, and who am I after all that I should be too good to have any book dedicated to me?

I'm sorry you are tied to Bensonhurst,[3] but nearly everyone gets tied to something. I often think life is like walking through a field, filled with traps, in the dark. Those that don't get caught are lucky. But then maybe the traps, if we get caught, "develop our personalities."

However, I'm getting beyond my depth. I may go to Toronto if I'm not too poor. Let you know later.

Sincerely yours,
Carl Becker

Love to Ida the more grumpy one.

1. LIG.
2. *The French Revolution and Napoleon* is dedicated "to Carl Becker, with great admiration and affection."
3. A neighborhood in Brooklyn, New York.

To James Truslow Adams

Ithaca, November 1, 1932[1]

Dear Mr. Adams,[2]

I am sorry if you think that my review of your book[3] did not do it justice. Perhaps it didn't. Still, it expresses, as well as I was able to do in short space, my judgment of it. Whether that judgment is right or wrong I feel sure that a different title would not have changed it. The title merely gave me a convenient lead for indicating what seemed to me to be the qualities of the work. I was quite aware that it is tragedy that is supposed to purge the soul by fear and pity. You will note that what I say is "banishes all sense of epic grandeur and *tragic conflict* which the story of American history is so well suited to convey." At first the editor of the *Review* raised the query as to the use of the words 'purge the soul by fear and pity' in connection with 'epic.' When I pointed out to him that the words as I used them referred to the above words 'tragic conflict' he felt that the sentence as it stood was quite all right. I still think so. The closing paragraph might have been written even if the book had had some other title. It does not say, or mean to imply, that the book should have been an epic or a tragedy: it merely says that while the book is an interesting and valuable tract for the times (and surely tracts for the times are now much called for) it leaves one without a sense of the epic and tragic which might have been found in the story of American history. It was intended as an indication of what the book was and what it was not.

Sincerely yours,
Carl Becker

1. James Truslow Adams Papers, COL.

2. Adams (1878–1949), an American historian, published many volumes of history, biography, geography, as well as encyclopedias.

3. *The Epic of America*, reviewed in *AHR*, XXXVII (1932), 558–561. For Adams' side of this controversy, see Allan Nevins, *James Truslow Adams: Historian of the American Dream* (Urbana, Ill., 1968), 79, 223–224. In 1922, Adams had written a review of CLB's *The Declaration of Independence* (see the *New Republic*, XXXII, 338)

which contained criticism quite bothersome to CLB. See his introduction to the 1942 edition, pp. vi–vii.

To Louis Gottschalk

Ithaca, November 10, 1932[1]

Dear Gottschalk,

Thanks for your remarks about my book.[2] What can I say in reply to such cordial approval except that I am very glad to have it, since you are one of that small number, and very special brand, of my former pupils whose judgments I especially respect. I think it is the best of my books—the best constructed, the best thought out, the best written. T. V. Smith[3] likes it very much also, although he very decidedly doesn't want to accept the underlying implications, and he tells me that he won't if he can help it.

Thanks also for the snapshots of Alexandre. It's quite obvious that he's a Bolshevik; like all the Bolsheviks he's sticking his tongue out at all the world. He should be sent to Andover prep school, and afterwards to Williams College. Still, we all like his impudence, and all send him our love, and send our love to you, and especially to Fruma. When are we going to see you all?

Cordially,
Carl Becker

1. CBCU.
2. *The Heavenly City of the Eighteenth-Century Philosophers.*
3. T. V. Smith (1890–1964) taught philosophy at the University of Texas (1919–1921), Chicago (1926–1948), and Syracuse (1948–1956). See his letter to CLB, October 26, 1932, in the Appendix.

To James Truslow Adams

Ithaca, November 21, 1932[1]

My dear Mr. Adams,

I have just received your note. I see no reason why an author should not comment on a reviewer's treatment of his book. I am rather glad you did in this case, since I was glad to learn that the title was not yours. It is quite possible that I made too much use of the title. I myself have never found reviews of my own books very satisfactory as a rule; not because the reviewers haven't lauded them sufficiently—they have been cordial enough; but chiefly because it is not often that they have even been aware of the precise thing I tried to do. Maybe they are to blame for that; maybe the books are to blame. I realize that my reviews of other people's books may be unsatisfactory in the same way.

I saw Allen Nevins last night and he says that your new book, "The March of Democracy," is having a very good sale. I am glad to hear it. I haven't as yet seen the book.

Very Sincerely Yours,
Carl Becker

1. Adams Papers, COL.

To William E. Dodd

Ithaca, November 29, 1932[1]

Dear Dodd,

It is very nice of you to want me at Chicago this summer; but the fact is that I have already agreed to give a couple of courses at Columbia again.

My book isn't history, certainly, nor is it law, although it was presented in the form of lectures to the law school. Perhaps it's philosophy,—or maybe what all the younger writers now are in the habit of calling "creative" criticism. Why may it not be creative criticism—don't leave out the 'creative.'

Are you one of the 3000000 people who voted for Roosevelt[2] in the belief that you were voting for T. R.? I voted for Thomas,[3] because I knew he couldn't be elected. I wouldn't want to be in any way responsible for the people that run things at Washington.

Thanks again for your kind invitation. Give my regards to Mrs. Dodd & Martha.

Sincerely,
Carl Becker

1. CBCU.
2. Franklin Delano Roosevelt.
3. Norman Thomas (1884–1968), clergyman, lecturer, author, Socialist leader, six-time candidate for president.

To Leo Gershoy

Clifton Springs, New York, [December 1932][1]

Dear Gershoy,

You may have heard that I had another attack of my old trouble. I have been laid up for three weeks—since last Saturday; and for the last week, since Tuesday a week ago, I have been here at the Sanitorium. After thorough examination, Dr. Mumford is positive (1) that there is no serious trouble, such as cancerous or other growths; (2) Pretty confidant that the trouble has arisen from a certain weakness in the intestines which makes it difficult for them to expell the feces entirely; this results in a gradual cloging of the lower bowel which in time sets up irritation and what he calls "reverse parastalsis" (spelling) & colitis (overflow of mucus in the intestines); & hence the pains which I suffer at those times: (3) He is confidant that this weakness of the intestines can be corrected by simple means.

I tell you all this because it will probably get about at Toronto that I am ill, and there are likely to be rumors spread all over the country (as there were from the Boston meeting a few years ago) that I have Cancer, or some incurable disease. If you hear any talk you can say with authority that my trouble is in no sense serious, & that I expect to be better in the next 5 years than I have in the last two. If any of my special cronies are around (George Andrews,[2] Hedger, Gottschalk, or any others) you can convey this information to them so that they may be in a position to scotch any rumors to the effect that I have one foot in the grave. I've suffered a lot of pain in the last three weeks, but pain, although as unpleasant as you like, isn't a sure symptom of anything serious. I'm going to live at least ten years more (barring motor accidents) and expect to criticise and advise and generally bore my friends as much as ever. I expect to be back in Ithaca towards the end of the week but can't be sure just when.

Give my regards to any one who happens to know me. And my particular love to Ida when you see her.

Sincerely yours,
Carl Becker

P.S. I was going to send you and Ida a copy of the Heavenly City for Christmas, but was too miserable to attend to it. I'll send it later. I've only seen one review—that of Krutch[3] in Herald Tribune *Books*. Not bad, but I note a little of the spirit of condesention which the 'literary-intelligencia' exhibit towards professors: the same kind that professors exhibit toward the literary intelligencia. However, I don't mind reviews—I've got over that long ago.

1. LIG. Clifton Springs, New York, is southeast of Rochester.
2. George Gordon Andrews (1887–1938) received his Ph.D. at Cornell, under Becker's direction, in 1921. He taught European history at the universities of South Dakota and Iowa.
3. Joseph Wood Krutch (1893–1971), journalist, educator, and literary critic, was an editor with *The Nation* (1924–1937) and taught English at Columbia (1932–1952).

To Mary Elizabeth Bohannon

Ithaca, January 22, 1933[1]

(Keep your courage UP!)
Dear Miss Bohannon,[2]

I have just sent off to the Council of Learned Societies, at its request, a recommendation favorable to your "Project of Work," and have emphasized the fact that without assistance you can't, at present, go on. I sincerely hope you get a grant.

N.B. I don't mean that the Society requested a *favorable* recommendation.

I have been laid up in bed for a few weeks—or rather was during the holidays and a week after. This time I went up to Clifton Springs Sanitorium for two weeks, and gave them a look in (literally): the results, although mainly negative, were encouraging: they say there is nothing serious the matter with me—no organic trouble or foreign growths in the way of cancer etc—There is an even chance that these attacks, which I have had on an average of one about every 10 months during the last two years, may be prevented, or at least abated, in the future.

N.B. I mention these uninteresting matters so that you can refute any rumors to the effect that I am dying of cancer or whatnot.

We have had a sad business here—the sudden death of Professor Guerlac[3] from Spinal Meningitus last Monday.

Don't forget that I get great pleasure out of giving you, as the English say, 'a leg up,' at every opportunity.

Very sincerely yours,
Carl Becker

1. Mary Elizabeth Bohannon Papers, CU.

2. Bohannon (1905–1963) received her Ph.D. at Cornell in 1932, and taught history at Wells College (1936–1963).

3. Othon G. Guerlac (1870–1933) taught Romance languages and literatures at Cornell (1900–1933) and was also the American correspondent of *Le Temps*.

To Mary Elizabeth Bohannon

Ithaca, February 8, 1933[1]

My dear Betty,

I was perfectly delighted the other day when Mr. Marcham[2] told me that you had the fellowship. Of course the only thing to do was to take it: you thus have a sure thing, and avoid the uncertainty and worry of waiting some weeks. Marcham tells me that at present rates of exchange you should have 300£ which you will no doubt know how to manage on. It is a great thing to be young and to be going to England for a year. I know you will have a fine time and will make the most of the chance. And by saying "the most" I do not mean that you will make as much as you hope or wish. One never does as well or as much in a given time, one never writes as good a book or as good an article, as one hopes or wishes or expects. Please remember that. I hope my letter helped a little. I don't think I often (except once in a [Moon's?] eye when I'm mistaken) say more for my friends than they can live up to; although I often say more than they (in their modesty) think they can.

(Excuse me. I thought I could get it all on two sides [of the stationery]; but I run on and on as you know). I gamble a little on my young friends, and on what could one better gamble on? And one of the reasons they do so well is that they're better than they know; and when I back them they feel it would be a pity to disappoint me, to let me down, and so they work a little harder, and perhaps with a little more confidence than they might otherwise. It's amazing what you all do for me, and how you all appreciate so highly the little I can really do, or do do, for you. If I do a little to keep you going and to keep your confidence up, it's no more than right, since you all do so much for me: You keep my confidence up; by turning out so well and being so nice and friendly you enable me to keep up the illusion that my 'teaching' (God save the mark!) is perhaps not all useless waste motion.

And so, congratulations, and all my best wishes. And I should be delighted if you would write to me whenever you feel in the mood (no 'duty' letters please!)

Sincerely yours
Carl Becker

1. Bohannon Papers, CU.
2. Frederick G. Marcham (1898————) received his Ph.D. at Cornell (1926) and taught English history at Cornell (1926–1971). His specialty is the Tudor-Stuart period.

To Arthur M. Schlesinger

Ithaca, February 14, 1933[1]

My dear Schlesinger,

Fox[2] has just forwarded to me your letter to him in comment on a letter of mine. My letter was in reply to a query from Fox at the time your book was sent out,—and his query was apropos of some comments I made to him last summer when I had your Ms. Let me say that whatever criticism I may have to make on the series or any book in it are made only in private and only to the editors.[3]

I have never made any secret of my lack of enthusiasm for the kind of thing these books attempt to do, and on the whole do as well as that kind of thing can be done. You may recall our first conversation about it in the 'dark backward and abysses of time' at that club on 5 Ave. when I was stoping. I then said much the same thing as I said in my letter to Fox. But from certain expressions in your note I have a notion that there was more or that you have read into it more, in my letter to Fox than I intended: more of a condemnatory note, more of a Judgment from on High. I certainly did not intend to take a superior tone or to condemn anyone or anything; but merely to express my attitude, preference, prejudice if you like. I think also that it was a mistake to use the word 'synthesis'—as it is usually a mistake to use a shopworn word that everyone is familiar with since each one will see the word in the light of his own preferences & performances. I certainly don't care any more than you do for the 'glib synthesis.' I do not think your book, or any of the books in the series, can be said to have presented a 'glib synthesis.' I do not think they present any snythesis at all—not in the sense in which I understand that word. I think your book (and most of the others) is a clear, straightforward presentation of a great mass of information about a great variety of activities, all excellently *classified* under certain subject rubrics, presented moreover with whatever comment is necessary to explicate & make intelligible the particular situation. That kind of book certainly has a right to exist, and I should never deny to others what I claim for myself—the privilege of writing whatever kind of book they like as well as they can. Your book is, in its kind, a most excellent one. The best, I should be inclined to say, in the series so far. My only point is that I personally do not care particularly for the kind. All facts are 'stubborn': taken in their fullness they become unmanageable; to make anything at all of them one must select & reject and emphasize & subordinate and foreshorten. I don't mean to say that you do not do this, that you present, or attempt to . . .

[*A page is missing.*]

. . . of information than with the species of book that make a synthesis or an interpretation in terms of general and related & coordinated ideas. They belong with such books as Lavisse, *Histoire de France* (probably the best of all co-operative social histories)[4] rather than with books that attempt and achieve as well as possible a real synthesis—such books for example as Bury's *The Idea of Progress*[5] or the one I mentioned in my letter to Fox, Burckhardt's *Renaissance in Italy*.[6] I think both kinds useful, I certainly think the authors of the one as well as of the other kind (supposing the results to be excellent in that kind) do "deserve the decent respect of mankind." And as for the readers, God bless them, let every man read what he finds interesting & useful. In the meantime everyone concerned, and especially you, my dear Schlesinger, has the decent respect of

Yours very sincerely,
Carl Becker

1. CBCU, rough draft.
2. Dixon Ryan Fox (1887–1946) taught history at Columbia (1912–1934), and was president of Union College (1934–1946). His specialties were early American and social history.
3. The book is Schlesinger's *The Rise of the City, 1878–1898* (New York, 1933); the series is "A History of American Life" (13 volumes), edited by Schlesinger and Fox. Becker was nominally one of the two consulting editors for this series. In fact, he played little part in its development and was criticized for allowing his name to be used "provided he would not have to do any work or even read the manuscripts. It does not seem a very scholarly way of earning money" (James Truslow Adams to Allan Nevins, Oct. 22, 1932, in Nevins, *James Truslow Adams: Historian of the American Dream* [Urbana, Ill., 1968], 174, 224).
4. Ernest Lavisse, ed., *Histoire de France* . . . (28 vols.; Paris, 1900–1922).
5. J. B. Bury, *The Idea of Progress: An Inquiry into Its Origin and Growth* (London, 1920). CLB reviewed the second edition in *AHR*, XXXVIII (1933), 304–306.
6. Jakob C. Burckhardt, *The Civilization of the Renaissance in Italy* (London, 1892).

To Ida Gershoy

Ithaca, February 23, 1933[1]

My dear Ida,

Ever since Leo wrote, long time ago, that you had had grip three times, I have intended to write to let you know quite positively that three times is too many in one short season. It reminds me of a sentence I picked out of a popular novel recently

"Beth was expecting her third child
within the month, and she was done up."

Any woman would be: a third child within a month is indeed too many. So it is with grip. Well, I indulge in the most flagrant 'wishful thinking' and am fully persuaded that you are now blooming again in all your customary darkly burnished splendor. As for myself, I'm in excellent health, and have a most greedy and grasping appetite which would cost you a lot *if* I were in N.Y. and *if* you should, as you usually do, insist on taking me out—to the Brevort and such like swell places—and paying for everything. There's many an *if*: but I'll be seeing you I hope next June if we don't cross on our ways.

Do you manage to live on your income? I hope not, because I can't, and it makes me unhappy to see anyone else doing it—especially my best friends in whom I like to be able to note at least *one* defect.

Very Sincerely yours,
Carl Becker

Regards to Leo, the author.

1. LIG.

To Leo Gershoy

Ithaca, March 1, 1933[1]

Dear Leo,

I have just read your review of Miss Anthony's *Marie Antoinette*. I just want to say that it's a model of what a review should be. Discriminating, quite to the point and put, as to form with every felicity. You may say, "a brief review—what's that to write home about?" But let me tell you, what very few people know, that to write a brief review and do a neat competent job of it, with nothing too much, with just enough, and without exaggerating minor defects or overdoing favorable appraisal—in short, to *place* the book just where it belongs: let me tell you that this is one of the most difficult of jobs. It isn't once in a donkey's years that I read a review that is a work of art, as a review may be. Yours is, and I congratulate you. Having reviewed some hundreds of books in the last thirty years, I know something about it.

I'm now doing Napoleon I, Emperor of the French, for the Ency. Soc. Sciences.—1000 (One thousand words).[2] Thats a job too—what to reject, what to put in, how to phrase it so as to include the maximum of information and still convey something of what the man was. Then next I have to write for the same repository an article on the Idea of Progress in 3500 words.[3] Sweet job!

Health first rate now—except that I sleep badly: but then I don't sleep as well any time these last ten years as I used to do—and never did: so it's no matter.

Sincerely yours,
Carl Becker

1. LIG.
2. "Napoleon I," *ESS* (1933).
3. "Progress," *ESS* (1934).

To Livingston Farrand

Ithaca, March 9, 1933[1]

Dear Mr. Farrand,

Yesterday you made to the faculty a statement announcing a cut in salaries for the coming year. The announcement, as you probably know, did not come as a surprise. Among the members of the faculty with whom I come in contact (not very many it is true, but representative enough) it has for some time been taken for granted that such a cut was inevitable; and the inevitable, although not pleasant, has been accepted I think in a very good spirit. Of course there has been criticism (there is always criticism—I have indulged in it myself) of the Trustees and 'the Administration' for wasteful expenditures; and I think it must be admitted that in the last twenty years virtually all of our universities have too much emphasized the tangible and visible at the expense of the impalpable and the essential values of higher education. But I realize that to place the sole responsibility on the Trustees and 'the Administration' is to do them an injustice; the faculties are in part responsible too. In a very real sense no one is responsible. A modern university, like modern society of which it is a part, is so complex an institution, and so integrated with the mechanized life of the time, that it seems to develope along a certain line, inevitably, by some impersonal interior law of its own, in spite of all that any one can do to direct it otherwise.

I suspect that to make the statement you made yesterday was not the most pleasant, that it was in fact perhaps the most unpleasant task you have had to perform during your term of office as president. I write this note merely to say that I appreciate, quite fully I think, the conscientiousness and ability with which you are meeting them; and that you have now, as you have always had, my own cordial support for whatever it is worth. It isn't, I am aware, worth much in a practical sense at least, since dealing with the sort of problems you have to face isn't in my bag of tricks at all. But I wish you to know that the present situation does not affect in the least my strong attachment to Cornell as an institution or my admiration for you as its president. For fifteen years Cornell has permitted me to feel that I am being paid a salary for doing essentially what I please; and no one has contributed more to this happy state of mind than yourself. I only wish that I might have done more for Cornell, and that, in the present emergency, I might do more to lighten the burden of your own responsibilities.

With the best of all possible wishes in the best of all possible worlds, I remain,

Very sincerely yours,
Carl Becker

1. Farrand Papers, CU.

To Frederick Lewis Allen

Ithaca, March 19, 1933[1]

Dear Mr. Allen,[2]

I wanted to tell you how much I enjoyed your book, *Only Yesterday*.[3] It's an amazingly vivid picture of the decade as it must have appeared to the general run of people who lived through it. Historians like myself like to see the past in long perspective; and we arrange events in an orderly sequence—a pattern that looks simple and logical; at least we try to do it—often enough we fail. No doubt that's one way to interpret the past; but another way is to reproduce the stream of hit and miss things that come and pass and are forgotten within the year. That's your way; and it enables one to realize how the great majority of people, including historians, see the events they live through as a kind of continuous news reel —one thing following another without much apparent connection. And I suppose that is especially characteristic of our age—more so than of earlier, more stable times.

I was much interested too in your report of Wilson in his last years. I too happened to have the privilege of visiting him, through the courtesy of Professor W^m E Dodd, together with several others —J. F. Jameson, G. S. Ford, Professor Cheyney and some others. He talked to us for half an hour, to all appearance with his customary vividness, sense of humor, etc. But I noticed that his mind did not make *transitions* easily. He would talk for five minutes of something—the Kaiser, or Clemenceau, or whatever; then he would drop it, and be silent, until he thought, or someone suggested, some other topic. He seemed a man at bay: desperately fighting still, but now what he was fighting for was really to hold on to the conviction that he hadn't wholly failed. I recall his saying "But we've got the League—*they can't take that away from me.*"

He talked a little about history (we were all historians): and said that people exaggerated the ability of people in high places to know all that was going on; & that a fault of historians was to assume that the actors in great events knew as much about everything and what was coming in the future as the historian did himself. If he had to write history again, he would try to *know as little as possible* about what happened after the particular time of which he was writing: then he might see it more as people did who were living it. You haven't had the disadvantage he deplored of knowing too much about what was to happen—in the 1930's.

Very sincerely yours,
Carl Becker

1. CBCU.
2. Allen (1890–1954) was an author and magazine editor with the *Atlantic Monthly, Century,* and *Harper's* (1923–1953).
3. A history of the 1920's (New York, 1931).

To Guy Stanton Ford

Ithaca, May 3, 1933[1]

Dear Ford,

I have read your address with great pleasure.[2] You put your finger on the really fundamental question—can we adapt ourselves to the rapidly changing conditions produced by science with sufficient rapidity to avoid a collapse. I hope so, and the American people, when sufficiently pressed with misfortune, can do more than many people think. It may be that the best thing in the end would be a continuation of the depression for several years. It's a horrible thought. But if 'prosperity' comes now I am afraid the old hit and miss system will continue. The real trouble is that all of the brains have gone into the production, sale, & transportation of wealth. No brains at all have been devoted to the question of whether people are going to have any money in their pockets to buy all these things. Something has got to be done about that.—What needs to be produced, & how much, where profits are to be [directed?] & under what security. If something isn't done about that side the end is desperation and revolution. The Germans follow a fool like Hitler in order to escape some other fool trying to wear the hat of Lenin. If we don't get some people who know something and are honest to do something here we will end in the same mess. I am not as optimistic as you *sound;* I don't know whether you are. But since you face the facts, your optimistic tone is the right one.

Sincerely yours,
Carl Becker

1. Guy Stanton Ford Papers, UM.
2. *Science and Civilization,* Day and Hour Series of the University of Minnesota, no. 1 (Minneapolis, 1933).

To Norman Spitzer

Ithaca, May 10, 1933[1]

Dear Mr. Spitzer,[2]

I signed your petition and am enclosing a small check all in behalf of the right of free speech. This I do because I am a liberal who believes that free speech is desirable, even for those who do not believe in it. I never could understand, however, how a communist, on his own principles, can claim the right of free speech, or expect to be granted it willingly. Communism, as I understand it, preaches the social revolution, the suppression by force of certain classes of people, and of all free speech for those who refused to support the communist ideal. You, if you are a communist, therefore, are essentially asking for free speech in order to establish a system which will deny free speech. Since you appeal to force

I can understand why you should *resist* oppression, but not why you should *resent* it. What the Hitlerites are doing to the Communists is exactly what the communists would do to the Hitlerites if they (the Communists) were in power. If I, as a liberal, wish communists to have free speech in this country it is not to advance their cause, but because I believe they will be weaker if let alone than if they are repressed.

Very sincerely yours,
Carl Becker

1. CBCU.
2. Norman Spitzer received his B.A. at Cornell in 1934.

To Conyers Read

Ithaca, [May 10, 1933][1]

Dear Read,[2]

Your letter startled me like a fire bell in the night—if you will allow me to coin a novel phrase. So you are "planning,"—(everybody is planning), but you are planning, actually planning, "revolutionary changes." I can't believe it. I remember a slight insurrection in the Association a number of years ago, but it was not planned by those high in office.[3] It is incredible. What is the Association coming to? It's another bit of evidence of the collapse of capitalism no doubt. But you don't say whether this revolution is according to the principles of dialectical determinism. How then can I say whether I approve of it or not?

I have not recovered from the shock, and there are so many things to say that I hardly know where to begin. I might as well begin with Beard. Since he is capable of being up to anything, I suppose he is at the bottom of the whole affair. At all events he is trying to drag me in, to lead me astray as it were; and with the worst sort of Jesuitism—the sort that is perfectly transparent. He knows perfectly well, and he knows that I know, and that I know that he knows, that he did not go all the way to Minneapolis to hear me spout. He was on his way with Mary Jane (for which I wish to praise something or someone, since it enabled me to meet that most intelligent and charming & much better half of the great Charles A.)[4] to California to deliver some lectures (for money I dare say) and merely stopped off at Minneapolis on his way. And so that's that, and if C. A. will get me a good chance to make some money in California and a leave of absence at just the right time, I will gladly travel all the way to Urbana to hear him do his stuff. And again I hope to meet the above mentioned and hence described Mary Jane. But can he do that? He cannot.

Now I am no Jesuit and I will give you a straightforward answer. I approve of the section on Historiography. I should like to be there and attend it. (I should like even to hear the president's address— a thing I haven't done in many years) I shouldn't greatly object to preside at all, although presiding isn't in my bag of tricks at all. But the plain & simple truth is that I can't be sure a week ahead whether I shall be able to come at all. Last December I intended to go to Toronto, and even sent my $12.50 for reservations; but at the time instead of being in the jamboree of an Hist Association Meeting I was in the Sanatorium at Clifton Springs—there's a notable difference, in case you don't know it. After five weeks of illness, I was very well apparently for three months; & then as suddenly as before was laid up again for four weeks. Now I'm coming to again. How long I will be up & about amazing my students & colleagues I don't know—long enough I hope to finish out this term & by good luck the Columbia summer session. Longer than that I hope. I always hope. But these attacks have been coming on at intervals of about six months for the last three years. The attacks appear to increase in length & the intervals between to decrease; so that maybe after awhile there will be no intervals. Then my friends will not need to worry or inquire about my health any more since they will know that it's always bad; and that will be, so far as being always [consistent?], all to the good. Now I wish you wouldn't mention this to a soul except Beard under confidence, for all sorts of wild tales get circulated, as e.g. that I have cancer of the stomach, am about to die and so on. There's nothing to it. I've been examined, x rayed to a finish & they can't find anything the matter. Obviously something is the matter, a weak spot somewhere in the stomach or intestines which breaks down on account of too much eating or eating the wrong foods or comb. of foods. It's a matter of finding by experiment what to eliminate. It's a matter of eating the right things, sparingly, & always going about hungry, with saliva dripping from my tongue every time I pass a nice smelly bake shop. I wouldn't tell you about all these wearisome matters except to have you & Beard understand why I can't undertake the job you wish me to. I can't because I simply can't count on being well enough to go anywhere or do anything not essential at any particular time. I'm teaching at Columbia this summer because I very much need the money & I'm trusting to fate not to break down in the midst of the session. I will, however, be glad to help in arranging the session by suggestion as to subject matter or as to men who are interested in the sort of thing you want. Send this letter to Beard if you like, but mum's the word in respect to my health,—because every now & then I get distressed letters from friends asking if it's true I've got cancer or spinal meningitus. Like [*two illegible words*], I'm doing as well as can be expected under the circumstances. But I have to be careful, & I cant promise to be well enough to go to Urbana, or to have energy or time enough to arrange a a program. I'm sorry, but there it is.

1. CBCU, draft.
2. Conyers Read (1881–1959) taught history at Chicago (1910–1920) and the University of Pennsylvania (1934–1951), specializing in the Tudor-Stuart period of English history. He was executive secretary of the American Historical Association (1933–1941).
3. See CLB to William E. Dodd, [early summer] 1915.
4. Mary R. Beard (1876–1958), educated at DePauw and Columbia, wrote extensively on women's history and collaborated on many books with her husband, Charles A. Beard, whom she married in 1900. See Charles A. Beard to CLB, May 14, 1933, in the Appendix.

To Leo Gershoy

Ithaca, May 15, 1933[1]

Dear Leo,

I must say you have a tough time—teaching for a salary, not good enough at the best, which has the habit of some streams that every now & then disappear under the earth. Well, I suppose it is true that those of us who have jobs at all ought to be thankful—or at least resigned. But in these days the word 'resigned' has an ominous sound.

I am now pretty well restored to normal. It's a matter of eliminating the foods, & combinations of foods, that disagree with me.

This is a slow process because it is difficult to find out what should be eliminated. But we are getting on with it, I judge so at least since most of the things I like best have been already eliminated. It's a matter of going around hungry all the time with mouth watering. I haven't got to that point yet, since I am rarely hungry.

All you say of my writing & "influence" is very nice and comforting. I know that relative to most so-called historical research and writing mine is good enough. But relative to some other standard it's not so notable. I know how good it is, and also what its defects are. Only it's not as good as I should like—which is always the case with anyone who is self-critical: and I want to do something better.

What I have done for you & others is quite all right if you & they think so. But there's no merit in it on my part. If I did it from a sense of duty, or in order to make a good impression, or something like that, then I might deserve a merit mark. But then it wouldn't be any good. If it's good at all it's good merely because I do it because it gives me pleasure, and there's no merit in doing what you like. So you can't "owe" me anything. I refuse to admit that my friends owe me anything—even a letter. Everything is already repaid & more.

Sincerely yours,
Carl Becker

1. LIG.

To William E. Dodd

Ithaca, June 11, 1933[1]

Dear Dodd,

The scholar in politics.[2] Well, I do congratulate you—if this job pleases you. You had better run over to Phil Allen's[3] and talk German with him on Mondays, Wednesdays, & Fridays to brush up. Learn all the expletives and hate words. If there's any more bonfires please do your best to get all of my books included. I'll give you copies for that purpose—I don't suppose there are any in Germany. The advertisement would do me good. By the way I never thought of you as a diplomat—a man who, when he means yes says no, when he means no says perhaps, & when he means perhaps says yes. Different from a woman who says perhaps when she means no, no when she means perhaps, and yes when she means no. I bet you are all three as proud as seven peacocks.

> Love to all,
> Carl Becker

1. Dodd Papers, LC.
2. On June 8, 1933, Roosevelt appointed Dodd ambassador to Germany.
3. Philip Schuyler Allen (1871–1937), professor of German at Chicago (1903–1937).

To Florence Mishnun Yohalem

Ithaca, [summer 1933][1]

Dear Florence,[2]

Your letter was posted by someone, since I received it. But I was glad to have the supplement too. Being in a hospital would be rather terrible if there were not compensation: and the compensation is that (1) one ceases to be responsible for anything, e.g. bills, the furnace, the ice box, etc.—, and (2) one is in some small way the center of attention—one is perhaps "an interesting case." This feeling of importance lasts as long as anyone will listen to a description of your case & what was done about it. When people begin to put on that bored look, you know that it's all washed up—the distinction is over. You see I've been through this, so I can sympathize with you & understand your feeling of deflation. However, there's always the Revolution, you know. Think of that—be cheerful.

> Ever sincerely,
> Carl Becker

1. FMY.
2. Yohalem (1904———) received her B.A. at Cornell (1925); she worked on the *Encyclopedia of the Social Sciences* (1929–1934), for the Social Security Board in Washington, D.C., and for the U.S. Department of Labor as a research economist (1942–1969).

To Livingston Farrand

New York, New York, July 15, 1933[1]

Dear Mr. Farrand,

I thought you might be interested to know that Dr. Holland has found my case sufficiently "interesting" (which means difficult I suppose) to keep in touch with it during the summer. The general result of the examination was much the same as at Clifton,—nothing organically or radically wrong with me. But Dr. Holland is more definite in ascribing the trouble to what they call a "loup" or "pouch" in the small intestine: the loup being caused by "adhesions." The pains are the result of 'tensions': as I understand this, it means a pull on the adhesions which excites the nerves of the abdominal wall. The pain is thus not dangerous at all, only uncomfortable. Holland is treating it by special diet and medication. But he spoke of an operation as a last resort. Said he had recently had a case like mine, which was cleared up by a slight operation which consisted in sniping a few of the adhesions. He thinks, or says, he does not believe an operation will be necessary. Until day before yesterday I have had a good deal of distress; but yesterday & today there have been no pains, & I begin to feel like a human being once more; which is good for me, & for those who have to live with me.

Sincerely,
Carl Becker

P.S. Considering what they did for me, & the bill I received, I feel like a dead beat. But after all I won't have much difficulty in getting over that.

1. Farrand Papers, CU.

To Mary Elizabeth Bohannon

New York, New York, July 25, 1933[1]

My dear Betty,

It was really very nice of you to write me such a long letter of impressions; and I am delighted to learn that you are finding everything as glamorous as you hoped. I never was abroad but once, and then late in life, when nothing could any longer be as glamorous as it should have been & would have been in my youth. As you say, everything was just as I had pictured it, so much so that it seemed as if I must have been there—in London, Paris—many times before. Still I enjoyed it—London especially. And Edinburg. You really ought to see Edinburg (but not Glasgow); it's a romantic place out of Scott's novels.[2]

I just had a letter from Crump[3]—one of his inimitable letters. I think he is the most interesting writer of letters I know; and I merely reply without any possibility of keeping my end up just to get another. Give them my love when you see them. I hope his health is better, or at least not worse.

I was in the NY Hospital two weeks: and their verdict, on the negative side, was much the same as that of Clifton Springs— nothing serious or organically wrong. But I think Dr. Holland is a bit more definite on the positive side. He locates the difficulty more definitely than the others. Of course he may be wrong. He is keeping in touch with me this summer, & is relying for the present on a strictly regulated diet and some medicines. I have had no real distress since July 13, although I am not very strong. The Summer school goes on easily enough (you know I reel off the same dope as always, so it's no trouble); & the rest of the day I do nothing but rest and pamper myself.

It's a good thing the B. M.[4] is not open longer. It won't then be possible for you to spend all your time there. Much better to run about & enjoy yourself, make friends, and saturate yourself with London and things English, & the English themselves. They're much the nicest people in Europe. They play the game better than anyone else. They're fundamentally honest and pessimistic (but not cynical) & deep down full of sentiment; but rather ashamed of all these qualities which they keep well down underneath a surface of good form. Their 'form' is not either coldness or snobbishness: it's just, as I say, playing the game without parading either their virtues or their vices. I was sure you would like them, and I'm glad you do.

Sincerely yours,
Carl Becker

1. Bohannon Papers, CU.
2. Sir Walter Scott (1771–1832), author of the Waverley Novels.
3. Charles George Crump (1862–1935), clerk in the Public Record Office, London. (1889–1923), editor of literary works, author of *The Logic of History* (London, 1919).
4. British Museum.

6. In Sickness, in Health, and in California, 1933-1935

To George Lincoln Burr

Ithaca, September 12, 1933[1]

Dear Burr,

On returning home, I found your address on liberty four hundred years ago,[2] which I have read with great pleasure. I am afraid we are entering another period in which liberty will be at a discount. The liberty that we prize—liberty of thought—means little or nothing to the mass of the people: & they seem disposed to support any leader or dogma which promises to give them bread and circuses. Bread & circuses are no doubt the first necessity. Perhaps liberty is merely a function of indifference which flourishes in ages of security and plenty. I have been invited to give the West Memorial lectures at Stanford in 1934–35 (3 lectures),—and I have an idea of trying to conjure up something to say about liberalism in the nineteenth century & the difficulties confronting it in recent times. The trouble is I don't know what I think about it—and won't know until I try to set it down on paper.[3]

Very sincerely yours,
Carl Becker

1. Burr Papers, CU.
2. "Liberals and Liberty Four Hundred Years Ago," *Proceedings of the Unitarian Historical Society,* III (1933), 1–21.
3. *Progress and Power* (New York, 1936), lectures given in April 1935.

To Val R. Lorwin

Ithaca, [September 1933][1]

Dear Lorwin,

I was glad to get your [budget?] of news about the job you have. It doesn't sound very fine; but I suppose you didn't expect it to be very fine when you took it. I don't suppose you will have your thesis[2] ready this June,—but perhaps you could get your exams off either this June or in September. Not that there is any great hurry about it, except that it would be a relief to have the business finished. By the way, when you left here you left a box of notes etc. They are in my office, and any time you want them let me know and I will send them on.

I've got a very lively seminary of about 15 people—mostly men. They are not all my majors by any means—the top-notchers from government & other fields of history come in to listen & take part in the confabs that go on. We discuss anything almost—except history as it is understood. I read them the paper on Communism—I prepared it for the public lecture at Columbia. I have the copy I read then. If you like I will send you the thing.

I'm working on the World History—i.e. a 200 page sketch of the history of man from the earliest times to the 18 c to take the place of the first 200 pages of Modern History. This is for schools that want to give only one year to European History. I've got the first chapter done—covering the history of Man 494000–6000 B.C.: and am working on the second—civilizations in Egypt, Crete, Mesopotamia, and India 3500–1000 B.C.—while the Greeks were still barbarians. It's rather interesting because I didn't know much about it.[3] I'm also writing a longish article for the *Nation* (if they want it) suggested by the recent correspondence in that journal about the sound doctrine of free speech and whether it should be accorded to Nazies & others who make use of it with the avowed intention of banishing it altogether. I am writing the article mainly to clear up my own ideas on the subject.[4]

Don't let Madge break down her health by working too hard— if it can be avoided,—and take care of yourself.

Sincerely,
Carl Becker

1. CBCU.
2. "Trade Unions in France," Ph.D. dissertation, Cornell, 1953; published as *The French Labor Movement* (Cambridge, Mass., 1954).
3. *Story of Civilization*, with Frederic Duncalf.
4. "Freedom of Speech," *The Nation*, CXXXVIII (Jan. 24, 1934), 94–96.

To Leo Gershoy

Ithaca, October 4, 1933[1]

Dear Leo,

I'm really sorry I neglected to let you know we were staying in New York until Sept 9, in time so that you wouldn't have delayed leaving Ithaca on our account. I hope it didn't interfere seriously with your plans. I'm glad indeed to know you are still on the payroll with a slight increase—is this time & a half for overtime? I'm especially glad you can see your way to a separate domicile—it will be a very good thing for you both.

I don't know how Miss Lorenz [sic] gets the idea I dislike her.[2] I never met her but once or twice, except as I meet all the library staff casually: I didn't dislike her at all. But you know I don't take a great shine to many people. The people I don't especially take to, I expect I treat rather casually. That's partly my country upbringing—I haven't any conventional manners. But it's partly that my mind is so little occupied with disliking people that I hardly ever ask the question—"do I dislike this person? Does this person dislike me?" I rather take it for granted that a person's "all right" whether I particularly take to them or not—and I suppose it doesn't occur to me that a young girl like Miss Lorenz would think it mattered if I liked her or not. However, I don't dislike many people. I'm indifferent to a good many, and I haven't much talent for palaver and putting people at ease.

Frederiksen came in today with an outline for a study of the actual working out of the system of administration under the Constituent—to what extent did the theory of separation of powers work out in practice. Did you put him up to this? I think he's got hold of it very well indeed.[3] He's a good sort in spite of his Y.M.C.A.-ism or whatever it was. I don't know his wife—I hope she doesn't think I dislike her. Lorwin isn't coming back—he has a minimum wage teaching in the extension department of Brooklyn College, which will give him bread (but no circuses) and some time to finish up his thesis.

I seem to be okay so far, except that I have no strength or pep or zest. Still a fellow can just muck along even if he isn't filled with inspiration and the *joie de vivre*. . . .

We all send our very best.

Sincerely,
Carl Becker

1. LIG.
2. Margaret Lorentz (1904–1971), cataloguer in the Cornell University Libraries (1926–1970).
3. Oliver Frederiksen (1894——), received his Ph.D. under Becker (1934) with a dissertation on "The Administrative Work of the Committee of the Constituent Assembly" (of France, 1789–1791).

To the editors of *The Nation*

Ithaca, October 16, 1933[1]

To the Editors of *The Nation*:

I have just read in *The Nation* for September 20 Mr. Villard's article on Sir Edward Grey,[2] the general purport of which I entirely approve. There is no doubt that Grey was made use of by the French from 1905 to 1914, and as a result found himself in a bad hole in August, 1914. It is equally obvious that his statements to the House in reply to queries about England's obligations to France were disingenuous. But I still think you fail to bring out the point on which Grey justified himself. It is this. All the conversations between Grey and Cambon[3] and the written statement prepared in 1912 were based on a supposition. The supposition was that *if* France and Germany found themselves at war, and *if* in that case Great Britain *should* come to the aid of France, then Great Britain could not give France the most effective support unless the military and naval experts had beforehand agreed on the way in which this support could best be given. Thus, for example, Haldane's[4] very efficient preparations for the sending of a British force to Belgium were not undertaken as the result of an agreement that Great Britain *would* support France in a war against Germany, but were undertaken in order that support might be most effective *in case* Great Britain *should* decide to give it.

So far as I know, neither Grey nor any other member of the British Cabinet ever signed any agreement or gave any verbal promise to support France in a war with Germany. In a strict legal sense, or in the sense of an international treaty obligation, Great Britain was not really bound to support France. But there is a little joker in the pack. The naval experts decided that the most effective use of the two navies would be realized if the French navy took over the protection of both British and French interests in the Mediterranean, while the British navy took over the protection of both British and French interests in the North Sea. Now as a matter of fact the two navies were so disposed just before the war broke out that when France found herself at war with Germany her north coast was unguarded against the German navy except by the British fleet. Did this create an obligation? Grey evidently thought so, and the Cabinet apparently agreed with him, since the Cabinet promised France on August 2 (at any rate before the British were at war with Germany) that if the Germans attacked the French coast the British navy would resist them. This was before Parliament had declared war. This promise was sufficient, if carried out, to involve Great Britain in a war with Germany whatever Parliament did. The whole business reminds me of scholastic discussions tending to prove that God is three in one, or the Jesuit casuistry of the seventeenth century designed to enable confessors to absolve the best people from sins whatever their intentions were.

I believe that Grey was never shrewd enough to know quite where his acts were leading him. It was his muddleheadedness, rather than any deliberate purpose, that got him into the hole he was in in 1914.

Carl Becker

1. *The Nation,* CXXXVII (Nov. 1, 1933), 510–511.

2. Grey (1862–1933) was British foreign secretary (1905–1916), and chancellor of Oxford University (1928–1933).

3. Pierre Paul Cambon (1843–1924), French ambassador to Britain (1898–1920). In November 1912 he exchanged with Grey a set of letters concerning military cooperation in the event of war.

4. Richard Burdon Haldane (1856–1928), Secretary of State for War (1905–1912) and Lord Chancellor of Britain (1912–1915).

To Leo Gershoy

Ithaca, October 30, 1933[1]

Dear Gershoy,

I and Conyers Read are arranging a session at the A. H. A. meeting at Urbana on historiography; and would like you to read a paper (about 20 minutes) if you can. The idea is to deal with history, not as a list of historians to be estimated in terms of some standard of excellence, but to deal with the ideas of history at any time as part of, and influenced by, the general preconceptions & ideas of that time. We have J. W. Swain[2] who will write a paper on Gibbon; Marcham, who will do something on the 17 Century. If you could do something on the 18 or 19 Centuries that would fill our bill admirably. Taine, whom you know something about, would be a good subject. One could show how the "new sciences" influenced him, also how the 19 Century aversion to the 18 Century philosophy of natural rights & Reason influenced him. But I don't need to select a subject for you, still less to tell you how to treat it. The question is whether you want to go to Urbana & read such a paper. I should like to know as soon as possible because the program committee is calling for names, etc.

Sincerely yours,
Carl Becker

1. LIG.
2. Joseph W. Swain (1891——) taught ancient history at Illinois (1919–1960). He specialized in ancient imperialism, early Christianity, and historiography.

To F. S. Rodkey

Ithaca, [November 1933][1]

Dear Rodkey,[2]

I don't think your article is very "radical." But what if it were? I wouldn't bother to ask that question. In so far as you are concerned with the question of whether your ideas are too radical or too conservative, you are letting your mind wander from the essential point, which is whether they are true or false, valid or invalid. I think in fact your ideas are very sound. They are apparently: (1) that the changes that may be necessary and that will be practicable depend upon a certain heritage which is vastly different than that of Russia; (2) that the objective of the Communist ideology, whatever may be said of its practice in Russia, is a more equalitarian & democratic society; (3) that this ideology is not essentially different from our own democratic ideology; (4) that therefore it should be possible for us to achieve that objective without resort to the violent revolutionary methods that have been applied in Russia.

This is all very good. I think, however, you have made it rather heavy reading and not as clear as you might by building your exposition around a clumsy academic terminology—*Dialectic Materialism*, "Mechanistic determinism" and the like. Also by some rather involved and slow-moving sentences. I don't know for whom this paper is intended; but it won't mean very much to the average person. You mention presenting such a point of view to the "man on the street." For him it would have to be put much simpler. And the less said about Russia and dialectic materialism the better. We might very well in 25 years or so come out with a regulated economy not very different from that which may prevail in Russia then. But if we do it will have to avoid carefully the Communist terminology & invent a new one. In fact we are already doing it. *National Industrial Recovery Act:* What could be more American or less alarming. These are all familiar words, saturated with American feeling. But Soviet, Communism, Marxism, Bolshevism, Dialectic Materialism—these words will not go down.

Professors are apt to be convinced, naturally enough, that great social changes can be brought about by deliberation & rational reflection. This is a great mistake. The average person—& this means 90%—cannot think at all in general terms. He can think pretty sensibly about specific concrete matters that touch him personally. It is the pressure of economic distress that alone has made it possible even to attempt anything that looks in the direction of a nationally planned or supervised economy. And such support as this attempt has had has been elicited, not because people understand intellectually what is being done or attempted, but because their emotions & their hopes have been mobilized. The N R A has been put over, in so far as it has been, in the same way precisely as the war was put over—that is, by appealing to people's "loyalty," by getting them to feel that they must "stand back of" the President, & that to criticize or question (that is to deliberate rationally & try to get at the merits of the scheme) is to be a "reactionary," a "Tory," etc. People can understand and enjoy a boycott much better than an argument.

Well, I think the N.R.A. is good if it is a beginning; but if it is to be only a beginning it is no good. We will have to go much farther in regulating our industrial system if we are to avoid worse things. The crux of the matter is *profits*. What is to be done with profits that machines pile up & now place in the control of a few private persons. These have got to be distributed, not directly but indirectly, in such a way as to enable the man of the people to buy what is essential. Even the capitalist himself ought to be intelligent enough to see that there is no use making millions of motor cars, even with the latest radiator caps, unless people have money in their pocket to buy them. How this management of profits is to be effected I don't know, but it can only be done from the point of view of the social interest. It won't do any longer to leave it to a few private gamblers & guessors. I hope we can do it without suppression of the traditional right of discussion & criticism. If we can't we shall have lost the best thing we have; & in the long run I think it will never be done successfully by choking off all ideas except those that square with an established & official dogma.

Sincerely
Carl Becker

1. *DWH*, 82–84.
2. Frederick S. Rodkey (1896———) taught history at Miami University (1921–1929) and at Illinois (1929–1958), specializing in eastern European history. He had been an undergraduate student of CLB's at Kansas (1914–1916), and in 1933 sent an article (later privately published as "An Historical Approach to the World Problems of Today") to CLB for criticism, wondering whether perhaps his article was too radical.

To Ida and Leo Gershoy

Ithaca, December 9, 1933[1]

Dear Ida,

I am delighted to know that you and Leo have at last realized the old dream of an apartment in New York. Now, in the intervals of scouring pots, you can get on with the writing of your thriller. You see I never forget important things like that, and I still confidently expect to have the Ms. laid before me for comment and admiration. You don't know that I am an authority on literary art. You couldn't know it, because it is only recently that I have become one. The evidence of it, which I will show you when you come to Ithaca, is a little purple ribbon that I am permitted to wear in my buttonhole, a ribbon given to me by the Academy of Arts and Letters. You see the significance of the little ribbon is that whenever you meet a person with the ribbon you know he, or she, is an artist: except for the ribbon you wouldn't know it. So you must be prepared to do me honor when you see the ribbon. And please tell

Dear Leo,

I am not going to Urbana. It's too far, and too expensive in time and money. Besides, I will be better off at home. I suppose you are going by the N.Y. Central in order to stop at Rochester. Otherwise of course you could take the Lehigh. I hope you will be able to stop here one way or another, and please let me know so that we can meet you. We have a room for you here. You had better write the Taine before you know too much. That's what I always do.

Sincerely,
Carl Becker

1. LIG.

To Leo Gershoy

Ithaca, December 20, 1933[1]

Dear Gershoy,

We will be expecting you on January 1, by one or the other trains. If possible please let us know which one, so that we can meet you.

I try to recall all my past actions, & fail to see what I have done for you and Ida except to mention now and then that you are both good fellows. I recommend you for the summer job, and Jordan[2] gladly accepts my suggestion because he is convinced that you do an exceptionally good job of teaching, and he is convinced of that because students, graduate & undergraduate, spread the good news about. That is all there is to it. If either of you imagine that maybe I accept the Columbia offers in order to make a place for you here, you are imagining a vain thing. You simply don't know me—I'm far too selfish to put myself out to any such tune as that. So neither of you need trudge around with a great packet of gratitude strapped to your backs. My famous pupils (some of them) idealize me more than is reasonable. I don't go so far as to charge them with "respecting" me; but they come very near it: love me if you can, but don't dare respect me or harbor gratitude. I have tacked up in my office the following.[3]

> "Hway gives me no assistance.
> There is nothing that I say,
> in which he does not delight."
> Confucius,
> Analects, XI. 3

Hway was a 'disciple.' Bernard Faÿ says I have few disciples.[4] I refuse to have any. You and Ida are not my disciples. You are my very dear friends, and I am your very humble, Obedient Servant,

Carl Becker

1. LIG.
2. Riverda H. Jordan (1873–1950), professor of education at Cornell (1921–1941), and director of the summer session (1924–1934).
3. CLB included this maxim in *Everyman His Own Historian* as part of the dedication to his former students.
4. Faÿ (1893———), French historian and lecturer, had written: "It is a great but rare pleasure for a European to read from time to time an essay or a book by Carl Becker who, of all contemporary American historians, seems by his detachment, his wisdom, and his profound understanding of his country, to be Turner's most faithful follower. Becker writes little, however, and, though he is a highly esteemed professor, he is training few disciples" ("An Invitation to American Historians," *Harper's Magazine*, CLXVI [Dec. 1932], 30).

To Guy Stanton Ford

Ithaca, January 13, 1934[1]

Dear Ford,

I am glad you liked Lerner's paper. Personally he is pure gold, one of the few people I most delight in, and he has an extraordinarily keen and profound intelligence, besides having a great fund of general knowledge in history, literature, and political philosophy. He was a Brookings Ph.D. in economics, but his main interest is in the history of ideas, especially political and social. He is teaching at Sarah Lawrence school, where his wife (also a Ph.D. from Brookings in economics) teaches literature. He is a born teacher, loves the job, and at the same time is very ambitious to write something very good. If I had a professors job in political science to fill I would jump at the chance to get him, young as he is. A difficulty is that his wife is such a live wire that she has to have a job also (in order to keep her self respect), so it would be difficult to deal with that situation. I don't know how they would work it out, but I know that Max would like a first class place somewhere. I tell you all this so that you will keep him in mind when you see a first class job going. Max is only about thirty years old, looks like a puckish boy, but is really all round the ablest chap I know anywhere round that age.

I was sorry not to be at Urbana, hope to be in Washington next year.

Sincerely yours,
Carl Becker

1. Ford Papers, UM.

To Leo Gershoy

Ithaca, [January 1934][1]

Dear Gershoy,

I have been going over my stuff to see if certain essays and reviews could be grouped in certain more or less together-hanging topics.[2] The result I send you. The last group needs a better name perhaps. It might be called applied psychology, or psychological interpretations. But I don't like the term 'psychology.' But the point is that these are specifically studies in the way in which minds seem to work. I don't suggest that these are the essays that should be published, or that all of them need be included. But on the whole I think these are the best. Some of the shorter ones, as I read them over, seem better than I had recalled. In some ways the one on Victor Hugo, although the subject is not important, is the best writing I ever did.[3] I also like "Labelling the Historians." You might send this on to Gottschalk if you like. The essay on Freedom of Speech will I think be in this weeks Nation.[4] I asked them to send you a copy, not knowing whether you subscribed for the Bumble Bee or not.

Sincerely yours,
Carl Becker

1. LIG.
2. For the volume *Everyman His Own Historian.*
3. "Juliet Drouet and Victor Hugo," in *ibid.*, 256–261.
4. "Freedom of Speech," *The Nation*, CXXXVIII (Jan. 24, 1934), 94–96.

To Val R. Lorwin

Ithaca, [winter 1934?][1]

Dear Lorwin,

I sent today by express the packet of notes I failed to give to the lad who came for your papers. I did not include the paper on Marx, as I said I would, because one or two of my seminary students wanted to read it.[2] I will send it on later.

I read it the other night to the Cosmospolitan Club, & had the honor of having my remarks "interpreted" by a Turk for the benefit of a group of Turks who could not understand English. A little white haired boy of German extraction heatedly objected to an unfriendly allusion in my paper to Hitler: and we had quite a discussion. I had said that Germany was at present a most "depressing spectacle." He said that Hitler was doing just what the Germans wanted, that they liked it. All I could say was that that was what made Germany a "depressing spectacle." However, to me the whole world is rather depressing now. I'm old enough to begin to carp about "the good old days."

Sincerely,
Carl Becker

1. CBCU.
2. "The Marxian Philosophy of History," first published in *Everyman His Own Historian*, 113–131.

To Carl Van Doren

Ithaca, March 9, 1934[1]

Dear Van Doren,

Of course you may include in your anthology "Everyman," or anything else I may have written. It is all very flattering to me. I think you will have no trouble in getting Macmillan's permission, since they have already authorized the republication of the article in a collection of my casual essays which some former students of mine propose, if a publisher can be interested, to print in a small volume. In my opinion "Everyman" is the best thing I have written on that subject, and I am glad you have chosen that one. Your opinion of it gives me much satisfaction, since I have such a high regard for your critical judgment. You will notice that the word "cannot" is throughout printed "can not." This is not my doing: the editor of the *Review*, although himself agreeing that the former is the generally used form, used the latter in deference to the traditional custom of the Review. You may use the form "cannot" if you agree with me that that is now the accepted usage. Maybe it will surprise you (but maybe not) to learn that several persons took the trouble to inform me that the price I set down for twenty tons of coal was excessive, figuring out to something more than $50.00 a ton. They seemed to think it strange that a historian should be as inaccurate as that. I need not tell you that this excessive price was thoroughly intended, and has a certain symbolical significance: it represents the effect of our coal bills upon our emotions when we first see them, and thus reinforces the general thesis of the paper that our prejudices enter in to our reconstruction of past events. It is of no importance, and you can "correct" it if you like. I had a number of "separates" of the address, and if any were left I should be glad to send you two for the purpose of preparing copy.

Sincerely yours,
Carl Becker

1. CBCU.

To Mary Elizabeth Bohannon

Ithaca, March 15, 1934[1]

Dear Betty,

In clearing up my desk I came upon your letter of Oct. 27 and November 19, which I fear I did not answer. If I did, it's all right; & if I didn't this is to say that, in spite of all appearance, I was very glad to get it, & to know that you are having the time of your life. Tell Crump that the poor man who took away the papers is not to be harshly treated, because the notion that documents are sacred is only an academic prejudice after all—a prejudice which those who have reached the age of discretion and philosophic security should divest themselves of. Consider that in the course of time all documents and books & other monuments of human creation will crumble to dust, & the Universe itself will become cold & inert. What price then all our little histories! The Alexandrian library was burnt, and Hitler has begun this useful process in our own time. We should know our history with much greater certainty and less trouble if the documents were fewer. What a blessing that we don't (like the Sumerians) use clay tablets which last forever, but paper & ink that become more and more less durable, so that within 100 years the carbon copies made during the world war will be quite illegible. Meantime, from the point of view of the moment, it will be a good thing for you to finish your book.

Sincerely,

Carl Becker

1. Bohannon Papers, **CU.**

To Leo Gershoy

Ithaca, June 2, 1934[1]

Dear Leo,

We shall be here at least until July 1; and although I should like to have you and Ida here as long as possible before we leave, I would not be so cruel as to suggest that you come before your class reunion is out of the way. Let us know in good time the day you expect to arrive. We want you to stop with us until you find a place to live.

Gottschalk writes that he is turning the Ms. & the project for the essays over to me.[2] Of course I expect to prepare the Ms. & see it through the press: but I should like him to decide on the publisher. I think also that it would be appropriate for him to write a brief preface indicating how & why the project started. If he does not, I will. The idea of reprinting these casual essays is a very flattering compliment to me: and those who are responsible for getting the thing done are not to be allowed to drop out unsung, forever remaining unmentioned, "mute, inglorious Miltons." Your contribution to knowledge, on the gaiety of nations, has to be mentioned at least. I am under such heavy obligations to my former students for their continuing appreciation and good will that if I *had* to pay up I should long since have been bankrupt. Luckily for me, I know you will never demand payment.

How does this here, now, business & professional woman, Ida, who is immersed in editorial & other duties, manage to break away and spend an idle summer in Ithaca? I know how fully occupied she must be, for the reason that never did she have time to send me a copy of the valuable periodical with which she is, or was, connected.[3] I had to borrow a copy from Gussie. Alas, after a life time of naive faith & optimistic endeavor, I am beginning to think that we live in an imperfect world! However, everything is forgiven, and we are all looking forward to seeing the lady who was once described thus: "My God, ain't she a swell dame!"

Sincerely yours,
Carl Becker

1. LIG.
2. *Everyman His Own Historian.*
3. The *Dance Observer.*

To Louis Gottschalk

New York, New York, [summer, 1934][1]

Dear Gottschalk,

Have just seen Crofts,[2] & he wants to get the essays out in October. I have all the essays except, *Everyman his own Historian,* and *The Letters & Memoirs of Madame Roland,* and *The Spirit of '76.* Have you by any chance offprints of these that could be used as copy? Of course the printer will dirty them up a bit, and you may not want your copies used even if you have them. I have copies at home, but no way to get at them. We can no doubt have them photostated from the Review if necessary.

Crofts also wants to put in a picture of me. I don't like this idea at all. It's a cheap kind of thing that is not done ordinarily; but Crofts' idea is that this is a special kind of book got out by my students, & that they would like it. What do you think?

The contract is signed & he evidently wants to get to work at once. I spoke about your idea of some special copies, but he said you had said nothing to him about it. If you want to have them you had better write to Crofts & explain the idea.

Sincerely yours,
Carl Becker

[*Written in the margin alongside the letter*]

The contract provides that the 50.00 to Holt for the F. J. Turner article shall come out of royalties. Was this your understanding?

1. CBCU.
2. Frederick S. Crofts (1883–1951), book publisher (1924–1951).

To Ida Gershoy

New York, New York, July 15, 1934[1]

Dear Ida,

Well, here we are in all our splendor. We ran into the tail end of a terrific hot spell of 14 days, but since a week ago today it has been moderate and enjoyable. Everything serene. We saw *Men in White* yesterday, and liked it. I always like plays better than anything, and can overlook defects with ease. Not that there were many defects in this one—it was really pretty fine.

I don't do anything except the two daily lectures, which trouble me very little. In the afternoons I read detective stories, sleep, take a bath and in the evening we go somewhere or ride about in the breezes. It's a lazy life.

Our home is occupied by some Eyetalian family, so I hear.

We saw the Lerners for an evening, and expect to see the Yohalems this week. We are trying to avoid the distinguished neighbors on our right, & to see as little of our relations as possible. It was nice seeing so much of you & Leo. With love from all,

Carl Becker

1. LIG.

To Ida Gershoy

Ithaca, [September 5, 1934][1]

Dear Ida,

I offer a thousand apologies for not answering your post card, & your invitation to come to Martha's Vineyard. One excuse is that the card got mislaid and I had not remembered your address. Not a very valid excuse, I think; but in any case we couldn't very well have come, much as we all regretted not seeing you and Leo again. However, I recall some plans about all meeting in Washington, D.C. this December. In February we shall probably be sailing from N.Y. for San Francisco, in which happy event we shall certainly see you.

Ithaca is nice & green now, and cool too. We have just returned (Monday night), and I have seen no one except Miss Hartman[2] (Leo's great friend), Gussie (who is always Gussie), and Marcham (who sang both your praises, (and that of your beer)) [sic]. All told, we had a nice vacation in N.Y.C. I did no work at all (except to read a Ms. of a not very good book, for which I received $25.00 (this will pay for the next dinner we all have together—in Washington, perhaps)).

Now I must to work some more—"work for the night is coming."

Ever Sincerely Yours,
Carl Becker

Ask Leo what's the witchazel [sic] in my office desk for?

Note: You are not to buy a copy of the *Essays* when they come out, because I am going to give you a copy, and properly inscribed & signed by yours truly.

1. LIG.
2. Margaret Hartman received an M.A. in history at Cornell (1935).

To the editors of *Time*

Ithaca, September 17, 1934[1]

Sirs:

Thanks for sending me a copy of *Letters*, Aug. 20, in which you published some remarks about me and a picture with my name under it. As Huck Finn said about the book "wrote" by Tom Sawyer, this account tells the truth "mainly," but nevertheless contains some "whoppers." Graduate students may read my *Modern History*, but I feel sure no professor of history would so far forget the decencies as to use a high-school textbook "as a reference work in graduate reading rooms." Thirty years ago it was an ordeal for me to face a class, but it no longer is so. I do not "tremble." On the contrary, nothing is more restful for me or, I should imagine, for the students either, than my lectures in modern history which are given at 3 P.M., a proper hour I have always thought for the siesta. If I cannot be heard beyond the front rows, so much the better, since no one wishes to be disturbed when taking a nap.

I am not opposed to examinations. Examinations are very useful as a means of determining whether a student should have a degree, and a degree is a useful thing to have, although it has little or nothing to do with education. I get a reputation for being opposed to examinations because I insist on attributing to them the value which they have and not the value which they haven't. In any case I am sure I never forgot a scheduled undergraduate examination, although one of my assistants who was charged with holding one once did. I feel very strongly about this, since faithfulness in small obligations is one of the minor virtues I cultivate assiduously in order to compensate for major defects.

Whoever said I referred to Theodore Roosevelt as "my hero" must be mistaken. No man is a hero to the scientific historian who valets him; and in any case if I had a hero it would certainly not be a verbose purveyor of platitudes. By the way, the picture under which you have placed my name is not a picture of me at all. I suspect you got this from a group photograph, taken by a newspaper man, of those who were given honorary degrees at Yale University in 1932. I was in the second row from the front, I think, and the names attributed to all the persons in that row were wrong, owing to the circumstances that the man who took the picture was given the names in the wrong order, which in turn was owing to the circumstance that two Yale professors, for what reason I don't know, were standing in that row as if they too were receiving honorary degrees on that day, which they were not. . . .

All of this reminds me of a story.

One morning a newspaper man remarked to his landlady: "The buckwheat cakes this year are not very good. It's not your fault. The buckwheat is not so good this year on account of the dry weather in August." "Oh, no," the landlady replied. "The buckwheat this year is just like always." The newspaper man then went down to the office and wrote for his paper an article on the current year's buckwheat crop, explaining that it was of inferior quality because of the dry weather in August. Upon returning home in the evening his landlady remarked brightly. "You was right about the buckwheat. I just now read in the paper where it said the buckwheat was spoiled on account of the dry spell in August."

Ten or 20 years hence graduate students will probably still be engaged in "scientific historical research," writing doctor's theses in which every statement of fact is supported by "the testimony of two independent witnesses not self-deceived." Such testimony will no doubt be found, then as now, in the "original sources," and no doubt newspapers will, then as now, be included among the original sources. This is nothing against the newspapers. As a historian I know how difficult it is to find out the truth about anything, and considering the conditions under which newspaper men have to work the wonder is that they get things as straight as they do.

Carl Becker

1. "*Time* magazine used to publish the letters it received separate from the magazine itself. In 1934 one *Time* reader wrote an appreciative letter on Carl Becker, stating that he was an outstanding prose writer and that Becker's high school history book was used "as a reference work in graduate reading rooms." *Time* published the letter, adding to it a picture it mistakenly thought to be Becker and an editorial note. The note explained that Becker was a shy, retiring, but

popular teacher at Cornell University who still 'trembles' when he faces a class and who lectures 'in a voice too weak to fill the room.' Becker, the editor reported, seldom reveals his own opinion on history. 'During a course in European History from 1815 to 1914 he made two comments—1) he referred to Theodore Roosevelt as "my hero"; 2) he admired Bismarck's honesty in admitting how unscrupulously he had altered the Ems telegram.' The editor went on to say that Becker opposed 'such academic restrictions on liberty as roll calls, examinations, required papers'; 'he has been known to forget to give examinations, requires no work at all in his seminars, but gets it nonetheless.' To all of this Becker responded with a letter *Time* published in its *Letters* September 17, 1934." (*DWH*, 160–163).

To Florence Mishnun Yohalem

Ithaca, November 7, 1934[1]

Dear Florence,

A week ago Monday I resumed work (I mean lectures), yesterday I exercised my sovereign power at the polls, and in spite of the strain I am feeling very well so far—better than I did last summer. I am sticking rigidly to the diet, boresome as it is, and hope in that way to keep at least out of bed. Meantime, I am plugging along with the lectures to be given at Stanford next April: it is very slow business because I don't know what it is that I want to say; I have to find out by writing, or trying to.

Millis replied to my note to the effect that there were no openings in his field. Hamilton has not replied at all.[2] Hamilton is no doubt the best bet. Meantime, you can practice the virtues of a good *hausfrau*, and see that Morton's slippers are warmed & ready when he returns from the brutal outside world. I hope he goes to Europe. I hope he makes a name for himself, and a fortune, & that you both live happily ever after as well as before.

With love,

Carl Becker

1. FMY.

2. Walter Millis (1899–1968), author and journalist, was an editorial writer for the *New York Herald Tribune* (1924–1954), and staff member of the Fund for the Republic (1954–1968). Walton Hamilton (1881–1958) taught economics at Amherst (1915–1923) and the Brookings Graduate School (1923–1928), and law at Yale (1928–

1948). In 1934–1935 he was a member of the National Recovery Administration Board.

To Morton Yohalem

Ithaca, [fall or winter, 1934][1]

Dear Morton,

How grand that you and Florence can go to Europe, even if your hands will be filled all the time with legal documents and such. My best wishes go with you both.

I am feeling very well now, and much stronger than last summer. A friend sent me a little grinding machine for extracting the juices from raw vegetables. You feed carrots, celery, cabbage, etc., into a hopper, and turn a crank, and the reprehensible pulp comes out one side, & the delectable juice out of the other. The juices are then mixed with fruit juices & the drink is not distasteful. This is a fine way to get the vitamins & alkaloids that I most need. I think it is a noble discovery.

I may go to Washington for the meeting, but maybe not. It will depend on (1) how well I feel, (2) how much money I have, and (3) how much work I have on hand.

I am writing the Stanford lectures, and one is done: two remain to do, and they require much doing.

We sail for California Feb 9. Panama-Pacific Line.

We all send our best wishes.

Sincerely,
Carl Becker

1. FMY.

To Leo Gershoy

Ithaca, December 14, 1934[1]

Dear Leo,

I have reserved a room at the Mayflower for Dec. 27–28, but I am not sure I shall go. If I go it will be by the Lehigh to Phila., and not through New York. The latter route would not give me the reduction in fare, and I am particularly short of cash on account

(1) of hospital & doctor's bills, and (2) on account of having to pay our boat fares to California before we leave. (There ought to be a reason (3), because three reasons is always the right number for a historian to advance for any statement; but I can't think of any other). I wish the boat line would adopt the installment buying plan. I should certainly like to see you & Ida, and if Ida will cross her heart to die and she be not there, I will do my best to squeeze out the what it takes.

I have read the first batch of page proof, but there is no hope now of getting the book out before January.[2] Blest if some of the stuff doesn't read quite sensibly. In one of the pieces I quoted Dickens to the effect that "the law is a ass." Of course the type setter knew better and sent it back in galley "an ass." I corrected his correction, & back it comes in page proof "an ass." I went to the shop and explained that this was a quote from a guy named Dickens.[3] Let my former brilliant students always remember that the correct form in English is "an ass"—it's a useful phrase, I find.

May you both be forever blessed and happy.

Carl Becker

1. LIG.
2. *Everyman His Own Historian.*
3. From Charles Dickens, *Oliver Twist* (London, 1837), 51; said by Mr. Bumble.

To Merle Curti

Ithaca, January 5, 1935[1]

Dear Curti,

I heard that you were at the Washington meeting, but I didn't catch a sight of you—it was a crowded meeting, & I was there only Thursday afternoon and Friday until 6:10. The *Social Frontier* came to the office today, or at least I got it today, and haven't read your article.[2] I suppose revolutionary principles always disappear after the Revolution is accomplished. This is due to a very simple fact: principles are made to justify revolutions & revolutions are made to obtain something desired; when the revolutionists get what they want they naturally are opposed to being dispossessed by revolutions. This is illustrated by early Christian revolt, Protestant revolt, the political revolutions in the 17–18 century, the Fascist & Hitler revolts, & the Communist revolution in Russia. Russia is now going nationalist and patriotic. Stalin says that "Equality of rewards & possession" is a "bourgeois sentimentalism."

I have been very well lately—better than for years. I have found the proper diet I think—I hope so at least. We are off to California by boat on the 9 of February. I will be at the Huntington Library for a month or two, and will give 3 lectures on the West Foundation at Stanford April 3–5. Back in June.

I will be glad to mention your book to Smith.[3] I should like to see it, but just now I am rushed with many things—writing my lectures, which is a devil of a job.

Sincerely,
Carl Becker

1. Curti Papers, SHSW; misdated Jan. 5, 1934.
2. "Our Revolutionary Tradition," *Social Frontier*, I (Dec. 1934), 10–13.
3. Curti, *The Social Ideas of American Educators* (New York, 1935). Smith, presumably, is Preserved Smith.

To Leo Gershoy

Ithaca, January 6, 1935[1]

Dear Leo,

I had a good time at Washington, but didn't see as much of you as I hoped. It was a crowded meeting, and someone was always wishing to see me about something. I weathered the storm all right, except for a slight cold, which hasn't bothered me at all; and in fact I am better & stronger than I have been for years: it must be the delectable vegetable juices. I am getting a "school girl complection." I know this to be so because I am taking the juice of an orange, rind & all, with carrot juice, which the booklet says will give that "school girl complection"; and I always believe what the book says, as you well know. Ida of course doesn't need to know how to get the school girl complection, so you needn't tell her the recipe: but you may tell her that I was very sorry not [to] see her in Washington.

The proof for the essays is all done, and Crofts has announced the book for January 15; but it won't be out til late in January unless they get busier than they have been. However, they promise it before I leave, which will be about the 6 of February. The boat sails on February 9—Panama Pacific Line, S.S. Virginia. We will see you then, and until then good luck & best wishes to both of you.

Carl Becker

1. LIG.

To Felix Frankfurter

Ithaca, January 10, 1935[1]

Dear Felix,

A thousand thanks for the honor and recognition involved, but there are any number of reasons why I could not accept the Harmsworth professorship even if it were offered to me.[2] The chief one is that I have never taught American history, and really know very little about it in those matters of detail that a teacher has to know at all times. Another reason is that I can't afford it. My standard of living is now up to the point where I can use a shaving stick (25 cents) instead of a shaving cake (ten cents) in a mug; and I don't think any one would be cruel enough to expect me, at my age, to drop down to the old level: I want to enjoy the short time there is before the Revolution comes to expropriate me and my shaving stick. A third reason is that we are all off to California, for a Sabbatical, and in order to give three lectures at Stanford on the West Foundation in April; sailing February 9, Panama Pacific Line, on the S.S. Virginia (and I expect you to be there to say *bon voyage,* if you can't think of anything more original), and I can't make arrangements, for a three or five year stay in England, from remote California.

These are reasons enough. Why don't you take it yourself? I hear that you made a ten-strike at Oxford. You, Sir, are the very person wanted, with your brilliance, your interest in the fate of the world at the present moment, and your unrivaled capacity to charm every one. And that reminds me. Why do we never see anything of each other, considering that the world is so small a place and that we are really next door neighbors? I know why—you are such a man of affairs with your hands always full to overflowing with business and good works and scholarly pursuits, while I am a miserable hermit always sitting behind a door never opened except for a suspicious crack when any one knocks from outside, as old OPPORTUNITY is now doing.

Again accept my thanks, and convey same to any and every misguided person who may have thought that I would be a proper man for the Harmsworth place. What you want is the unusual combination of a perfectly SOUND SCHOLAR and an accomplished PUBLIC PERSON. Am I that person, I ask you? Echo and Felix alike answer, NO!

Very sincerely yours,
Carl Becker

1. CBCU.
2. A visiting professorship at Oxford University.

To Leo Gershoy

Ithaca, January 15, 1935[1]

Dear Leo,

I know of no reason at all for Croft's taking a different attitude towards you than formerly. I doubt if there's anything in it, more than a bit of indigestion on his part, or some other irritation of the moment with which you had nothing to do.

Our plans are for Maude to visit Edith for a few days & to arrive in New York on the 8 of February. Fred and I will be in New York probably from the 5 to the 9th, & he will probably stop with the Lerners in Scarsdale: I also, if they have room, unless there is a bed in your flat where I could sleep for a night or two. If there isn't it's no matter.

A small party would be very nice—but not "in honor" of me or my book. If people like to see me that is all the honor I desire—anything else is merely formal flub-dub. I shall be free so far as I know, so that you can arrange your party at any time that is convenient for those you wish to invite. Don't make it too large. I believe the boat (S.S. Virginia, Panama Pacific Lines) sails on the 9th of February at noon: I mean I believe it sails at noon, I am sure it is the 9th.

I am indeed very well. After I got home I had a cold, but for the first time since the memory of me seemeth not to the contrary it did not distress me at all—I went about my small affairs as usual. If I stop with you Ida will have to have golden carrots & oranges (California Sun Kissed) to grind up in my little Health Mill, which I shall carry with me as a primitive man carries a charmed object. Forget about the Crofts business.

Sincerely,

Carl Becker

I think the Book will not be out before I leave. Your cards are the wrong size, unhappy man! I use 4 × 5½. That's my originality.

1. LIG.

To Val R. Lorwin

Ithaca, [January 1935][1]

Dear Lorwin,

Don't disparage poor Taft[2] too much. Think what it would be like to edit the papers of U. S. Grant, J. A. Garfield, G. Harding, or Coolidge. The list could be extended—backwards. It is not strange that Presidents are not always exceptional men; it is strange that there have been as many as there have been who are exceptional. Consider two facts: (1) the fact that presidents are chosen by politicians for the purpose of getting votes from the people; (2) that our electoral system makes it necessary to choose them from that particular state that is of a strategic importance because it may go to either party. How long has it been since we have had a citizen of Pa. for president? And why is that? The ablest man, intellectually, that has been prominent in the Republican party in my time is Elihu Root.[3] He could not be president, because he often said something. You don't expect to see water rise above its source; why do you always expect political talent to do so. You ought to abandon this devotion to magic.

I am more concerned about your eyes than about your disillusionment about Taft. Have you had them examined by an occulist that knows something besides the mechanisms of optics? You probably need an occulist who is also a physician, and understands that there may be [remote?] physical or psychical causes of weak eyes. However, they cost money, it is true; but eyes are of primary importance to you.

We are leaving for California, the home of sun-kissed oranges, on Feb. 9,—and will be in Pasadena for a month, possibly longer. The Huntington Library, San Marino, California, will reach me.

My regards to Madge, and both of you be merry if possible, & not worry about the sad state of the world more than is necessary to squeeze something out of it for yourselves.

Sincerely,
Carl Becker

1. CBCU.

2. William Howard Taft (1857–1930), President of the United States (1909–1913), and Chief Justice of the United States (1921–1930).

3. Root (1845–1937) was Secretary of War (1899–1904), Secretary of State (1905–1909), U.S. Senator from New York (1909–1915).

To Ida Gershoy

Ithaca, January 30, 1935[1]

Dear Ida,

The Brevoort! All my recollections tell me that this is far too swell for the likes of me. It costs too much and would make me feel inferior. There must be some more moderate, dingy, humble place where I could feel that I belong to the exploiting, capitalist classes, and that is a pleasant feeling.

However, I will be coming on the Diamond,[2] on Monday, the 4th, arriving about 8 P.M.: and will come at once to your place, and then we can fight it out about the Brevoort. I told you you were not to feel a wretch. You may be one, and since we have been cautioned to withhold judgment of a man until he is dead, I reserve my opinion. But my whole philosophy is that although we are all manifestly miserable sinners, we are *not* to feel that we are sinners: we are sinners in the sight of God, which is quite enough without being sinners in our own sight. I am not God, & so you are not a wretch.

Monday, the 4th then. Maude will be in N.Y. on the 8th. She says to have our party before she arrives, & then on the 8th we can have a dinner all by ourselves and with the Lerners if they are available. This dinner is on me, and not at the Brevoort!

As ever,
Carl Becker

1. LIG.
2. "The Black Diamond," a Lehigh Valley train connecting New York City and Buffalo.

To Ida Gershoy

On board S.S. Virginia, [February 1935][1]

Dear Ida,

Yesterday we sat on deck without rugs or coats: today some palm beach suits have appeared: as for the Professor, he has not ventured to do more than to change from red woolen underwear into cotton. It is all very pleasant and restful. Fred has picked up two young married women—but is not enthusiastic. I am working on my lectures in the morning, but not very furiously. We are now approaching the Florida coast, although it is not yet (3 P.M.) visible. Tomorrow at 9 A.M. we are expected to be in Havana, leaving at 8 P.M. Excursions are arranged in parties of 6 or 7, to drive about & see the sights. In the afternoon we shall probably walk about seeing what appears interesting. I have proposed—with my usual inconsistency—to go to the Casino but not to gamble: I can do with vicarious experience. My grinder is in the kitchen, & I get my glass of vegetable cocktail for lunch & dinner: the food is marvelous. There appear to be few interesting people aboard. If you & Leo were here it would be more pleasanter yet already. I threw you a penny as part payment on the 20 cents, but Anita got it of course.

Thanks for everything: we had a grand time in New York.

Sincerely,
Carl Becker

Maude & Fred send their best.

1. LIG.

To Leo and Ida Gershoy

Los Angeles, California, March 4, 1935[1]
Dear Ida and Leo,

We have acquired a Super-Hubert—5 passenger Essex Sedan—Model 1928 (or maybe 1929)—horse power 2—speed 35 m.p.h.—pickup O. We went over to Santa Monica on the ocean. Once we passed another car. So you see!

The latest example of delicate California sensibility. A lady recently died, and as a novel and gracious attention her cherished automobile was towed behind the hearse that carried her to the cemetary. *Quelle sentiment!*

Sincerely,
Carl Becker

P.S. oranges
     carrots   } very cheap here

1. LIG.

To Leo Gershoy

Pasadena, California, March 16, 1935[1]
Dear Leo,

There's nothing to say about your poor mother, except that it's better now as it is, and that I'm sorry that you've had all this to distress you. Nevertheless, time passes & all things with it, which is a blessing after all.

I'm doing my daily out at the Huntington Library, and don't care much for it. It's a kind of monastic place, & the revered memory of the great & good man Mr. Huntingtin hangs heavy upon it.[2] There are very few people there—one or two or three permanent researchers, the others temporary. Virtually all English Lit people—a couple of dessicated females, and half a dozen men, none of whom, except two, are more than ordinary. It's a show place, with magnificent grounds and an art gallery in the old house—some very good Reynolds & Gainsboroughs in it. The prize is "The Blue Boy."[3] People come in crowds every day it is open to the public. Poor Farrand[4] is between his researchers & the outside world, & his business is to find reasons to give to his trustees & others for spending money for "research in the Humanities." We had a conference on this the other day, in which all the good old reasons were brought out. It seems that we researchers are "preserving civilization"—did you know that?

Love to Ida from all.

Carl Becker

We will be going to Palo Alto about April 1.

1. LIG.
2. Henry E. Huntingtin (1850–1927), lumberman, railway official, and corporation director, owned one of the finest private collections of English literature and Americana, for which he endowed a library and gallery in San Marino, California.
3. Sir Joshua Reynolds (1723–1792), portrait painter; Thomas Gainsborough (1727–1788), painter of "The Blue Boy."
4. Max Farrand, brother of Livingston Farrand, president of Cornell.

To Gussie E. Gaskill

Palo Alto, California, April 13, 1935[1]

Dear Gussie,

I have been so occupied in finishing up my lectures that I haven't been able to do any thing else much, and so your letter gets set aside from day to day. We came up here about the first of April, and have a comfortable bungalo of six rooms, all for what in Ithaca would be regarded as a nominal sum—$45.00 per month. Every thing here is relatively cheap, and everyone who has anything to sell is overwhelmingly attentive. The climate has rather let them down, since it has been raining off and on and remains chilly after the rainy cool season should, they say, be over. However, it is all very satisfactory to me: I have only to think what it might very well be in Ithaca. I should like to take the California climate back home with me (except that I might keep some rain for the summer), but there is not much else that I should wish to take—unless the oranges & grapefruit and celery. We bought a second hand Essex in Pasadena, model 1928, for $95.00, and it is serving us faithfully. True, it won't go more than 35 miles an hour, it has no pick up, & its horsepower must be about 10; but the great thing is that it never fails to go. The Gershoys call their car Hubert, & so we call ours Super-Hubert, ours being a five passenger sedan. I never saw so many second hand cars for sale as in Pasadena and round about. They stand in rows on every street corner nearly—thousands of them, many looking almost new. I don't know how they manage to sell them, but at any rate they offer cash for used cars. We hope to sell ours again for $50.00.

I didn't see the man you mentioned around the Huntington Library; and I don't think he could have been there, since there aren't many people any way, and I had every chance to see every one. It's a rather curious place—a curious atmosphere: a cross between a monastic retreat for scholarly minds and a private estate opened to the public on special days. If you are a part of it you have to lower your voice in awe when mentioning Mr. Huntington. It's somewhat the attitude that Mr. Burr has for Andrew D. White. However, it is a fine place for any one who is interested in English literature in the Elizabethan times, or in certain aspects of American history. Its weakness of course is that it has no adequate collection of the tools & [authorities?] that scholars in any field are always using.

I expect we shall hang around here until we return (S.S. Virginia, May 25), taking trips on the side. We are going to the big redwood country, & such other places as we can reach with Super-Hubert. I have been asked to talk to the graduate history students in Stanford & at Berkeley, and to give an address before the Oakland forum on the "Situation in Europe." The two former invitations I have accepted, but the latter not. Damn the situation in Europe, and I don't know anything about it anyway.

We expect to arrive in New York about the 9–10 of June. Give my regards to Willis & anyone else handy.

Faithfully,
Carl Becker

1. GEG.

To Anita M. Lerner

Palo Alto, April 13, 1935[1]

Dear Anita,

I got your letter a long time ago, so that it is now all deciphered. I wish you didn't live on trains all the time. You see we have moved to Palo Alto, where we shall probably remain (as headquarters) until our return, which will be by S.S. Virginia, Panama Pacific Line, arriving New York about 15–16 June. The bright & glamorous prospect of a trip to Hawai [sic] is clouded, since it costs too much: but we shall go up to the big red wood country & whatever other places we can conveniently reach with our car, which is an Essex, 1928, that we bought in Pasadena for $95.00. The Gershoys have a two seater which they call "Hubert" for some reason: we call ours "Super-Hubert," since it is a five passenger. It goes 35 an hour, has a horsepower of about 5, and no pick-up. Still, we passed a car once, and the great thing is that it always goes. In short, a poor thing, but mine own. We hope to sell it for $50.00. This is a pretty desperately hard up community especially round Los Angeles— and you wouldn't wonder if you could see the great stretches of country all laid out in building blocks, with cement sidewalks and macadam roads (and of course water & gas pipes underground), and no houses. I never saw so many used cars for sale—every garage & every street corner, nearly, in Pasadena, Hollywood, etc. filled with them—mostly pretty new ones. They say ⅓ of the population round Los Angeles is on the relief list. Of course you can live out here much more cheaply. We have a six room bungalo, comfortable enough, for 45 a month—and food is cheap (except meat, I suppose, we don't buy any, since we take all our meals except breakfast out). There's an excellent restaurant down the road that gives you a swell French dinner for 65 cents—What Amos and Andy call "Horses Doves," Soup, fruit salad, broiled chicken, vegetables, salad bowl, dessert & coffee—*and* a bucket of swell French bread.

The climate is not quite up to snuff—since it rains a good deal after the rainy season should be over (so they say!). But it's all very nice to my way of thinking. The flowers are blooming and oranges (down in Pasadena, not up here) ripening on the trees.

I have been working like a slave on my lectures—a terrific job: but I see the end now—and a good thing too, since they have to be given April 23–5.

I read about a riot in Harlem. Did Max go down there to live, or was it caused by something else.

Presently we are going to explore China town in San Francisco, and we hope to pick up a toy or a Joss stick[2] for the Lerners; may their shadow never grow less!

All send love,
Carl Becker

1. AML.
2. A thin stick of fragrant tinder mixed with clay, used by the Chinese as incense.

To Elias R. B. Willis

Carmel-by-the-Sea, California, May 3, 1935[1]

Dear Willis,

We are down here for a week at the principal seaside beach in this part of the country. It is a very nice beach—about the cleanest sand I've seen; and very nice hilly, wooded country rising up from the sea. Bright sun and not too cold for lying on the beach, but a little too cold for much bathing, although a few people do go out. It never really gets warm enough on this coast unless you are a cold-blooded fish. There's a very attractive 17 mile drive along the coast, and a couple of "seal rocks"—rocks where seals congregate. They are interesting creatures—their barking is quite human.

The lectures went off O.K. as far as I could judge. I shall put them aside for a few months, and then get them in shape to print.[2] Everything considered, it's been a very pleasant go all round. I've talked to the grad students at Berkeley and will do so at Stanford this coming week. I think the hard times have made quite a dent on the young instructors and grad students in both institutions—they both appear jarred out of their complacency, & quite as alert and "advanced" as the Cornell bunch. The older professors of course appear not to know that anything has happened since 1914.

We are going up into the big redwood country the latter part of next week I think; and then home, arriving in New York on the S.S. Virginia about June 10. Health is O.K.

Sincerely,
Becker

    1. CBCU.
    2. *Progress and Power.*

To Ida Gershoy

Palo Alto, May 5, 1935[1]

Dear Ida,

I have been a long time answering your letter, but I have been busy revising the last chapter of Modern History. This I have now finished, and for a few weeks I expect to be a man of immense leisure. Last week we spent at Carmel, a very attractive seaside place, with a very fine beach—which is a rare thing on the west coast. The weather was fine and invigorating, warm enough to lie on the beach, but rather too cold for bathing although Fred did go in once for about 60 seconds.

We picked up a little souvenir for you, which will arrive shortly. You had better take the felt off the bottom (it's half off already) and replace it with thin rubber so that the things won't slip so easily. They are made of something that grows as a parasite on the big redwood trees.

I feel honored by your indignations with Crofts. But why so hot, little children! The book is of slight importance in the general scheme of things, and of course Crofts can't be expected to advertise it much since it will have only a limited sale, and I expect he is reaching most of the people who are likely to buy it with the leaflets he has sent out. Wilbur wrote me that they were troubled by the delay in getting reviews out. I don't know to what journals they have sent it. But there is a review in the Nation by Elisio Vivas, a philosopher in the U. of Wisconsin:[2] a pointed and intelligent review, which is something rare enough. So, patience!

The lectures seemed to go off well enough—about 500 people, and they kept coming, which is something. Now I will put them aside for a few months, so that I can get an objective view of them. They will need to be gone over, and elaborated a little for the press. Probably they will be published by the Stanford Press. I am having some copies made of them as they stand, and I am going to send one copy to you & Leo, if you will promise, hand on heart, to give me your quite unprejudiced critical opinion. Not to praise, but, if necessary, to bury Caesar is what I want. You must renounce all friendship for the time being, or rather you must bring real friendship to the test by just being the good intelligent impersonal critics you know how to be when other people's writings are concerned.

Probably I will bring the copy along with me and give it to you when we arrive in New York. We will sail on the same boat (SS Virginia, Pan American Line) May 25 and are due to arrive in N.Y. June 10, which I think is a Monday.

We will be seeing you then. We all send our loves.

Sincerely,
Carl Becker

1. LIG.
2. Eliseo Vivas (1901——) taught philosophy at Wisconsin (1935–1944), Chicago (1944–1947), Ohio State (1947–1951), and Northwestern (1951——).

To Anita M. Lerner

Ithaca, [July 26, 1935][1]

Anita, darling,

You are instructed to make secret and confidential inquiries into the activities of a fella named Max. The circumstances are these: about a month ago I sent to him a MS entitled, *Progress & Power*, with a request that he read it and give me his honest opinion of it. What you are to find out is whether he has so far wasted his time as to read this MS and so far stultified his intelligence as to form an opinion of it. You are to keep this inquiry dark, under your hat, on the q.t., as the saying is, etc. The kind of gumshoe business that is expected of a detective employed by a man to find out about the goings on of his wife. And report to me without disturbing his meditations.

It's pretty hot here, but hotter in N.Y. I expect. Did you know we were in a great flood?[2] And were caught out in the country & had to stay all night at a farm house (but there wasn't any farmer's daughter!)? Well, we were. Adventure!

Ever yours,
Carl Becker

1. AML.
2. During a twenty-four hour period, July 7-8, 1935, 7.9 inches of rain fell in Tompkins County.

To Leo and Ida Gershoy

Ithaca, August 24, 1935[1]

Dear $\left\{ \begin{array}{l} \text{Leo and Ida} \\ \\ \text{Ida and Leo} \end{array} \right\}$

I have here done my best to maintain an impartial attitude. Each one takes precedence of the other in turn, although Ida's precedence occurs on the lower level, which seems right because after all is said and done "the sex" ought to be kept in a slightly inferior position.

Anyhow it was ever so nice to get your two letters, and still nicer to know that you have had a splendid time. In spite of all the sly innuendoe, I can still see that. I hoped you would be driving up to Ithaca, but I see you won't return soon enough for that. Anyhow, we expect to be somewhere on the Jersey coast for the first three weeks in September. On our way home we might stop in N.Y. I don't know whether we will or not. I should like to see you—you can take that as a permanent state of mind.

I have had a couple of letters from Crump. They were delighted with your visits, and Crump almost apologized to me for being too old & feeble to be as entertaining as he ought to be to visitors from the U.S.A. I expect he is pretty feeble, but he still writes the most deliciously humorous letters. They are both very wonderful people I think, and I'm glad you liked them. Laski of course is Laski.[2]

Poor Hull is also very feeble—it's a kind of a sad duty now to see him. Burr returned from California on the buss [sic], had a heart attack on the bus, and another after he arrived home. He is now in Philadelphia near the Lea Library working on the introduction to the Lea book on Witchcraft.[3] He said it would be better in Philadelphia for him since it wasn't so hilly: so he now lives in a dormitory room on the third floor (no elevator) still it's true that Phila. is not so hilly as Ithaca. He fears his mind is weakening, and is very cheerful & stoic about it.

Dreadfully hot here. It's pulled me down a little, but otherwise I'm O.K. If you see Laistner[4] you might tell him that he missed seeing Lois Gibbons (Good God!) who was here. She has a job at the Woman's College in Oxford, Ohio.

Cheers, most frightfully, too.

Carl Becker

1. LIG.
2. Harold J. Laski (1893–1950), professor of political science at the University of London (1920–1950).
3. Henry Charles Lea, *Materials toward a History of Witchcraft . . .* , with an introduction by George Lincoln Burr (3 vols; Philadelphia, 1939).
4. Max L. W. Laistner (1890–1959) taught ancient history at the University of London (1921–1925) and Cornell (1925–1959).

To Max Lerner

Ithaca, October 5, 1935[1]

Dear Max,

I was very much disappointed not to have seen you again. I had dinner with the Gershoy's at a restaurant, after which we were at their apartment until eleven: we must have got back after you telephoned. I wish you lived around the corner so that I could talk to you whenever I needed to—or didn't need to. I need to very often because you always have some fresh information or point of view that keeps me from intellectual hardening of the arteries. Just now I need you because I have taken up the ms. on *Progress and Power* in order to prepare it for the press. I confess it reads better than I expected it would, so that I am not as reluctant to publish it as I was. But I have always realized that the last part of the third lecture—the end of the third section particularly—needs revising. It is too much foreshortened, and the last paragraphs of the third section take on the character of a discussion of current issues, which is not in harmony with the aloof view of human activities from Mt. Olympus. What needs to be added I think is some elaboration of the point I have briefly suggested—viz. that there is a great gap between the intellectual levels of apprehension, as I have put it, that is between the matter-of-fact apprehension of the few (scientists, technologists, etc.) and the apprehension of the many who still live on the level of primitive fears and tabus. This is of course the sociologists famous "cultural lag." The difficulty is that the thing as written is *set* like a concrete structure, and it is the devil and all to break down a wall and enlarge it. This is why I am very much in need of whatever general or detailed comments you have made or wish to make about the thing as a whole. I know you are terribly busy, and it is an imposition to burden you still more; but I should really appreciate whatever comments you wish to make as soon as you can conveniently send them to me. The ms., as I said, you can send to Leo Gershoy, 44 West 12 St. . . .

> Ever faithfully yours,
> Carl Becker

1. Max Lerner Papers, Yale University Library.

To Merle Curti

Ithaca, October 12, 1935[1]

Dear Curti,

Thanks very much for your very friendly review of my essays. I liked your mentioning the fact that I have injected a little psychology into my writings. It's the thing I've definitely tried to do, but not many historians seem to notice it, for the reason, I suppose, that I make no use of technical jargon. Harry Barnes has several times referred to me as one of the "new historians"; but I never could find that he understood very well why I was one—from his point of view: I don't claim to be "new" or old or anything that a label can be attached to. You might have said more, you know, in the way of adverse criticism—cultivating my garden, always ending in a sterile skepticism, etc.

Very sincerely,
Carl Becker

1. Curti Papers, SHSW.

7. "A Well Known Communistic Writer," 1935-1939

To Isaiah Bowman

Ithaca, November 8, 1935[1]

Dear Bowman,[2]

Greenfield[3] has written me about your inquiry into the activities in Washington respecting Communistic teaching in the schools, and the effort to exclude my book *Modern History*. I wish to express my great appreciation for your willingness to take the time and trouble you have about it. The information you gathered is encouraging, and is confirmed by what my publishers also have found out. The school authorities are evidently fighting for independence from political & patrioteer interference, and they need all the support they can get. Personally I don't care what these people think of me or my writings.

As I should be in Baltimore for a short visit in late January, I hope to see you again at that time.

Sincerely yours,
Carl Becker

1. Isaiah Bowman Papers, The Johns Hopkins University Library.
2. Bowman (1878–1950) was director of the American Geographical Society (1915–1935) and president of Johns Hopkins (1935–1949).
3. Kent Roberts Greenfield (1893–1967), professor of modern European history at Johns Hopkins (1930–1946), Chief Historian for the U.S. Department of the Army (1946–1958).

To W. Stull Holt

Ithaca, November 11, 1935[1]

Dear Holt,

I ought to apologize very abjectly for having forgotten my correspondence with you and Greenfield last June. I must be getting old, since I don't recall ever before having forgotten anything as complimentary as that to me. However, your mentioning it did recall it to my mind, and today in going over the correspondence the details came back to me. The precise time was not fixed, except that I suggested the latter part of January. I could manage a week and possibly ten days before and during our examination period at the close of the first term. I don't know if I mentioned any topics for the two public lectures. I have thought I might talk about the general conditions that have conditioned the general wars in Europe during the last 300 years, and the movement towards internationalism & peace during the same time. The general title might be, "War and Peace in Europe in Modern Times," and the individual titles, (1) "The Conditions of War," and (2) "The Traditions of Peace." The precise wording could be determined later. I will try to hit upon a more appropriate wording if these subjects seem to you and Greenfield proper ones,—and I will also consider more carefully the exact time that I can best come.

The talk I gave at the Brookings School was never written except that some of the ideas appear in "Everyman His Own Historian." But in the informal talks to the graduate students I can start the ball rolling by some remarks on historical sources & the nature & validity of historical evidence. If they will ask questions I expect I can keep the thing alive.

Very sincerely yours,
Carl Becker

1. CBCU.

To Leo Gershoy

Ithaca, November 18, 1935[1]

Dear Gershoy,

I am much relieved to find that you have such a favorable opinion of *Progress and Power*. Your judgment may not be infallible (especially where my work is concerned), but it is one of the best I know, and so I rely upon it. I know what you mean in what you say about the closing pages. I have had the same feeling, and I have as a matter of fact been revising these pages—I mean the closing pages of the third section—the *tone* was not proper to the aloof olympian view that characterizes the former parts. I realize also that the first lecture—that is the first part of it, is in a different tone than the later ones. This is an artistic defect, and if there is any excuse for it it is that the speaker & his audience have not yet placed themselves on the Olympian Heights. I don't know whether this is a valid excuse or not. However, I will take careful account of the pages you have noted. You needn't be so modest about "instructing" the professor. It is really true that if I have been able to keep my mind reasonably open, & abreast of what is new in ideas and points of view, it is in no small part due to a few young fellows like you. If my intellectual associations had been confined to the learned professors of my own generation, I should be far more dead & impervious to new ideas than I am—which God forbid.

Max [Lerner] wrote me ten days ago or more about the Nation offer, & wanted my advice. He said it had to be decided by Monday (last). So far as I gave him advice it was to stick to Harvard if they would keep him on. He wants to write books and to make some impression on the thought of his time; and he would have a better opportunity to do this in Harvard than at 20 Vesey St. But Max is a divided personality. His mind is critical, philosophical, aloof, well suited to an intellectual apprehension of the world; but his heart is soft and his emotions are all for saving the world by promoting the revolution. Besides, there is Anita who wants to preserve her self-respect by paying her way; and since they want to live together that would be more difficult if Max is in Harvard. In New York they can live together, Anita can help make the money for supporting the eminently bourgeois establishment they have built up, and Max can do his bit to promote the revolution that is designed to destroy it. It's a complex world.

I have recently recommended your name for consideration at California, Nebraska, & Washington University at St. Louis. I think, from a talk I had with Dean Heller of the latter institution, that you may hear from Washington University. I know you won't hear from Nebraska, & I guess you won't hear from California. I don't know whether you would care to go too far from New York.

I have made the rash decision not to teach anywhere next summer, and shall ask for your appointment here if you would like it. There is a new Director of Summer School who may have ideas of his own, but I expect he will take my recommendation. Maude has suddenly taken a great fancy for New York and can't be persuaded to go to California. The reason may have something to do with Fred. Anyhow she has visions of a sojourn in New York next summer on our way to the Jersey coast, where I expect to lie in the sun—and concoct a little of the famous *World History*.[2] I hope at least that our "movements & tendencies" (yours & ours) during the summer will bring us together a little while. . . .

Well, this is a long screed, but thanks very much for reading the Ms. Ida doesn't deign to send her criticisms, but I will heap coals of fire on her black curls by sending my love. I hope the coals don't burn the curls because I think they are quite nice.

Sincerely yours,
Carl Becker

1. LIG.
2. *Story of Civilization.*

To W. Stull Holt

Ithaca, November 26, 1935[1]

Dear Holt,

Our examination comes at the close of January and runs over into the first week of February. But we have a week before exams begin during which professors may at their discretion discontinue lectures. The idea is that students will thus be free for a week for wide & leisurely "general reading" which of course they have no time for while lectures are on. I think they mostly spend this free week sleeping till noon and going to the movies in the afternoon. However, my idea was to come to Baltimore for this week, coming down perhaps on the Wednesday or Thursday of the week preceding. This would make the dates approximately January 16–25. If this isn't satisfactory to you let me know.

I am looking forward to being with you (although you have every reason not to think so). The only thing that worries me is the fear that if the audience of the general talks are large I may not be heard very well. My voice doesn't carry well, and sometimes it's worse than others. If the room is good in its acoustics I will perhaps get on well enough with 250 people. I should like to get them off my chest as early in the visit as possible, although that isn't of great importance.

If you have seen the Washington papers you will perhaps know that I am said to be "a well known Communistic writer," attested by "records" in the Library of Congress & by several books to my credit or discredit.[2]

Sincerely yours,
Carl Becker

1. CBCU.
2. See CLB to the editor of the *Washington Herald,* Nov. 26, 1935.

To the editor of the *Washington Herald*

Ithaca, November 26, 1935[1]

Editor of the Washington Herald:

In your issue of November 21 I am charged with being a Communist, and with approving the Soviet system in Russia. These charges are based upon extracts taken from my school text book, "Modern History."[2] They are false in every sense. I am not and never have been a Communist, I do not subscribe to the revolutionary doctrines of Marx, I do not approve of the methods of Lenin in Russia, or of the Soviet system of government. I have never done anything to promote Communism in this country or to advocate a revolutionary change in the American system of government. I much prefer the system we have to Russian Communism or to any of the forms of Fascist dictatorship. The reported statement of George E. Sullivan[3] that I am a "well known communistic writer" is not only false but ridiculous. Any one who knows me, or has read my writings, or listened to my lectures in Cornell University, would know it to be so. My views on Communism are explicitly set forth in "Everyman His Own Historian" (F. S. Crofts. N.Y. 1935) pp. 112–131.[4] Furthermore, there will shortly appear in the New Republic a review of that book by Louis Hacker, who deplores the fact that I am an old fashioned Liberal, and that my thinking is confused because I do not understand and subscribe to the Marxian Communist interpretation of history.[5]

Your reporter conveys the impression that I am a Communist and a supporter of the Soviet system by the simple method of taking statements out of their context. He quotes this passage from my book.

"Instead of talking about the ideal society we should like to have, let us study history and see what kind of changes the future has in store for us, whether we like them or not. History shows us, according to Marx, that in every age," etc.

The impression here created is that I am quoting Marx to support my own views about what the future has in store for us. This is false. What I say in my book is this:

"It is no use, says Marx, to write nice books describing an ideal society. . . . All historical changes, he said, are brought about by silent economic forces that are stronger than men's wills and desires. A proper study of history shows that this has been so in the past. Why should we not expect it to be so in the future? Instead of talking about the ideal society we should like to have, let us study history and see what kind of changes the future has in store for us. History shows us, according to Marx," etc.

I should think it impossible for any intelligent person, who reads the two paragraphs on page 534 which contain the extracts quoted by your reporter, to suppose that I am quoting Marx in support of my own views. It is obvious that I am merely stating the views of Marx.

Your reporter quotes also a number of statements in my book about Lenin, the establishment of the Soviet system, the output of Russian industries, the aim of the Russian revolution to transform society. He quotes a statement that the Russian revolution is an "important" event. He gives a list of books which I "recommend." He implies that these statements and this list of recommended books is evidence that I approve of the Russian revolution, that I admire Lenin, and that I "recommend" books for the purpose of propagating Russian Communism. This is in no case true. The statements I make are statements of fact about Lenin and the Russian revolution. In no sense do they imply that I approve of Lenin or the Russian revolution. In saying that the Russian revolution is "important" I do not mean that it is good. Do those who wish to exclude my book from the schools think the Russian revolution is *not* important? Obviously they think it is very important —important in the sense that an earthquake is important. It is important in the sense that it is a force in the modern world to be reckoned with. If it is a force in the world, especially if it is a dangerous force, what should Americans do about it? Ignore it? Refuse to allow students in high schools to learn anything about it? If Communism and the Russian revolution are important and dangerous forces I should think that American citizens, and students who are citizens and will soon be voters, ought to learn what Communism teaches, what it has done in Russia, and what it aims to do elsewhere. In my text book I tell students what Communism teaches, what it has done in Russia, and what it aims to do. Because I tell what Communism is, does not mean that I approve of it; because I tell what Lenin thought and did, does not mean that I admire him, or believe what he believed, or approve of what he did. The function of a historian is to tell as accurately as he can what happened. It is for the reader, and, in the case of high school students, it is for the student with the aid of the teacher, to form his own opinions as to what historical characters are admirable, and what events are good.

I recommend certain books in order that the students may acquire further information, and I recommend books which express different views of the same subject. Some of the authors recommended for a further study of the Russian revolution favor, and some oppose, the Soviet system for Russia. W. H. Chamberlin's books on Russia are so hostile to the Soviet system that the author, according to his own statement, would not now be permitted to enter the country.[6] B. Russell is an English mathematician.[7] He is not a Communist. He is opposed to revolution as a method of solving social problems. He is opposed to the Soviet system of government. H. N. Brailsford is an English Liberal who describes how the Soviet system works. He is opposed to it. A. Wickstead writes about life under the Soviets. He is not a Communist, and he does not favor the Soviet system of government. Trotsky is a Communist. He was associated with Lenin in establishing the Soviet system. He tells what he did and thought, and why. A few years ago he was driven out of Russia for disagreeing with the policies of the Soviet government. The two other writers are, if not Communists, in sympathy with the Russian system. Of the writers "recommended," the majority, and the first on the list, are strongly opposed to the Russian system. Obviously I cannot agree with the views of all the writers I recommend. If I did I should have to agree to diverse and irreconcilable views.

"Modern History" is a story of what has occurred in modern times. In it I have studiously refrained from imposing my personal views on students and teachers. Mr. Sullivan has either not read my books or has misunderstood what I have said in them. He will find my views of Communism explicitly set forth in "Everyman His Own Historian," pp. 112–131. On page 125 he will find the following confession of faith.

"I have no faith in force and repression as the primary means of achieving the good life. I am not a non-resistance pacifist. Any government is probably better than none, and all governments rest at last upon force. But I believe that the essential test of civilized society is the extent to which law and public authority rest on free discussion and voluntary consent. A resort to force . . . may sometimes be necessary to prevent society from falling into virtual anarchy; but the resort to force in place of persuasion is so far a confession of failure. I have no faith in the possibility of abolishing oppression by suppressing oppressors. I have no faith in the infallibility of any man, or any group of men, or in the dogmas or doctrines of any man or group of men, except in so far as they can stand the test of free criticism and analysis. . . . I believe that all the great and permanently valuable achievements of civilization have been won by the free play of intelligence in opposition to, or in spite of, the pressure of mass emotion and the effort of organized authority to enforce conformity in conduct and opinion. I do not believe that there has been or that there will be a high civilization in any country in which the mind of man is limited to the expression of ideas authorized by public authority. Dictatorship is as old as European society; and whether it be the dictatorship of a Stalin, a Mussolini, or a Hitler, it does not become something new and admirable by being dressed up in new and mystical ideology. I recognize it as a possibility that our modern, com-

plex, machine civilization may so far fall into confusion that a dictatorship may in fact replace the present regime; but I refuse to recognize this outcome as inherently desirable, and I refuse to join in any effort to make it inevitable."
If this makes me out a Communist, then there is no meaning in words.

The article in which I was charged with being a Communist will no doubt be widely circulated through the country. I feel sure that you do not wish to represent any one in a false light. I therefore ask you to publish this letter, and to give it the same prominence that was given to the charge which it refutes.

Yours truly,
Carl Becker

1. CBCU.
2. 1931.
3. Sullivan (1881–?) was a journalist, author of *The Road to Victory* (1942) and *The Great Deception* (1946).
4. "The Marxian Philosophy of History."
5. See CLB to the editor of the *New Republic*, Jan. 8, 1936, in response to Hacker's review. Louis Hacker (1899——) taught economics at Columbia (1935–1967). His specialty is American political and economic history.
6. William H. Chamberlin (1897——), journalist, editor, and author of *The Russian Revolution, 1917–1921* (2 vols; 1935), *Russia's Iron Age* (1934), *The Soviet Planned Economic Order* (1931), and *Soviet Russia: A Living Record and a History* (1930).
7. Bertrand A. W. Russell (1872–1970), British mathematician and philosopher.

To Wilma Pugh

Ithaca, November 26, 1935[1]

Dear Wilma,[2]

I am glad you are having your fling in Paris at last. If you learn a little French, & do a little work in the Bibliotheque, that will raise your market value. There are more positions going this year than I have heard of in the four years before. True they are all for men; although Miss Lois Gibbons did get a job of sorts. However, I think maybe next year may turn up some vacancies in women's colleges too. Some of the old timers ought to die or resign, even if there are no new positions created.

However, don't spend all the time in the Bibliotheque. Buzz around and have a good time, and see as much as you can of French life & people & places. That will do you good, and will be always something to remember. Besides, it's a part of your education.

Everything is about the same here, except that we are uniting our various departments of history into one department with an elected chairman. It won't change matters much, but will simplify administration for the Dean's office. I have about 19 in my seminary, & we have moved to Willard Straight. I don't see any first class people in it—I mean top-notchers.

Just now the Hearst papers are Red Hunting in the Washington D.C. schools, and I have been celebrated as a "well known communistic writer." I think we can hold them off from throwing out the book—at least we are making a "defense" for the Washington school authorities to use.

I hope to hear from you again about your work & play,—& to see you here in Ithaca. I shall be here until about the 20 June I expect.

Sincerely yours,
Carl Becker

1. CBCU.
2. Pugh (1906——), received her Ph.D. at Cornell in 1931, and taught French history at Stephens College (1931–1935), Lindenwood College (1936–1939), and Mt. Holyoke College (1943——).

To Leo and Ida Gershoy

Ithaca, December 26, 1935[1]

Dear Leo & Ida,

Your special delivery arrived this morning when I was shaving. I thought of course that it was a summons for deportation, and was relieved to learn that it was nothing more than a Christmas greeting.

I'm all right now I think; but I have had this fall a succession of crosses, laid upon me by Providence for my sins and for strengthening my character. Item—lumbago; item—just a touch of my old intestinal trouble; item—a swolen tonsil with a slight infection, making it hard for me to talk, a severe deprivation to one of my nature; item—a little "athletes foot" or ringworm on the back of my hand. But now I think I am back to normal, or very nearly so.

Did the Junior Executive[2] tell you that he has to go out to Chicago for a big conference of salesmen? He is beginning to look down on the old man now—he knows so much about type, and "space points," and "set ups," and "color printing." If you get a chance, just put him wise to the fact that the old man knows a thing or two also. Not that the old man does, but family discipline needs to be maintained if possible.

Who is your candidate for President of Cornell? P. Smith[3] wrote me that he heard that the Trustees were considering Arthur Treman.[4] Notestein has a high opinion of Prof. Baxter[5] of Harvard, which lets him out. Westerman[6] thought Carleton Hayes[7] or a Prof. Haig[8] of Columbia would do. Dick Fox,[9] and Whitke[10] of Ohio State have been mentioned. I am beginning to think that I might do myself. Or how would Leo Gershoy strike you.

Maude sends her love,

Sincerely,

Carl Becker

1. LIG.
2. CLB's son, Frederick.
3. Preserved Smith.
4. CLB may have confused Arthur B. Treman with his cousin Robert E. Treman (1888–1953), who received his B.A. at Cornell (1909), became a prominent Ithaca businessman, fund raiser for Cornell, alumni trustee (1931–1953), and director of the National Association for the Advancement of Colored People.
5. James Phinney Baxter III (1893——), professor of American history at Harvard (1925–1937), president of Williams College (1937–1961).
6. William L. Westermann (1873–1954) taught ancient history at Wisconsin (1908–1920), Cornell (1920–1923), and Columbia (1923–1948).
7. Carleton J. H. Hayes (1882–1964), taught modern European history at Columbia (1907–1950), and was U.S. ambassador to Spain (1942–1945).
8. Robert M. Haig (1887–1953), professor of political economy at Columbia (1912–1952).
9. Dixon Ryan Fox, president of Union College (1934–1946).

10. Carl Wittke (1892–1970) taught American history at Ohio State (1916–1937), Oberlin (1937–1948), and Western Reserve (1948–1963).

To the editor of the *New Republic*

Ithaca, January 8, 1936[1]

Sir:

Thanks very much for sending me Louis Hacker's review of me and my book [p. 260].[2] I will not take advantage of your offer of space for a "reply" to his remarks. Since Mr. Hacker has done me the signal honor of selecting me as a "case," an objective item in social history well worth examination, it would be out of place for me to reply. "No method," says Max Planck,[3] "that transforms an object is suitable for examining it." How unsuitable then would I be as an object for methodical examination, if like the electron when exposed to light, I should be suddenly and uncertainly perturbed by the examination. My part, obviously, is to look natural when posed as an object interesting to science, to remain indifferent and undeflected so long as there is any call for my services as a datum in sociology. Mr. Hacker has discussed my "case" with frankness and ability; if there is to be further discussion, it must be by an observer who regards the phenomenon as sufficiently important to merit further exploration. The datum can contribute to the advancement of learning only by remaining quiescent.

Besides, Mr. Hacker has said so many nice things about my writing that it would be ungenerous for me to question his right (as a critic of my book) to be distressed because I have chosen to write about the things that interest me rather than about the things that interest him, or his right to deplore the fact that my "fine and independent mind" has not been sufficiently fine and independent to subscribe to the Marxian philosophy of history.[4]

Carl Becker

1. *New Republic*, LXXXV (Jan. 8, 1936), 256.
2. Hacker reviewed *Everyman His Own Historian*, in an essay called "Historian of Revolutions."
3. Planck (1858–1947) was a German physicist who introduced the quantum theory, for which he received the Nobel Prize in 1918.
4. See Felix Frankfurter to CLB, Jan. 11, 1936, in the Appendix.

To Leo and Ida Gershoy

Ithaca, February 6, 1936[1]

Dear Children,

You certainly think of the nicest things to do! The book isn't in the library yet, and I wanted it, especially here when I am lying around the house all day. I read about 150 pages yesterday, and of course it is a very fine book.[2] Considering that the author is a philosopher, the characters are well individualized. But then Santayana is more than a philosopher. He says of himself that he is not a learned man at all—"almost a poet." He is, like Plato, a poet philosopher, with a fine sense of humor, and an intuitive understanding of people—even of people whom you wouldn't suppose he ever had much to do with.

I try to think of nice things to do for people I like, but nothing ever seems to occur to me. I'm working on it now, and hope before I die to think of something nice to do for you—something that will please & surprise you.

I'm planning to go to Johns Hopkins about the 14 of March for a week. Maude hopes to come to New York then to see Fred, & the plan is for me to come home by way of New York for the week end. I will see you then. I'm now nearly as well as usual, but it's a slow business. I expect to begin "teaching" on Monday. I'm very glad you are to be in Ithaca this summer.

Sincerely yours,
Carl Becker

1. LIG.
2. Presumably George Santayana's *The Last Puritan: A Memoir in the Form of a Novel* (New York, 1936).

To Florence Mishnun Yohalem

Ithaca, February 12, 1936[1]

Dear Florence,

Well, I'm glad at last to get a line on your gaddings about. I supposed that your European debauch would not outlast the summer: & here you are back again—living in the crassest luxury, as I can see. A lawyer living on the spoils of big business, and his wife —no longer a person with a name even—doing nothing. The kept classes, as Veblen said—well, you & Morton have nothing on me now—no use spouting the class conflict & the Revolution to me. I should merely sneer out of the corner of my cynical mouth. For all that, I'm delighted you are both buzzing about the world and learning to pronounce matches in seventeen languages—what could be more socially useful.

Many things have happened since I saw you last. We had a fine time in California—a swell trip, and a good vacation. The lectures are going through the Press.—"Progress & Power," Stanford Press. Rather a fantastic performance which your critical mind will see all kinds of holes in. Last July Ithaca had a grand flood—we were out at Fontainbleu Inn having dinner, and had to stop at a farm house all night. Ten inches of water running down Court and Aurora Streets: Enfield & Taughanack Park temporarily ruined. It supplied topics for conversation all summer.

In September we went to the Jersey coast, & I basked in the sun and finished up an article for the new *Journal of Social Philosophy*. I'm sending you a copy.[2] This Christmas not so good—in the hospital again with the old trouble, pretty grim, but now I am O.K. again, or appear so. In March I am going to Johns Hopkins for a week to sit around and be an inspiration to the graduate students.

Fred has a job in the publicity department of Silver Burdett Co., and is delighted with the job & the people. I infer he does it pretty well or he wouldn't like it so much. He seems a more mature person already, and more confident & cheerful. We are pretty lonely.

Give our best wishes to Morton & his matches.

Sincerely yours,
Carl Becker

1. FMY.
2. "New Liberties for Old," *Journal of Social Philosophy*, I (1936), 101–121.

To Leo Gershoy

Ithaca, February 13, 1936[1]

Dear Leo,

I haven't seen Petry,[2] but I am sure the courses you outline will be quite all right. Of course personally I think the specialized course should be entitled "The Rise of Petty Bourgeois Sensibilities," and the general "Fascism—The Last Ditch of Finance Capitalism." But what is the use of suggesting these titles, since my favorite pupil has suddenly turned parvenu & baldly expresses his refusal to accept subversive criticism. Alas, what has happened to the "Becker Cult"? The last refuge of my egoistic nature appears to be collapsing. If you have corrupted Ida I am lost indeed.

I'm back on the job—manfully struggling with the task of lecturing three times a week—and meeting a seminary!

Sincerely,
Carl Becker

1. LIG.
2. Loren C. Petry (1887–1970) taught botany at Cornell (1922–1955) and was director of the summer session (1934–1944) and director of veterans' education (1944–1948).

To Harry Elmer Barnes

Ithaca, February 29, 1936[1]

Dear Barnes,

I have never thought of publishing the article on what is a historical fact.[2] It is not in shape for publication, because the subject is a difficult one. I am not sure I could find the ms. now. Mencken asked me if I had the thing in shape for publication some years ago, when he was editing the Mercury.—I dare say you put him up to it. There are too many things written anyway, and the longer I live the more I agree with A. A. Milne.[3] "The only reason I have ever found for writing anything is because I want to write it." The piece helped to clear up my ideas, and so served its purpose.

I am putting through the press three lectures delivered last year at Stanford. The thing is called "Progress & Power," and will appear within the next month or so. It's just unorthodox and outlandish enough to be (possibly) interesting to a fellow of your stripe—a newspaper man who knows a lot about what happened before 1900, and is naive enough still to think that the Human Race is amenable to treatment. . . .

I suppose you know I was denounced in Washington, D.C. by the Patriot Lunatic Fringe as a "well known Communistic writer"—on account of my little milk & water book Modern History. If you don't want to be connected with a dangerous Red you had better burn this.

> Sincerely,
> Carl Becker

1. Barnes Papers, University of Wyoming Library.
2. CLB never did. He read versions of it to the Research Club of Cornell (April 1926) and to the American Historical Association (Dec. 1926). It was posthumously published as "What Are Historical Facts?" *Western Political Quarterly,* VIII (1955), 327–340, and reprinted in *DWH,* 41–64.
3. Milne (1882–1956) was the author of *Winnie-the-Pooh* (1926), *Now We Are Six* (1927), and *The House at Pooh Corner* (1928).

To Guy Stanton Ford

New York, New York, April 10, 1936[1]

Dear Ford,

Someone sent me a clipping containing your review of my *Everyman.* I didn't know that you recommended me for the Turner. I was of course describing the remembered impression Turner made on me—a green boy from the sticks: and I have often wondered if it corresponded to the impression he made on others. I'm glad to know that you can recognize the man in the description. Several other old students of Turner's have said it was the Turner they know.

Turner the man & teacher was much more than Turner the writer. His writings do not do him justice: & his long books are less good than his articles. He had not the synthetic mind. His last book is not so good as his first one. His reputation is beginning to diminish, &, if the communist point of view gains prestige, will continue to do so no doubt. So I am glad if I have managed to get in print some fairly vivid picture of the personality, the man as he impressed several generations of young men.

Paxon [sic][2] pointed out to me last winter that an astonishingly small number of Turners Ph.D.'s had turned out more than mediocre. I didn't know that, but I have been impressed with the fact that a great many men of distinction in other fields than American history, & in other fields than history, have been greatly influenced by Turner's writings. So many of his "disciples" (true to the character of disciples) never have understood what Turner was really driving at. It was unfortunate that he used the term "western" as synonymous with "frontier": the result has been that many dubs have supposed that they are following in Turner's footsteps by counting the pigs in some county in the middle or far west.

I've been laid up here for three or four weeks, but expect to return to Ithaca within the next week or ten days.

Sincerely,
Carl Becker

1. Ford Papers, UM.
2. Frederic L. Paxson (1877–1948) taught American history at Colorado (1903–1906), Michigan (1906–1910), Wisconsin (1910–1932), the University of California at Berkeley (1932–1947).

To the editor of the *New Republic*

Ithaca, September 30, 1936[1]

Emerson said of the Abolitionists: "They may be wrong-headed, but they are wrong-headed in the right direction." Candidates for the office of President of the United States (those that have any chance of being elected; the others, knowing well that they will not be called upon to make good, can afford to say what they think, even if they can think straight) are usually (practically always for the duration of the campaign) wrong-headed; but some of them, some of the time, may be wrong-headed in the right direction. The only candidates who have any chance of being elected are Mr. Roosevelt and Mr. Landon.[2] During the campaign they and their supporters naturally confine themselves to generalities which, like the famous statement agreed to by the Jansenists and the Jesuits for the good of religion, may be taken to mean one thing or another as you please. Nevertheless, allowing for campaign hokum and the necessary limitations and disingenuousness of minds long habituated by the political game to following the line of least intelligence, it seems to me that there is an underlying difference between the attitude of Mr. Roosevelt and that of Mr. Landon. Mr. Landon believes, or appears to believe, that the economic and industrial problems that are now pressing for some solution can best

be solved by reducing the government regulation of private business enterprise to the minimum; while Mr. Roosevelt believes, or
appears to believe, that governmental regulation of some sort is
essential for their solution. I shall therefore vote for Mr. Roosevelt
because I believe that however wrong-headed he may have been
and may still be he is at least wrong-headed in the right direction,
whereas Mr. Landon suffers the grave disadvantage of being not
only wrong-headed but wrong-headed in the wrong direction.

Carl Becker.

1. *New Republic,* LXXXVIII (Sept. 30, 1936), 224. The editors had
written to ninety-seven "well known Americans who have in general
taken a progressive political position, asking them for whom they
would vote in this year's national election."
2. Alfred M. Landon (1887——), governor of Kansas (1933–1937),
Republican nominee for president (1936).

To Florence Mishnun Yohalem

Ithaca, November 8, 1936[1]

Dear Florence,

It is good that you should again be a bachelor girl, earning her
own living. It will give you a sense of independence, and, I hope,
a greater assurance that you are after all good for something. However, I dare say you will find reasons for thinking what you are
doing is futile—has no "social content" or significance. That is
really not a thing to worry about. Most of us are necessarily busy
doing whatever we can do, either to earn a living or for the fun of
doing it, or, in the happiest instances, for both reasons: the social
significance has to take care of itself. Is this cynical? I don't think
so, for the reason that if we are doing useful or necessary work,
and if it is the thing we can do best or best like to do, it will do more
"good" than if we insist on doing something more obviously "good"
which we are not particularly fitted to do.[2] Find consolation in the
fact that if you were doing anything else you would be, probably,
no better satisfied. I say "probably" because the dissatisfaction is
subjective rather than objective in origin. So at least I think.

Well, excuse the sermon and the prig who gives it. I am very
well, and it is a pleasure to find how good food can really taste: I

had forgotten. I am doing my teaching, and have recovered a certain zest for writing ("creative writing", I should say). The creative writing takes the form of a text-book, and two lectures to be delivered at Johns Hopkins sometime in April.

I have been reading Carl Van Doren's *Three Worlds,*[3] which I find interesting in itself, and especially because his recollection of his boyhood in Illinois up to the time he left the University is so extraordinarily like my own recollection, in respect to manner of life & social habits & customs, as to be amusing: by changing a few names, incidents, and events, it could be presented as a history of my life up to the age of 22.

I hope Morton isn't allowing his uncle to manage his life: and I hope you won't forget him and I hope he won't forget you and I hope neither of you will forget me and mine: for we are all, I think, very nice children.

Maude sends her best.

Sincerely yours,
Carl Becker

1. FMY.
2. CLB again takes up this question of "doing good" in his letter to Thomas Reed Powell, Dec. 3, 1944.
3. *Three Worlds* (New York, 1936), an autobiography.

To Morris Bishop

Ithaca, November 22, 1936[1]

Dear Bishop,[2]

If a man wants to go in for egoism in a really big way, there's nothing like self-renunciation, is there? I've finished your book,[3] and I know a lot more about Pascal than I did, although I knew a good bit before. There's a very favorable review in today's Herald Tribune Books—perhaps you have seen it. I think you did a grand job—excellently organized, excellently written, sound scholarship, acute and penetrating judgments, above all wisdom (rarer than all the others) in your estimate of an exceedingly difficult character.

I think I agree with you in every esential matter. There is a small point. "We are rejecting specific testimonies on the basis of an *a priori* theory" (p. 178). This goes to the heart of the question as to the value of testimony in establishing historical facts. The testimonies here referred to establish the fact that the witnesses had a certain experience, but not, I think, that their interpretation of the experience is correct. History (that is, our knowledge of it,) rests on testimony—"the testimony of two independent witnesses, not self-deceived," as Bernheim lays down the rule for historians in his *Lehrbuch;*[4] but there is always a point beyond which we will not accept any amount of testimony—we say the witnesses are "self-deceived." That point is reached when the witnesses testify to something which conflicts with our settled conviction (*a priori* theory, but based on experience none the less) as to what can and cannot happen. This proves nothing of course as to what can or cannot happen, but only indicates that historical knowledge for us, or any other age, rests in the last analysis on our general philosophy of the world and how it behaves. Pascal, scientist though he was, readily accepted the miracle of the Thorn. If miracles can be established by testimony of witnesses, they are established as well as any other events. Hume[5] tried to prove that miracles can't happen. His argument is that it is easier to believe that any number of witnesses can be mistaken than it is to believe that the natural order is ever subject to supernatural intervention. That proves nothing except that Hume didn't believe in miracles. De Maistre somewhere maintains (probably in his book on *The Pope*)[6] that we *must* believe any event that is supported by a certain number of reliable witnesses. This proves only that DeMaistre was predisposed to believe anything that would support the truth of Catholic Christian teaching. Well, I agree with Hume, and I expect you do too; but I agree with Justice Holmes[7] that "Truth is only the system of my limitations". Probably you agree with all this, but it isn't clear from the context—or wasn't to me at least. I hope all this doesn't bore you in any case.

By the way, I suppose you are familiar with Brunetiere's essay on the Jansenist-Jesuit quarrell.[8] I think his summary of what the Jesuits in their "Probabilism", were up to, is excellent. It is much the same as yours.

Sincerely,
Carl Becker

1. Morris Bishop Papers, Ithaca, N.Y.

2. Bishop (1893——) received his B.A., M.A., and Ph.D. degrees at Cornell (1913, 1914, 1926), where he taught Romance languages and literatures (1921–1960). He has written biographies, essays, verse, and a murder mystery set at Cornell, *The Widening Stain.*

3. *Pascal: The Life of Genius* (New York, 1936).

4. Ernst Bernheim, *Lehrbuch der historischen Methode* (Leipzig, 1889).

5. David Hume (1711–1776), British philosopher and historian.

6. Joseph Marie, Comte de Maistre (1753–1821), political and religious philosopher, author of *Du Pape.*

7. Oliver Wendell Holmes (1841–1935), justice of the Supreme Court of Massachusetts (1882–1902) and of the United States (1902–1932), author of several books on law and society.

8. Ferdinand Brunetière (1849–1906) was a French critic who tried to apply the theory of evolution to literary history.

To Leo and Ida Gershoy

Ithaca, November 29, 1936[1]

Dear Wanderers on the face of the earth, Beloved Gugenheimers!,

I have received your cards etc. which indicate that you have been among the heathen peoples, who all appear to speak a foreign language & to have been born in foreign countries. It seems rather dangerous, and I wonder if it is quite right. I do hope that by now you are back in a safe & sane country where people do not do the things that are not done.

The papers today tell me that some statesman in Albany has found out that Cornell is a center of Communism.[2] Since all the State Schools are going to be investigated, I'm afraid the worst will come out. You might write to J. Stalin & tell him that the International Revolution can't be long soft-pedalled now that Cornell has taken it up. Cornell is bad business when she gets going. I will probably lose my job. Don't tell anyone that you are my pupils—favorite pupils.

We have a new president—Mr. Something Day, now of the Rockefeller Foundation.[3] I don't know anything about him, except that he is better than some of the ginks and Bilboes that were seriously considered—he must be! We hope for the best and expect the worst.

Nothing new here—except the Communism, and of course that isn't new. . . .

My health is very fine, and I am putting on weight—ten pounds since I came home—and am getting stronger. A certain zest for work and writing. Am going to Johns Hopkins for a week in April, to give two public lectures and sit about with the grad students and spread abroad the old illusion of wisdom etc. Expect to go to Providence for the A.H.A. meeting.

Maude sends her best love, and I do too,

As ever,
Carl Becker

1. LIG.

2. State Senator John J. McNaboe. See Morris Bishop, *A History of Cornell* (Ithaca, 1962), 493–494.

3. Edmund Ezra Day (1883–1951) taught economics at Dartmouth (1907–1910), Harvard (1910–1923), and Michigan (1923–1928). After serving the Rockefeller Foundation as director for the social sciences (1928–1937), he was president of Cornell (1937–1949).

To Leo and Ida Gershoy

Ithaca, December 25, 1936[1]

Dear Frents,

Am thenkink maybe these littel missel on Senta Clas should, by you who is always in England travellink, meb your 'Ebrew herts beating varmish for the nativf Amerika, and such for hunnert per cent Kleinz Amerikan kinder vat is geboren and livinck by Bointenhoist am Brooklyn.

Mit best wish and apology for Mr. K-A-P-L-I-N fromm New Yorker.[2]

Your kind frent,
Carl Becker

1. LIG.

2. Cf. Leo Rosten, *The Education of H*y*m*a*n K*a*p*l*a*n* (New York, 1937).

To Felix Frankfurter

Ithaca, January 3, 1937[1]

Dear Frankfurter,

Returning from Providence, I find your little volume,[2] with its friendly and flattering inscription, on my desk. I like your rehabilitation of Taney.[3] Poor man, he suffered from the verbosity which is the vice of lawyers & judges—not of course, teachers of law! If he had decided the Dred Scott case[4] in three pages instead of thirty (or whatever number it was) he would not have occupied the bad eminence he has. However, in that case he would have been far less well known, and maybe that is the main thing.

I have a great advantage over you. I studied "sound political science" (under Burgess),[5] and the result is that it was settled once for all, so that I have never had to bother about it since. But you have had to study it all your life, and still you aren't sure, you are afflicted with doubts, and are always looking up authorities. I wrote a long paper on the 14 Amendment clause on Due Process of Law. Unfortunately, the thing was never published, & is now lost —it would have made unnecessary such masses of writing!

I was patched up last September by a very good surgeon, and I think I am over the troubles I have had for the last five years. At all events my health is now very good.

Why didn't you come to Providence? Why is the universe so badly arranged that I never see you any more? I threaten to come to Cambridge some day just to see if you are as lively and optimistic as ever—and as grey as I am. So beware, & be prepared.

With kind regards to Mrs. Frankfurter,

Cordially yours,
Carl Becker

1. CBCU.
2. *The Commerce Clause under Marshall, Taney, and Waite* (Chapel Hill, N.C., 1937).
3. Roger B. Taney (1777–1864), Chief Justice of the United States (1836–1864).
4. On March 6, 1857, Taney held that Scott (and therefore all Negro slaves or their descendants) was not a citizen of the United States or of the state of Missouri, and thus was not entitled to sue in the Federal courts.
5. John W. Burgess (1844–1931) taught political science and constitutional law at Columbia (1876–1912).

To Val R. Lorwin

Ithaca, [February 1937]¹

Dear Lorwin,

The dates for the Baltimore sojourn are March 29–April 4. I don't really know whether I can get down to Washington or not, because I am expected to be more or less "on tap" at Hopkins for the graduate students. That is what they really have me down there for—the public lectures are a necessary condition of getting the money. But of course I can see you if you come to Baltimore.

Your Taft skit is really illuminating—if it is fairly representative, as I dare say it is. I do not see anything to get excited about in R's proposal for the Court:² I am not opposed to the Court as an institution, or to its powers: because I think civil liberties are safer in the hands of 9 or 15 jurists, however "old," than in the hands of elected legislators. The only trouble with the court temporarily is the excessive percentage in its personnel of intellectual desiccation. The President's plan aims to get rid of this: it does not change in any way the power of the Court or the structure of government. That's why I like it. Probably the President will concede something in the way of raising the age limit, or slowing up the process of making new appointments. I haven't your faith in the virtue or wisdom of the "people," or of the representatives they are likely to choose. I dislike all the schemes for amending the Constitution, except that of Lippman [sic],³ who suggests adding to the list of specific powers granted by the Const. to Congress. Liberals & radicals think the Court a nuisance when they have a liberal President & Congress. But suppose you get a thoroughly reactionary President & Congress, and no Court to put a little check on it. Then they might regret the abolition of Court power to check it.

Give my best regards to Madge, and to Hammy.

Sincerely yours,
Carl Becker

1. CBCU.

2. On February 5, 1937, Roosevelt submitted to Congress a plan for reorganizing the Federal judiciary. The proposal included an increase in the membership of the Supreme Court from nine to fifteen if judges who had reached the age of seventy declined to retire.

3. Walter Lippmann (1889———), journalist, author, and critic. See Lippmann's *The New Imperative* (New York, 1935) and *An Inquiry into the Principles of the Good Society* (Boston, 1937).

To Leo and Ida Gershoy

Ithaca, February 7, 1937[1]

Dear Ida & Leo,

I am just emerging from a two week reading of 200 term papers, am still alive and well. So you see! The papers are unusually good, which lightened the drudgery of reading them, but increases the labor, for I feel that a good paper calls for comment. In one of them there was a most illuminating comment, a piece of unconscious humor. The chap had been reading Morris Bishop's *Pascal*, which came to him on the Book of the Month Club list, and this inspired him to write his paper. In explaining all this he remarked: "Having read this book with as much thoroughness as it is possible to read any book in school" etc. One is so busy "studying" for exams that it is difficult to find time for irrevelant activities, such as reading books. I had supposed that school was precisely the place to read books thoroughly, but it seems I was mistaken. Nevertheless, the paper was a very good one.

The most mildest-and-without-snow-or-cold-winter we have ever had. Since December 10, chains on the car only twice, and each time for one day only. I tell you this so you can be sorry you didn't stay at home.

I went to Providence for the meeting of the A.H.A.—a terrible crush of about 1000 registrations: difficult to see anyone except by accident. Yet I had a good time. I heard people say the best papers were by Gottschalk and Knappen. McIlwain didn't do himself justice in the Pres. Ad:[2] but then very few do. Helen Sullivan came down from Boston, & I had dinner with her, and heard all about her adventure in Spain. She got out before the war it seems; but thinks she has got hold of something interesting in connection with some 16 century political philosopher—I've forgotten the name, never having heard of it, being so ignorant as anything.

Have got George Andrews to teach in summer school, since my favorite pupil is not available. I expect we shall be in Jersey again

—if the royalties hold up sufficiently—probably at the same place, although we looked at cottages farther down at Spring Lake. Very nice, but $100 more expensive, which is not so good. I hope you will be home in time to come and see us. Hope you are improving both your minds like anything, and are not becoming so English that people will mistake you for Rhodes Scholars. Are you loyal to King Geo VI—that's the principal question. Did you note Mr. Baldwin's indiscretion when he made his famous speech on the abdication?[3] He said in effect that, not having had time to prepare a speech, he would have to be content with telling the simple truth briefly & clearly. He should have been asked to resign after that.

The chief news here is that F.D.R. has "struck a fatal Blow at the Foundations of Our System of Government"—by recommending the addition of members to the Supreme Court. The Herald Tribune is wearing black sleeve bands. The Constitution will be no more when you return. You will have to get used to living in a strange country.

The chief news in our domicile is that Maude is Treasurer for the Committee that is collecting money for Spanish Relief. It's her first venture into Public Activity. A woman called up and wanted to know whether the Loyalists were Communist or Facist. Maude didn't know, but by some chance I did: so the honor of the family was saved. I think she is a wise woman to live contentedly without knowing what Communists or Facists are or which is which. It's what I aim at, but not with much success: with this much success, however, that I only know what I think Communists and Facists are, and don't see much difference between them.

I'm struggling along peacefully with the World History. And just now have to read for Crofts a very dull Ms. on European Civilization by Boak, Hyma, and Slosson.[4] All facts are created equal, but at different times and places. The Greeks were a remarkable people, likewise the Egyptions, likewise the Babylonians, likewise the Jews; but they have different names, which enables one to tell them apart. Feudalism arose in a time of confusion and disorder, but it is not known when the term *client* was replaced by the term *vassal* —I bet you don't know. The Crusades were religious movements, also political and economic. You see I have learned a lot by reading the Ms. and later will get $50.00.

Here's a new Kaplan story. A self-made Professor, who went not to college, said he didn't regret it: he didn't care if he wasn't an alma mater of any college. Neither do I. Do you?
Go to the Beeksteak Club and take off your hat.
Maude joins me in love & best wishes.

Carl Becker

1. LIG.
2. Charles H. McIlwain, "The Historian's Part in a Changing World," *AHR*, XLII (1937), 207–224.
3. Stanley Baldwin (1867–1947), three times Prime Minister of Great Britain, notably in 1936, when Edward VIII abdicated.
4. Arthur E. R. Boak, Albert Hyma, and Preston Slosson, *The Growth of European Civilization* (2 vols.; New York, 1938).

To Val R. Lorwin

Ithaca, [late February 1937][1]

Dear Lorwin,

I do not wish to concur in this proposal[2] for two reasons: (1) because, being a member of the Council, I think it inappropriate for me to do so even if I favored it; (2) because I do not favor it in any case. The present system of asking members to signify their preferences was adopted many years ago as the result of a flare up against an "inside ring", & with the purpose of making the management more "democratic."[3] It has failed to do that, for the reason that very few members ever signify their preferences. Since this is due to indifference, & the feeling that the matter can best be left to the nominating committee, it will not be corrected by changing the mechanism. To make the nomination of those who receive a majority of votes mandatory would make possible the very thing you mention—nomination by small cliques. At present the nominating committee takes into consideration the preferences expressed by the few who return the ballots, but is not bound by them, and should not be since the number is negligible. For these reasons I think a representative committee can do the job better than it could be done by any scheme designed to make the elections "democratic." There is no way of making elections "democratic," because there is no way of getting the whole body of the Association to take a sufficient interest to form an intelligent opinion. Any such scheme would result in a few interested persons, motivated by "loyalty" to friends or "patrons" or to localities, playing politics and "putting over" their particular interests. I think as it is there is too much attention paid to pacifying certain regions that are large in square miles but small in talent: there would be more of it if elections were or could be made "democratic." The Association is and always has been very well managed on the whole, and I feel sure that attempts to make the technique more democratic will not improve matters—on the contrary.

Sincerely yours,
Carl Becker

1. CBCU.
2. CLB is replying to a letter from Lorwin, February 16, 1937, which enclosed a "memorandum on The American Historical Association election procedure . . . being sent to people all around the country, mostly by some historians with the National Archives and The National Park Service; also some in university posts, such as Howard Beale. If you agree with its purpose and want to sign it, that will greatly help." (CBCU).
3. See Jacob E. Cooke, *Frederic Bancroft, Historian* (Norman, Okla., 1957), 98–102, for Bancroft's attempt to reform the Association in 1915–1916.

To Florence Mishnun Yohalem

Baltimore, Maryland, March 30, 1937[1]

Dear Florence,

I should love to come down to Washington to see you, but fear it won't be possible. They keep me pretty busy here. There are not only the two lectures (which are at 5 oclock today & tomorrow), but sitting in with the graduate students & professors in a kind of general seminary every day. Besides, there are some luncheons (one with the President, & one with H. L. Mencken), and people to dinner every night. It's enjoyable, but after all pretty exhausting, and I don't think I ought to run off. You see what they are really paying me for is not so much the public lectures, but for sitting around & letting the graduate students look at the great man & ask questions. I am pretty well, and feel so; but I haven't after all any superabundance of energy. If you could run off some afternoon, I have free time from about 2 to 4:30 P.M. Why not? I am stopping now with Prof K. R. Greenfield The Tudor Arms apts. But probably Thursday & Friday I shall be with Prof W. Stull Holt. I don't know his address. Friday I shall be running off to N.Y. on some late afternoon train. Couldn't you come up Thursday?

As ever,
Carl Becker

1. FMY.

To Max Lerner

Ithaca, April 11, 1937[1]

Overture—*Don't Forget to Answer This!*
Dear Max,
    Do you know of a first rate man to write an article for the Yale Review on the Spanish War?[2] Someone who knows Spanish history and Spanish politics in the 19–20 century to get it in perspective, and to get it solidly based, without being twisted out of shape by either a communist or fascist or democratic bias. This is asking a good deal; but it doesn't mean that the author should be so "objective" as to have no opinions. It means only that we want a man who knows the subject and can present it intelligently to American readers without making it a propagandist tract. It isn't necessary for him to have been in Spain during the war: better not, on the whole. The kind of men we don't want are such men as Louis Fischer[3] or Ralph Bates[4]—good as they both are in their way. I thought with your wide acquaintance of writers you might suggest a man or men. The article would be wanted probably for the September issue—to be ready early in August.
    I thought Stalbergs[5] article on Trotzky's [sic] book[6] a very good one—the best thing I've read of his. I had a good time at your highbrow house. Give my love to Anita.

Sincerely,
Carl Becker

1. Lerner Papers, YU.
2. CLB served on the editorial board of the *Yale Review* from 1937 until his death in 1945.

3. Louis Fischer (1896–1970), journalist, author, and lecturer specializing in European politics and Soviet affairs. He traveled and studied in Spain in 1936.

4. Ralph Bates (1899――), an English novelist, went to Spain in 1923 and lived there until the end of the Civil War. Spain was the subject of all his earlier novels.

5. Jonah Stalberg (1894–1955) came to the United States from Russia in 1923. He established St. Nicholas Orthodox Church in Portland, Oregon (1925–1938), and subsequently became a prominent churchman and lecturer in this country.

6. Leon Trotsky, *In Defense of the Soviet Union* (New York, 1937) or *Lessons of October* (New York, 1937).

To Max Lerner

Ithaca, [April 1937][1]

Dear Max,

Thanks for the suggestions for the Spanish article. I've sent them on to the proper person.

I've read your introduction to the book, Adam Smith His Wealth of Nations.[2] It's well done—that is it brings out what you want effectively. What else might have been said, I don't know A. S. well enough to know. Perhaps a word to the effect that A. S. planned to write a complete synthetic philosophy, a la Spencer,[3] only in the 18 c climate. The W. of N. was to have been only a part, and by no means the most important. I've always understood (perhaps wrongly) that he set more store by the Moral Sentiments. In the 18 c. they were hard put to it to find some *natural* quality on which to rest a belief in virtue, morality, etc. Something to take the place of divine authority. *Sympathy* was thought much of in this connection. Diderot[4] tried to make something of it.

I like your point about the book being a *result* of the *milieu,* and then becoming a *cause* in its own right—something added to the milieu which created it. It's a safe line to take in the treacherous matter of Old Historical Cause and Effect.

Sincerely,
Carl Becker

1. Lerner Papers, YU.
2. New York: Modern Library, 1937 (sixty-page introduction).
3. Herbert Spencer (1820–1903), British philosopher and sociologist.
4. Denis Diderot (1713–1784), French philosophe and writer.

To Anita M. Lerner

April 25, 1937[1]

Dear Anita,[2]

. . . . .

I suppose there is a technique of writing which one has to acquire; but before you can write really well you have to forget all about the technique. So far as I am concerned, the art consists in getting clear concrete pictures of the thing you are trying to convey, and then finding exactly the words to convey it exactly & vividly.

Book reviewing is supposed to be something any one can do. In fact it is something of an art—so much needs to be put in so short space. There should be a brief clear idea of what the author has tried to do: some pertinent comment on the extent to which he succeeds or fails or both; and some *placing* of the book in its *genre*.

Generally speaking, it's a good plan to go from A to B to C. But it can be overdone. And some minds don't work that way. You have a quick intuitive mind that sees the whole in terms of this that or the other aspect of it. It's usually right: but you have a hard time working out its reasons. You often say a lot that seems to go from Z to D to Y to A: but give you time and you get all the letters in the end. What you need to do in writing is to get clear in mind what are the high spots, & the order: then build these up with the aid of all the apparently disconnected insights that come to you: but the [pungent?] disconnected bits must be subordinated to the main theme for illustrative purposes.

Well, here's a lecture, and no good, because no one can teach anyone else anything about how to learn to write. Your review of the Tolstoi book was a real gem—it *brought the book out* in terms of the people concerned without any aid from any general theory of things.

Laski's foible is to be omniscient & omnipresent & omnivocal—a bit on the ex cathedra side. I know how you feel.[3]

By the way, are these Linds you mention the Middletown Linds [sic]?[4] If he reviews my book I should like to know where. It's been out 18 months and I haven't seen any serious review of it yet.

Best wishes,
Carl Becker

1. AML.
2. Two brief introductory paragraphs have been deleted.
3. Laski reviewed CLB's *Progress and Power* in the *New Republic*, LXXXVIII (Sept. 16, 1936), 162–163.
4. Robert S. and Helen M. Lynd, *Middletown: A Study in Contemporary American Culture* (New York, 1929); and *Middletown in Transition: A Study in Cultural Conflicts* (New York, 1937).

To Leo and Ida Gershoy

Sea Bright, New Jersey, August 20, 1937[1]

Dear Leo & Ida,

I am very glad you have had a grand time. Is it a part of having a grand time that Leo goes off to France and leaves Ida in London to pay old bills and contract new ones? Or is it merely that Ida couldn't contract debts in France? It seems hardly possible. However, I trust you will be returning on the same ship. And by the way, what ship is it to be? Please let me know, because we shall be pulling out of here almost on the day of your arrival, & if we see you it will be in New York. The situation is this. I have to go up to New Haven to attend a meeting of the board of editors of the Yale Review either on Sept. 20 or 21. The plan is to drive up to New York & leave Maude there until I return from New Haven. If then we know the boat and the date of arrival, & if the latter happens to be the 20 or 21 or thereabouts we can get in touch with you. We don't want to miss any chance of seeing you.

We have had a good summer, although it has been pretty hot. I am the color of a red Indian, and am well enough—fine in fact, except for a slight set-back this last week. A bit too much sun, I think. I am scribbling away on the World History, & have got to the point where I can see the end—thank God! I have also written a short paper to be read at Phila. next December—Random Remarks about Constitutions.[2] I dread going back to the academic grind. I should like to retire right now & never meet another class or get within smelling distance of another masters or doctors thesis or term paper, or committee meeting. Maybe I can do so within a year or so.

Please arrive before we leave, & in any case let us know the boat & the date.

With love,
from Carl Becker

1. LIG.
2. "Afterthoughts on Constitutions," *Yale Review*, XXVII (1938), 450–462.

To Max Lerner

Ithaca, March 25, 1938[1]

Dear Max,

Thanks for sending me your article. It is a penetrating and essentially a sound exposition of historical events. But I think you dismiss too easily the notion that unrestrained majority rule carries with it a danger of dictatorship and suppression of civil liberties. You can have majority rule without periodical voting. There is a majority rule in a real sense in Russia, Germany, Italy. There was majority rule under Napoleon and Peisistratus. Under Napoleon, Hitler, Stalin voting is not unknown. Under proper conditions, when fear and emotion run strongly, the people is a great beast. Individual representatives of the people are ordinarily good fellows, humane and sensible in respect to anything they can understand. But collectively they can easily become something else. You have a romantic faith in the humanity and good sense of the people which I do not share. I have no desire to protect the minorities that so largely control economic welfare in their own interest. But the danger is that the people, in freeing themselves from this minority, will willingly sacrifice the minorities that are represented by people like you and me who believe, at least I do and I hope you do too, that in the long run no freedom can be worth much that does not include freedom to discuss the ends and means of social organization. The people would sacrifice this easily if by so doing they thought they were getting what they wanted. Believe me, it is a real danger, a danger which may come from majorities as well as from minorities. In the Greek world, when democracy reached a certain point it emerged as Tyranny. On the basis of that experience Aristotle was right enough in maintaining that Democracy was a degenerate form of Polity, as Plutocracy was a degenerate form of Aristocracy. It might be maintained plausibly that modern experience is repeating that of the Greeks.

And with all your virtues heavy upon you, may God have you in his holy keeping!

Carl Becker

1. Lerner Papers, YU.

To Charles A. Beard

Spring Lake, New Jersey, [September 1938][1]
Dear Beard,

Just read your article on Nevins book.[2] Very good. What they can't forgive you for is saying (if you did say it—it's so reported) that history is an act of faith, or something like that. If you had said that history is a science and gives us the truth about the past, why you could then have said all you have said (which virtually demonstrates that history is not a science) and all would have been well. You are casting doubt on the absolute value & truth of their studies—that's why they call you a defeatist. Don't mind—as I know you don't. I have been called a "milk & water liberal," a "well known Communist writer," a "defeatist," and a "social fascist"—whatever that last may be. In these days there is a terrific pressure on everyone to be *loyal* to some cause or group or individual. You are expected to join something and hate in unison. Well, good hunting. And very best regards to Mary Jane.

Sincerely
Carl Becker

1. CBCU.
2. Allan Nevins, *Gateway to History*, reviewed in *The Nation,* CXLVII (Sept. 24, 1938), 300–302.

To Guy Stanton Ford

Ithaca, September 29, 1938[1]
Carl Becker is glad to have Guy Ford, his Book,[2] but glader to have his friendly salutation. In turn the boy from Blackhawk who made good salutes the boy from Bremer who made gooder—who made, as Hyman Kaplan would say, "good, better, high cless."

1. Ford Papers, UM.
2. *Dictatorship in the Modern World* (Minneapolis, 1935).

To Robert Morris Ogden

Ithaca, October 15, 1938[1]

Dear Ogden,[2]

Thanks very much for sending me a copy of your book.[3] I heard you present some of it to "The Circle",[4] and now I have been reading the completed work with profound interest and great admiration. Your fundamental idea has long been a notion of mine, but I had neither the knowledge nor the patience to make it explicit as you have done. It always seemed to me that every one, or nearly every one, is capable of aesthetic appreciation, and that this appreciation runs throughout all behavior and is not confined to what is called "fine art." There is a satisfaction in doing almost anything as expertly as it can be done, or in seeing others do it, merely for the expertness of the doing and quite apart from any practical advantage involved. It may be washing dishes, or throwing a foreward pass, or making a table, or painting a Mona Lisa. In each case the expertness is a form of art, and the satisfaction derived from it is an aesthetic satisfaction: the quality, intensity, value of the art or the satisfaction may of course differ greatly. Your differentiation of the practical from the fine arts seems to me admirable. But then the whole book is admirable. I don't know how you find the time to do all the things you do. It must be because you do it with so little lost motion, so expertly, in short as an artist.

Cordially yours,

Carl Becker

1. Robert M. Ogden Papers CU.

2. Ogden (1877–1959) taught psychology at Tennessee (1905–1914), Kansas (1914–1916), and Cornell (1916–1945), where he was also dean of the College of Arts and Sciences (1923–1945).

3. *The Psychology of Art* (New York, 1938).

4. The Gentleman's Intellectual Recreation Circle of Cornell University, described as "a self-constituted group of the *cognoscenti, literati,* and *illuminati,* which, during the academic year, meets one evening a month to hear and eviscerate a learned paper and drink beer—in short, a socially minded research club from which some of

the best minds on campus have been excluded." Becker was an original member of The Circle, formed in March 1934.

To Harry Elmer Barnes

Ithaca, October 22, 1938[1]

Dear Barnes,

Thanks for your note. Authors rarely write to their reviewers[2] except through the columns of the journal where the review appears, and then to complain that the review isn't good enough. I had a letter from a publishing house the other day, and the writer took occasion to hint that I had given you what for. That surprised me, and I am sorry if that is the impression the review leaves. I said in so many words that it was about the best book on the subject for the general public. I suppose if a reviewer resorts to a little harmless humor some readers will inevitably think he must have it in for the author. Henry Adams told me, through Jameson, that I ought to beware because humor was dangerous for a historian.[3] However, if you don't think I've blasted your book, it doesn't matter to me.

Sincerely,
Carl Becker

1. CBCU.
2. CLB reviewed Barnes's *The History of Historical Writing*, in *AHR*, XLIV (1938), 20–28.
3. Adams (1838–1918) was a historian, biographer, essayist, and editor. See CLB to the editor of the *American Historical Review*, Jan. 31, 1945.

To the editor of the *New Republic*

Ithaca, [autumn 1938][1]

I have a letter from the New Republic which asks me to note any books during the last thirty or forty years which have impressed me or influenced my thinking. Undoubtedly many books have influenced my thinking, or at least clarified ideas I already had (which is about the only way books influence thinking anyway). Those I can think of offhand are the following:

Sumner's 'Folkways,' which impressed me with the relativity of custom and ideas. Freud's 'Introduction to Psychoanalysis,' which made explicit the notion that the wish is father to the thought. Vaihinger's "Als Ob,' which came to me in the English translation. 'As If,' and confirmed me in the notion that social thinking is shaped by certain unexamined preconceptions current at the time. Whitehead's 'Science and the Modern World' and 'Adventures of Ideas' had the same sort of influence. Croce's 'History, Its Theory and Practice' helped to shape my ideas about history, which I set forth in the address, 'Everyman His Own Historian.'

What little I know about the new science has come largely through the popular works of Eddington, Whitehead and Bertrand Russell. (The latter's books on social matters are amusing but superficial.) Whitehead's little volume on mathematics in the Home University Library I found very useful. John Dewey's books I find hard to understand, but his ideas, coming to me through other writers, have confirmed a native tendency to pragmatic theory. Warner Fite's 'Moral Philosophy' is, I think, the only book on that subject that ever made any impression on me, but that hit the right spot somehow.

I hope this may in some sense answer the request as you wish it to be answered.

Carl Becker

1. *New Republic*, LXXXXVII (Dec. 7, 1938), 135; published in Malcolm Cowley, ed., *Books That Changed Our Minds* (New York, 1939), 5–6.

To Louis Gottschalk

Ithaca, December 26, 1938[1]

Dear Gottschalk,

I am at last out of the hospital, and seem to be on the road to recovery. Am sorry not to be able to take advantage of your kind invitation. However, I had not expected to go to the meeting anyway, apart from illness. I have just read your article on Trotsky.[2] Very acute, without being unjust to Trotsky. I confess not to know what a revolution can be, apart from the historical events which exhibit it; & in that sense no revolution is ever betrayed. What is betrayed are the hopes & expectations of leaders who wish it might have taken another course. In this sense every revolution is betrayed, because history is a cynical, tough old nut that always betrays our ideal aspirations. In the case of the Russian revolution history betrayed the Marxist utopian dream, just as in the French Revolution history betrayed the liberal democratic dream of equality & fraternity. Your point about Trotsky's attitude towards Kerensky etc. is very well taken. Marxists ought, on their own theory of the class struggle, to take it for granted that the bourgeois classes will fight for their interests. Christian, or even liberal philosophy, would justify me, for example, in sacrificing my interests for the welfare of mankind; but on the basis of Marxian philosophy, I would be a fool to work for Communism. I am a professor, that is to say a tool of Capitalism which supports me; and why should I not, therefore, fight for my class & my own interests.

Give my regards to Leo & all the people who remember me. And love to Fruma and Alexandre.

Sincerely,
Carl Becker

1. CBCU.
2. "Leon Trotsky and the Natural History of Revolutions," *American Journal of Socioliogy*, XLIV (1938), 339–354.

To Charles A. Beard

Ithaca, December 27, 1938[1]

Dear Beard,

Thanks for your very nice letter. I have now come to the surface again, and am as well as usual, so that I can go on doing half a he-man's job.

Have you seen a new book by Maurice Mandelbaum on "The Problem of Historical Knowledge"?[2] It is a "refutation of relativism." The "relativists" are certain "practising historians and philosophers." They are introduced in the order of least importance. The first one introduced is Carl Becker, the second Charles Beard. His heavy guns are, naturally, reserved for the philosophers, Croce, Dilthey, & Mannheim—people who may be expected to know what they are talking about.[3] It is an elaborate affair, but quite confused, and the crucial refutation is achieved by denying that there is, as the relativists claim, any distinction between "facts" and "interpretation" of facts. The historical account is a "tissue of facts" and nothing else; & the tissue of facts set forth in their natural context provide their own meaning. A clumsy work, but as you are given quite a run around you might be interested. I am reviewing it for the Philosophical Review.[4]

God keep and preserve you, and please give my love to Mary Jane. I always recall with great pleasure our talks in Minneapolis and on the train, & it seems a kind of perversity of fate that we do not see more of each other.

Sincerely,
Carl Becker

1. CBCU.
2. *The Problem of Historical Knowledge: An Answer to Relativism* (New York, 1938).
3. Benedetto Croce (1866–1952), Wilhelm Dilthey (1833–1911), and Karl Mannheim (1893–1947).
4. *Philosophical Review*, XLIX (1940), 361–364.

To Henry W. Edgerton

Ithaca, December 29, 1938[1]

Dear Henry,[2]

Your letter reached me in the hospital, from which I returned on Christmas Eve. I seem now to be as well as usual, needing to recover a little weight & strength however. I always go on the optimistic assumption that the current attack will be the last one—an assumption which eight years of experience thoroughly refutes. However, life is impossible unless lived on illusions. One of your illusions seems to be that every word in what I write is thoroughly considered and must have some particular reason for being where it is. The truth is that my writings are not designed to be subject to the formidable analysis of the legal mind. They crumble up under such analysis like a paper house subject to a match. I am glad that you liked the article.³ Everyone seems to like it—even Barnes who wrote me that his book was justified, if for no other reason because it inspired me to write one of my essays. The fact is I don't think it so devastating as many of my correspondents seem to think. After all I said that the book was the best thing in English for the general reader, and it was designed for the general reader. But if a critic indulges in a little playful humor at the expence of a writer's foibles, many readers think he must have no use for that writer's book. Henry Adams once told Jameson that my humor was very agreeable to him, but that he (Jameson) ought to warn the young man that humor was a dangerous quality in a historian.

Well, I hope you and Alice are enjoying your wealth and fame and may God have you in his Most Holy keeping, for the new year and for many New Years to come.

Sincerely,
Carl Becker

1. CBCU.
2. Edgerton (1889–1970), a lawyer and judge, received his B.A. at Cornell (1910), and taught law there (1916–1921, 1929–1937), before becoming a judge in the U.S. Court of Appeals for Washington, D.C. (1937–1962). A distinguished civil libertarian, he was one of CLB's best friends.
3. CLB's essay-review of Barnes's *History of Historical Writing*.

To Charles A. Beard

Ithaca, [February 1939]¹

I read with great interest your article on Turner,² who as you perhaps know was my teacher in Wisconsin, and the most stimulating one I ever had. (I might except Robinson, but for the fact that I had only one seminary with him). I think Turner was fed up with the genetic view of institutions that held the field at Johns Hopkins in his day—the view that free institutions were "inherited" from the so-called German Mark. His whole point was that American institutions were not inherited from Germany, brought over here from England, and set up intact, as it were; but that customary habits and ways of thought were brought over from England, and then transformed by the new and strangely different environment. In short, the explanation of American institutions was to be found, not in the German forest, but in the American wilderness.

I think you are quite right in thinking he exaggerated the "individualism" of the frontier. Of course the frontier promoted initiative and self-reliance. You had to have guts to survive. But conformity was essential too. Individual liberty could be exercised only within a narrow framework of conduct and thought. And cooperation in the community was absolutely essential. I think this is the explanation of the fact that in the west, which produces individuals with plenty of intiative and independence, eccentricities which go beyond the narrow limits of the common mores are likely to be more frowned on than elsewhere.

There was a fundamental inconsistency in Turner's general philosophy. His thesis was that the "peculiar" (how often he used the word) American ideas and institutions were essentially the result of the environment of a new country. If so, the conclusion would be that as these conditions of a new country disappeared and came to resemble those of older civilizations, the peculiar ideas and institutions would be modified and perhaps disappear altogether. But Turner, although never explicitly drawing this conclusion, never liked explicitly to admit it either. He was so in love with America and its ideas, that he clung to the notion that our blessed liberty, equality, and fraternity was not only something new in the world, but that it would always somehow remain what it was.

Paxon once called my attention to the fact that Turner never turned out more than three or four Ph.D.'s who ever amounted to anything. I think one of the reasons is that most of his admiring disciples, who went into American history, felt that to be a follower of Turner you had to study the "frontier", and this meant to study the history of the "West," and they understood Turner so little that this meant you had to gether "data" on the west—perhaps count the hogs in some county in Iowa. The first rate people whom he influenced are to be found in other fields than American history, or in other fields than history for that matter.

I shall be interested to see your review of Mandelbaum.[3]

1. From an incomplete draft, CBCU.

2. "The Frontier in American History," *New Republic,* XCVII (Feb. 1, 1939), 359–362; reprinted in Cowley, ed., *Books That Changed Our Minds,* 61–71.

3. *The Problem of Historical Knowledge* (1938).

To Alfred A. Knopf

Ithaca, June 9, 1939[1]

Dear Mr. Knopf,

Your congratulations are very agreeable to me, however much I really hate honorary degrees.[2] The first time you receive an honorary degree it is nice enough: the second time, a little stale: the third time, it verges on the ridiculous. However, I don't want to be ungracious: and Nick Butler[3] really puts on a good show.

Sincerely yours,
Carl Becker

1. AAK.

2. Becker received a Litt. D. at Columbia in 1939.

3. Nicholas Murray Butler (1862–1947), president of Columbia (1901–1945).

8. War, Retirement, and
Renewed Vigor, 1939-1943

To May Elish Markewich

Ithaca, October 17, 1939[1]

Dear Mrs. Markewich,[2]

Thanks very much for your friendly note. It seems clear what the allies are fighting for: but whether they will obtain all of it by fighting is another matter. I think they will defeat Germany if the war goes on, more easily than the last time, because Germany is in no condition to stand a long war. But while they may get rid of Hitler, I can't see war as an effective method of establishing a "new order" in Europe. Heaven knows what will come of it.

Give my regards to your husband,

Very sincerely,
Carl Becker

1. May Elish Markewich Papers, New York, N.Y.
2. Markewich received her B.A. at Cornell in 1928.

To Carl Horwich

Ithaca, April 29, 1940[1]

Dear Mr. Horwich,[2]

I have no objection to your taking my works for a subject for a thesis. As to my life, I'm afraid there is little in it that is of much interest. You will find the main points in Who's Who. My father's ancestors came to New York in 1775 from Amsterdam. His mother's name was Van Brocklin, which seems to indicate Dutch extraction. My father was born in Jefferson Co. N.Y. near Carthage, moved to Iowa in 1867: & I was born on his farm 16 miles from

Waterloo, & lived there until the age of eleven, when we moved to Waterloo, where I went to school, graduating from the high school in 1892. During three summers I worked on my uncle's farm. Otherwise my life has been the usual uneventful academic life. You will find some material in a pamphlet, issued by Silver Burdett Co. for publicity purposes in connection with my text books, which you can get by writing to my son, Frederick Becker, Silver Burdett Co., 45 East 17 St. N.Y. The report of the Librarian of Cornell University for some years past has contained a list of works published each year by the faculty.

I have just come home from the hospital, & this is the best I can do now. Perhaps later I could help you on specific matters which you might like to know about.

Sincerely,
Carl Becker

1. CBCU.
2. Horwich was a graduate student in history at Wayne State University in Detroit. His M.A. thesis was "Carl Becker: A Study of Liberalism and the History of Ideas," 1941. A copy given to CLB is in the Olin Library, Cornell University.

To Louis Gottschalk

Ithaca, May 3, 1940[1]

Dear Gottschalk,

I had a pretty tough time, but am now on the road to recovery. Renewed lectures this week, what there is of them—two a week. Fifteen months of uninterrupted good health gave me some reason to hope that maybe I was through with these attacks. However—I keep on hoping in spite of ten years experience which makes the hope look rather forlorn.

The Virginia lectures are postponed until October or November next.

I will be retiring at the end of next year—age 68. Very glad to do so, although I haven't too much to live on—enough, however, to get on with. As rackets go, teaching & writing is one of the best, or at least for me it is. But enough is enough, and after forty years of it I am willing to kiss it good bye.

McNeil [sic][2] is doing very well, and got some sort of assistant-ship, although just what I don't know as the awards were made when I was in the hospital.

Give my love to Fruma,

Sincerely,
Carl Becker

1. CBCU.
2. William H. McNeill (1917——) received his B.A. and M.A. at Chicago (1938, 1939), and his Ph.D. at Cornell (1947). He has taught at Chicago since 1947.

To Carl Horwich

Ithaca, [June 11, 1940][1]

Dear Mr. Horwich,

I send you some additional titles & virtually all the reviews.

I think you need to think a little more about the phrase "historical facts." You seem to make no distinction between an event and a fact. The word fact is merely a symbol which expresses our conviction that something is true: the fact is only as solid & sure as our evidence for believing it. To me anything is a fact so long as I am convinced it is true. But when does an alleged event become a historical "fact": how many people have to believe it a fact to make it one? Many alleged events were regarded as "facts" in the Middle Ages by virtually all the people who counted: now they are regarded as myths. And certain events are taken as facts for a long time & by virtually all historians, only to be disproved. The story of Galileo & the Leaning Tower of Pisa has been regarded as a fact for 300 years. Now it is clear that Galileo never dropped weights from the Leaning Tower.

The point is that historians do "create the facts" in this sense: that our conviction that it is a fact rests upon *evidence* and *inferences* we make from the evidence: and an alleged event becomes a fact for us when the evidence & the inferences we draw are sufficient to convince us. At any time, therefore, "facts" depend upon what we can accept as valid evidence & proper inferences. This capacity to accept evidence & assent to inferences is always changing. Always keep this in mind: a fact is not something objective & material in the outer world,—but only something the mind is convinced is true.

Sincerely,
Carl Becker

1. CBCU.

To Louis Gottschalk

Ithaca, August 28, 1940[1]

Dear Gottschalk,

I returned to Ithaca Monday; and am making a very good recovery. The operation, a pretty drastic one, they assure me will put an end to the gastric troubles that I have had for the last ten years. I hope so. The operation (a fairly common one now) consists in cutting out about ¾ of the stomach—the part where ulcers bleed & which secretes the acids that are disasterous. Out of the ¼ remaining they make you a new stomach, which gradually & very accomodatingly enlarges to something like the normal size. Already I can eat fairly normal meals with no feeling of being stuffed. It's now a matter of regaining strength, especially in the legs. In respect to legs, I'm like Chaucer's Clerk of Oxenford:

> "As lene weare his legs as is a rake,
> There was no calf ye seen."[2]

Give my love to Fruma, & Mrs. Becker joins in best wishes to you both & to the children.

Sincerely,
Carl Becker

1. CBCU.
2. CLB must have been quoting from memory (or else writing a parody of Chaucer), because the lines are altered from the original. See *The Canterbury Tales*, General Prologue, lines 287 and 591–592, where Chaucer writes of the reeve's legs.

To Leo and Ida Gershoy

Ithaca, August 30, 1940[1]

Dear Children,

Arrived home Monday without feeling tired. (In spite of Ida's conspiring behind my back, *not* in a Drawing Room—ha! ha!) Am doing very well, and getting around a little, but getting back my strength is slow business. My legs are weak, and like those of Chaucer's Clerk of Oxenford:

"As lene weare his legs as is a rake,
There was no calf ye seen."

I don't know whether we will get up to Lake George. It depends on how long it takes me to get reasonably strong. However, everything is O.K. at present. Good appetite and no ill effects. Haven't had my apple cobbler yet, but will in good time.

Enjoy yourselves. Let there be *Incidents* in your life that you would not want known at Sarah Lawrence or on Eleventh St.

I may be in Charlottesville on Thanksgiving—the thought just occurred to me.

Be of good courage,
Carl Becker

1. LIG.

To Ida Gershoy

Ithaca, September 28, 1940[1]

Dear Ida,

Your letter delights me because it exhibits you at the top of your wit & full of prunes & spinach & the joy of life. We must go to Truro[2] if it sets people up like that.

I have done nothing but loaf for five weeks. It's a slower business than I hoped. I haven't gained a pound of the 15 I lost. Everything is all right, I'm told, but the normal result of such an operation is that the eating of meals, although enjoyable, is followed by a certain amount of faintness induced by a tendency to diarrhea. They are working on this, but say it will disappear only as the patched up stomach gets adjusted to its task. Meantime, it leaves me with little strength or zest for work of any kind. (Two lectures a week, which begin next week, I don't count as work: there's not much strength even for them, & no zest at all, but I will pull them off somehow.) We didn't get to Lake George, but may drive up for a weekend towards the middle of October if the weather is good.

You shouldn't begrudge Leo an affair. It would no doubt guarantee him a more "richly satisfying life" & enable him to "express his personality more fully."—à la Max![3] The same applies to you. But neither of you will ever venture—you are too well brought up & effectively inhibited. *Bourgeois!*

Maude is flourishing. And so am I really. It's only that the recovery is taking more time than I had expected.

Regards to the Mountain Goat.

Carl

1. LIG.
2. Near Provincetown, Massachusetts, on Cape Cod.
3. Lerner.

To Leo Gershoy

Ithaca, October 16, 1940[1]

Dear Leo,

I am getting on very well, and two lectures a week on a subject which, having forgotten so much about it, I can speak with the greatest confidence, is no strain at all. On the contrary, it provides a slight stimulation.

We drove up to Lake George last Friday, returning Sunday. Saturday we drove up the west side of the Lake to Ticonderoga, & in the afternoon parked by the lake shore and listened to the Army-Cornell game. The weather was perfect Indian Summer. I thought we had some fine color here in October: but never, in my born days, have I seen such a riotous, unrestrained & unashamed display of brilliant barbaric color as on that day.

I have read half or more of Taylor's book, which is all I care for. So please keep it.

We are preparing for Thanksgiving! You can ask Ida to figure out what that means.

> Love to you both,
> Carl Becker

P.S. The Virginia lectures are now set for Nov. 12, 13, 14. May stop in New York on way home. Will let you know.

1. LIG.

To Alfred A. Knopf

Ithaca, April 23, 1941[1]

Dear Mr. Knopf,

It is very agreeable to me to have your good opinion (which I value highly) of my book, and to know that you would much like to publish an elaboration of the ideas therein.[2] The older I grow the less I am interested in elaboration, and the more I like to get down to essentials. I have really said my say on democracy (in this book and in four or five articles in the Yale Review in the last four or five years) and it would be rather boring to undertake an elaborated rehash of them. Besides, I am committed to give the (six) Messenger lectures here in 1942–1943, and as I write so slowly it will take most of my time to prepare them. I should really like to have a book published under your imprint, but as it happens I have had little to do with selecting publishers. I hope to live long enough to write a book the publication of which is not already arranged for. Meantime, I regret very much that it is not possible for me to undertake the project which you present with so much effectiveness. As matters stand now it really isn't possible for me to do it.

> Very cordially yours,
> Carl Becker

1. AAK.
2. *Modern Democracy*, three lectures delivered at the University of Virginia on the Page-Barbour Foundation, November 12–14, 1940.

To Leo Gershoy

Ithaca, May 1, 1941[1]

Dear Leo,

Your letter did not arrive before I left Ithaca. I should have been glad to meet your gang; and I had originally planned to take dinner with you in New York, stay the night there, & return by the Lehigh. But Gussie's plan for driving me down & back made it more convenient to stay out at Hartsdale.

I have written to *Professor* J. Selwyn Schapiro[2] commending you highly.

I see that my successor has been announced—DeKiewit of Iowa.[3] A good fellow I think, but his work is chiefly in British imperial history, although of course he will give courses on Modern European history. I had nothing to do with it, & was glad enough not to have had. I can tell you in confidence (since I had it in confidence from Laistner) that you were considered for the place (and in my opinion ought to have been appointed). I think Laistner supported you, but he told me that there was no possibility of a sufficient unanimity in the department. I'm terribly sorry, but I can understand that it was essential to have someone that the department could agree on: & I know you would not have wanted the job without such agreement. I have long hoped that you would be my successor. This is strictly confidential of course.

Sincerely,
Carl Becker

1. LIG.

2. Schapiro (1879——) taught modern European history at the City College of New York (1907–1947). His specialties were anticlericalism and the history of liberalism.

3. Cornelis W. de Kiewiet (1902——) taught history at the University of Iowa (1929–1941) and Cornell (1941–1948); he served Cornell as dean, provost, and acting president (1945–1951), and then became president of the University of Rochester (1951–1961). His specialty was British imperial history.

To Max Lerner

Ithaca, May 9, 1941[1]

Dear Max,

I saw Anita for a short time in December when I was at the Hist meeting. I don't get about much, except to go up to New Haven for a Board meeting occasionally, and then I am in New York only on the way.

Glad you liked the book.[2] Your colleague (isn't he) reviewed it for the Nation,[3] and Leo Gershoy will have a review for the June Yale Review.

I am retiring this June from active teaching. As rackets go, teaching is a good one, but after 42 years of it one is content. I am not sorry to be done with it, but sorry only that I have reached the age when one is not sorry to be done with it.

The second term of next year I will be at Smith College, on the Neilson Research Professorship. They are paying me a good bit, apparently for residing in the community and giving them the benefit of my distinguished presence. I can't afford to turn down money, especially money obtained under false pretences.

Sincerely,

Carl Becker

1. Lerner Papers, YU.
2. *Modern Democracy.*
3. Reviewed warmly by Reinhold Niebuhr in *The Nation,* CLII (April 12, 1941), 441.

To Ida Gershoy

Ithaca, June 10, 1941[1]

Dear Ida,

We expect to drive down to see Fred sometime in late June, but I can't promise to make the Cape—it's a long way off the road home. However—as Reggie Fortune[2] is always saying.

Tonight Maude & I are going by invitation to dinner at the Spring Side Inn on Lake Owasco. The invitation comes from the incorporated body of history grad. students, and is I suppose staged in honor of my retirement, and maybe involves the presentation of a present, & certainly involves, for me, a few remarks, in my well known well chosen words. I don't care for it much, except as an evidence of good will; but still they are a nice & lively bunch and with Gussie their guide, mentor, & friend along, it won't be stogy.

Maude's mouth already begins to water at the thought of lobster: & therefore she, as well as I sends her love,

Carl Becker

1. LIG.
2. Plump, drawling hero of many detective stories written by Henry C. Bailey, an English author. CLB loved detective stories.

To Louis Gottschalk

Cape Cod, Massachusetts, July 18, 1941[1]
Dear Gottschalk,

Your letter was forwarded to me here, where I am spending two weeks. Such letters are a consolation and a great reward for all the effort a teacher puts in to what often seems a futile business.[2] I get a good many, and they enable me to feel that, little as I can understand what it is, there must have been something valuable that I did for many people.

Retiring doesn't mean any great change to me, since for the last few years I taught only the two hour course on Fr. Rev. & Nap. and the seminary. I am, after 40 years, glad to be done with it, only perhaps a little sorry to have reached the age when I am glad to be done with it. They have appointed me "Cornell Historian." What my duties are I can't find out, except that there is a general expectation that I will occupy myself some how with the history of Cornell University.[3] I have been invited to give the Messenger Lectures (six lectures) in 1942–43: and the president suggested that I might choose for them some aspect of Cornell history. I have therefore planned to devote the six lectures to the Founding of Cornell University. I hope to relate it to the broad general subject of education so as to bring out the fact that the founding of Cornell was a significant aspect of the general trend in modern times toward history & Science. What else can I do to justify my appointment after this is done, I don't know. The effect of the appointment, whether that was its purpose, is to boost my retiring allowance to a respectible figure.

I am going to Smith for the second semester. The appointment is on the Neilson Research Professorship. The duties are negligible, except to live in Northampton, & the pay is generous.

Maude joins me in best of wishes to you & Fruma and the noble progeny.

Sincerely,
Carl Becker

1. CBCU.
2. Gottschalk's letter of July 15, 1941, is in the Appendix. Cf. CLB to Frederick Jackson Turner, May 16, 1910.
3. On April 27, 1940, CLB had delivered an address, "The Cornell Tradition: Freedom and Responsibility," to celebrate the seventy-fifth anniversary of Cornell's charter. See CLB, *Cornell University: Founders and the Founding*, 193–204.

To Alfred A. Knopf

Ithaca, August 7, 1941[1]

Dear Knopf,

I am intending to write the Introduction for the Declaration[2] as soon as I finish a review of Shirer's Berlin Diary for the Yale Review.[3] It should be in your hands within a week or two at latest.

It must be a great satisfaction to publish a book that is not only a great book but a best seller as well.[4] In the review I've tried to explain why the book is a good one, and also to convey something of the fine intelligence and character of the author. I don't know when I've come to admire an author so much from simply reading his book.

Sincerely,
Carl Becker

1. AAK.
2. In 1942, Knopf published a second edition of *The Declaration of Independence* (1st ed., 1922), for which CLB wrote a thirteen-page introduction.

3. William L. Shirer, *Berlin Diary, 1934–1941* (New York, 1941), reviewed in *Yale Review*, XXXI (1941), 173–176.
4. Shirer's *Diary* was published by Knopf.

To Leo Gershoy

Ithaca, September 24, 1941[1]

Dear Leo,

Knopf has just asked me to read a German Ms. on the Fall of Napoleon's Dictatorship. I've set him on to you.

How does the base ball star of Wellfleet like it in the class room? I suppose it doesn't matter where he is so long as there are plenty of girls around. Thanks be, that I don't have to go back to the class room. The freshmen, every year, look more inane and lumpish than the year before, and the grey caps make them look more inane than they naturally would.

We had Carl Jadwin[2] for a week, while Fred & Betty went off to the Adarondacs for a vacation. Just as they left Maude fell down and hurt her knee, & had to go to bed for two days. So all the hard work fell to me. I can do everything. He's beautiful like his grandmother, and very good like his grandfather. If you want to see something worth while go up to 68 Hartsdale Ave., someday about 4 P.M. or 11 A.M. I'm dedicating my book of essays to him.

I've got one Messenger Lecture done, or virtually so. The others will be easier.

We will be coming to Hartsdale the weekend of Oct. 18–20. Hope to see you and Ida (to whom my love) then.

All the best,
Carl Becker

1. LIG.
2. CLB's grandson, Carl Jadwin Becker, born November 10, 1940.

To Henry W. Edgerton

Ithaca, [late December 1941][1]

Dear Henry,

Thanks for your letter.[2] You read books with *attention*—a rare bird! I know the common phrase is "Government of men": but I used the other because it leaves no ambiguity.³ "Govt of men" might mean that men are the governed—as Lincoln's government *of* the people. Probably I should have used the phrase that is usually used.

As to the Courts—of course I know judges, like other men, are bound to be influenced by their personal & class bias: but in the essay I was trying to bring out what seems to me the fact that this anti-intellectual view could be, and has been, carried too far: & that in fact *the logical end of it is the Nazi* philosophy. I agree that to know our opinions are biased is the best guarantee that the bias will be overcome so far as possible; and to know that judges opinions are influenced by their class conditioning should be all to the good. What I had in mind was that it's possible to take the attitude that if opinions are the result of bias & emotion & interest,—well, what the hell, then let's make our opinions mere servants of interest. This is what I had in mind about the courts—if they are, or are generally thought to be, *nothing* more than instruments in the hands of a class,—then they lose half their value. I didn't bring it out clearly enough.⁴

Sincerely,
Carl Becker

P.S. Glad to hear Ann is doing well. I suppose Alice is behaving as well as she can.

1. CBCU.
2. Dec. 15, 1941; in CBCU.
3. In *New Liberties for Old.* Becker wrote, "In the early nineteenth century the adherents of democracy were apt to say . . . that democracy is a government by laws and not a government by men" (128).
4. See *ibid.,* 136, 144.

To Leo and Ida Gershoy

Ithaca, [December 1941]¹

Little boys and girls should never fight,
Nor let their angry passions rise,
Nor loudly yell.
For if they always do what's right,

>And ask forgiveness every night—
>Who can tell?—
>As like as not
>On Christmas night
>They'll win a prize!

1. LIG; written by CLB on his Christmas card to the Gershoys.

To Anita M. Lerner

Northampton, Massachusetts, February 12, 1942[1]

Dear Anita,

I am enclosing a letter of information about women's colleges which might interest you. No need to return the letter. If you want to apply to President Jaqua,[2] you can of course refer to me. You can do that at any time anyway.

Am having a good time here. Max lectured here last night, and I met the girl—his wife now, isn't she?[3] Max is an effective lecturer, but there is a Marxian formula, although not very obtrusive, [peering?] through his interpretation—a bad time in the past, owing to evil men or conditions: a time of persecution & injustice: then the revolution when all is to be set right by the people. This is now applied to the last 20 years, the present war, & the post-war reconstruction. (This is only a new version of Christian philosophy —Decline and fall of man: time of trial & [?]: end of world & Church Triumphant.) Max is therefore very gloomy about the present moment, but extremely idealistic & optimistic about what can be made of democracy in the future. Still, it's good tonic for the times.

Love & thoughts,
Carl

1. AML.
2. Ernest Jaqua (1883–1972), president of Scripps College (1926–1942).
3. The Lerners were divorced in 1940.

To Mary Elizabeth Bohannon

Northampton, March 4, 1942[1]

Dear Betty,

Thanks for sending on Mrs. Crump's letter, and for your own. I'm living here in the hotel—very comfortable; and I'm really having a good time here at Smith. They are all most kind and obliging, and very good natured in attending my conferences, and very generous in their approval of everything I do. It's a really fine place, —a wholesome, husky bunch of girls: a democratic place with no pretense or finishing school snobishness, so far as I can see.

Of course I've met Miss Wilson,[2] and I think she is a very sound person. I gave a lecture the other day in a large introductory course on Modern history which she has something to do with—at her request. It's strange how, in spite of age, and shrunk shanks, and short breath, and a mind becoming dulled, the tounge wags on with a certain fluency.

I think the new President, Davis, (from Cornell as you know) is very much liked here.[3] Of course he isn't regarded as God Almighty and Jupiter Olympus, as Mr. Nielson [sic][4] was—but that could hardly be, and maybe it's better so. I heard a new story about him (Nielson). Maybe you've heard it. In connection with the report that got into the newspapers that the Amherst boys had said "Smith girls were easiest to kiss." Of course it raised one of those tempests in a teapot; and you can imagine what the average college president would have done—lectured the girls solemnly for half an hour. Well, at the first general chapel the girls were there wondering what President Nielson would say. He conducted the chapel service as usual, then started to leave the platform—the girls' eyes goggling out at the prospect of having nothing said. Then, suddenly, he turned back: "Oh! I forgot to say: If you must kiss, kiss gentlemen—gentlemen kiss but don't tell." And walked off.

Sincerely,
Carl Becker

1. CBCU.
2. Jean S. Wilson (1903——) taught history at Smith College (1927–1969), specializing in Tudor-Stuart England.

3. Herbert J. Davis (1893–1967) taught English literature at Cornell (1937–1940), and served as president of Smith (1940–1949).
4. William A. Neilson (1869–1946), president of Smith College (1917–1939).

To Max Lerner

Northampton, March 11, 1942[1]

Dear Max,

I was asked to make a talk at the Tuesday luncheon the defense organization has here every week—usually with speakers; and it was suggested that they would like to hear any comment I cared to make on your address. I didn't disagree with it very sharply. I told them what I told you—that I thought you were too pessimistic about the present, & too optimistic about what might come out of the war. I don't think there is as much contrast between the "people" whom you think are all right & the top hats and industrialists whom you think are mucking things up. I think, by & large, they are all more or less all right: they all want to win the war, & will do what is necessary in so far as they can *realize* what we're up against. But most people—high or low—not having imagination, can't really realize it. If we had hell bombed out of us for six months, as the English have had, then they would realize it, but I fear we never will have that. I told the story my daughter-in-law told me—of going into a White Plains grocery. Two women were ahead of her. One bulldozed the fellow into selling her five pounds of sugar, saying she was giving a big party, and "just *must* have it."

When the fellow went to get it, she turned to the other woman and said: "That makes 135 pounds I've got now." Well, I suppose she's all right too—just a silly ordinary suburban woman, who'se probably kind to her mother. But how many like her? A good many I'm afraid. They know we are at war, but they really don't understand anything about it. Then I thought we had a full time job on our hands to win the war, without revolutionizing the social structure at the same time—not that it won't be revolutionized a good deal. In short, I seemed to see in the pattern of your lecture the familiar Marxian formula, telescoped to fit fifty years of confusion—the bad boys getting the good people into a jam, then the Social Revolution, in which the bad boys will be ousted, then the good

times coming. But I said it was a very effective, moving talk and
would do a lot of good.

My lecture here, which opened the series, will be published in
the March Yale Review—out next Monday.[2]

Sincerely,

Carl Becker

1. Lerner Papers, YU.
2. "Making Democracy Safe in the World," *Yale Review*, XXXI
(1942), 433–453.

To Alice Durand Edgerton

Northampton, March 13, 1942[1]

Dear Alice,[2]

I have here some notes taken by you of a conversation between
Charles H. Hull and Olis Wood, sister-in-law of Ezra Cornell, in
which she gives her recollections of Ezra.[3] It's all extremely interesting: but I should like to know if you remember the incident,
and what your impression was of the old lady. Particularly, did she
seem to be an admirer of Ezra, or was she a little prejudiced against
him. She says there was a time when he went off on various
schemes, & the family at the Nook—her sister and three or four
children—had to be supported by her father, Mr. Wood, because
they had no money, and no credit. This might have prejudiced her.
Another point—how old was she, & did she seem to be intelligent
and capable of recalling these incidents clearly.

I want to form a judgment as to her reliability, especially because she says that Ezra was strongly opposed to the consolidation
of the electric telegraph companies into the Western Union, but
was forced to come in because his own company was virtually
bankrupt. Hull said the same, but whether he had any other evidence I don't know. This is of course entirely contrary to the story
told in all the biographies, which make out that Ezra was the
leader in organizing the Western Union. Any information you can
give me will be appreciated.[4]

How are you all? I hope Ann and John are doing nicely, and that
Henry is behaving as well as can be expected. I'm having a fine

time up here, with lots of leisure to work; and it's a very good college, as far as I can determine. Not a flake of snow since the 4 February, & only a little then. Sunshine, and mild weather. Ithaca and roundabout have had heavy blizzards, but I think most of it has disappeared.

All best wishes,
Carl Becker

1. CBCU.
2. Wife of Judge Henry W. Edgerton.
3. Ezra Cornell (1807–1874) devised a means for insulating telegraph wires on poles, and became a chief figure in a new industry. In 1855 he joined in the founding of The Western Union Telegraph Co. A decade later he provided the endowment necessary to establish Cornell University.
4. See CLB, *Cornell University: Founders and the Founding*, ch. iii, "Circumstances and the Man: Ezra Cornell."

To Alice Durand Edgerton

Northampton, [March 1942][1]
Dear Alice,

In my letter I said it was Ezra Cornell's sister in law that Hull had the interview with. It was I've found his brother in law. The name seems to be Olis E. Wood. But it may be Otis.[2]

Sincerely,
Carl Becker

1. CBCU.
2. It is.

To Ida Gershoy

Northampton, March 30, 1942[1]

Mrs Ida P. Gershoy,
14 E. 11 St.
New York City

Dear Madame,
   I take my pen in hand to let you know that I am well and hope you are the same.

> Yours respectfully,
>   Carl L. Becker, Litt. D.
>   Nielson Professor of History
>   Smith College,
>   Northampton, Mass.

P.S. What the hell do you mean writing that snooty letter? Write me a nice letter and I'll tell you all the news of Ithaca & Hartsdale.

   1. LIG.

To Ida Gershoy

Northampton, [April 1942][1]

Dear Ida,
   Well! At last!!
   I'm coming to New York this 25 of April as ever was: and will call you up sometime in the evening, as you are probably "at the office." Or if not you can call me at Freds. Maude will be here Thursday & Friday as well. But I have to come home Monday.
   The news is that C. J.[2] got his mother's nail polish & smeared it all over his face & clothes so he looked like a red Indian for some time. And then he found a beer bottle in the kitchen half full, &

took it to the fireplace & mixed the beer & ashes, & smeared this on his face. He's evidently going to be an actor.
We'll see you Sunday somewhere.

Love,
Carl

1. LIG.
2. Grandson Carl Jadwin.

To Richard M. Leighton

Ithaca, June 5, 1942[1]

Dear Leighton,[2]

I was glad to hear from you; & to know (I had already heard it) that you were doing something more interesting at least than carrying a gun and peeling potatoes. I hope you may get something you like even better. Your article is very good—that is, it's a good idea, I don't know for whom it is written: if for the average run of men, perhaps the phrasing is at times a bit heavy on the understanding.

I hear from Gussie what is known about Ford[3] and McNeil. Scot Lytle[4] is being called in shortly, and Spaulding also.[5] I think they are short this coming year of good material,—if I recall rightly there were two vacancies in the Modern history fellowship —and neither is filled. Are about 1200 in Summer School, which has already started.

I had a swell time at Smith, with nothing to do, & its a good college, & a good faculty. But I'm glad to be back in Ithaca. I had hoped to go to Cape Cod for a month, but with the gas restrictions there is not much use; so we expect to be here all summer, barring a train trip to N.Y. maybe for a weekend. I would surely be very glad if you could get off and come to Ithaca for a few days. Drop me a line when you haven't anything better to do.

Sincerely,
Carl Becker

1. Richard M. Leighton Papers, Alexandria, Va.
2. Leighton (1914———) received his Ph.D. at Cornell (1941); he worked in the Office of Military History, Department of the Army

(1948–1959) and at the Industrial College of the Armed Forces
(1959——).

3. Robert A. D. Ford (1915——) received his M.A. at Cornell (1939),
entered the Canadian foreign service in 1940, and became Canadian
ambassador to the U.S.S.R. in 1963.

4. Scott Lytle (1918——) received his Ph.D. at Cornell (1948), and
has taught modern European history at the University of Washington
since 1949.

5. William L. Spalding, Jr., received his Ph.D. at Cornell (1949),
taught history at South Carolina (1949–1951), Vassar (1951–1956),
Osaka University, in Japan (1956–1958); since 1960 he has worked
for the Central Intelligence Agency as a specialist on northeast Asia.

To Jessie Becker

Ithaca, June 26, 1942[1]

Dear Jessie,[2]

I am remembering your birthday, July 1, with a little check. You
can go with some friends to dinner, and then buy some fire crack-
ers. Do you remember how we used to make so much of the 4th of
July? At least the boys did, I think Ann[3] was scared. I don't know
about you. We used to get up at 4 oclock. If I had 50 cents, that
was as much as I ever had: but we certainly had more fun out of it
than I've ever had out of 50 cents since.

I remember when you were born—a bright warm day. I was sent
off in the morning to spend the day with the Vittman boys—it
seemed to me very funny they should make a point of it—and when
I came home at 6 oclock there you were.

I hope you have many happy returns.

Maude is doing fine—hasn't had any pains since coming home.
She has to follow a diet and take medicine,—which burns her up
because she never before had an illness—was never before in a
hospital bed.

With love,
Carl Lotus

1. CBCU.

2. CLB's youngest sister, who worked for thirty years in the office
of the Clerk of the District Court in Waterloo, Iowa.

3. A younger sister of CLB who became a school teacher.

To Thomas Reed Powell

Ithaca, July 10, 1942[1]

Dear Reed,[2]

Thanks for sending me your off-springs. I liked them all, as I do all your writings. I liked especially your confession and avoidance in the matter of a philosophy of law.[3] But it was after all a low-down trick to play on the sponsors of the series. They asked for a philosophy of law, and I should think that, in these crucial times, you might have complied with so reasonable a request. That is to say, you should have given them a philosophy of law that could be used to defeat Hitler.

I am writing six lectures to be given on the Messenger Foundation here at Cornell next spring. Subject: The Founding of Cornell University—to fit in with celebration of the 75th anniversary of the opening of the institution, Oct. 1868. I will send you a copy if you want. Meantime, I have a collection of essays called "New Liberties for Old."[4] Maybe I sent you a copy. If not, I will be glad to if you care to be bothered—no obligation to read of course.

What do you think of the world? It's different from what it seemed to be in 1916 when we played tennis at Columbia U.

Give my best to Molly and to all the little Powells, who are, after all, not so little now.

Sincerely,
Carl Becker

P.S. Am now Professor Emeritus, and liking it a lot.

1. CBCU.
2. Thomas Reed Powell (1880–1955) taught law at Columbia (1911–1925) and Harvard (1925–1949).
3. "My Philosophy of Law," from a book of the same title (Boston, 1941), 269–280.
4. *New Liberties for Old.*

To Leo Gershoy

August 5, 1942[1]

Dear Leo,

Yesterday I turned up an envelope addressed to you, and opening it found it was your speech on The Historian in War Time. I must have intended to return it and then mislaid it somehow. If you still want it let me know, and in any case all apologies.

But what I want especially is to know what has become of you & Ida. Did you get to the Cape, or are you, like every other important person, working in Washington?

Or is Ida in uniform working in a munitions factory? I'd love to see her handling a lath or riviting an air plane. . . .

We are sitting around. Maude is doing fine, but she has to watch her step, and take three or four medicines—no lobster, no sweet corn, no melons, etc. And it burns her up to see me eating blueberry pie and anything else. Anyway she hasn't had any return of the intestinal pain. We have an A and a B card, and feel very superior.

Am working on the Messenger lectures: and you would be astounded to see me going every morning like any other Academic slave, to research in the library, with 3x5 cards—only they're 4x5½. Am turning up a lot of stuff in the Cornell and White Papers down in the vault. So for once I can make a contribution— two dozen new little facts, or at least eighteen. And I'm having a researcher to go through the N.Y. newspapers for 1865.[2] If this goes on I'll have to have a secretary and a dispatch case. It won't last long however, and then I'll begin spinning it out of my head as usual.

Maude sends her love,

Sincerely,
Carl Becker

1. LIG.
2. In preparation for CLB, *Cornell University: Founders and the Founding.*

To Louis Gottschalk

Ithaca, [September 1942][1]

Dear Gottschalk,[2]

I understood Redfield[3] to be asking me to make a study of how historians actually had been using the human document—something quite too elaborate & painful for me to undertake. But chiefly my refusal was because I had already more than I could easily handle on my hands.

As to the authors being trained in Thompson's & Schmitt's seminars—I took that as implied in the Preface. I doubt if any or all of the historians you mention had been included it would have been necessary to modify what I said: and I still maintain that Croce is better known outside the narrow company of professional historians than any of the group of historians included: and that he will bulk larger, say in a hundred years from now in any history of European thought. However, maybe you are right that I'm too hard on the historians.

Maude is not very well just now. She is having a good deal of pain and inconvenience generally from what the doctors diagnose as colitus. I'm going to have a specialist on "alergy" test her to see if he can't devise a more proper diet.

Otherwise all is well.

Best & affectionate wishes to Fruma.

Sincerely,
Carl Becker

There is no demerit in not being the type that gets ulcers. On the contrary!

1. CBCU.
2. CLB is answering Gottschalk's letter of August 30, 1942 (CBCU): "I've been pretty sore at you of late. You refused to do the volume on 'the use of the human document in the study of history' for the Social Science Research Council. (Remember Redfield's request a few months ago—on my suggestion?) As a result, I've had to do it. . . . On top of that, I've just read your review of Schmitt's collection of essays on

'modern historians' and note you say those students were trained by Schmitt and Thompson. They were not! At least six of them are my Ph.D.'s. . . ."

3. Robert Redfield (1897–1958) taught anthropology at Chicago (1927–1958).

To Leo Gershoy

Ithaca, October 7, 1942[1]

Dear Leo,

I have read your two chapters and they seem to me most admirable.[2] You have a grasp of the whole and its relations that isn't exhibited in any book known to me. In some spots—ends of paragraphs or transitions it may need a little polishing. Maybe here and there there are too many adjectives. But if it's all as good as this you need have no fear of its reception.

You use the phrase "legal despotism." Shouldn't it be "legal absolutism"? The persistent tradition from Roman times down, among the legal fraternity & juristic writers was the distinction between "absolutism" and "despotism." The King was regarded as acting constitutionally when he exerted absolute power in the political sphere of public law: but it was widely maintained that the King acted unconstitutionally when he ignored the restraints imposed by civil law guaranteeing the rights of the individual. To act so was to act "despotically." This is developed by McIllwain in his Messenger Lectures:[3] and a Harvard PhD wrote a thesis on it for the 16 C. One of my students worked it out to some extent for the 18 century. I can't this minute think of his name—he was here only a year. I can get the thesis for you if you want it. Dick Leighton wrote a thesis on the Influence of the French Rev. on English Political Ideas.[4] A good study, but far too long, as he was the first to recognize.

I'll keep the Ms. if you say so, or return by regular mail.

Sincerely,

Carl

P.S. What profound significance is in the yellow & blue paper?

1. LIG.

2. *From Despotism to Revolution, 1763–1789* (New York, 1944).

3. Charles H. McIlwain, *Constitutionalism, Ancient and Modern* (Ithaca, 1940), originally presented as the Messenger Lectures at Cornell, 1938–1939.
4. Richard M. Leighton, "The Tradition of the English Constitution in France on the Eve of the Revolution," Ph.D. dissertation, Cornell, 1941.

To Leo and Ida Gershoy

Ithaca, December 25, 1942[1]

Dear Leo & Ida,

I see in the papers where thousands of Jewish boys in England have agreed to stand watch while their Christian comrades in arms celebrate Christmas day. These boys keep the ancient faith. But would you and Ida come to Ithaca and watch while Maude and I eat Christmas dinner? Not you! You have to celebrate Christmas as if you were Christians. You even work on your own Sabbath— if you call it work.

Well, have your fun while you can—the Lord will settle you in the End.

Maude is ever so much better, but can't eat any mince pie & cheese!

As ever,
Carl Becker

1. LIG.

To Florence and Morton Yohalem

Ithaca, December 27, 1942[1]

Dear Florence & Morton,

I was glad to get your card. Have been trying to find out your address for a long time. I suppose Wash. DC is swallowing up Pa. Mad. & Va. How does it go in Bedlam!

This is a great retreat; and much as always except for 1000 Naval people hip-hipping to class, to meals, and to barracks—or should I say to ships. Sage College is now a thing of Decks, passageways, and bulkheads. When you ask for leave to go down town you ask for leave to "go ashore."[2]

I'm very happy in retirement. Just enough writing to keep me busy in the morning, & in the afternoon there's billiards and solitaire, and dozing in dressing gown and slippers before the fire.

Am giving the Messenger Lectures in April (6) on The Founding of Cornell University, in celebration of 75 Anniversary of the opening in 1868. It's good fun; and I've done some "research" believe it or not, and have, or will, add something to knowledge. I know when Ezra Cornell went to Maine, which was in July 1843, something Charles Hull hadn't found out. That's a triumph isn't it?

Health is excellent: but Maude, for the first time in her life, has been ill. Colitus. Hospital, an operation. I believe you don't ever get entirely over colitus: but she is much better as a result of the operation, and is fairly comfortable most of the time, and gets out and around.

Best wishes from both of us for the New Year.

Sincerely,
Carl Becker

1. FMY.
2. See Bishop, *History of Cornell,* ch. xxxvi, for Cornell during World War II.

To Florence and Morton Yohalem

Ithaca, March 19, 1943[1]

Dear Florence and Morton,

Awfully glad to hear there's a new Yohalem in the world. May he and you be ever blest! From all accounts he will live in a new and better world, and as a contribution to that new and better world some congressman has already publically sobbed at the thought that the "Mothers" of this country may not be able to welcome their boys home on the first boat after the war is over because he will be needed to police conquered countries! I have written something about the new and better world, & will send you an offprint if I get any.[2]

You speak of the pessimism & discouragement that exists among the war workers in Washington. Don't take it too seriously. Washington is the worst place in the country, and a small desk in a small office in a mamouth administration is the worst place in Washington to get an objective view of what is being done. Considering the difficulties, and the extent of the enterprise, & the fact that it has to be done in terms of our political system, we are doing a very good job—better than the last war by far. Save up your capacity for pessimism until the war is over—there'll be more use for it then.

By July we will have about 5000 navy & army men at Cornell, and the university will be virtually a military school—with women and incompetents taught on the side. Am I glad that I am retired! Health excellent—but poor Maude has been laid low with intestinal colitus for a year, and has a pretty thin time. It's a messy trouble, and difficult to do much for, but we keep hoping.

I have just about finished the Messenger Lectures which I will give next month,—on the "Founding of Cornell U."—it's the 75 anniversary of the opening in 1868. I've had a lot of fun with it, & have really done "research" in unpublished documents, and have discovered some facts not known before—for example, that E. Cornell went to Georgia in 1843, which was something (the date I mean, that Charles Hull didn't know; and if that ain't something, I don't know what is), so I'm a real scholar at last.

Also will give the Penrose Lect. at the Am. Phil. Society in Philadelphia April 22, on the Pol. Phil of T. Jefferson—its the celebration of the 200 anniversary of his birth.[3] So you see I'm going in for anniversaries: and since you are so near I expect to see you at the lecture (if they allow the uninitiated and benighted to enter the Sacred Halls), if not at the lecture at least some time on that day.

Our grandson, Carl Jadwin, 2 yrs 4 mo. is thriving, and talking a blue streak, and is of course the most beautiful, and intelligent, and in every way lovely and paragonish boy that ever was. They have to keep telling him not to throw things about the room. "Don't throw things, Carl." The other morning Fred was in a hurry to get off, and got up from the breakfast table, and threw his napkin down on the table. Then C. J. had him: "Don't srow sings, daddy!" he said.

As ever
Carl Becker

Maude sends her regards & best wishes.

1. FMY.
2. "How New Will the Better World Be?" *Yale Review*, XXXII (1943), 417–439.
3. "What Is Still Living in the Political Philosophy of Thomas Jefferson?" *American Philosophical Society Proceedings*, LXXXVII (1943), 201–210.

To Alfred A. Knopf

Ithaca, March 26, 1943[1]

Dear Knopf,

Glad you liked the article.[2] The University is having 1000 off-prints made for circulation; and this article & the one last month were taken as the basis of discussion in a committee here that is linked with similar committees in Yale, Harvard, *etc* for discussing post war reconstruction. Many people liked the article; but [it] is astonishing what a large number of academic people (tender-minded & humane, as they are) still stick to the idea that you can create political power by resolutions: so that if you only resolve to have a federal world state & provide it with a constitution and a "police force," the job is done. Imagine a "police force" (that's the ambiguous word they use) arresting Joe Stalin or the British Empire, or the USA and taking them off to the jug—or better still all three at once.

If you have the right man a life of Geo. Bancroft should be a fine thing.[3] He was a man, not only of ability as a historian, but of an interesting mind and personality. The conventional idea among historians is that he was a bad historian but a fine writer. I hope your man corrects this. I think he was a good historian but a bad writer.

The other B—I know little about, except that he collected a library.[4] If he didn't do more than that I shouldn't think his life would be worth a biography—except to collectors and historians.

I am in excellent health, and we have gas enough to drive in (two miles from the U. & the town) "backwards and forwards" as a woman who used to work for us put it.

April 22 I am to give the Penrose Lecture at the Am. Phil. Soc.

in Phila, in celebration of the 200 Anniversary of T. Jefferson's birth. "What is Still Living in the Pol Phil of T. Jeff."

Sincerely,

Carl Becker

1. AAK.
2. "How New Will the Better World Be?" *Yale Review*, XXXII (1943), 417–439.
3. Russel B. Nye, *George Bancroft: Brahmin Rebel* (New York, 1944), awarded the second Alfred A. Knopf Fellowship in Biography.
4. Hubert Howe Bancroft (1832–1918) began collecting Pacific Coast historical documents in 1858, which when turned over to the University of California in 1905 numbered sixty-thousand volumes.

To Alfred A. Knopf

Ithaca, April 13, 1943[1]

Dear Knopf,

The address on Jefferson will be published in the proceedings of the American Philosophical Society, as I suppose. It may be that they plan to publish all of the speeches made at this celebration—which is a 3 day show—in a separate volume. Anyhow I'm pretty sure to have some off prints, and will be glad to send you one.

As you say, there is ample room for a good life of Jefferson, and even of Franklin. Van Doren knew every thing there was to be known about what Franklin did and said: but one can read the book without somehow ever coming to know the juicy and salacious old codger himself.[2] He is one of my admired heroes, and I had a good deal of fun writing 10 000 words on him for the D. of Am. Biog:[3] condensing everything & squeezing every thing important in, and summing him up in the last three or four paragraphs.

Fred lives in Hartsdale, which is virtually a part of Scarsdale— divided from it by the tracks,—& so not far from White Plains. It's the next station out beyond Scarsdale. I should like nothing better than to be under your roof; and I hope to be; but I don't get about much, and burrow most of the time in my own den.

Sincerely,

Carl Becker

1. AAK.
2. Carl Van Doren, *Benjamin Franklin* (New York, 1938).
3. "Benjamin Franklin," *DAB* (1931), posthumously published as a book with an introduction by Julian P. Boyd (Ithaca, 1946).

To Alfred Kazin

Ithaca, May 4, 1943[1]

Dear Mr. Kazin,[2]

I have been reading your recent book[3] with great interest and enjoyment. Your judgments strike me as sound and penetrating—those of a man capable of standing off, as it were, from his time and place and seeing it in a long perspective. This seems to me—and I take it to you—to be just what most of our writers since 1900 have not been able to do. One may say that they won two freedoms: freedom from the idea that it was necessary to revere and look up to and imitate European writers, especially British writers; and freedom from the squeamishness of Victorian writers, American and British. These freedoms were worth winning: but most of our writers seem to have thought that since it wasn't necessary to imitate foreign writers it wasn't necessary to know anything about them; and that since they had freed themselves from the squeamishness of the 19 century it wasn't necessary to know anything about the 19 century. Trying to avoid provincialism, they mostly end up with the worst kind of provincialism—the provincialism of being little interested in and knowing almost nothing about any time or place but their own. They so often strike me (perhaps it's merely the prejudice of a historian) as failing because they know almost no history earlier than 1900: & many of them—the most vocal—appear to belong to a mutual admiration society, of which the members go round in circles, slapping each other on the back for being brave fellows and estimating the literary merit of their respective works by the number of copies sold. No doubt there were exceptions: but taking some of the most effective—such as Dreiser, Lewis, and Hemingway[4]—vivid & powerful as they are, how much it might have added to their "genius" if they had taken the trouble to acquire some mastery and understanding of the history of European Civilization, & even of American civilization—and of course by history I mean to include the

history of literature which is the best key to the history of civilization. I suppose most of them think Howells an old maid and James
an old fogy:[5] but I'm not sure Howells wasn't a better writer (and
this means thinker) than any of them; and I'm quite sure James
was.

Your judgment of both of these men seems to me extraordinarily
good, and especially well balanced. (Some critics now find as
much too much in James as others have found too little)—and
this is the more extraordinary if, as I am told, you are a very young
man.

Since I am an old man—70 next Sept—I will take the liberty
(but hope you won't think it one) to say that you have got something badly needed—a discriminating critical sense. I hope you
have the opportunity to make the fullest use of it.

Sincerely,
Carl Becker

1. Alfred M. Kazin Papers, New York, N.Y.
2. Kazin (1915——), essayist and literary critic, professor of English at the State University of New York at Stony Brook (1963——).
3. *On Native Grounds: An Interpretation of Modern American Prose
Literature* (New York, 1942).
4. Theodore Dreiser (1871–1945), Sinclair Lewis (1884–1951), and
Ernest Hemingway (1899–1961).
5. William Dean Howells (1837–1919) and Henry James (1843–
1916).

To Charles A. Beard

Ithaca, May 10, 1943[1]

Dear Beard,

I recently received from Alfred Knopf a copy of your edition of
"The Law of Civilization and Decay";[2] and I have read with the
greatest interest your fine introduction which traces so clearly
the history of the writing of that book, and disposes once for all
of the myth that the book was as much the work of Henry as of
Brooks. It also throws some more light on the extraordinary minds
of the Adamses—especially that of Henry. How obsessed the man
was with the notion that there could be no success in life for an
Adams except in politics. His first thought about the book was

that to publish it would ruin Brooks' ambition for a political career! For all his bluster, Henry Adams was a timid man; and for all his professed modesty, a vain one.

I read the "Law of Civilization" many years ago when I was writing the "Beginnings of the American People," and I then found it extraordinarily suggestive. Its chief value, I think, if my recollection is not wholly at fault, is in its suggestive interpretation of particular periods or historical events. But as a law of history or of civilization, it provides too limited an explanation, and in any case one that is incapable of proof in any sense. It deals with concepts—"civilization," "concentration," "force," "energy," etc.—without even attempting to define them with any precision. Without this precision of definition, physical science can't do a thing, and doesn't profess to be able to. But Brooks and Henry wish to find a law of history or of civilization in terms of the direction and momentum of social energies and forces ("Lines of force," as Henry calls them), while admitting that none of these terms can be precisely defined, to say nothing of measuring them. Henry ends by saying that he had not solved any problem, had not indeed even been able to state what the problem was.

What both their philosophies come to is the notion that men, like physical nature, are condemned to an endless repetition of the same activities. Well, it looks a good deal that way if one takes a short time view—four hundred or four thousand years. But if one takes a longer view, or even the four thousand year view looked at from a different angle, it seems to me that man is the only creature that can, I will not say learn, but appropriate the learning of others for his own use. Every tiger, as Ortega Y Gasset[3] says, is "a first tiger," beginning all over again from scratch, learning the same things the first tiger had to learn. Man at least doesn't have to do that; and even in four thousand years, to say nothing of four hundred thousand, he has managed always to store up a little more knowledge about his own nature and the nature of the world in which he lives; so that he can, and does, although slowly, transform his activities instead of exactly and endlessly repeating them.

Fortunately for the physicist, the electron cannot acquire a knowledge of physics. If it could, every law of the electron discovered by the physicist up to date could be used by the electron to modify its behavior, in the future, and so dish all laws of physics. This subject matter of the sociologist, which is man, can do just that. What the sociologist learns about the behavior of his subject matter in the past, his subject matter can learn, and this learning he can use to modify his behavior in the future. This is why I think all attempts to discover laws of history by following the methods of the natural sciences are futile.

Forgive me this long lecture, which is quite unnecessary since you have thought your way around and through this insoluable problem far more thoroughly than I have. I only want you to know that any thing from your pen is always an event for me. I wish there were more of them. But I particularly wish that you and Mary Jane may be forever happy and blest—if that is at all possible in this hellish world.

Sincerely,
Carl Becker

1. CBCU.

2. Brooks Adams, *The Law of Civilization and Decay: An Essay on History* (New York, 1895), with an introduction by Beard (New York, 1943).

3. José Ortega y Gasset (1883–1955), Spanish philosopher and humanist.

9. Retrospection and Reflection on a Better World, 1943-1945

To Walter Francis Willcox

Ithaca, [May 1943][1]

Dear Willcox:[2]

It cannot be said that any decision or agreement was reached by the group as a result of the discussion on May 8th.[3] But as a result of the discussion I am rather clearer in my own mind on the questions discussed.

I am convinced that during the war it is desirable for the United States to recognize the governments in exile, since they are the only existing governments of the countries concerned. But this does not mean that we will necessarily continue to recognize them after the war. Whether it does or not will depend in part upon the attitude of the people of their countries towards those governments.

In respect to the policy of the United States regarding the establishment of governments in the conquered countries after the war, I think we should be guided by two general assumptions.

One is stated in the Atlantic Charter: "the right of all peoples to choose the form of government under which they will live." This is what we are fighting for, for ourselves, and for the allied and conquered countries.

The other assumption is that the United Nations (and for Europe this means especially Russia) should work cooperatively instead of competitively on post-war reconstruction. If they cannot do this there is little hope for any better international situation than existed before the war.

In respect to the establishment of governments and of boundaries in some of the conquered countries these two assumptions may conflict. If all the people comprised in Poland before the war, for example, are united in wishing to live under a Polish government, the United States will have to choose between supporting self-determination for the Poles, at the risk of breaking with Russia, or concede some Polish territory and people to Russia which means abandoning self-determination to that extent. I think it is more important to work in harmonious relations with Russia than it is to stick to the principle of self-determination for the Poles through thick and thin. The role of the United States should be that of a mediator, attempting to bring the interested parties together in some settlement that will satisfy both as far as possible.

The same sort of difficulty will exist in most of the Balkan countries. I cannot conceive that it will be possible to draw boundaries in the Balkans that will satisfy the national and other aspirations of all the people concerned, including Russia. The role of the United States, as a country less directly interested than any other of the great powers, should be the same as in respect to Poland.

In respect to Norway, Denmark, Holland, Belgium, and France these difficulties will not arise, will be far less serious. These are well defined "nations," capable of deciding with a fair degree of unity what form of government they want. No one covets any of their territory. I should think there would be no serious opposition to their retaining their former European limits or establishing any form of government they wish. It may be that some larger plan of European reconstruction would require a limitation of the independence of the first four in foreign relations, and to that they might object. If so the policy of the United States can be determined only at the time and in consideration of all the circumstances.

France presents a different problem. I think Great Britain, Russia, and the United States would wish France restored and made as powerful as conditions permit, in order to be a balance against Germany. It will be desirable for the other three countries to work with France as well as with one another if a stable European international situation is to emerge. But France will probably wish her African possessions restored and say that she cannot be as strong a balance against Germany as the Allies desired unless she has them. Should the United States insist on the principle of self-determination for the peoples of North Africa? What are the "nations" of North Africa? If they are to be freed from France, what about Spanish Morocco? Our policy in respect to North Africa should be the same as in respect to Poland and the Balkans. Harmonious cooperation between the United States, Great Britain, Russia, and a restored France is of greater importance than the complete satisfaction of the political aspirations of the North African tribes.

The same question may arise in respect to Great Britain and India. The British government has already said that India is a problem for Great Britain to settle. If we say it is a question to be settled by international agreement, the British might well say that the question of Puerto Rico and the Philippines is no less so. I think the wise policy for the United States is to leave India to the British.

> Sincerely,
> Carl Becker

1. CBCU.
2. Willcox (1861–1964) was professor of economics and statistics at Cornell (1891–1931), and dean of the College of Arts and Sciences (1902–1907).
3. CLB's weekly luncheon group.

To Leo Gershoy

Ithaca, July 10, 1943[1]

Dear Leo,

Well, well! So you're going to be some use at last. Will you have a nice hot uniform? Probably not. Will you broadcast? If so you must let me know, I want to hear you. I have a great respect for people who can broadcast. I heard Andy Biemiller broadcast the other night—but maybe you didn't know Andy; he was a card—joined the Dekes and wouldn't wear a hard boiled shirt: wouldn't study during study hours, and had Jews for friends. They labored and prayed with the boy but he told them "to hell with it." He's socialist member of the Wisconsin legislature now.

You make me envious off there near the ocean: but of course now that you are a two job family you have more money than you know what to do with, and your social level is far above mine, so that envy is the proper attitude.

Glad you got the book off.² I'm half way through my little book for Knopf, and hope to have it finished by first of September or thereabouts.³

Maude sends love. She is better, improving slowly, with set backs some days. But ever so much better than a year ago.

Fred & Betty & C. J. will be here next month.—

My address at the Phil. Soc. on Jefferson will be out soon. Tell Ida I'll appease her by sending a copy.

Sincerely,
Carl Becker

P.S. I sent the recommend off today.

1. LIG.
2. *From Despotism to Revolution, 1763–1789* (1944).
3. *How New Will the Better World Be?*

To Leo Gershoy

Ithaca, September 4, 1943¹

Dear Leo,

I hear you are in Washington, and I am writing to get your address. I have an offprint I want to impose on you, & especially Ida.

Fred & Betty have been here for two weeks, and C. J. for nearly four. We love him much, but four weeks is a long time. He's not much trouble as children go, but full of energy and it's a strain for doddering old people like me. The other day Betty asked him: "Do you love Mommy, Carl?" "Yes." "Do you love Daddy?" "No, I can't love everybody." I think he had something there.

Am writing the last (7th) chapter of the book for Knopf—"How New Will the Better World Be?" Expect to send it off before the end of September.

Give us all the dope on the new job and everything, and how it feels to be giving your life blood for your country.

As ever,
Carl Becker

Maude sends love. She is about the same—a little better I think.

1. LIG.

To Alfred A. Knopf

Ithaca, October 18, 1943[1]

Dear Knopf,

Thanks for your wire. I am glad you find the thing good. After finishing a book I cannot judge it objectively, because it is too familiar. It's like saying a word over & over again until it ceases to have any meaning. Certainly the subject is "timely," and I believe the principal ideas are sound.

I have been asked to go to Washington for a couple of months to do some work in connection with the probable effects of certain policies on German morale—am not certain just what it is. It's for the army apparently. Of course these projects spring up & then as often as not collapse. But if it goes through I shall be going within a week or ten days. Will let you know the address.

Am sending herewith the preface & front matter.

Sincerely,
Carl Becker

1. AAK.

To Leo and Ida Gershoy

Ithaca, October 24, 1943[1]

Dear Leo and/or Ida,

Did I answer your long, four-page letter written at such top-speed that I was a whole day making it out? I don't think so. You were at the top of your form, I remember, every fourth line a wise crack, and every second wise crack at my expense. Why so much hilarity? I don't think it was because you were rid of Ida for the time being. I think it was because you were off on an adventure, and all was yet in confusion—not even in your office. You were not cut out for a professor. Always want to try something new. What you would really like would be to be in Africa or Italy in uniform, lying in the open, demonstrating that your bicepts are hard & that you can take it like any other roughneck. There was some grandeloquence about shedding your life blood for native land, etc.; and I thought at first the F.B.I. may have been after you & shot you in the leg when you ran away; but it turned out only to be a quart donated to a hospital. Very tame. I hope Ida has got you in hand by now.

Maybe I'll be seeing you. Have been asked by Frank Monaghan (Major)[2] to work two months in Washington with Gottschalk, Earle,[3] Schmitt, and some others on a job of reporting for the army. If it doesn't blow up, will be in Washington this week probably. But if they find that I'm a Communist with friends among the Jews, I suppose it will be all off.

Fred has a chance for a commission in the Navy doing additional work on Navy College programs. If that goes through he will also be in Wash. sooner or later. C. J. is in fine form. He says "I'm going on the train on Tuesday to grandfather's house."

Maude sends love.

Sincerely,
Carl Becker

1. LIG.

2. Frank Monaghan (1904–1969) received his B.A. (1927) and M.A. (1928) at Cornell, taught history at New York University and Yale (1931–1943), served as a consultant to the War Department during the War, and wrote and edited various historical publications.

3. Edward Mead Earle (1894–1954) taught history at Columbia (1920–1934), then became a member of the Institute for Advanced Study, in Princeton (1934–1954). His specialty was American foreign policy.

To Merle Curti

Ithaca, October 25, 1943[1]

Dear Curti,

I am informed that you are seriously considering the offer of a professorship here at Cornell. No doubt Wisconsin can easily meet any salary we can offer you; so that your decision must be made on other grounds.

You must of course make the decision on the basis of your personal desires and needs about which I can know nothing. But I should like to say that it will be a matter of satisfaction to me personally if you decide to come. I always think of Cornell as about the kind of university which, if I could have had one made to order for my peculiar frailties and abilities, I should have chosen. It's a place where you can do very much as you please. You can have as much or as little formal, official, social life as you like. You can pick a few congenial people and ignore all the rest. You will teach the courses you desire, and not a heavy schedule. You will find probably less administrative duties than any place you have ever been. All the time I have spent in administrative duties, within the department or outside of it, during 25 years has been really so trivial that my opportunity to do my own work wouldn't have been bettered if there had been no administrative duties at all. There is no place I know of where professors are so free to do what they like, or so unaware of anything mandatory coming from the administration.[2] If you like a quiet small town (20000), which you can have as much or as little to do with as you like, and a moderate sized university which will allow you the maximum of freedom to do the work you want to do, I think you will like Cornell very much. There are almost no feuds or petty rivalries— certainly none in the history dept. and none within the "Social Sciences" departments that I know of. Besides, Ithaca is a beautiful countryside—if that means anything.

Of course, I am describing Cornell as I knew it before I retired (July, 1941). It is now a very different place, turned over to the Army and Navy, and God knows whether it will ever be the place it was before. But I suppose that is true of all the universities.

Very sincerely,
Carl Becker

1. Curti Papers, SHSW.
2. Cf. CLB, "The Cornell Tradition: Freedom and Responsibility," in *Cornell University: Founders and the Founding*, 193–204.

To Edmund Ezra Day

Ithaca, November 1, 1943[1]

Dear Mr. Day,

I have been asked to go down to Washington for six weeks or two months to work with some other men on a report for the War Department. It's something to do with the probable effects of certain policies on German morale, I think. I am going down tonight. I can't shed my blood for my country, but I can shed ink, and since they asked me to go I thought I ought to. I hope this is proper work for a University Historian. The Messenger Lectures should be out this month.

Sincerely yours,
Carl Becker

1. Edmund Ezra Day Papers, CU.

To Alfred A. Knopf

Washington, D.C., November 4, 1943[1]

Dear Knopf

This will be my address for some weeks in all probability. They have us out at the Pentagon Building, where I'm told 34000 people work. I don't pretend to be able to find my way around in it. It's a maze, a warren, a labyrinth, or whatever you will. The phone extensions run up into the 4000's at least. I can't tell you what we're doing because I don't know very well myself.

Sincerely,
Carl Becker

1. AAK.

To Richard M. Leighton

Washington, D.C., November 6, 1943[1]

Dear Leighton,

I heard you were on the history project, and I am glad indeed you are. It will be along the line of your interest and training and will occupy you for the duration and maybe longer.

I am at the above address. Have been invited to make one of a committee of historians to make an "objective" report to General Arnold on the probable effect of military pressure, especially bombings, on German strength and morale. A project that must be finished within two months. At present our locale is 2717 in the air force building; but we expect to be shifted shortly to the Pentagon. The work isn't hard & is, some of it, interesting; but the hours (including time going & coming) are long. I hope we can get together some time. I am mostly free after about 7:30. Not much chance of meeting at the Pentagon, or of having any time to talk if we did. Maybe some evening we could manage to leave together and have dinner.

Sincerely,
Carl Becker

1. Leighton Papers.

To Leo Gershoy

Ithaca, January 15, 1944[1]

Dear Leo,

I have a communication (I mean a Directive) from Sarah Lawrence asking me to suggest some people, male or female, 35–50 years of age, to take the place of Miss Warren who is retiring. I haven't the slightest idea of anyone. If you could suggest anyone I should be obliged. Probably you know all about it, and have already been asked.

We've had the best January on record—no snow & no cold weather, but two weeks of sunshine!

I'm OK & Maude is rather better I think, but with some days not so good as others.

The Washington business tired me out a good deal, although I didn't realize it until I got home. But I'm all right now. Working on an article for the *Yale Review*—on the Hard Boiled Age 1919–1939—which I will call (the article I mean) "What we didn't know hurt us a lot."[2] I've got to the point, towards the end, where it seems junk. I don't know how to draw it together and end it. However, I'll probably discover some meretricious trick to cover up its weakness and hoodwink some readers—if it ever gets by Helen McAfee.[3]

How's Ida & her famous back. I hope the one is better and the other just as good—I hope I don't need to say which is which—

Sincerely,
Carl

1. LIG.
2. *Yale Review,* XXXIII (1944), 385–404.
3. Managing editor of the *Yale Review.*

To Louis Gottschalk

Ithaca, February 23, 1944[1]

Dear Gottschalk,

Thanks for the reprint. I have heard no more of the Report than you.[2] I don't think it matters either. I think 12–15,000 dollars for a report which contained nothing that could not have been got together by any one or two people in OSS[3] was a waste of money. But if they are going to waste it I had just as soon they wasted it on me & you as any other way.

I am including a folder which will tell you about the new book.[4] The jacket recommendations by Beard, Van Doren, et Cet place me like Humpty Dumpty on a high wall. Here's hoping I don't fall off.

Mrs. Bradfords name is Margery. Her husbands initials are E. F.[5] Faculty wives I don't, in general, cotton to much. But Margery I like ever so much. She's a real person, & a real scholar too—not a pseudo intellectual.

I have been asked to give a series of lectures at U. of Michigan, on a new Cook Foundation devoted to "American Institutions & their Preservation." Since this is the first of the series I thought it appropriate as well as easiest for me to do, to discuss the broad question of rights & liberties on which American Institutions rest. So I have called the lectures "Freedom and Responsibility in the American Way of Life." Have one lecture done, & a second well advanced. Probably will give them next Fall. Best of all is the pay off—$3000—the highest any one has yet offered me to shoot off my mouth.

Sincerely,
Carl Becker

1. CBCU.
2. An unpublished report on German morale prepared for General H. H. Arnold by a group of historians, including CLB. See Wesley

Frank Craven *et al.*, *The Army Air Forces in World War II*, II (Chicago, 1949), 704, 711.
3. Office of Strategic Services.
4. *How New Will the Better World Be?*
5. Marjorie Campbell Bradford. Eugene F. Bradford (1889–1972) taught English literature at Syracuse University (1913–1928), received his Ph.D. at Harvard (1927), was director of admissions and registrar at Cornell (1928–1957) and a member of the university faculty.

To Leo and Ida Gershoy

Ithaca, March 20, 1944[1]

Dear Ida & Leo,

If you are going to spend a fortune, why spend it on newspaper reviews? Why not buy the book? In fact you ought to buy ten copies. Miss Speed, in the Cornell Library, bought 9 copies of The Founding of Cornell University. I shouldn't think the wife of a professor, and of my favorite pupil would consent to be outdone by a mere library assistant. So I suggest 10 copies of "How New Will the Better World Be?" Just to be on the safe side. The reviews are very good so far as I have seen them—and the sales also—about 3000 copies sold before Mr. 14, the official date of publication—bringing a royalty check large enough, nearly, to pay first quarter income tax on April 15.

We'll be glad to see Leo's new book. Of course, not being in H. E. Barnes' and C. Becker's class, he can't expect to get out two books within five months.

I knew about Geo. Zook—industrious worker and slave and master of all the cliches of thought & speech ever struck off.[2]

Fred has his commission as Ensign: but before taking his job in Washington he has to have 8 weeks of naval indoctrination—& is now at Ft. Schuyler in the Bronx. Likes it very much, after 3 weeks. Betty & the great C. J. were here for two weeks. In N.Y. C. J. saw a double-decker bus: & he said there was a bus with another on top. He asked me: "How do the people get out of the top bus?" The inquiring mind.

Maude gets on well & cheerfully, but has to spend much time getting rid of gas, etc. It's a pretty boresome business, but she keeps up better than I would—considering there seems to be not much prospect of cure.

Am working on the Michigan lectures—have got two finished out of the five, and a third nearly done. Probably will be given next fall. Sorry to say that will be a third book within 10 months.[3]

Did I tell you the army has ordered 75000 copies of Modern History[4] in 3 paper volumes for use among the doughboys. You may picture them, in their fox holes, whenever they have a few minutes to spare, pulling a copy out of their pockets and reading about Karl Marx and the classless society!

Maude sends love.

As ever,

Carl Becker

1. LIG.

2. George F. Zook (1885–1951) received his Ph.D. at Cornell in 1914, taught European history at Pennsylvania State (1912–1920), was president of the University of Akron (1925–1933), president of the American Council on Education (1934–1950), and author of various books and reports on American education.

3. *Freedom and Responsibility in the American Way of Life.*

4. CLB, *Modern History: The Rise of a Democratic, Scientific, and Industrial Civilization.*

To the editor of the *Cornell Bulletin*

Ithaca, May 26, 1944[1]

To the Editor of The Bulletin:

In a recent issue of The Bulletin, you refer to the famous message "What hath God wrought?" said to have been sent from Washington to Baltimore on May 24, 1863. According to the traditional story this was the "first message ever flashed over the telegraph." Just to keep that record straight, it should be pointed out that whatever message was sent on May 24 was not the first one "flashed over the telegraph." It can hardly be supposed that Ezra Cornell or anyone else would complete the entire line before testing it to see if it worked all right; and in fact we know that from time to time, during the progress of construction, sending instruments were attached to the wires and messages were sent to Washington for that purpose. These messages probably ran somewhat as follows: "Can you get it?" "Yes, but not clearly." "What's the trouble with the damned thing" "Signals run together. Are you well grounded? Test your connections." Something of that sort. Moreover, although the first message sent from Washington to Baltimore was undoubtedly sent on May 24, it is not at all certain that "What hath God Wrought?" was that first message. Ezra Cornell, who was in a position to know what occurred, said that it was not until many years later that he first heard of such a message having been sent. He at least did not believe it ever was sent, either on May 24 or any other time.

This is merely to keep the record clear, not with any desire to destroy a myth. Myths often serve a useful purpose because even if not true they symbolize something that is true and worth remembering. The story of George Washington and the cherry tree is a myth, but it has served to impress on the minds of people a fact of first rate importance—namely, that George Washington happened to be a man of absolute integrity. Someone (it may have been Voltaire) said that if God did not exist it would be necessary to invent him. The famous message "What hath God wrought?" should have been sent on May 24, 1863. Maybe it was; if not, then someone had the good sense and foresight to invent the myth. It serves the useful purpose of symbolizing an important truth—namely, that when, after years of effort, it became possible to send intelligible messages a distance of fifty miles over telegraph wires something of great significance had indeed been "wrought" by God's will, or man's ingenuity, or both working together.

Carl Becker

1. *Cornell Bulletin,* May 26, 1944, p. 4.

To the editor of *Common Sense*

Ithaca, June 1944[1]

I recognize the right of Mr. Rex Stout,[2] and other members of the Writers' War Board, to hold and express freely whatever opinions about Germany and the Germans, and about the activities of the German exiles in this country, they may think true and useful. I am not sufficiently familiar with the activities of the Writers' War

Board to know whether it professes to speak for the "writers" of the United States. But if the opinions of Mr. Stout, as quoted in the *Common Sense* editorial represent the opinions of the Writers' War Board, I should like to say that the Writers' War Board cannot be taken to speak for me.

I am, like Mr. Stout, entirely in favor of dealing with Germany and the Germans "realistically and competently"; but I do not agree with him that "we cannot do that unless we are aware of the utter hatefulness of Germany and the Germans." On the contrary I agree with Edmund Burke,[3] who said that he did not know how to draw an indictment against an entire nation; and I think that to regard all Germans without distinction as utterly hateful is to be romantic and deluded rather than realistic and competent.

Carl Becker

1. *Common Sense,* XIII (June 1944), 211.
2. Stout (1886——) is the author of the Nero Wolfe mystery stories.
3. Burke (1729–1797) was a British politician and writer.

To Leo Gershoy

Ithaca, June 12, 1944[1]

Dear Leo,

Am awaiting the opus which hasn't come yet. Of course it's a good book. Why would anyone write a book unless it was a good one, any more than any one would do anything that was not for him, for the moment, and all things considered, the best thing to do. Glad you like your job, hectic as it is. Don't worry about not becoming a practiced and efficient liar. You'll succeed. You must be good already since you have been promoted—and if you could only tell the truth what good would it do to send you to N.Y. to talk with the French people: Do they ever by any chance tell the truth? They are going to have an alibi for the collapse of 1940 before they are through—one part of it will be that G.B.[2] didn't support them properly, another that we furnished aid too little & too late, and a third that we adopted the wrong policy after we came. They certainly want a lot considering the poor show they put on and the fact that if it wasn't for G.B. & the USA they would be done for forever.

Fred & family are all moved down to Washington. Have one of the Navy[?] houses at 4817 South 29 St. Fairlington, Arlington, Va. Navy moved them down gratis. Maude is about the same, a little better I think. I'm OK. Was in N.Y. 27 May to receive an award for distinguished service to the teaching of the Social Studies from the Assoc. of Teachers of the S.S. in N.Y. City. It's what they do when your hair gets white. Have agreed to give an address at Colgate on July 27. This is a meeting of a state organization to educate the people on P. war reconstruction. D. R. Fox got me into it. No money—great for the cause. Got a letter from the manager of publicity who said he must have biography and "four glossy prints," also newspaper "mats" if I had them; but anyhow "four glossies." I told him to consult the Who's Who and go to hell for his mats and glossy prints.

Have four of the five lectures done for the Michigan show, & will finish the 5th in July. Let me tell you this will be a good book too.

C. J. is having the time of his life in Washington—can go in and out doors without being taken down an elevator & has plenty of ground to play on and sidewalks to ride his tricycle. In N.Y. I had dinner with them at a hotel in White Plains. We had only a sandwich because of late breakfast, but C. J. had the dinner— soup, lamb, potatoes, carrots, a big roll, & ice cream—all of which he ate without spilling a drop on himself or the table. When he was finished, he said: "Tell the man to bring me some more dinner."

Sorry about Ida's back; but I don't believe in it because she does whatever she likes, back or no back. I think probably there is no back.

Maude sends best wishes.

Carl Becker

1. LIG.
2. Great Britain.

To Alfred A. Knopf

Ithaca, July 13, 1944[1]

Dear Knopf,

Thanks for sending me a copy of Mr. Postgate's[2] letter. It is true that the Communist Manifesto was published in 1848. Please put that on the list of corrections if and when.

In respect to his remarks about Dr. Johnson's[3] famous phrase, "Patriotism is the last refuge of a scoundrel," there is this to be said:

1. Mr. Postgate says that the particular "patriot" Johnson had in mind was Wilkes.[4] Very likely it was.

2. He says that a "patriot" in Johnson's day was not a person who said, "my country, right or wrong." I did not say or imply that it was.

3. He says that a "patriot" in Johnson's day was a "seditious revolutionary." But George III called himself, or was called by others, a "patriot king." Would Mr. Postgate then conclude (here's the place for Mr. Postgate to look for an "undistributed middle term," as the logicians say) that George III was a seditious revolutionary?

4. He concludes from all this that I have mistaken the meaning of Johnson's phrase. This is a non-sequitur of a rather obvious sort which comes of confusing the meaning of Johnson's phrase with the particular persons and circumstances to which he applied it. I did not say or imply anything at all about the meaning of Johnson's phrase except the meaning that is clearly conveyed by the words themselves. Whatever Johnson may have meant by the word "patriotism," and whoever he may have had in mind when he used the word, the phrase itself can only mean one thing— that a scoundrel, having been driven out of all other refuges, finds a last refuge in the word "patriotism." All that I have said or implied is that when we hear in our time people shout, "my country, right or wrong," we are apt to agree with Dr. Johnson that patriotism is the last refuge of a scoundrel. We can certainly agree with Johnson's statement without having in mind the same sort of scoundrels that he had, and without meaning the same

thing he meant by the word patriotism. Mr. Postgate seems to have missed the point of my statement altogether. He seems to think that I was using Johnson's phrase in support of a definition of patriotism, and that I committed a "howler" because Johnson's idea of patriotism was entirely different from mine. I wasn't trying to define patriotism, but only indicating the way in which people often use the word to justify conduct which cannot be otherwise easily justified. If Johnson's phrase means anything, that is precisely the meaning he intended to convey by it.

A good many people have thought the title of my book "odd." I have always thought such people must be very literal minded, not very quick on the uptake, perhaps lacking in a sense of humor, in short, a little odd themselves.

Sincerely,
Carl Becker

1. AAK.

2. Raymond W. Postgate (1896——), journalist, author, and editor, was Knopf's European representative (1930–1949). His letter discussed *How New Will the Better World Be?*

3. Samuel Johnson (1709–1784), English lexicographer, essayist, and poet.

4. John Wilkes (1727–1797), English politician and polemicist.

To Louis Gottschalk

Ithaca, September 3, 1944[1]

Dear Gottschalk,

Thanks for your article on Causes of Revolution.[2] I think what you say suits me as well as any description could. I like particularly your emphasis on the fact that we can't count on people *not learning* from experience. That puts it in the safest way no doubt. But by & large the fundamental difference between the social studies and the natural sciences, or perhaps I should say the physical sciences, is that the subject matter of the latter cannot change its habits by learning, while the subject matter of the social studies can & does change its habits by learning. And the important thing is that part of this learning is learning what the social scientist or historian has discovered about its behavior in the past. Hence you may say that any theory about the behavior of man in the past, in so far as men accept it and act on it, falsifies the theory because it introduces a new condition into the factors that determine the behavior of men in the future. The Marxian theory had this effect because millions of men accepted it as true whether it was or not, & for that reason acted differently than they would have done if the theory had never been published. If Marx wanted his theory to remain valid (supposing it was valid for the past) for the future, he should have kept it to himself. I have expressed this difference by saying that "fortunately for the physicist the atom cannot acquire a knowledge of physics."

Of course the concept of "cause" is a difficult one to define. There is always as you say the question of what is the cause of the cause, & this takes you back to the first cause, which leaves the question unanswered. The physicist therefore dispenses with the concept altogether, & is content to describe sequences and relations, reducing them to mathematics whenever possible. But the historian cannot dispense with causes, except in so far as he is a mere antiquarian or statistician. I think the reason is that he deals not only with the action of men, but with their purposes, desires, aspirations etc. That is men's actions have value & purpose: and if we write history in such a way as to give it meaning and significance we have to take account of these values & purposes, to explain *why* men behave as they do, what they aim to accomplish, & whether they succeed or not. In explaining all this we use "cause" in the same way we do in practical life,—as, for example, the cause of missing my train was that my watch was slow. In history therefore, our causes are not on the scientific level or the philosophical level, but on the practical level of every day life. They are our best estimates or judgments. The causes of the French Rev must therefore in this sense be multiple, and they were different according to the historian & according to the age in which he writes. This does not mean that historians at any time can't reach a degree of agreement, but one historian will emphasize one factor more than another. It is rare that you can place your finger on one factor and say that without this the Rev would not have occurred. You can come close to it in explaining the American Civil War. You can say with confidence, I think, that without the presence of Negro slavery the Civil War would not have occurred. American historians have been too clever by half in finding other causes of the Civil War. Of course you can say that even with slavery if people had not come to regard it as a moral evil there would not have been the "irrepressible conflict" over it, & so no war. But if there had been no slavery there would have been no occasion for thinking about it as an evil. The only way you can eliminate slavery as the fundamental cause, is to ask what were the causes of slavery existing in the U.S.—& of course this takes you on the long trek through the dark backward & abysm of time to the ultimate cause of all things—which is of no use to the historian.

Well, I like your article very much. You have evidently given a lot of thought to this subject.

I don't see anything in the course of events that seems to falsify our famous report to General Arnold, except that when the invasion occurred the entire German air force did *not* come up into the air to be conveniently destroyed at one stroke, as Monaghan & Earle & all the air people were convinced it would do. But I've often wondered whether it was worth 12 or 15000 dollars to make a report of that sort, however good.[3]

Sincerely,
Carl Becker

1. CBCU.
2. "Causes of Revolution," *American Journal of Sociology*, L (1944), 1–8.
3. See CLB to Louis Gottschalk, Feb. 23, 1944.

To Robert N. Campbell

Ithaca, October 1, 1944[1]

Dear Mr. Campbell,[2]

Thanks for your letter and the inclosures. I found your idea of a League of Independent Voters interesting, and no doubt it would be a useful organization, if there were sufficient funds to handle the preparation and circulation of information. I don't know whether it was your idea that part of it would be active all the time or merely in election years. In either case a good deal of money would be needed, and a considerable research organization. It requires an enormous amount of research to find out anything reliable about issues, what various congressmen have done in connection with them, etc.

Two points occur to me. One is that there are many "independent" voters who are independent only in the sense that they are not strongly attached to either party, but their decision to vote for one or the other is not based on any considered or reasoned understanding of the situation. These probably your organization wouldn't reach.

The other point is that the old parties would not be greatly influenced by the platform of the organization. They would regard the League as they do any other body of voters—something to give any [sic] eye to, and to conciliate by putting another weasel worded plank in their platforms. However, the thing that is needed is more non-partisan action by intelligent citizens. Every sort of an organization with that aim is useful, and I think your scheme is the most suggestive I have come across.

I raised the question the other day in a luncheon discussion, and Professor Cornelius de Kiewet [sic] made the point that a group of faculty people in Cornell, or any university might organize for producing accurate, non-partisan information for use by any body or bodies that wanted or could use it. Such an organization might fit in with yours. In any case, I think you might find it worth while to send your brochure to him. He is an exceedingly able and public-spirited man.

I am naturally glad you liked my book. It has had a pretty wide sale.

Sincerely,
Carl Becker

1. CBCU.
2. Robert N. Campbell, a government employee, had written to CLB from Washington, D.C., on September 19, 1944.

To Louis Gottschalk

Ithaca, October 7, 1944[1]

Dear Gottschalk,

Thanks for your pamphlet.[2] I think I agree with it mostly. I think, however, that the real weakness of the League [of Nations] was that it was and could be only an agency of the member states, & could do nothing that the great powers were not willing to approve because they had the real power. A police force would not alter that fact. If the great powers do not quarrel no police force is necessary; if they do and one becomes the aggressor or supports an agressor, no police force would be adequate. This fact is brought out in the Dumbarton Oaks Conference; Russia realizes that power remains in the hands of the states that have it, and she isn't going to pretend to give it up by promising something that wouldn't alter that fact anyway.

I'm sorry you had so much difficulty reading my writing. I should have transcribed those notes on a typewriter.

I'm giving the Michigan lectures in the week of Dec 4–8 inclusive.

Sincerely,
Carl Becker

1. CBCU.
2. "Lessons of Modern History for World Peace," in Lyman Bryson, ed., *Approaches to World Peace* (New York, 1944).

To the editor of the *American Magazine*

Ithaca, October 1944[1]

Dear Sir:

The article *You Don't Elect the President* (Sept., p. 34) points out that the Electoral System makes it possible for a candidate to be elected President of the United States although a majority of the voters have cast their votes for someone else.

I happen to have at hand statistics of elections covering 28 presidential elections from 1828 to 1936, inclusive.

The important conclusions to be drawn from these are that:

In 17 out of those 28 elections the successful candidate received a majority of the total popular vote cast for all parties.

In 9 elections the successful candidate received less than half of the total votes, but still received more votes than his chief rival.

In only 2 elections has a candidate been elected president even though he received fewer popular votes cast than his chief rival received.

The important thing about the electoral system is not that it permits one to say, "You don't elect the president" (in any reasonable meaning of that phrase), but that it makes it difficult, if not impossible, for any major party to be organized on strictly sectional or class lines and hope to win the election.

Dr. Carl Becker

1. *American Magazine,* CXXXVIII (Dec. 1944), 4.

To Alfred A. Knopf

Ithaca, October 20, 1944[1]

Dear Knopf,

Glad to know the book is still going.[2] I still get letters about it every now and then—all favorable now. I am writing another book —or part of one: a new World History for high schools. My part of it can, I hope, be made by a condensation of the text book on Modern History. In any case it will occupy me for the next eight or ten months I think. I have to make a living, or think I do, and this is the easiest way to get a substantial return that will run over a period of ten years.

Sincerely,
Carl Becker

1. AAK.
2. *How New Will the Better World Be?*

To Leo and Ida Gershoy

Ithaca, November 20, 1944[1]

I wonder where the Gershoys are?
They often wander very far.
They may be in the Honey Pot—
Or in the Cooky Jar.

But I do hope they're *Not*
Fallen down the Penny Slot!

> Inquiring friend,
> Carl Becker

1. LIG.

To Thomas Reed Powell

Ithaca, November 29, 1944[1]

Dear Reed,

The Michigan lectures will be published sometime next spring—probably by an arrangement between Alfred Knopf and the U. of M. Press.

I haven't received the "one or two things" of yours mentioned in your letter—unless the carbon on Free speech inclosed is one of them. This analysis reveals the Tribune [*New York Herald Tribune*] very clearly. Aside from it's election editorials, I have found its editorials extremely able. But it had to support Dewey,[2] and was hard put to it to make anything of him. Just before the election it reached its all time low, I thought, by pointing out two vital issues in the campaign—(1) Roosevelts health; (2) the Truth about What happened at Pearl Harbor.

Apart from party affiliations, the Tribune was, when Dewey was nominated, in virtually the same position as Walter Lippmann—strongly in favor of the war & post war cooperation, but very critical of the New Deal and some of Roosevelt's decisions on foreign policy. But whereas Lippmann was free from party committments and could therefore see that Dewey wouldn't do, the Tribune, being committed to the G. O. P. had to make do with what specious arguments it could invent. I wonder if the man who did the editorials believed what he said, or was merely hewing to the party line because it was his job?

> Sincerely,
> Carl Becker

1. CBCU.
2. Thomas E. Dewey (1902–1971) was the Republican candidate for president in 1944.

To Thomas Reed Powell

Ithaca, December 3, 1944[1]

Dear Reed,

The "two or three" things you said you were sending me came yesterday. I liked them all, as I like all of your "things"—probably because we have minds that work in the same way. I liked especially the paper[2] in which you raised the question whether it is possible to think without thinking about thinking and about the something that you are thinking about. I am one of those who are more interested in finding out so far as possible what men are like & how they think than in "doing them good," which I rationalize by saying that the way I can do them most good is to find out what they are like, what they do and why they do it and why they think its a good thing to do it.

You may not care to "do good" any more than I do. But you do *me* good anyway. So if you have any more "things" to send, please do so.

With all best wishes for you and yours,

Carl Becker

1. CBCU.
2. See "Authority and Freedom in a Democratic Society: Constitution, Legislatures, Courts," *Columbia Law Review,* XLIV (1944), 473–487.

To Mildred J. Headings

Ithaca, December 14, 1944[1]

Dear Miss Headings,[2]

I have looked through your MS and read considerable parts of it.[3] You have a fine lot of material with all the necessary documentation. But your organization could be improved a good deal. Since the main subject is Masonry during the Third Republic, I think you have far too much on the earlier period. All that you need to say about Masonry before the middle of the nineteenth century or thereabouts could be put in an introductory chapter. This should be a relatively brief sketch, with not too many notes, of the origin, organization, and general character of the order in the 18 century, and an indication of how it was changed as a result of the Revolution and the democratic trends of the early nineteenth century. This would give you the necessary background for the more detailed study of the order under the Third Republic. I should think the first three chapters, or the greater part of them, could be compressed into this one introductory chapter.

The chapter on "Philanthropy" seems too short in comparison with the others; and I should think this material could be included in one of the others, or distributed among some of them. The later chapters that deal with the main subject are on the whole very good, but they are rather in the nature of separate studies on various aspects of Masonry than organic parts of the general subject of Masonry under the Republic. A good part of the art of writing a book consists in having at all times a clear idea of your subject as a whole, and of the various chapters as organic parts of it which are related to each other and to the general subject in a more or less necessary or at least a logical way. This organic structure should be made clear to the reader, and he should always be kept aware of it, so that he always knows where he has been, where he is, and where he is going. This can best be done by indicating in a general way at the beginning what the subject of the book is and what in general you are attempting to do with it; and then at the close of each chapter or at the beginning of the succeeding one, or both, make the transition clear—that is to say, make it clear why the next chapter naturally follows the one just completed. This can be done in a few sentences usually. This sense of continuity and logical order is very important, and it should be made apparent, not only in the transitions from one chapter to another, but throughout—particularly in the transitions from one paragraph to another. Of course this requires a careful thinking through of the subject and all its parts. I think your book can be much improved along these lines. I don't think it means much rewriting, but probably some condensation here and there and maybe some rearrangement of the material. But at all events, much can be done by drawing the whole together in the way I have suggested in respect to the transitions from chapter to chapter. The great thing is, *never leave a reader wondering where he has been and is at the end of a chapter, or where he is and where he is going at the beginning of the next one.* But of course in order to do this you must be yourself very sure just where you are at all times, and why you are there and how you got there.

We have had a bad blizzard here, and have not yet got shoveled out. But I will be returning your MS as soon as possible by American Express.

Very sincerely,
Carl Becker

1. CBCU.
2. Headings (1908———) received her M.A. (1931) and Ph.D. (1938) at Cornell and teaches history at Hood College (1942———).
3. *French Freemasonry under the Third Republic* (Baltimore, 1949).

To Alfred A. Knopf

Ithaca, December 20, 1944[1]

Dear Knopf,

I find that I may, through inadvertence, have got myself or you or both of us into a mess, which you will very likely say is no more than was to be expected. The question concerns the use I have made in the Michigan lectures of matter in "How New Will the Better World Be?", and in a book now in process of publication by the Cornell Press.[2]

I have, as you know, published a good deal on the general subject of democracy and the democratic ideology. In preparing the Michigan lectures, I therefore found it virtually impossible in certain chapters not to say again in substance what I had already said elsewhere. Naturally I tried to say it in a sufficiently different form to make it acceptable; but now on making a more careful comparison I find that there is in certain lectures a greater amount of similarity, and in places, of identity of phrasing than I thought. There is in any case more than I like. You may like it even less. I will give you the essential facts, accept your judgment, and do what is necessary under the circumstances.

The similarities occur in Lectures I, IV, and V.

Lecture V deals with "Private Economic Enterprise," and in this lecture I have developed the same general argument as in Chapter

VI ("What Kind of Collectivism do we Want?") in "How New Will the Better World Be?" The matter is in some places condensed, in others elaborated, and there is in the Michigan lecture a good deal that does not appear in the chapter on Collectivism. But there are a good many paragraphs and pages in which the phrasing is very similar, and in some cases identical.

Lectures I and IV. After the first four Michigan lectures were written in the first draft, I was asked to give one of a series of lectures on the general subject of civil liberties here at Cornell. For this lecture (which I called "Political Freedom—American Style.") I made use of four or five pages of Michigan Lecture I, and a somewhat larger part of Lecture IV. Here also there is condensation, elaboration, and a certain amount of rearrangement; but the material is much the same, and in some cases, especially in Lecture IV, the phraseology is substantially the same. The lecture given here at Cornell is one of five which are now in process of publication by the Cornell Press.

Two points arise. One is whether you will think you have been sold a pig in a poke, have, in fact, had palmed off on you a MS supposed to be fresh which is in considerable part a rehash of old stuff. The other point concerns copyright. The Cornell Press may think the use I have made of material in their book in the Michigan lectures I and IV, if published by you, an infringement of their copyright. I will in any case consult Mr. Reynolds[3] of the Cornell Press, and get his permission, which I have no doubt he will give provided we mention the matter in the preface or elsewhere. It is, therefore, mainly a question of how the matter strikes you. I know you will be quite frank, and probably tell me off for being incapable of managing my affairs.

I mentioned this matter to Dean Stason,[4] who seemed not concerned, and said he would mention it to you when he saw you in New York, which he expected to do this week. But maybe I did not sufficiently stress the matter to him, and indeed I was not then as aware of the possible seriousness of the matter as I am now after making a more careful comparison.

I had a very good time in Ann Arbor, and the lectures were very favorably received.

With regards and apologies,
As ever,
Carl Becker

1. AAK.
2. In *Safeguarding Civil Liberty Today* (Ithaca, 1945), 1–31.
3. Victor Reynolds (1905———), director of Cornell University Press (1943–1963), later of the University Press of Virginia (1963–1971).
4. E. Blythe Stason (1892–1972), dean of the law school, University of Michigan (1939–1960).

To James Duane Squires

Ithaca, December 22, 1944[1]

Dear Squires,[2]

We were even too optimistic—thinking the war would end in Europe in 1944. And I remember that Earle and Monaghan were positive that when the invasion came the entire German air force would come off the ground in a desperate effort to block it, which would give the Allied air force the long-waited opportunity to destroy it. I remember also suggesting that we put a qualificating phrase in the report to the effect that it was just possible the Germans would conserve a part of their air force for the time when they made the final stand on the German frontier, and that Earle & Monaghan laughed this to scorn. Also Schmitt and others did not agree with some of us that the Russians would be slowed up when they got to the German frontier, because of German desperation in defending the home land & longer lines of communication for the Russians. I think we got this in the report however.

The only event which has failed to justify our report is the failure of the Germans to throw all they had into blocking the invasion.

I haven't heard anything about the Report since we were notified that it was received with thanks.

But the other day a fellow from the State Dept. called me as [sic] saying that Schmitt was a candidate for a position in that Dept, and wanting to know what I could tell him.

With all best wishes,
Carl Becker

1. CBCU.
2. Squires (1904———), professor of history at Colby Junior College (1933———), was a historical consultant to the U.S. Army Air Force (1943–1944) and to the War Records Commission, New Hampshire (1944–1945).

To Leo and Ida Gershoy

Ithaca, December 22, 1944[1]

Dear Children,

Merry Xmas to you. We have had 15 inches of snow—unprecedented this early in the year—and today, or last night, the glass registered 10° below zero. To hell with winter!

Have recently returned from Ann Arbor, where I had a good time, and (or because) the lectures were received with great favor.

Going to Ann Arbor, I lost my bag. At Detroit, in the dim morning light I set my bag on a porter's truck & told him I wanted the Ann Arbor train. He said to go on to the gate and he would find me. So I did, & presently along came a porter & truck with one bag on it that looked exactly like mine. Instead of making sure I took it, and in my room at Ann Arbor found it was some other fellow's bag. The lectures were in my bag. It was a blow in the plexus. I telephoned at once to the lost & found dept. of the Mich. Central, and there they had the bag and said they would send it on by the next train. It relieved me, and the whole affair quite set me up—I discovered that in an emergency I could [employ] celerity, judgment, and common sense. You may expect therefore, the next time you see me, to meet a more confident and conceited fellow than even you supposed I was.

Maude joins me in all good wishes for Xmas day and all other days that ever will be.

Carl

1. LIG.

To Anita M. Lerner

Ithaca, December 30, 1944[1]

Dear Anita,

You do bob up in the most unexpected places. I heard you were in Chapel Hill, N.C., and here you are in Boulder, Col. I've been there, and it's a lovely place. It should be restful for you and fine for the children. That is, it should be restful because its a small quiet place: but the climate is exhilerating, and God knows you don't need any exhilerating. What you will be like in the mountain air, I don't know—skipping like a mountain goat, I expect. Let me not see it! And, alas, I won't because I shall in all probability never get as far from Ithaca as that again. However, my health is very good, no more pain, and you can never tell.

Maude, poor dear, is not so well. Not serious apparently, but also apparently not entirely curable—intestinal colitus, if that means anything to you. A messy business, that keeps her close to her bed & bath room a good part of the time.

Another book is on the way, the nature of which you will see by the enclosure. The older I get the more difficult it is to write anything without plagrizing my previous works—a sign that my mind is drying up, like incomes, at the source.

Well, Maude joins me in saying, be happy and let who will be good: and in all best wishes for your new venture, whatever it is.

As ever,
Carl Becker

1. AML.

To Rudolph E. Freund

Ithaca, January 12, 1945[1]

Dear Mr. Freund,[2]

Thanks for sending me a copy of your paper on Turner.[3] Turner evidently will not down! Who writes critical essays about Channing,[4] Osgood, or a dozen others long after they died? It's a good sign—a good sign that there's something in his ideas, or a good sign that people are not inclined to swallow them whole.

I don't think I have any criticisms to make of your article. It brings out many interesting and important points, and particularly perhaps that Turner never felt any too sure of the "frontier theory" —of what it was or how to work it out. The only thing he felt sure of was that the frontier conditions had a great significance for American history which was right enough. The difficulty that troubled him at last, whether he knew precisely what the difficulty was I don't know, was that the old type of "liberty" and "equality" of individual initiative etc. which developed under frontier conditions seemed to be disappearing. He wanted to think, that a "peculiar" sort of freedom was the result of America's development under frontier conditions, which was true enough; but (2) that this type would endure which was not true. But if he had ever thought out his fundamental premise, he must have realized that it could not be. In his premise was that American ideas & institutions were the peculiar product of this environment—they were derived from the American wilderness not the Teutonic forest. But if so, then as the environment—the wilderness—changed, the institutions would change. He loved the relatively simple conditions of the Wisconsin of his youth—its buoyancy, freedom, initiative, equality, good will, absence of cynicism & *arriere penseés;*[5] that's one reason he was never happy at Harvard. And when he saw that the "closing of the frontier" meant that the old simple conditions would disappear, he feared that the "peculiar" and superior type of American freedom might not endure after all.

Thanking you again, and with best regards,

Carl Becker

1. Rudolph E. Freund Papers, North Carolina State University Archives, Raleigh.
2. Freund (1901–1955) taught agricultural economics at North Carolina State College (1946–1953).
3. "Turner's Theory of Social Evolution," mimeographed essay, subsequently published in *Agricultural History,* XIX (April 1945), 78–87.
4. Edward Channing (1856–1931) taught history at Harvard (1883–1931), specializing in American history.
5. Backward, or second, thoughts.

To Carl G. Gustavson

January 15, 1945[1]

Dear Gustavson,[2]

Thanks for your article. I did not know you had had that sort of difficulty; and the amount of it and method of correcting it is extremely interesting—and remarkably well written.[3] It is, I think, a well known fact now, that when parents force children who are normally left handed to use the other hand, they are apt to fall into stammering or other abnormalities. I don't gather that that was your case, but your cure illustrates the case.

I was hoping you could stay on at Miami: but the prospective at Vanderbilt seems marvelously suited to your interests and training. I don't know much about the U of V. but have an impression it is one of the better southern colleges. I have written to Bulkley, giving you a strong send off. I've always had great confidence in your ability—partly because you are not the run of the mill sort who enter graduate school. (You know the Germans have a saying that "a professor is one who thinks *otherwise*"); and partly because you were so deeply interested in matters of the mind. Let me know how it comes out.

The enclosed circular will tell you what I have been up to. Will be published this Spring by Alfred Knopf.

Sincerely,

Carl Becker

1. Carl G. Gustavson Papers, Athens, Ohio.
2. Gustavson (1915——) received his Ph.D. at Cornell (1942), taught at Miami University (1943–1945) and Ohio University (1945——), specializing in modern European history and historiography.
3. Gustavson had sent CLB an offprint of an article on speech correction which had been published in the *Quarterly Journal of Speech*. "I had been curing myself of stammering," he wrote to the editor of this collection, "meanwhile at Cornell preferring to appear slightly—ah—backward, rather than betray the speech defect."

To Mrs. Max M. Kesterson

Ithaca, January 26, 1945[1]

Dear Mrs. Kesterson,[2]

I am glad you liked my book.[3] A good many people have, judging from the number of letters I get; and the sale of the book has been very good. I don't know what to say about myself that would be of any help to you. The main facts about my career are in "Who's Who in America," which you can find in the Grand Rapids libraries. I have published a good number of books, some of which are listed in the front of my book; and all of them are listed in Who's Who.

Some of the things I suggested in the book, such as an international organization, and an agency to stabilize exchanges, have already been started at Dumbarton Oaks and Bretton Woods. Other things, such as an agency for international trade, investments, and distribution of raw materials, etc., are yet to come, if they come at all. The most significant recent event is the fracas in Greece. Roosevelt and Churchill have said all along that they were in favor of allowing all liberated people to choose their own government after the war when it can be done by peaceful elections. But the Greeks, or some of them, apparently are not willing to wait, but prefer to decide it now, and not by election but by force. The question is, in how many European countries can the question be decided by peaceful election? What will happen in Germany? This is one of the disturbing things. Another is whether the USA, Russia, and Great Britain can work together for a settlement of Germany and eastern Europe. If they can't the prospects are dark indeed. Of course there will be differences, and we shouldn't be alarmed because there are differences in respect to Poland, Greece, etc. There are bound to be such differences. But I do not see any reason to suppose there need be any irreconcilable differences, such as would make an international organization useless. What we should recognize is that Poland and Eastern Europe is not a major interest for us, and that Russia is bound to get what she thinks indispensable there; just as we would regard the West Indies and South America a major interest for the U.S., and would, if similar questions should arise there, insist on getting what we regarded as essential.

In general I am not too pessimistic about the future in respect to international affairs. The prospects seem to be better than we have any right to have supposed, three years ago, they would be. This does not mean that I think there will be any new or ideal world. That is foolish. The world will be much what it has been; but I do not think Germany, or Japan, will ever have another chance to repeat their present schemes; and unless irreconcilable conflicts arise between Russia on the one hand, and Great Britain and the U.S. on the other over the German settlement, I see no likelihood of serious differences between them anywhere else. Of course a good deal depends on whether we can get the 150 billion income and the 60 million jobs that are said to be necessary.

Very sincerely yours,
Carl Becker

1. CBCU.
2. Mrs. Kesterson was the wife of the managing editor of the *Grand Rapids* (Mich.) *Press*.
3. *How New Will the Better World Be?*

To Leo Gershoy

Ithaca, January 29, 1945[1]

Dear Leo,

What ho! Lt. Colonel! Well, I never did! Beware of pride. Pride goeth before a *Fall*, and a haughty spirit before *Destruction!* So you're going on the grand tour. Don't forget to take a couple of extra powdered wigs, buckled shoes, and the snuff box. And a spy glass— for the mountains, to marvel at the wonders of Nature. And don't get mixed up in the black market. Do you trust Ida? But of course you have to, and anyway she can't expect to do better than a Lt. Col.

Haven't seen the Jan. copy of the A.H.A. I read Barzun's[2] review in something or other. Don't expect too much of reviewers. They mostly don't know nothin', and never made or unmade no one's reputation nohow.

The new book has just gone to Knopf. Probably out about April. I suppose I'll have to send Ida a copy. We are as usual, only we have blizzards all the time. My driveway is like a tunnel, with snow on both sides five feet high. Had to shovel it out myself once. Worked two hours steady, and poor old back as good as ever—or better. So there's life in the professor still.

Maude is about as usual—gets out with Edith every other day or so, if weather permits. We would both like to see you and Ida, but what chance is there for mere civilians with Lt. Cols.?

As ever,

Carl Becker

P.S. Did you know Harold Landin?[3] He's in France somewhere— and a lot of other Cornellians. And did you know Andy Biemiller? The fellow who wrote an estimate of the character of History 42 once, and said that Prof. Becker "has few equals and no peers." He's in Congress, representing Milwaukee on the Socialist ticket.

1. LIG.
2. Jacques Barzun (1907———) teaches history at Columbia (1927———), specializing in modern cultural history.

3. Landin (1903——) received his Ph.D. at Cornell (1928), taught history at Ohio State (1929–1942), and worked for the U.S. government during and after World War II.

To the editor of the *American Historical Review*

Ithaca, January 31, 1945[1]

In reading the extremely interesting Bryce-Jameson correspondence published in the January number of the Review,[2] I find that Mr. Stock[3] thought it worth while to include Bryce's[4] note of acknowledgement to Jameson for sending him "the little essay on Kansas."[5] This reminded me that at the same time Jameson sent a copy of the little essay to another valued friend, and from him received also a note of acknowledgement. The other friend was Henry Adams. Since the note is pure Henry Adams, and adds something to the gaiety of nations, which is especially needed just now, it occurred to me that your readers might be interested in seeing it. Here it is.

Sincerely yours,
Carl Becker

[Washington, D.C., March 22, 1911]

My dear Mr. Jameson,

Of course I have at once read the paper of Professor Becker, which is charming. If I were he, I should be a little afraid of indulging so freely my fancy for humor, but to elderly men somewhat desperately bored by commonplaces, humor is the single redeeming chance of literature, and they lap it up like a thirsty dog. A light touch is to them the finger of God. Even poor dear Emerson, whose sense of humor was extremely diluted, and who could see none in Aristophanes, was said to define God as infinite risibility, and this is one of the aphorisms which greatly reconciles me to Emerson's very homeopathic deity. Professor Becker shaves dangerously near laughing at us now and then.[6] I enjoy not only the laugh, but also the restraint which holds it back. . . . I do not know whether it is possible to do battle with the Philistine in

American Universities, but I earnestly hope he will try. Yet, no! I would be his friend, and I wish him no serious wrong.

> Ever yrs.
> Henry Adams.

1. Published in *AHR*, L (1945), 675–676. The original, in CBCU, is addressed to Guy Stanton Ford.

2. Leo Francis Stock, ed., "Some Bryce-Jameson Correspondence," *AHR*, L (1945), 261–298.

3. Stock (1878–1954) was a staff member of the Division of Historical Research of the Carnegie Institution (1910–1945) and professor of American history at Catholic University (1919–1941).

4. James Bryce (1838–1922), Regius Professor of Civil Law at Oxford (1870–1893), Liberal M.P. (1880–1906), ambassador to the United States (1907–1913), made three visits to the United States (1870, 1881, 1883); he wrote *The American Commonwealth* (1888).

5. CLB, "Kansas," in *Essays in American History Dedicated to Frederick Jackson Turner, by His Former Pupils* (New York, 1910).

6. See CLB to Harry Elmer Barnes, Oct. 22, 1938.

To Carl Jadwin Becker

Ithaca, February 14, 1945[1]

To My Valentine, C. J.   Feb. 14, 1945
> Clump, clump, clump—
> Upstairs and downstairs,—
> What is that noise?
> Maybe Carl Jadwin
> Looking for his toys.
> Maybe his Elephant,
> Maybe his bear.
> He'll find it somehow
> If it's anywhere.

> Pat, pat, pat—
> Now where's he going?
> Out in the yard.
> Maybe it's snowing.
> Maybe he's looking
> For the Popsicle man,

Running to the corner
As fast as he can.
What he'll do next
There's no way of knowing.

Whatever he does—
This grandson of mine—
He's a nice rascal
And my own Valentine!

Ithaca Grandfather.

1. CBCU.

To Mrs. Max M. Kesterson

Ithaca, February 16, 1945[1]

Dear Mrs. Kesterson,

It would contribute to clear thinking if we would drop the word "appeasement." In 1939 Chamberlain[2] tried to arrange a compromise with Hitler. He said in effect, we will concede the Sudeten lands if you will promise not to ask more. That proved to be a mistake because Hitler couldn't be trusted. He wouldn't really concede anything or keep any promise. Someone then hit on the word "appeasement." The word has a bad sound because it suggests knuckling down, pleading, begging; and so, since appeasement was bad in Munich people think it must always be bad; and now if a country concedes anything to another it's called appeasement and is condemned.

The proper word is compromise, conciliation, concession. Now in private and public life the art of getting on without fighting is sensible compromise. You can't live a week with your children, friends, or neighbors without making concessions, without adopting a policy of "appeasement" if you want to use that word. Of course it is necessary for the others to make concessions too. The same in international affairs. If countries are to live together without fighting they must compromise their disputes. Compromise, conciliation, appeasement if you like,—whatever word you use, the thing itself is the essence of politics. The question then, in any particular case, is not whether you are making concessions or appeasing someone, but whether you are making the right concessions, or are conceding too much or too little. That is a question of judgment. Now I say that concession or appeasement at Munich was a mistake because as it turned out Hitler couldn't be trusted to keep a promise of any sort. Compromise with Hitler was impossible. But I think compromise with Russia about Poland and the Balkans is possible and wise, because the hope of an international settlement and organization for keeping peace in Europe depends first of all on the possibility of Russia, Great Britain, and the U.S. working together. If they can't work together then there is slight chance of preventing war in another thirty years. Therefore it is unwise to try to force our solution of Poland and thereby risk the danger of breaking with Russia. We have an interest in Eastern Europe but not a major interest. Russia has the major interest there because she is on the spot and has to live with these people. Russia insists on certain Polish territory. If she insists on it she will have it, because she is on the spot and has the power. It is never wise to insist on something you can't back up; and we couldn't force Russia to back down on the Polish question if we wanted to. Russia may have an interest in Mexico and the West Indies, but not a major interest. What would we think if Russia should insist on our giving up Puerto Rico because our control of it violates the Atlantic Charter? What good would it do Russia to insist? She couldn't force us to give it up anyway. Of course we have an interest in any part of the world where there is danger to international peace. That is why we want an international organization to preserve the peace. But we haven't a major interest in every part of the world; and if we are to have the international organization we must manage to get on with the great Powers, because unless the great powers can work together no international organization can be effective. If we are to get on with them —with Russia, Great Britain, China, France—we must recognize that in certain parts of the world their interests are superior to ours, and be willing to concede their right to have what they regard as essential, always of course on the condition that they concede the same right to us in those parts of the world where our interest is superior.

The Atlantic Charter is a statement of ideal principles and ends.

These are ends to work towards; but it is useless to suppose that these ideal principles can be applied in particular circumstances with complete success. The Polish question is a particularly complex problem, and Americans don't understand how complicated. The people in the territory demanded by Russia are mostly not Poles, and they are mostly of the Greek Church religion, as the Russian people are, and not of the Roman Catholic faith as the Poles are. During the war there have been two underground organizations in Poland, one allied with the government in Exile in London, the other hostile to that government and sympathetic with Russia. From the point of view of race, religion, and historic tradition, there are good grounds for the Russian demand; there are good grounds for the demand of the government in exile. There is here a complex situation, a complicated conflict of ideas and interests which simply cannot be solved by saying that every people "must be permitted to choose the government under which it will live."

Of course, if you think Stalin is no more to be trusted than Hitler, and that he is out to dominate Europe and the world by spreading Communism, why then you are right to say we should concede nothing to him. But in that case you must be prepared to give up any hope of an international agreement that will be of any use whatever in preserving the peace of Europe. Apparently at the recent conference Roosevelt and Churchill, while conceding Russia's demands on the boundary, got some concessions from Stalin on the composition of the Polish government which all three would recognize. This seems to me the essence of wise statesmanship. There were concessions (appeasement) on both sides; but naturally Russia didn't make major concessions in respect to Eastern Europe where she has the major interest, has made the major sacrifices in the war, and has in any case the major power.

I hope this may have been of some assistance to you. I think we Americans are terribly afraid of being duped by what we regard as the wily Europeans. This fear leads us to run to one or other of two extremes: either we wish to keep entirely out of European affairs; or else, if we take any part, we think we must run the whole show. We have to learn that it is necessary to take a part, but only our proper part; and that we are as apt to be duped by being too suspicious of the Europeans as we are by being too credulous.

Very sincerely yours,
Carl Becker

1. CBCU.
2. Neville Chamberlain (1869–1940) was Prime Minister of Great Britain (1937–1940), and attempted to negotiate a peaceful settlement with Hitler in September 1938.

To the editor of the *Cornell Alumni News*

Ithaca, March 1945[1]

To the Editor:

For a long time now, a certain number of people with inquiring minds have wanted to know who was the author of the words, "Above all nations is humanity," which are inscribed on the stone seat that stands in front of Goldwin Smith Hall. Various suggestions have been made: Goldwin Smith,[2] Mazzini,[3] Goethe,[4] some Stoic philosopher. So far as I know, no one has as yet suggested Gerald K. Smith,[5] the Gentleman from Montana, or the hair-pulling Rankin from Mississippi.[6] I have not made any special researches for the purpose of answering this momentous question, but the other day I came, quite by accident, on two bits of evidence that throw some light on it.

The first is taken from the first number of The Cornell Era, November 28, 1868: "Goldwin Smith has arrived and entered upon his course. He is a tall, slight, dark-haired man—an Englishman— 'loving England well, but loving humanity more'—deeply interested in America and American institutions," etc. The implication here is that the writer had heard Goldwin Smith use the phrase quoted, or something similar.

The second bit of evidence is more to the point. It is a statement in Andrew D. White's hand, written in lead pencil, and dated September 18, 1872 (*White Papers* in the Cornell University Library): "Dr. Lyons, a Presbyterian professor, is greatly exercised by the inscription on the stone seat placed in the University grounds. The

seat bears the inscription, 'Above all nations is Humanity,' which
. . . written by one Englishman and carved by another, was under
the circumstances very appropriate. It evidently was intended to
show that an Englishman, Goldwin Smith, recognized a tie with his
new associates here stronger than nationality.—A. D. W."

This makes it clear that Goldwin Smith wrote or suggested the
phrase to be inscribed on the seat. Of course, he may have been
quoting some one else; but in that case I think he would undoubtedly have added the name of the author.

—Carl Becker

1. *Cornell Alumni News*, XLVII (May 1, 1945), 430–431. There is
an early draft of this letter, dated March 2, 1945, in CBCU.
2. Goldwin Smith (1823–1910), Regius Professor of Modern History
at Oxford (1858–1866), professor of history at Cornell (1868–1871),
settled in Toronto in 1871, where he wrote extensively and became active in public affairs. He bequeathed most of his large fortune to Cornell.
3. Giuseppe Mazzini (1805–1872), Italian patriot and revolutionary
prophet of European nationalism.
4. Johann W. von Goethe (1749–1832), German poet, natural philosopher, critic, journalist, statesman, and educator.
5. Gerald L. K. Smith (1898———), radio personality, political lecturer, head of the America First Party, editor of *The Cross and the
Flag*.
6. John E. Rankin (1882–1960), U.S. representative from Mississippi (1921–1953).

To H. L. Mencken

Ithaca, March 14, 1945[1]

Dear Mencken,

Thanks for your learned brocure on Hell & swearing.[2] Swearing
is going out of fashion in academic circles—if it ever was in. I
keep it up in a half hearted way, and am looked upon with kindly
indulgence as an eccentric because I sometimes say damn or to hell
with it.

As ever,
Carl Becker

1. Mencken Papers, New York Public Library.
2. Mencken, "American Profanity," *American Speech*, XIX (Dec. 1944), 241–249.

To Leo Gershoy

Ithaca, March 14, 1945[1]

Dear Leo,

Thanks for your letter, and its brief news about the Paris atmosphere and the Parisians. I got a lovely Christmas card from Harold Landin, with pictures of Paris and American doughboys and French girls, etc., all very lively. I suppose you're having the time of your life. Even if you are very busy you can't be more so than you were here. Ida feels deserted, and very much out of it since this is the first time according to her that you have gone abroad without her tagging along—so she says.

Nothing new here, except that our winter broke very suddenly the last week in February, and its been very nice and spring like now for two weeks. Fred is in New York this week and next week will be in Florida—some conference of the editorial groups in the Navy. I don't know when the Michigan lectures will be out, but sometime this Spring I suppose. I am now working on the new World History for Silver Burdett Co.[2] —a high school text which will include a proper amount about the Far East, which will be done by a Dr. Han of U.C. at Los Angeles. The Ancient and medieval part to the 18 century will be done by Painter of John Hopkins.[3] My part is mainly to reduce Modern History to the allowed space, with some additions relating to the U.S.A. and South America. Mainly paste and scissors.

Be a brave good boy and give my regards to Lorwin and any others who may be interested.

As ever,
Carl Becker

1. LIG.
2. *The Past That Lives Today* (New York, 1952).
3. Yu-Shan Han (1899———) taught Chinese history at the University of California, Los Angeles (1941–1966); Sidney Painter (1902–1960) taught medieval history at The Johns Hopkins University (1931–1960).

To Jessie Becker

Ithaca, March 21, 1945[1]

Dear Jessie,

I was glad to get the account of the flood. I don't remember any floods in my time, and I don't see how the river gets such a head of water in that level country, but of course if there is enough snow or rain you can get a flood anywhere.

I may get a few off-prints of my article.[2] They don't often print any articles separately; but they have printed a few of mine, and they may this time. If they do I will send you one. You oughtn't to complain about the Electoral System. The only Presidents that slipped into the White House by the aid of the Electoral System, without having a plurality of the popular vote, were both Republicans—Hayes in 1876 and Harrison in 1888.[3] If it hadn't been for the electoral system we should have had two more Democratic Presidents, and you wouldn't have liked that. The election of Tilden[4] in 1876 would have given Father heart failure. The election of Cleveland[5] in 1884 nearly did. He thought the end of the world had come. Looking back on those elections it is easy to see it didn't make any difference worth mentioning which side won. The fact is that there is very little difference between the two major parties, and either one can represent the will of the people well enough. And the Electoral System is one of the reasons why the parties are so much alike, and can't be organized on purely class or sectional lines. That is why it is on the whole a good system.

Our winter is over, and in fact it broke suddenly the last of February. We had two days last week with the thermometer at 73 degrees. That's too hot, coming at this time of year.

As ever,

from your brother

Maude keeps about the same. She gets out every other day or so, but can't get away very well except from about 3:30 to 6. It's not serious, but very disagreeable and discouraging.

1. CBCU.
2. "The Will of the People," *Yale Review*, XXXIV (1945), 385–404.

3. Rutherford B. Hayes (1822–1893), U.S. President (1877–1881); Benjamin Harrison (1833–1901), President (1889–1893).

4. Samuel J. Tilden (1814–86), lawyer, Democratic politician, and unsuccessful candidate for President in 1876.

5. Grover Cleveland (1837–1908), President (1885–1889, 1893–1897).

Appendix: Eight Letters to and about Carl L. Becker

From Iris Calderhead[1]

New York, New York, August 27, 1932[2]

Dear Mr. Becker:

I have an impulse to tell you something, and in this weary and heavy-laden world perhaps impulses are to be obeyed. There was something much more than the casual renewal of a friendship in our meeting after twenty years.

To the people who knew my husband[3] he was of the breed of Prometheus—even the Irishman—the gentleman of the press—who had been told to come get his "story" said to me—me, mind you, who had lived with this man—Mrs. Walker, perhaps you don't know—but God! *this* was a man."

I am aware of the strangeness of writing this to you, but hear me. I had lived to be 42 years old and had never seen death. The night the realization came—and it came quickly, we said goodbye to our beautiful life and then he said, read to me. I had to read—as I had many times through our years together—continuously so that the voice without a break would keep him lulled to sleep. The book I picked up at random was a history dedicated to *you*.

I have never until this week been able to recall the name of it, a biography of Gambetta.[4] I do not recall the name of the author; but the affectionate and grateful sentiments of the dedication to you, brought you to my mind. There was something strangely sustaining in the memory as I read monotonously through the long vigil.

There was a recollection of the sense of perspective that you were talking about last night. The calm poise, the even balance, the acute sensitivity that are yours to such an extraordinary degree —somehow reached across the years to me. Hour after hour, with every minute an eternity in the presence of death, everything is thrown into greater significance.

There you are—I thought I should like you to know. It made seeing you again something more precious than a passing episode.

Iris Calderhead

1. Calderhead (Mrs. John Brisben Walker) had been a student of CLB's at Kansas (B.A., 1910).

2. CBCU.

3. John Brisben Walker (1847–1931), editor, founded *Cosmopolitan Magazine* in 1889, and organized The Mobile Company of America in 1899.

4. I have not been able to locate such a book; but Mrs. Walker may very likely have meant Louis Gottschalk's *Jean Paul Marat: A Study in Radicalism* (New York, 1927), which is dedicated to CLB.

From T. V. Smith[1]

Chicago, October 26, 1932[2]

Dear Colleague:

Yes, I had a most elevating week-end. I was going up to Minneapolis, and I decided that as I went up bodily I ought to go up intellectually. So I took your "Heavenly City"[3] with me, and climbed its dialectical ladder inch by inch as the locomotive climbed the Minnesota hills. I passed through the "climates of opinion" as the train left the fog of Chicago and the flatness of Illinois behind. I negotiated "the laws of nature" as we went through the rolling hills of Wisconsin. "The new history" I identify with the restless Mississippi, since I finished the chapter as we crossed that divide. As darkness fell over us and the Minnesota hills grew in ominous dusk to the size of mountains and the mountains lost themselves in identity with the low-hanging clouds, I plunged into "the uses of posterity" and finally as the lights of Minneapolis ended the trip, I ended the book—coming out on the other side of posterity, almost beyond good and evil.

And then under the spell of the double-trip, elevated in mind and elevated in body, I spent the evening in bed at the hotel going back over the toilsome road and integrating my two journeys into one whole of enjoyment and significance.

Perhaps your book's philosophy, even if it isn't history. Whether it is or not, we'll let that pass. It is great writing without a doubt, and I suspect great thinking. After all, to generalize your own ad hoc observation regarding the philosophers at issue, philosophy is never Philosophy, you know. For Philosophy feeds on philosophy, and philosophy feeds upon the rawer stuff of life. Your book Philosophy? I know not. But philosophy? Without a doubt. Never did history and philosophy and life seem so close together and never seemed so fatuous any talk of compartmentization, as the hour after I finished your book. It is a real experience to have somebody take you by the hand and without so much as a warning take you up beyond acquisitive quarrels and show you the seamlessness of the entire realm of being. You almost did that for me.

Yet ringing in my ears your "it is unlikely that these tricks do the dead any harm, and it is certain that they do us much good." I could smile tolerantly at the humbler gait of those of us who must grow to more and more from less and less. It ain't right what nature has given some men, in the light of how little she has given some of the rest of us. But my gratitude at last has outrun my envy for even this outrageous distribution of talent among the children of nature.

I got such an aesthetic kick out of your book that I have had little desire as yet to assess it analytically. For a fact, I had no intention to be converted by you; for if Hume went down in the dust of tradition, then all the foundation for my own bellicosity would turn to dust. Now I did not mean to give up my own prejudice again mediaevalism and even against Christianity in every form. So I was going to let you rave on, enjoy you but not believe a damn conclusion you drew. Perhaps I may be able to rise from my initial defeat; but I must acknowledge that the subtle way in which (p. 109) you knocked even Hume's historical neutrality out from under me, has made quite a dent in my complacency, yea in my conviction. Well, let me put it this way: If there was such a little difference between Hume and those early woe-begoners, then that little difference is more precious to me than ever before!

But without a doubt you get closer to our (I mean my own) prejudices in the last chapter. That still remains the bone if not also the blood of my own rationalization. Now, however, I know the uses of posterity, I shall continue to use it. That really is a grand climax for your logical position, and somehow or other it gathers in its overtones the aesthetic echoes from the early chapters and ends the book in an organic unity of logic and axiology—that's Minneapolis by night.

Thanks for the copy you so kindly gave me. Thanks for the high enjoyment of the book.

YOURS,
T. V. Smith

1. T. V. Smith (1890–1964) taught philosophy at Chicago (1926–1948) and at Syracuse (1948–1956).
2. CBCU.
3. *The Heavenly City of the Eighteenth-Century Philosophers.*

From Charles A. Beard

New Milford, Connecticut, May 14, 1933[1]

Dear Becker,

Conyers Read sent me your devasating, crushing, inescapable rejoinder to his invitation.[2] I am ruined and weep bitter tears. Even at the risk of shortening your precious life I am tempted to mandamus you anyhow, especially since you never come to see me. It is true that I was on my way West when you burbled in Minneapolis, but durn your skin I did not have to stop three days in that burg in order to get there or go out of my way hundreds of miles. I did that because you were President and I wanted to be at the show. Still I will not quarrel with you more on that point.

Anyhow, you can help Read out by outlining a program on historiography, suggest speakers, and a chairman. I beg of you to do that much. I command you to do it on pain of expulsion from the heavenly city. And if possible, pray come to Urbana and take a hand. At least send us a five page paper. We need your help. Nobody can take your place. If you cannot lend us a hand, lend us a little finger; that is a hell of a lot.

As ever,
Yours,
Charles A. Beard

1. CBCU.
2. See CLB to Conyers Read, May 10, 1933.

From Robert R. Palmer[1]

Chicago, July 10, 1934[2]

Dear Mr. Becker—

. . . . .

There is one matter which I neglected before I left Ithaca and which I want to say something of now. That is to tell you how much I feel that I received from Cornell and in particular from you. I was aware of it before I left, but it was brought home to me with more force after I got back and went down to the U. of Chicago and heard some of my friends there tell me about their troubles. If I know anything now, or ever learn anything, about what to do with ideas and how to express them, or how to tell the woods from the trees, I shall always think that I owed it mostly to you, and partly too to a certain spirit among some of the students at Cornell which itself exists largely because of the influence in high-quarters—i.e. Room 3 of Boardman Hall. I know too, better than some of my esteemed colleagues who have never studied except at Cornell, what you mean by your phrase "trained to death in the graduate schools." It's a rare privilege, I'm sure, among American universities, to be able to get a Ph.D. degree without feeling as if you'd been through a wringer. One person here has even told me that, now of all times, I've lost that scholarly look!

I'm looking forward to seeing you in New York—and rather hoping, I must confess (when I ought to be hoping a little more energetically for a job) to manage somehow to get back to Ithaca next year, where I can "be around" and also get to work on that book.

Yours most sincerely,
Robert Palmer

1. Palmer (1909—) received his Ph.D. at Cornell in 1934, taught European history at Princeton (1936–1963, 1966–1969), Washington University (1963–1966), and Yale (1969——). His special interest is the late eighteenth century.
2. CBCU.

From Felix Frankfurter

Cambridge, Massachusetts, January 11, 1936[1]

Dear Carl,

I rejoice that the Washington affair blew up.[2] After all we are learning that liberty isn't a gift but a conquest, even though one doesn't see why a fellow who has paid as much for it as you have should have to pay more. But this is to tell you how exquisite I deemed your reply to Hacker.[3] No wonder the papacy is an undying institution! The Pope seems to be in all of us. Hacker writes as though God had talked to him with detailed economic disclosures on Sinai. But I always thought you were a gentle and a kind fellow. I don't know anything more cruel if not contemptuous, than to stick a very small needle into a very big balloon. The good Lord— or what lords there are off the Supreme Court—bless you!

Ever yours,
FF.

Prof. Carl Becker

P.S. I know about the Red Book,[4] but I don't know it. I am told that I would know a lot about myself that I don't know now, were I to read it. We are in for one of the bitterest of political years, and I wish you would write a piece recalling the sweet and lovely days when similar amenities were indulged in against that destroyer and atheist, one T. Jefferson.

1. CBCU.
2. See CLB to the editor of the *Washington Herald*, Nov. 26, 1935.
3. See CLB to the editor of the *New Republic*, Jan. 8, 1936.
4. Elizabeth Dilling, *The Red Network: A "Who's Who" and Handbook of Radicalism for Patriots* (Kenilworth, Ill., 1934, 1935).

From Harry C. Strong[1]

Duluth, Minnesota, December 13, 1938[2]

Dear Mr. Becker: —

My vanity flattered by their invitation, I agreed last fall with a group of women to speak to them on "The Philosophy of History" which I toned down to "Some Interpretations of History." In preparing my paper I made a free and beneficial use of your "Declaration of Independence" and of your essays in the volume "Every Man His Own Historian." If putting your work to such a use seems to you a profanation of it, please call Miss Mary Elizabeth Bohannon onto the carpet and give her a good talking to. Since I am nigh thirty years away from academic halls, I submitted my first draft to Betty, and she tactfully suggested that maybe I would want to make some changes if I should read those works of yours. Resulting changes to the good were numerous.

Betty's father recently said I would doubtless also enjoy your "Heavenly City of the Eighteenth Century Philosophers." While reading and rereading it, I figured my great delight in your writings is due to my feeling that they put me into the same kind of happy land in history that I dwelt in in philosophy when taking lectures under William James at Harvard in the late nineties.

This is the first "fan letter" I have even written and I somehow feel abashed and apologetic in doing it. I hope you will not mind, and please believe me,—you can toss this into your waste basket unanswered with no hurt to my feelings.

Sincerely

Harry C. Strong

1. Henry Carter Strong (1875–1949) attended the Graduate School of Arts and Sciences at Harvard, 1896–1899.
2. CBCU.

From Louis Gottschalk

Chicago, July 15, 1941[1]

Dear Mr. Becker,

I have put off writing this letter several times. It is the kind of letter I ought to write but find no relish in writing. Yet as your first (or at least first surviving) Ph.D., I feel called upon to say something about your retirement from Cornell.

Retirement may carry some pleasant connotations to you, and if it does, I shall not be surprised. The hope of having an assured, if small, income and no assigned duties sometimes seems very attractive to one who is still a quarter of a century from retirement age and feels he can do nothing well because there are so many things that have to be done at the same time. But *your* retirement is so keen a personal blow to me that I feel very differently about it and perhaps more personally than you do yourself. To me you represented Cornell. As long as you were there, I had a solid and warm association with Ithaca, much stronger than six years of residence and occasional visits subsequently could have caused. I don't know whether you ever realized it (though I suspect you did), but it is true that no other single person had a greater effect upon moulding my character, no other person was as much present in my mind as a model. That influence, of course, remains, but it is no longer associated with Cornell, which has become a place where the geography alone and no personal touch are familiar. Cornell meant Becker to me; Cornell is now in retirement as far as I am concerned. It doesn't console me that that is as inevitable as time, that institutions last while men pass on. But I am grateful that you have been spared us this long and hope that you may be around to guide us until my own retirement or longer.

McNeill[2] tells me you are going to Smith for a while next year. That sounds like uncommon good sense for Smith. Also that you are going to write a history of Cornell. Perhaps that will recapture for me that part of my youth which your retirement has rendered largely empty. Whatever you do and wherever you go, my deepest affection and respect go with you.

Please remember me to Mrs. Becker and Frederick and his family.

Faithfully yours,
Louis Gottschalk

1. CBCU.
2. William H. McNeill.

From Allan Nevins

New York, New York, September 9, 1941[1]

Dear Becker:

Ever since I heard that you have retired from active teaching I have been minded to send you a note of congratulation or condolence—I don't know which you would expect. Retirement always reminds me of a story current in my Scottish community in western Illinois about old McPheeters. He was attending a tent-revival, and in his Scotch-Presbyterian fashion obviously disapproving of the Methodist revivalist's methods. At one point the preacher called on all in the audience who wanted to go to heaven to stand up. Everybody rose but McPheeters, who remained clamped to his chair. "What," cried the preacher, "do you not wish to go to heaven, sir?" "Aye," drily rejoined old McPheeters, "but not jist yit." That is the way most of my colleagues seem to feel about retirement. I must say, and this is no idle flattery, that I could hardly believe in the fact of your retirement; you seem to me, I will not say perennially young, but perennially in early middle age.

That this is a fact, and that you will prove it by a steadier flow of the books and articles which you alone can write, we are all confident. I hope that you will enjoy your broader margin of leisure, and will find much opportunity for that lecturing which I am told you will begin at Smith this next spring. I wish that some of that lecturing might be done on Morningside Heights.

These are grim days for the world. The failure to comprehend just how grim they are, the widespread apathy, the prevalent spirit of "Let Russia and England do it," dishearten me more than they amaze me. I wish I might have a good talk with you, and exchange ideas upon some of the social and political changes I have seen in the making in Great Britain.

Cordially yours,
Allan Nevins

1. CBCU.

BIBLIOGRAPHY
AND INDEX

Bibliography

MANUSCRIPT COLLECTIONS

Department of Manuscripts and University Archives, Olin Library, Cornell University, Ithaca, N.Y.

Carl L. Becker Papers.
Mary Elizabeth Bohannon Papers.
George Lincoln Burr Papers.
Edmund Ezra Day Papers.
Livingston Farrand Papers.
Charles Hull Papers.
Jared T. Newman Papers.
Robert M. Ogden Papers.

Columbia University Library, New York, N.Y.

James Truslow Adams Papers.
Henry Johnson Papers.

Harvard University, Cambridge, Mass.

Wendell P. Garrison Papers. Houghton Library.
Arthur M. Schlesinger Papers. University Archives.

Henry E. Huntington Library and Art Gallery, San Marino, Calif.

Max Farrand Papers.
Frederick Jackson Turner Papers.

Johns Hopkins University Library, Baltimore, Md.

Isaiah Bowman Papers.

Library of Congress, Washington, D.C.

William E. Dodd Papers.
Felix Frankfurter Papers.

New York Public Library

H. L. Mencken Papers.

North Carolina State University Archives, Raleigh
Rudolph E. Freund Papers.

Pennsylvania State University Library, State College, Pa.

Fred Lewis Pattee Papers.
State College Literary Club Papers.

State Historical Society of Wisconsin, Madison.

Merle Curti Papers.
Frederick Jackson Turner Papers.

University of Kansas Library

James W. Gleed Papers.

University of Minnesota Library, Minneapolis

Guy Stanton Ford Papers.
August C. Krey Papers.

University of Wyoming Library, Laramie

Harry Elmer Barnes Papers.

Yale University Library, New Haven, Conn.

Ralph H. Gabriel Papers.
Max Lerner Papers.
Wallace Notestein Papers.

Private Collections

Morris Bishop, Ithaca, N.Y.
Gussie Esther Gaskill, Ithaca, N.Y.
Leo and Ida Gershoy, New York, N.Y.
Carl G. Gustavson, Athens, Ohio.
Oron J. Hale, Charlottesville, Va.
Alfred M. Kazin, New York, N.Y.
Alfred A. Knopf, Purchase, N.Y.
Richard M. Leighton, Alexandria, Va.
Anita Marburg Lerner, Columbia, Md.
May Elish Markewich, New York, N.Y.
Florence and Morton Yohalem, Washington, D.C.

BOOKS BY CARL L. BECKER

America's War Aims and Peace Program. Washington, D.C.: Committee on Public Information, War Information Series, 1918.
The Beginnings of the American People. Boston: Houghton Mifflin, 1915.
Benjamin Franklin. Ithaca: Cornell University Press, 1946.
Cornell University: Founders and the Founding. Ithaca: Cornell University Press, 1943.

The Declaration of Independence: A Study in the History of Political Ideas. New York: Harcourt, Brace, 1922.
The Eve of the Revolution. New Haven: Yale University Press, 1918.
Everyman His Own Historian: Essays on History and Politics. New York: Crofts, 1935.
Freedom and Responsibility in the American Way of Life. New York: Knopf, 1945.
German Attempts to Divide Belgium. Boston: World Peace Foundation, 1918.
The Heavenly City of the Eighteenth-Century Philosophers. New Haven: Yale University Press, 1932.
The History of Political Parties in the Province of New York, 1760–1776. Madison: University of Wisconsin Press, 1909.
How New Will the Better World Be? New York: Knopf, 1944.
Modern Democracy. New Haven: Yale University Press, 1941.
Modern History: The Rise of a Democratic, Scientific, and Industrial Civilization. New York: Silver Burdett, 1931.
New Liberties for Old. New Haven: Yale University Press, 1941.
Progress and Power. Palo Alto, Calif.: Stanford University Press, 1936.
Story of Civilization. With Frederick Duncalf. New York: Silver Burdett, 1938.
The United States: An Experiment in Democracy. New York: Harper, 1920.

SECONDARY SOURCES

Billington, Ray Allen. *Frederick Jackson Turner: Historian, Scholar, Teacher*. New York, 1973.
Blakey, George T. *Historians on the Homefront: American Propagandists for the Great War*. Lexington, Ky., 1970.
Boyd, Julian P. "Benjamin Franklin and Carl Becker." Preface to CLB, *Benjamin Franklin*, vii–xii. Ithaca, 1946.
Braeman, John, and John C. Rule. "Carl Becker: Twentieth Century Philosophe," *American Quarterly*, XIII (1961), 534–539.
Brown, Robert E. *Carl Becker on History and the American Revolution*. East Lansing, Mich., 1970.
Cairns, John C. "Carl Becker: An American Liberal," *Journal of Politics*, XVI (1954), 623–644.
Craddock, Richard S. "The Views of Professional American Historians on the Values and Purposes of Historical Study." Ph.D. dissertation, Duke University, 1969.
Destler, Chester M. "The Crocean Origin of Becker's Historical Relativism," *History and Theory*, IX (1970), 335–342. Reply by Hayden V. White, *ibid.*, X (1971), 222–227.
Ford, Guy Stanton. "Carl Lotus Becker," *The American Philosophical*

Society Year Book for 1945 (1946), 338–346. Contains a lengthy, intimate reminiscence by Leo Gershoy.

Gershoy, Leo. Introduction to CLB, *Progress and Power*, ix–xxxvii. New York, 1949.

Gold, Milton. "In Search of a Historian," *Centennial Review*, VII (1963), 282–305.

Gottschalk, Louis. "Carl Becker: Skeptic or Humanist?" *Journal of Modern History*, XVIII (1946), 160–162.

Hawke, David F. "Carl L. Becker." M.S. thesis, University of Wisconsin, 1950. Contains an invaluable chronological bibliography of CLB's writings, including book reviews.

Hexter, J. H. *The History Primer*, esp. 53. New York, 1971.

Holt, W. Stull. *Historical Scholarship in the United States and Other Essays*, chs. i & iv. Seattle, 1967.

Horwich, Carl. "Carl Becker: A Study of Liberalism and the History of Ideas." M.A. thesis, Wayne State University, 1941.

Jacobs, Wilbur R., ed. *The Historical World of Frederick Jackson Turner, with Selections from His Correspondence*. New Haven, 1968. Includes a number of letters from Turner to and about CLB.

Kammen, Michael. Essay review of Robert E. Brown, *Carl Becker on History and the American Revolution*. In *History and Theory*, XI (1972), 359–368.

Klein, Milton M. "Detachment and the Writing of American History: The Dilemma of Carl Becker." In Alden T. Vaughan and George A. Billias, eds., *Perspectives on Early American History: Essays in Honor of Richard B. Morris*. New York, 1973.

Krutch, Joseph Wood. "Carl Becker," *The Nation*, CLX (1945), 490–501.

Malin, James C. *Essays on Historiography*, chs. i, iv. Lawrence, Kan., 1946.

Mandelbaum, Maurice. *The Problem of Historical Knowledge: An Answer to Relativism*. New York, 1938.

Mason, Bernard. "The Heritage of Carl Becker: The Historiography of the Revolution in New York," *New-York Historical Society Quarterly*, LIII (1969), 127–147.

Noble, David. "Carl Becker: Science, Relativism, and the Dilemma of Diderot," *Ethics*, LXVII (1957), 233–248.

Palmer, Robert R. "The Age of the Democratic Revolution." In *The Historian's Workshop: Original Essays by Sixteen Historians*, ed. L. P. Curtis, Jr., 167–186, esp. 170. New York, 1970.

Penick, James L., Jr. "Carl Becker and the Jewel of Consistency," *Antioch Review*, XXVI (1966), 235–246.

Rockwood, Raymond O., ed. *Carl Becker's Heavenly City Revisited*. Ithaca, 1958. Studies resulting from a symposium at Colgate University, October 13, 1956.

Rule, John C., and Ralph D. Handen. "Bibliography of Works on Carl Lotus Becker and Charles Austin Beard, 1945–1963," *History and Theory,* V (1966), 302–314.

Sabine, George H. "Carl Lotus Becker." Introductory essay to CLB, *Freedom and Responsibility in the American Way of Life,* vii–xlii. New York, 1945.

Skotheim, Robert A. *American Intellectual Histories and Historians,* 109–123. Princeton, N.J., 1966.

Smith, Charlotte Watkins. *Carl Becker: On History & the Climate of Opinion.* Ithaca, 1956.

Snyder, Phil L. "Carl L. Becker and the Great War: A Crisis for a Humane Intelligence," *Western Political Quarterly,* IX (1956), 1–10.

——, ed. *Detachment and the Writing of History: Essays and Letters of Carl L. Becker.* Ithaca, 1958. Includes eight of CLB's letters.

Strout, Cushing. *The Pragmatic Revolt in American History: Carl Becker and Charles Beard.* New Haven, 1958.

Tucker, Louis L. Introduction to CLB, *The Spirit of '76,* 1–13. Albany, 1971.

Wilkins, Burleigh Taylor. *Carl Becker: A Biographical Study in American Intellectual History.* Cambridge, Mass., 1961.

Willis, E. R. B. "Carl Lotus Becker." In *Cornell University: Necrology of the Faculty, 1944–45,* 24–27. Ithaca, 1945.

Zagorin, Perez. "Carl Becker on History: Professor Becker's Two Histories: A Skeptical Fallacy," *AHR,* LXII (1956), 1–11. Observations by Leo Gershoy and Hilary Conroy, *ibid.,* 12–17, 1055–1057.

Index

Abbott, Wilbur Cortez, xviii, 4-5, 6n2, 10
Adams, Brooks, 301-302
Adams, Ephraim D., 144, 145n3
Adams, Henry, xix, xxvi, xxvii, 60, 263 & n3, 267, 301-302, 338
    letter from, to Jameson, 338-339
Adams, James Truslow, 168n2
    letters to, 168, 169
Adams, Sam, 72, 115
Allen, Frederick Lewis, 180n2
    letter to, 179
Allen, Phil, 185, 186n3
American Historical Association, 32-33, 61-63, 147, 182-184, 249, 252, 254-255, 337
American Historical Review, 13, 79, 338
American Magazine
    letter to, 324
Andrews, Charles M., 34, 35-36 & n4, 83, 84n2
Andrews, George G., xxvi, 171, 172n2, 252
Arnold, General H. H., 311, 313 & n2, 422
Association of Teachers of Social Studies in New York City, 318
Atlantic Charter, the, 341-342
Atlantic Monthly, 13
Augustine, St., 154

Baker, Ray Stannard, 86, 87 & n2, 88
Baldwin, Stanley, 253, 254n3
Bancroft, Frederic, 32, 33n3
Bancroft, George, xix, 298
Bancroft, Hubert H., 298, 299n4
Barber, Marshall A., 39, 42, 45-46 & n3
Barère de Vieuzac, Bertrand, 103, 151
Barnes, Harry Elmer, 107n2, 115, 116, 130, 267, 314
    letters to, 105, 107, 114, 242, 263

Barzun, Jacques, 337 & n2
Bates, Frank G., 10 & n8
Bates, Ralph, 256, 257n4
Baxter, James Phinney, III, 238 & n5
Beard, Charles A., xxi, xxiv, 59, 60 & n4, 153 & n3, 182-184, 313
    letters to, 261, 265, 267, 301, 351
Beard, Mary, 182-183, 184n4, 261, 266
Becker, Betty (Mrs. Frederick), 307, 314, 381
Becker, Carl Jadwin, 281, 288, 297, 307, 309, 314, 318
    letter to, 339
Becker, Carl L.
    aesthetic appreciation, 262
    and the American Historical Association, 61-63, 147, 182-184, 249, 252, 254-255
    biographical sketch, xv-xxviii
    on book reviewing and reviewers, xxv, 37, 168, 177, 258
    on books that influenced him, 263-264, 300-301
    on California and Stanford, 127-131, 217-223
    on censureship and freedom of speech, 145, 181-182, 190
    and Columbian Exposition of 1893, 120-121
    and Cornell, 38, 79, 132-133, 237, 248, 279-280, 295, 309-311, 314
    as a critic, xx, 168-170, 175, 194-196, 327-328
    on democracy, 83-84, 134, 195, 281-282
    on the depression and the New Deal, 181, 195-196, 251, 253, 282, 326
    on European history and government, 3, 18, 22, 26, 150-151, 154, 161, 281, 294, 317
    on faculty wives, 313

365

Becker, Carl L. (*cont.*)
finances, 209-210, 220, 253, 271, 313, 325
on Fredrick J. Turner and his influence, 15-17, 75-76, 88-89, 105, 117, 267-268, 333-334
health, 121, 144, 162, 171, 172, 176, 178, 183-184, 184-185, 186-187, 188, 192, 208, 209, 211, 214, 222, 237, 241, 244, 249, 264, 265, 266, 271, 273, 274-275, 318, 333
on historical knowledge, problems of, 32, 50, 52, 141-142, 247, 272-273
historical relativism, 153, 156-158, 261, 265-266
historical study, the nature of, 17-19, 52, 156-157, 179
on historical writing, synthesis in, 175
on history, causation in, 320-322
history, large factors in, 59, 78-79, 180, 189
history and historical study, the uses of, 15-17, 23, 156-157, 180, 302
history and literature, 34, 175
history and psychology, xxi, xxviii, 50, 83-84, 226-227, 327
history and science, 34, 52, 207, 239, 302-303
honors, 165, 197, 212, 269 & n2
and Ithaca, N.Y., 48, 57, 64, 205, 218-219, 224, 241, 310
on Jews and anti-Semitism, 124, 145, 161-162
law, 250
lectureships, 109, 228-229, 249, 251, 255, 271, 276, 279, 281, 291-292, 296, 297-299, 307, 311, 313, 315, 318, 324, 326, 329-330, 331, 332, 345
on the meaning and philosophy of life, 120-121, 123, 167, 245
myths and history, 316
the natural-rights philosophy, 79-81
on patriotism, 319-320
on politics and international relations after World War I, 66, 69-74, 77, 87-88, 119-120
and professional meetings, 26, 74
as a prophet, xxiii
publications, preparing of, 144, 148-149, 154, 190, 201, 223, 225-226, 228-229, 241-243,

280, 296-297, 307, 312-314, 349-351
on radicalism, socialism, and communism, 181-182, 194-195, 228, 232-237, 242-243, 261, 309, 321, 353
and religion, 50, 124, 182-184; *see also* Becker, Carl L., on Jews and anti-Semitism
retirement, 278, 279-280, 354
on revolutions, 11, 81, 83, 96-97, 210-211, 265, 320-322
self-evaluation, xvii, 31, 47, 75-76, 191
on sex, 129
skepticism, 63, 207, 302
sociology, 303
as a teacher, xx-xxi, 20, 21, 103, 206, 231, 352, 355
on teachers and students, 109-111, 112-113, 118-119, 173-174, 203, 206-207, 320-322
on teaching history, 23, 84-85, 126, 131
on theatre, 204
on totalitarianism, 260, 294
travel, 89-100, 108, 187-188
on the United States governmental system, 72-73, 214, 244, 324-325, 346
on United States history, 11, 31-32, 79-80, 81, 83, 321-322
on universities, 14, 36-37, 42-43, 68, 132, 178-179
and World War I, 58, 60, 106, 119, 192-193
and World War II, 270, 285, 304-306, 308, 310-313, 316-317, 331, 335-336, 340-343
on writing and literary form, xxi-xxii, 17-20, 21-22, 24-25, 29, 30-32, 33-35, 75, 103, 104, 154-155, 156-157, 162, 166, 185, 266-267, 300, 328
Becker, Edith, 213, 337
Becker, Frederick, 30, 135, 143, 147, 152, 158, 165, 213, 216, 231, 238, 240, 241, 271, 278, 288, 307, 314, 318, 345
letters to, 89, 96, 97, 99
Becker, Jessie, 290n2
letters to, 290, 346
Becker, Marie, 121, 122n2
Becker, Maude Ranney, 30, 90n2, 130, 165, 213, 216, 231, 240, 253, 275, 278, 279, 290, 292, 293, 295, 296, 297, 307, 308,

Becker, Maude Ranney (*cont.*)
  312, 314, 318, 332, 333, 337,
  346
  letters to, 90, 91, 92, 93
Becker family, history, xv, 65, 270-
  271, 346
Bell, Herbert C. F., 104 & n3
Bernheim, Ernest, 247, 248n4
Biemiller, Andrew J., 163, 164n4,
  306, 337
Bishop, Morris, 248n2, 252
  letter to, 246
Blood, Charles H., 54n2
  letter to, 54
Boak, Arthur E. R., 253, 254n4
Bohannon, Mary Elizabeth, 173n2,
  354
  letters to, 172, 173, 187, 202, 284
Boorstin, Daniel, xix
Boucher, Chauncey, 134, 135n3
Bowman, Isaiah, 228n2
  letter to, 228
Bradford, Eugene, xxvi, 313, 314n5
Bradford, Gamaliel, 34, 35 & n4
Bradford, Margery, 313, 314n5
Brailsford, H. N., 234
Bretton Woods Conference, 336
Brunetière, Ferdinand, 247, 248n8
Bruun, Geoffrey, 121, 122n3
  letter to, 150
Bryan, William Jennings, 25 & n5,
  60
Bryce, James, 338-339 & n4
Burckhardt, Jakob C., 175
Burgess, John W., 250 & n5
Burke, Edmund, 317 & n3
Burr, George Lincoln, 37, 38 & n5,
  48, 51, 56, 65, 69, 78, 123, 129,
  149, 153, 219, 225
  letters to, 46, 49, 52, 53, 58, 107,
  189
Bury, J. B., 175
Butler, Nicholas Murray, 111,
  112n4, 269 & n3
Byrne, Eugene H., 165 & n3

Calderhead, Iris, 349n1
  letter to CLB, 348
Calhoun, John C., 32, 80 & n4, 81
Cambon, Pierre Paul, 191, 192n3
Campbell, Robert N., 323n2
  letter to, 322-323
Carruth, William H., 39, 45-46n3
Chamberlain, Neville, 340, 343n2
Chamberlin, W. H., 234, 236n6
Channing, Edward, 333, 334n4
Chaucer, Geoffrey, 273 & n2, 274

Cheyney, Edward Potts, 34, 35-36n4,
  180
Chicago, University of, 64-65, 133-
  134, 352
Churchill, Winston, 336
"The Circle," 262 & n4
Clemenceau-Jacquemarie, Madeline,
  127, 128n5
Cleveland, Grover, 346, 347n5
Clinton, DeWitt, letters of, 5
Coffin, Victor, 57 & n4
Colby, Frank M., 34, 35n4
Colgate University, 318
Columbia University, 5
Common Sense
  letter to, 316-317
Coolidge, Calvin, 214
Cornell, Ezra, 286, 287, 296, 297,
  315-316
Cornell Alumni News
  letter to, 343
Cornell Bulletin
  letter to, 315
Cornell Daily Sun
  letters to, 109, 112, 115
Cornell Era, 343
Cornell University, xx, xxv-xxvi, 47-
  48, 49-50, 64-65, 67, 69, 101,
  178-179, 237, 271, 277, 297, 310,
  352
  Boardman Hall, 352
  Goldwin Smith Hall, 343
  Sage College, 295
  see also Becker, Carl L., and
  Cornell
Cornell University Press, 329, 330
Cox, James M., 77
Crawford, Clarence C., 7-8 & n3, 10
  letter to, 56
Croce, Benedetto, xviii, 264, 266 &
  n3, 293
Crofts, Frederick S., 203-204 & n2,
  211-212, 213-214, 222, 253
Crump, Charles George, 188 & n3,
  202, 224
Crump, Mrs. Charles G., 284
Curti, Merle, 120n2, 130
  letters to, 119, 210, 226, 309

Dartmouth College, xx, 5
Davenport, Herbert J., xxvi, 122,
  123n3
Davies, Samuel, 81 & n3
Davis, Herbert J., 284, 285n3
Davis, William W., 57 & n3
Day, Edmund Ezra, 248, 249n3
  letter to, 310

Debs, Eugene V., 74 & n8
De Kiewiet, Cornelis W., 277 & n3, 323
Dewey, John, xviii, 264
Dewey, Thomas, 326 & n2
Dial, The, 56
    letter to, 17
Dickens, Charles, 210
Dictionary of American Biography, 299
Diderot, Denis, 257
Dielmann, Rita H., 94, 95n3
Dilthey, Wilhelm, 266 & n3
Disraeli, Benjamin, 104
Dodd, Martha, 135, 144, 170
Dodd, William E., xxiii, 25n2, 34, 35-36n4, 125, 155, 180
    letters to, 24, 25, 27, 28, 31, 36, 37, 60, 61, 62, 64, 69, 71, 74, 77, 79, 81, 82, 86, 144, 156, 157, 170, 185
Dodd, Mrs. William E., 144, 170
Dodd, William (son), 135
Dodd, Mead & Co., 5
Donaldson, Norman V., 154n2
    letter to, 154
Dow, Earle W., 4, 6n5
Dred Scott case, 250 & n4
Dreiser, Theodore, 300, 301n4
Dumas, Alexandre, 18, 20n5
Dumbarton Oaks Conference, 324, 336
Dunning, William A., 34, 35 & n4

Earle, Edward Mead, 309 & n3, 331
Eddington, Sir Arthur S., 264
Edgerton, Alice Durand, 286n2
    letters to, 286, 287
Edgerton, Henry W., xxvi, 267n2
    letters to, 266, 281
Edwards, Everett E., 89n2
    letter to, 88
Emerson, Ralph Waldo, 244, 338
Erie Canal, 5

Fabre-Luce, Alfred, 114 & n2
Farrand, Livingston, 111, 112n3, 132
    letters to, 178, 186
Farrand, Max, 117n2, 218
    letter to, 159
Faÿ, Bernard, 198 & n4
Fay, Sidney B., 106, 107n3
Ferguson, Wallace K., 121, 122n4
Fischer, Louis, 256, 257n3
Fish, Carl R., 25 & n4, 34, 35-36 & n4
Fite, Warner, 264

Ford, Guy Stanton, 29, 30n3, 48, 58, 61-62, 180
    letters to, 180, 198, 243, 261
Ford, Henry, 115
Ford, Robert A. D., 289, 290n3
Fortune, Reggie, 278
Fox, Dixon Ryan, 174, 175, 176n2, 238 & n9, 318
Frankfurter, Felix, 118n2
    letters to, 118, 212
    letter to CLB, 353
Franklin, Benjamin, xvii, xxvi, 299
Franklin, Edward C., 39, 45-46n3
Frederiksen, Oliver, 191, 192n3
Freud, Sigmund, xviii, 264
Freund, Rudolph E., 334n2
    letter to, 333
Fuertes, Louis Agassiz, 121, 122n5

Galileo, 272
Garfield, James A., 214
Garland, Hamlin, xviii
Garrison, Wendell Phillips, 8, 9n1, 118
Garrison, William Lloyd, 8, 9n4
Gaskill, Gussie E., xxv, 109n2, 203, 205, 277, 279, 289
    letters to, 108, 128, 218
George III, 13, 319
George IV, 253
Gershoy, Ida, xxv, 114, 122, 141, 145-146, 147, 148, 153, 165-166, 167, 171-172, 197-198, 202-203, 219, 220, 242, 276, 281, 292, 307, 312, 318, 337, 345
    letters to, 152, 176, 197, 204, 205, 210, 211, 215, 216, 217, 222, 224, 231, 237, 240, 248, 249, 252, 274, 278, 282, 288, 295, 308, 314, 325-326, 332
Gershoy, Leo, xxv, 102n2, 108, 124, 176-177, 197, 205, 216, 219, 220, 223, 225, 226, 265, 275, 278
    letters to, 101, 102, 103, 114, 115, 120, 122, 126, 133, 141, 145, 146, 148, 152, 153, 161, 165, 166, 167, 171, 177, 184, 191, 194, 197, 199, 202, 209, 211, 213, 217, 224, 229, 237, 240, 241, 248, 249, 252, 274, 275, 277, 281, 282, 292, 294, 295, 306, 307, 308, 312, 314, 317, 325-326, 332, 337, 345
Gibbons, Lois O., 123 & n5, 225, 236
Gleed, James W., 45n2
    letter to, 39
Goethe, Johann W. von, 343, 344n4
Golder, Frank A., 127 & n3

Gottschalk, Alexandre, 264
Gottschalk, Fruma, 144, 145n4, 169,
    265, 272, 273
    letter to, 164
Gottschalk, Laura, *see* Riding, Laura
Gottschalk, Louis, 102 & n5, 109,
    115-116, 135, 144, 166, 171, 200,
    203, 252, 309
    letters to, 169, 203, 264, 271, 273,
    279, 293, 313, 320, 323
    letter to CLB, 354
Grant, Ulysses S., 214
Grant, William Lawson, 34, 35-36n4
Graves, Beryl Pritchard, 109n4
Graves, Nancy Nicholson, 109n4
Graves, Robert, 108, 109n4
Great Awakening, 28
Green, James W., 9, 10n5
Green, John Richard, 33, 35n3
Greene, Evarts B., 61, 62n2
Greenfield, Kent Roberts, 228 & n3,
    229, 255
Grey, Edward, 107, 108n3, 192,
    193n2
Guedalla, Philip, 115, 116n2
Guerlac, Othon, xxvi, 173 & n3
Gustavson, Carl G., 335n2
    letter to, 334

Hacker, Louis, 232, 236n5, 239, 253
Hackney, Edward T., 43-44, 46n9
Haig, Robert M., 238 & n8
Haldane, Richard Burdon, 192,
    193n4
Hale, Oron J., 164n2
    letter to, 163
Hamilton, Walton, 208 & n2, 209
Han, Yu-Shan, 345 & n3
Hanover, N.H., 5
Harding, Warren G., 72, 214
Harrison, William H., 346, 347n3
Hartman, Margaret, 205, 206n2
Harvard University, 12, 334
Harvey, George, 25 & n6
Haskins, Charles H., xviii, 37, 38n4,
    61, 76, 149
Hatch, Lloyd, 101, 102n4
Hayes, Carlton J. H., 111, 112n5,
    238n7
Hayes, Rutherford B., 346, 347n3
Headings, Mildred J., 328n2
    letter to, 327
Hedger, George Andrews, 53, 54n2,
    171
Hemingway, Ernest, 116, 300, 301n4
Henderson, Charles R., 36, 37n3
Hitler, Adolf, 181, 182, 200, 202,
    211, 235, 260, 291, 340

Hodder, Florence Moon, 130
Hodder, Frank H., 10 & n6, 32, 39,
    40, 43, 130
Holmes, Oliver Wendell, 247, 248n7
Holt, Henry, 88
Holt, W. Stull, 156n2
    letters to, 155, 228, 231, 255
Hooker, Richard, 81, 82n5
Hoover, Herbert, 66
Horwich, Carl, 271n2
    letters to, 270, 272
Howells, William D., xviii, 301 & n5
Hugo, Victor, 200
Hull, Charles, 49n2, 53, 69, 99, 121,
    149, 225, 286, 296, 297
    letters to, 48, 51, 133
Hull, Mary, 99, 133
Humble, Henry W., 9, 10n4
Hume, David, 247, 248n5, 350
Huntington, Henry E., 217, 218n2
Huntington Library, 159, 211, 215,
    217-218, 219
Hutchinson, Thomas, 72, 142, 145
Hutson, Charles W., 17-20 & n2
Hyma, Albert, 253, 254n4

Jackson, Andrew, 32
James, Henry, xviii, 301 & n5
James, William, xviii, 354
Jameson, J. Franklin, 32, 33n6, 58,
    60, 153, 180, 263, 267
    letters to, 68, 78, 116, 338-339
Jane, L. Cecil, 50-51 & n3
Jaqua, Ernest, 283 & n2
Jefferson, Thomas, xix, xxvi, xxvii,
    xxviii, 104, 152, 297, 299, 307,
    353
Johnson, Allen, 31, 32-33n2
Johnson, Henry, 85n2
    letters to, 84, 85
Johnson, Dr. Samuel, 319-320 & n3
Johnson, William S., 57 & n3
Jordan, Riverda H., 197, 198n2

Kansas, 24, 25, 26n7
Kansas, University of, xx, 4, 5, 7,
    9-10, 11, 13, 14, 39-45
Kaplan, Hyman, 249, 254, 261
Kay, George F., 42, 46n7
Kazin, Alfred, 301n2
    letter to, 300
Kellogg, Vernon L., 39, 45-46n3
Kesterson, Mrs. Max M., 336n2
    letters to, 335, 340
Knappen, Marshall, 112, 113 & n2,
    114-115, 144, 252
Knopf, Alfred A., 104n2, 108, 281,
    301, 326, 337

Knopf, Alfred A. (*cont.*)
  letters to, 104, 269, 276, 280, 298, 299, 308, 311, 319, 325, 329
Koch, Theodore W., 43, 46n8
Krey, August C., 131n2
  letter to, 131
Krutch, Joseph Wood, 172 & n3

Laistner, Max L. W., 225 & n4, 277
Lamb, John, papers of, 5
Landin, Harold, 337, 338n3, 345
Landon, Alfred, 244, 245n2
Langer, William L., 146, 147n2, 148
Laski, Harold, 224, 258, 259n3
Latané, John H., 32, 33n4
Lavisse, Ernest, 18, 20n6, 175
Lea, Henry Charles, 225 & n3
League for Independent Voters, 322
League of Nations, xxiii, 323-324; *see also* Becker, Carl L., on politics and international relations after World War I
Leighton, Richard M., 289n2, 294, 295n4
  letters to, 289, 311
Leland, Waldo G., 61-62 & n4, 79
Lenin, V. I., 181, 233-234
Leonardo da Vinci, 19-20
Lerner, Anita M., xxv, 136n2, 161, 205, 221, 230
  letters to, 135, 136, 139, 140, 143, 151, 158, 220, 223, 258, 283, 332
Lerner, Constance, 135
  letters to, 136, 138, 140, 147, 150, 151, 164
Lerner, Max, xxv, 135, 136n2, 198-199, 221, 223-224, 230, 275, 283
  letters to, 136, 151, 225, 256, 257, 278, 285
Lestrade, Gaëtan Combes de, 4n2
  letter to, 3
Lewis, Sinclair, 300, 301n4
Lincoln, Abraham, xxvi, 69
Lingelbach, William E., 145, 146n3
Lippmann, Walter, 251, 252n3, 326
Locke, John, 81, 82n4
Lodge, Henry Cabot, 73, 74n7
Loeb, Isidor, 4, 6n4
Lorentz, Margaret, 191, 192n2
Lorwin, Val R., 162, 163n4, 191, 345
  letters to, 190, 200, 214, 251, 254
Louisiana Purchase, 5
Luchaire, Achille, 17, 18, 20n4
Lunt, William E., 57 & n2
Lynd, Robert S. and Helen M., 258, 259n4
Lytle, Scott, 289, 290n4

Macaulay, Thomas B., 17, 18, 20n3
Maistre, Comte Joseph Marie de, 247, 248n6
Mandelbaum, Maurice, 265, 268
Mannheim, Karl, 266 & n3
Marcham, Frederick G., 173, 174n2, 194, 205
Marie Antoinette, 125
Markewich, May E., 270n2
  letter to, 270
Marvin, Frank O., 39, 45-46n3
Marx, Karl, 233, 315
Masonry (in French Third Republic), 327-328
Mather, Cotton, xix
Mazzini, Giuseppe, 343, 344n3
McClung, Clarence E., 39, 45-46n3
McCormick self-binder reaper, 11-12
McIlwain, Charles, 252, 294, 295n3
McKinley, William, 70
McLaughlin, Andrew C., 32, 33-35
McNeill, William H., 272 & n2, 289, 355
Meiklejohn, Alexander, 66n2
  letters to, 66, 68
Mencken, H. L., 142n2, 242, 255
  letters to, 141, 344
Michigan, University of, 313; *see also* Becker, Carl L., lectureships
Miller, Perry, xix
Millis, Harry A., 43, 65 & n2
Millis, Walter, 208 & n2
Milne, A. A., 242, 243n3
Minnesota, University of, xx, 45
Missouri, University of, 4
"Mona Lisa" (by Leonardo), 19-20, 262
Monaghan, Frank, 309 & n2, 331
Montesquieu, 127
Moore, William U., 9, 10n3, 42
Munro, William B., 35n2, 61-62
  letter to, 33
Mussolini, Benito, 235

Napoleon, 122, 177, 281
Nation, The, 8, 75, 86
  letter to, 192
Neilson, William A., 284, 285n4
Nevins, Allan, 122, 123n4, 166, 170, 261
  letter to CLB, 355
New Republic
  letters to, 239, 244, 263
New York Herald Tribune, 326
New York Public Library, 5
Newhall, Richard Ager, 63n2
  letters to, 63, 66, 124

Newman, Jared Treman, 75n2
 letter to, 75
Niebuhr, Reinhold, 278 & n3
Nock, Albert Jay, xxvii
Notestein, Wallace, 9, 10n2, 66, 90,
 91n4, 92, 104, 123, 129-130,
 145, 238
 letters to, 21, 29, 38

Ogden, Robert M., 51, 52n2, 132,
 263n2
 letter to, 262
Ortega y Gasset, José, 302 & n3
Osgood, Herbert Levi, xviii, 5, 6n6,
 333

Packard, Laurence B., 102 & n2, 104
Painter, Sidney, 345 & n3
Palmer, Robert R., 352n1
 letter to CLB, 352
Palmerston, Henry John Temple, 115
Parkman, Francis, 33, 35n3
Pascal, Blaise, 246-247
Pater, Walter, 18, 19, 20n7
Patterson, David L., 10 & n7, 11
Paxson, Frederic L., 31, 32n2, 34,
 35-36n4, 243, 244n2, 268
Pennsylvania State University, xx
Perry, Mabel, 126n2
 letter to, 125
Petry, Loren, xxvi, 241, 242n2
Phillips, Ulrich B., 160 & n2
Planck, Max, 239 & n3
Plato, 50, 240
Poincaré, Raymond, 106, 107
Pooley, William V., 37, 38n6
Postgate, Raymond W., 319-320n2
Powell, Thomas Reed, 291n2
 letters to, 291, 326, 327
Prescott, Frederick C., 90, 91n4, 92
Prince, Dr. Thomas, 81
Pugh, Wilma, 237n2
 letter to, 236

Rankin, John E., 343, 344n6
Read, Conyers, 184n2, 194, 351
 letter to, 182
Redfield, Robert, 293, 294n3
Renan, Ernest, 17, 20n4
Reynolds, Victor, 330, 331n3
Rhodes, James Ford, 34, 35-36n4
Riding, Laura Reichenthal Gott-
 schalk Jackson, 94 & n2, 108
Robespierre, Maximilien, 151
Robinson, James H., xviii, xxviii,
 115 & n5, 116, 130, 267
Rockefeller, John D., 134, 135n4

Rodkey, F. S., 196n2
 letter to, 194
Roland, Mme, 117 & n2, 129-130
Roosevelt, Franklin D., 170, 244,
 251, 253, 326, 330
Roosevelt, Theodore, 25 & n5, 34,
 35-36 & n4, 170, 206
Root, Elihu, 214, 215n3
Rousseau, Jean Jacques, 22 & n3
Russell, Bertrand, xix, 234, 236n7,
 264

Sabine, George, xxvi
Saint-Just, Louis de, 150
Salmon, Lucy, 145, 146n2
Santayana, George, 240 & n2
Scammon, Richard E., 42, 46n6
Schapiro, J. Selwyn, 277 & n2
Schevill, Ferdinand, 158 & n2
Schlesinger, Arthur M., 59n2, 78, 114,
 145
 letters to, 59, 142, 174
Schmitt, Bernadotte E., 133, 135n2,
 309, 331
Schurman, Jacob G., xvii, 67 & n3
Shakespeare, William, xxvi, 162-163
Shirer, William, 280
Sill, Henry A., 46, 48n2
Silver Burdett (publishers), 345
Sioussat, St. George L., 20 & n9
Slosson, Preston, 253, 254n4
Small, Albion W., 26, 27n3
Smith, Adam, 257
Smith, Albert W., 67 & n4, 68
Smith, Alfred E., 125 & n3
Smith, Gerald L. K., 343, 344n5
Smith, Goldwin, 343, 344n2
Smith, Preserved, 78 & n2, 211 & n3,
 238
Smith, T. V., 169 & n3, 351n1
 letter to CLB, 349
Smith College, 278, 280, 284, 289,
 355
Snow, Francis H., 39, 45n3
Spanish Civil War, 252, 253, 256
Spalding, William L., 289, 290n5
Spencer, Herbert, 257 & n3
Spitzer, Norman, 182n2
 letter to, 181
Squires, James Duane, 331n2
 letter to, 331
Stalberg, Jonah, 256, 257n5
Stalin, Josef, 211, 248, 298, 342
Stason, E. Blythe, 330, 331n4
Stephenson, Carl, 144
Stevenson, Robert L., 18, 19, 20n7
Stock, Leo Francis, 338, 339n3
Stout, Rex, 316-317 & n2

Strong, Frank A., 10, 11n9, 40, 42, 46n4
Strong, Henry Carter, 354n1
  letter to CLB, 353
Sullivan, George E., 232, 236n3
Sullivan, Helen, xxv, 122, 123n2, 129, 252
Sumner, William Graham, xviii, 264
Supreme Court, the, 251, 253, 282
Swain, Joseph W., 194 & n2
Sweet, Alfred H., 57 & n2

Taft, William H., 214-215 & n2, 251
Taine, Hippolyte Adolphe, 194, 197
Taney, Roger B., 250 & n3
Telegraph, first message sent, 315-316
Templin, Olin, 40, 45-46n3
Thayer, William Roscoe, 34, 35n4, 64 & n3
Thomas, Norman, 170
Thompson, James Westfall, 293
Thwaites, Reuben Gold, 11, 12n2, 15
Tilden, Samuel J., 346, 347n4
Time, xx, 206, 207-208n1
Titchener, Edward B., 121, 122n6
Tolstoy, Leo, xxvi, 258
Treman, Arthur, 238 & n4
Treman, Robert E., 238n4
Trotsky, Leon, 234, 256, 257n6, 264-265
Truro, Massachusetts, 274
Turner, Fredrick Jackson, xviii, xxvi, 35, 88-89, 116, 118, 153, 159-160, 204, 243-244, 267-268, 333
  letters to, 4, 6, 7, 11, 12, 13, 15, 20, 24, 26, 31, 56, 75, 105, 117, 129, 131, 148, 154
Tyler, Lyon G., 29, 30n4

Vaihinger, Hans, 264
Van Doren, Carl, 104, 246, 299, 313
  letters to, 82, 201
Van Loon, Hendrik Willem, 53, 54n3
Van Tyne, Claude H., 24n2, 34, 35n4, 37
  letters to, 22, 63
Vanderbilt University, 335
Veblen, Thorstein, 60, 241
Versailles, Treaty of, xxiii; *see also* Becker, Carl L., on politics and international relations after World War I
Villard, Oswald Garrison, 87, 88n3, 192

Vivas, Elisio, 222, 223n2
Voltaire, 122, 316

Walker, Arthur T., 40, 45-46n3
Walpole, Horace, on George III, 13
Washington, George, 316
Washington Herald
  letter to, 232-236
Webster, Daniel, 32
Wells, H. G., 111, 112n6, 122
Westermann, William L., 238 & n6
Whitaker, Arthur P., 149 & n3
White, Albert B., 38 & n2
White, Andrew D., 123 & n6, 133, 219, 343
Whitehead, Alfred North, xviii, 264
Wickstead, A., 234
Wigmore, Dean J. H., 118 & n3
Wilcox, Walter Francis, xxvi, 306n2
  letter to, 304
Wilhelmi, Henelia, 9, 10n3
Wilkes, John, 319, 320n4
Williamson, Robert D., 145, 146n4
Willis, E. R. B., xxvi, 125n2, 219
  letters to, 124, 128, 221
Williston, Samuel W., 39, 45-46 & n3
Wilson, Edmund, xxviii
Wilson, Jean S., 284 & n2
Wilson, Woodrow, 25 & n6, 69-70, 72-73, 74, 83, 86-87, 88, 180
Wisconsin, University of, 6, 7, 12-13, 14
Wittke, Carl, 238, 239n10
Wood, Otis E., 286, 287
World War I, xxiv; *see also* Becker, Carl L., and World War I
Writers War Board, World War II, 317
Wynkoop, Jeremiah, 109

Yale Review, 256, 257, 259, 276, 280, 286, 312
Yohalem, Florence Mishnun, xxv, 186n2, 205
  letters to, 186, 208, 240, 245, 255, 295, 296
Yohalem, Morton, xxv, 129 & n2, 205, 208, 241, 246
  letters to, 209, 295, 296
Young, Allyn A., 160 & n3
Young, Catharine (Mrs. Masters), 102 & n3, 108, 109n3, 127, 128n4
Young, John Wesley, 42, 46n5

Zook, George F., 314, 315n2

"What Is the Good of History?"

Designed by R. E. Rosenbaum.
Composed by Kingsport Press, Inc.,
in 9 point linotype Primer, 3 points leaded,
with display lines in Palatino.
Printed letterpress from type by Kingsport Press
on Warren's Olde Style, 60 pound basis.
Bound by Kingsport Press
in Holliston book cloth
and stamped in All Purpose foil.

Library of Congress Cataloging in Publication Data
(For library cataloging purposes only)

Becker, Carl Lotus, 1873–1945.
  "What is the good of history?"

  Bibliography: p.
  1. Becker, Carl Lotus, 1873–1945. I. Kammen, Michael G., ed.
II. Title.
D15.B33A4 1973   973.3'072'024 [B]   73–2849
ISBN 0–8014–0778–8